ORPHANS OF PETRARCH

Publications of the Center for Medieval
and Renaissance Studies 25
University of California, Los Angeles

Publications of the
UCLA Center for Medieval and Renaissance Studies

1. Jeffrey Burton Russell, *Dissent and Reform in the Early Middle Ages* (1965)
2. C. D. O'Malley, editor, *Leonardo's Legacy: An International Symposium* (1968)
3. Richard H. Rouse, *Serial Bibliographies for Medieval Studies* (1969)
4. Speros Vryonis, Jr., *The Decline of Medieval Hellenism in Asia Minor and the Process of Islamization from the Eleventh Through the Fifteenth Century* (1971)
5. Stanley Chodorow, *Christian Political Theory and Church Politics in the Mid-Twelfth Century: The Ecclesiology of Gratian's Decretum* (1972)
6. Joseph J. Duggan, *The Song of Roland: Formulaic Style and Poetic Craft* (1973)
7. Ernest A. Moody, *Studies in Medieval Philosophy, Science, and Logic: Collected Papers 1933–1969* (1975)
8. Marc Bloch, *Slavery and Serfdom in the Middle Ages: Selected Essays* (1975)
9. Michael J. B. Allen, *Marsilio Ficino: The* Philebus *Commentary, A Critical Edition and Translation* (1975)
10. Richard C. Dales, *Marius: On the Elements, A Critical Edition and Translation* (1976)
11. Duane J. Osheim, *An Italian Lordship: The Bishopric of Lucca in the Late Middle Ages* (1977)
12. Robert Somerville, *Pope Alexander III and the Council of Tours (1163): A Study of Ecclesiastical Politics and Institutions in the Twelfth Century* (1977)
13. Lynn White, jr., *Medieval Religion and Technology: Collected Essays* (1978)
14. Michael J. B. Allen, *Marsilio Ficino and the Phaedran Charioteer: Introduction, Texts, Translations* (1981)
15. Barnabas Bernard Hughes, O. F. M., *Jordanus de Nemore: De numeris datis, A Critical Edition and Translation* (1981)
16. Caroline Walker Bynum, *Jesus as Mother: Studies in the Spirituality of the High Middle Ages* (1982)
17. Carlo M. Cipolla, *The Monetary Policy of Fourteenth-Century Florence* (1983)

ORPHANS OF PETRARCH

POETRY AND THEORY IN THE SPANISH RENAISSANCE

Ignacio Navarrete

University of California Press

Berkeley · Los Angeles · London

University of California Press
Berkeley and Los Angeles, California

University of California Press, Ltd.
London, England

© 1994 by
The Regents of the University of California

Library of Congress Cataloging-in-Publication Data
Navarrete, Ignacio Enrique, 1954–
    Orphans of Petrarch : poetry and theory in the Spanish
Renaissance / Ignacio Navarrete.
        p. cm.—(Publications of the UCLA Center for Medi-
eval and Renaissance Studies; 25)
        Based on the author's doctoral thesis, Indiana Univer-
sity, 1985.
        Includes bibliographical references and index.
        ISBN 0–520–08373–3 (alk. paper)
        1. Spanish poetry—Classical period, 1500–1700—His-
tory and criticism.   2. Petrarchism.   3. Poetry.   I. Title.   II.
Series:
        Publications of the Center for Medieval and Renaissance
Studies; 25.
    PQ6066.N38   1994   93-4559
    861'.309—dc20   CIP

Printed in the United States of America
1 2 3 4 5 6 7 8 9

Contents

Acknowledgments

Translations from Petrarch's *Rime sparse* are taken from *Petrarch's Lyric Poems: The "Rime sparse" and Other Lyrics,* edited and translated by Robert Durling (Cambridge, Mass.: Harvard University Press, 1976). All other translations, unless otherwise indicated, are my own. I have tried to render them into modern colloquial English, guided more by the sense than by the style of the original, but occasionally I have been forced to follow the original more closely in order to capture an important detail.

I am deeply grateful to the many readers and commentators whose suggestions have done so much to improve this study. They made many valuable suggestions, but are not to blame when I failed to take their advice. The following people read some or all of the manuscript, at various stages of completion: Emilie Bergmann, Anne Cruz, Edward Dudley, Charles Faulhaber, Daniel Javitch, William Kennedy, Ronald Martínez, Giuseppe Mazzotta, John Polt, and Joseph V. Ricapito. The latter directed the dissertation on which this book is based; he has been for many years a mentor and friend. C. Clifford Flanigan and Frank Warnke taught me a good deal about scholarship and generosity. Many other friends, teachers, and colleagues also provided guidance and advice. Many students, over the years, helped me develop ideas, particularly participants in my 1991 seminar on Spanish Petrarchism, and my research assistants: Anne Gatschet, Kevin Duncliffe, and Elisabeth Anton. I am grateful to them all, as well as to Doris Kretschmer at the University of California Press and to H. Abigail Bok of the UCLA Center for Medieval and Renaissance Studies.

Financial support from Kansas State University, from the NEH Yale University Petrarch Institute, and from the University of California helped me to complete this study; I am especially grateful to the latter for a President's Research Fellowship in the Humanities, which allowed me to spend a year on leave during which the bulk of this book was written, and to the Center for Medieval and Renaissance Studies at the University of California, Los Angeles for its sponsorship. I am also grateful to the University of Illinois, the Hispanic Society of America, the Lilly Library at Indiana University, and the Bancroft Library at the University of California, Berkeley, for making their collections of Renaissance books available to me.

A very abbreviated version of chapter 2 was published as "The Spanish Appropriation of Castiglione," in *The Yearbook of Comparative and General Literature* 39 (1990–91): 35–46; an earlier version of the first section of chapter 3 was published as "Boscán's Rewriting of Petrarch's *Canzoniere*," in *Romanic Review* 81 (1990): 256–269; and an earlier version of the first two sections of chapter 4 was published as "Decentering Garcilaso: Herrera's Attack on the Canon," in *PMLA* 106 (1991): 21–33.

This book is dedicated to my wife, Hester, whose love, patience, and support cannot be measured.

1

Introduction

For more than a century, Petrarchism was the driving force in Spanish lyric poetry, as poets and theorists from Juan del Encina to Francisco de Quevedo pondered and exemplified the generic, thematic, stylistic, and even ethical ramifications of imitating an Italian poet who had been dead for more than 150 years. Petrarch was the great model for Renaissance poets throughout Europe, thanks partly to his canonization in Italy as the model poet for vernacular lyric poetry; in Spain, as elsewhere, the imitation of Petrarch was an aspect of the larger phenomenon of copying Italian styles in painting, architecture, education, and even courtiership. Petrarchism was a particularly vital force in Spain, however, for the combination of Spanish political domination over Italy, and a continuing sense of cultural inferiority, led Spanish poets to respond to perceived crises in the national lyric tradition by continuously rereading, reinterpreting, and reappropriating Petrarch's work. For successive generations of Spanish poets Petrarch became an alternative model, and a defense against the overwhelming stature of national predecessors who were thus reduced to the status of siblings. As such, although there is continuity in his influence throughout this period, there occurred major changes in the nature of that influence. He was consistently a source of poetic renewal, so it is those poets most concerned with transforming Spanish poetry who were the ones most self-conscious about the conflict between their role as imitators of Petrarch and their differences of age, nation, and temperament.

Yet the importance of Spanish Renaissance lyric goes beyond literary history and aesthetic value. Petrarch's power to engender Spanish imitators was not due to the strength of his poetry alone, nor to Italianism as a literary fashion. Belatedness was inherent in Italian Petrarchism, its endowment as the vernacular heir to the humanist tradition, but it was compounded by uniquely Spanish concerns about national cultural backwardness and competition with

Italy; the determination to claim the European heritage for Spain resulted in a metonymic association between Petrarchist lyric and the Spanish empire. Lyric poetry thus played a unique role in the Spanish struggle for cultural self-justification. Although Spain was the first powerful and unified nation-state in Europe and had the first self-conscious national literature, its poets spent more than a century trying to create a body of literature that befitted its imperial stature, and in particular that matched the cultural achievements already attained in Italy. In classical theory the epic was more noble, but it was also contingent on military achievement. Lyric poetry, as the most nonmimetic genre, became the arena of the struggle for a modern cultural legitimacy independent of military conquest, which paradoxically gave the lyric a social dimension: poetry was not just a pastime for amateurs or an expression of emotion but a vocation ultimately parallel to that of the warrior, and one calling for equal dedication. The concern with national backwardness was a consequence of what Ernst Robert Curtius diagnosed as, but mis-labeled, Spain's "cultural belatedness" (541), which more recently has been called the "Spanish difference," and which casts an important sideways light on literary developments throughout Europe.

The remainder of this introduction first examines the ideology of Petrarchism in Italy, particularly the consequences of Bembo's ap-propriation of the historiographical models of the classical human-ists and their application to the vernacular; when examined in the context of Petrarch's theories of history and of imitation, we see how Bembo both crystallizes Petrarch as a unique model and provides a degree of freedom by subjecting him to what Thomas Greene (88–93) called the humanist hermeneutic. Second, I look at the rise of indigenous Spanish forms of vernacular humanism and cultural be-latedness as they develop in the eulogies written after the death of the marqués de Santillana, and which come to a head in the linguis-tic and literary treatises of the Salamanca circle in the 1490s. There, we see the *translatio studii* as the key trope explicating the still-emergent state of Spanish literature, and the inexorable connection between imperial rule and cultural dominance. Finally, the introduc-tion briefly addresses questions about methodology, particularly the ways in which I qualify and historicize Harold Bloom's theory of poetic belatedness in order to make it useful for this study, and the

relationship I see between his revisionary ratios and issues of inter-
textuality and hermeneutics.

BEMBO, PETRARCH, AND RENAISSANCE
BELATEDNESS

In its strictest sense, Petrarchism is the result of the transfer to the
vernacular of models of literary history originally elaborated within
the context of an attempt to ameliorate composition in Latin
through the imitation of Cicero. The figure most associated with this
transfer, both during the Renaissance and today, is Pietro Bembo,
who in his landmark dialogue-treatise, the *Prose della volgar lingua*,
proposed the strict imitation of Petrarch and Boccaccio as a solution
to the problem of creating a national literary language for Italy.
Bembo in his youth developed a reputation as a strict Ciceronian in
matters of Latin style, and his theory of imitation was first worked
out in an exchange of letters with Gianfrancesco Pico della Miran-
dola, in which he rejected the eclectic approach promoted by earlier
generations of Renaissance writers, particularly those associated
with the Florentine Neoplatonists. To Bembo, imitation involves
copying not only the style but "if you please, the same organizing
principle which he has used whom you have set before you as an
example" (Scott, 11); hence copying stylistic details alone, an inevi-
table consequence of eclectic imitation, would only result in a trav-
esty. Imitation also gives a work a certain resonance; describing his
own early attempts to avoid imitation, he concludes, "It pleased me
and I experimented in it as far as I could, but all my thought, care,
and study, all my labor was vexatious and void; for I invented noth-
ing which could not easily have been drawn from the old writers;
and when I tried to avoid that, it lacked the charm, the propriety,
the majesty of those ages" (Scott, 13). Cicero and Virgil themselves
attained this majesty by imitating their Greek predecessors, and
they thus showed the way for Bembo and his contemporaries who,
if they are diligent in their imitations, may someday hope to surpass
their classical models. But for now this is only an elusive hope, as
"it is not so arduous to surpass the one whom you equal as to equal
the one whom you imitate" (Scott, 16).

As Ferruccio Ulivi pointed out, Bembo and the other humanist
partisans of a strict Ciceronianism nourished a phenomenological

concept of literary creation that emphasized process, as opposed to that metaphysical one which lay at the heart of Ficinian thought, which emphasized the emanation of ideas (23).[1] Thomas Greene, elaborating on Ulivi's distinction, focuses on the conflict between "*inventio* and *elocutio,* or *res* and *verba,* or expressionism and formalism, between creativity as spontaneous nature and creativity as discipline, between impulse and method, or between beauty as variety and beauty as unity, between color and purity" (175). He thus identifies the dispute over Ciceronian imitation with perennial aesthetic issues in the history of literature, though at the cost of the historical specificity of the issues involved. Although he correctly sees Pico, an advocate of the eclectic approach, as grounded in humanist historiography—that is, emphasizing the difference between antiquity and the sixteenth century and the freedom of the modern writer to pick and choose—he overlooks that it is Bembo who locates a writer in the historical process of reading and writing, and who has no illusions about the easy restoration of antiquity.[2]

As Greene further notes, between Bembo's letter to Pico and his discussion of poetry in the *Prose,* "his theoretical outlook did not significantly change" (175). Yet this consistency is in itself remarkable, for the *Prose* contains the first overt application of imitation theory, previously reserved for the more exalted area of Latin prose composition, to the vernacular. In order to transfer his ideas, Bembo had to preserve not only his phenomenological outlook but also the humanist conception of history as divisible into a tripartite structure comprising classical achievements, medieval decline, and Renaissance renewal. The process by which Bembo establishes Petrarch as a model therefore deserves closer scrutiny. To appropriate the humanist scheme of history, Bembo begins by justifying the use of Italian rather than Latin; the Romans, he argues, composed in their own language, even though they valued the literary accomplishments of the Greeks more highly than their own. Had they ignored the rule of composing in the native language, they would have written in Greek, while the Greeks themselves would have written in Phoenician, and they in turn in Egyptian, and so on. In this way, Bembo describes each culture's sense of inferiority to a preceding one, which is itself largely forgotten as the new cultures arise.[3] Thus language, and with it literature, are at any moment of time caught in an uncomfortable position of feeling inferior to the past and anxious about the future. Moreover, this cycle occurred not only in antiquity but in the recent past as well: Bembo declares that the *scuola siciliana* of thirteenth-century Italian poetry is only a name to him, and that although the Provençals were extremely influential and worthy of study, their language is as good as dead. This discussion of Provençal, in the *Prose*, directly precedes the statement of the *questione della lingua*—considering all the dialects spoken in Italy, which should a writer employ?—and therefore Bembo places the discussion about contemporary language in a context of past literatures that have come to grief. Bembo thus implies that this fate may hang over Italian as well, and that the *Prose* represents an attempt to ward it off.

As alternative solutions to the language problem, Bembo entertains two possibilities. The first is the *lingua cortegiana*, the common language spoken by courtiers throughout the peninsula. This however is rejected as being too unstable and lacking in uniformity. Moreover, speakers alone cannot guarantee immortality to a language:

> Né la latina lingua chiamiamo noi lingua, solo che per cagion di Plauto, di Terenzio, di Virgilio, di Varrone, di Cicerone e degli altri che, scrivendo, hanno fatto che ella è lingua.
> (110, *Prose* 1.14)

> Not even Latin would we call a language, were it not for Plautus, for Terence, for Virgil, for Varro, for Cicero, and for the others who, by writing, made it into a language.

Here Bembo moves from arguing that writers insure that a language will be studied in ages to come to asserting that only writers make up the language. He concludes that Tuscan must become the literary language of Italy, for it was the principal heir to the Provençal tradition and, more importantly, because it is the most developed dialect in Italy:

> Perciò che se io volessi dire che la fiorentina lingua più regolata si vede essere, più vaga, più pura che la provenzale, i miei due Toschi vi porrei dinanzi, il Boccaccio e il Petrarca senza più.
> (110, *Prose* 1.14)

> Thus if I wished to say that the Florentine language is clearly more ordered, more beautiful, and more pure than Provençal, I would put before you my two Tuscans, Petrarch and Boccaccio, and no more.

Petrarch and Boccaccio, however, lived almost 150 years before the composition of the *Prose.* By citing them rather than more contemporary Tuscans, Bembo underlines the endangered state of Italian poetry, courting the same fate that had earlier befallen the Sicilians. Yet by positing this gap, and turning to Petrarch and Boccaccio as models, Bembo saddles the vernacular with the same sense of cultural inferiority with which the humanists had earlier burdened Latin composition. By turning away from Latin (in the *Prose* at least), Bembo rejects the humanist ideal; but his method for improving the vernacular was derived from humanist practice. Again and again as Bembo repeats his key point—that Petrarch and Boccaccio have never been surpassed and that Italian literature in fact has decayed since the time they wrote—he appropriates for the vernacular the key elements of the humanist tripartite division of history: the notion of a dark age, and the practice of scholarship and imitation as the only means to recuperate the level attained by long-dead predecessors.

Ultimately, Bembo concludes the discussion of vernacular imitation with a nearly necromantic model of imitation, a description of artists in Rome disinterring ancient monuments and dutifully sketching the paintings, sculptures, and buildings. Reversing Petrarch's description of strolling through Rome and imagining what lay beneath the ruins, Bembo presents a city in the course of recovering its ancient cultural artifacts in such a way that modernity begins to merge with the predecessor that formerly lay underneath. This process of recovery, by providing adequate models, is responsible for the achievements of Michelangelo and Raphael, both of whom have become so proficient in their art that it would be difficult to tell their work from that of their antique models. If imitation can accomplish such results with the plastic arts, it should be able to accomplish far more for literature, "così leggiadra e così gentile" (so graceful and so noble, 184). While there is now an overabundance of books in Latin, however, the vernacular is most in need of development: the many vernacular writers have produced few works in prose or in verse worthy of preservation, and only the same process of imitation can lead to the restoration of poetry. Thus Bembo establishes a heuristic equivalence among Latin literature, the architectural and artistic monuments of ancient Rome, and the state of modern Italian letters. All three are subject to the same his-

torical model adopted by Petrarch to define the humanist move-
ment, yet while the first has been fully recovered through a plethora
of books, and the second is now literally being exhumed for study,
the necessary archaeology for the restoration of the vernacular has
scarcely begun.

Bembo's understanding of Petrarchist imitation is primarily lin-
guistic and stylistic, and his appreciation of Petrarch's phonetic
structure led Cesare Segre to characterize it as "linguistic hedo-
nism." Yet even if his precepts were not easily transferred outside
Italy, and were often resisted within it, he was tremendously influ-
ential in other ways. By displacing to the vernacular realm the theo-
retical foundations of Ciceronianism, he provided an ideological
framework that justified the effort to illustrate the languages of con-
temporary Europe. From Ciceronianism, however, he also brought
to the realm of the vernacular the tripartite historiography of the
humanists, and the attendant sense of deficiency, which made Pe-
trarchism the truest form of Renaissance vernacular lyric poetry, for
it reflects the idea of decadence and rebirth inherent in the idea of
a renaissance. Thus his theories were self-serving, for from the *Prose*
there emerge two sets of linguistic heroes, Petrarch and Boccaccio
in the fourteenth century as the original illustrators of the language,
and Bembo himself as the vanguard of its restoration. Moreover, his
fame as a Tuscan scholar brought his poetry a canonical status sec-
ond only to Petrarch's, further increasing his influence abroad (see
Cruz, *Imitación*, 24–34). Bembo's popularity, like that of contempo-
raries such as Sannazaro and Ariosto, may partly have been due—
as Curtius argued (34 n. 44)—to a fashion for things Italian; but his
legacy was a model of literary history and of Petrarch's place within
it as the only modern classic, the standard against which lyric poets,
both Italians and foreigners, must measure themselves.

To appreciate more fully Bembo's position in the development of
vernacular humanism, we can situate him in a context that includes
Petrarch's own views on literary history and imitation, and the sub-
sequent history of what we might call the trope of the continual
Renaissance. In his history of the Renaissance as a historical con-
cept, Wallace Ferguson credited Petrarch with conflating models
drawn from civic and sacred history to posit the tripartite division
of time into the ancient Greco-Roman world, an intervening "dark
age," and the contemporary, incipient revival.[4] Moreover, by re-

jecting any continuity with ancient Rome through the Holy Roman Empire (an idea still held by Dante a generation earlier), Petrarch was free to see the end of the republic, rather than the collapse of the empire, as the first step in a decline that included the cultural as well as the political spheres, while conversely the recovery of civic virtue would entail not only the founding of a new republic, but also the exhumation of culture through the cultivation of Latin and the study of Roman literature, particularly Cicero. Beginning with Petrarch, the two major tools for the humanist restoration of ancient standards of literary culture became scholarship, for the purification of model texts, and imitation, as a guide for the development of the moderns (see Ulivi, 9). Ferguson's view of Petrarch as the source of humanist theories of alienation from antiquity is echoed by Greene, who sees Petrarch as the founder of the "humanist hermeneutic," the recognition that classical texts had a meaning in ancient times that can be recuperated only through scholarship, not through the atemporal allegorical and anagogic modes of interpretation practiced during the Middle Ages. Greene takes as paradigmatic Petrarch's description of a stroll through Rome, in the course of which he evokes the historical associations of the mounds and ruins he encounters. The passage echoes the eighth book of the *Aeneid* in which, as Aeneas walks through the site of the future Rome, the poet cites the buildings and monuments that will some day stand in the same locations. But Petrarch's retrospective tour, by emphasizing the decayed state of the scene, also underlines the fact that Rome is gone for good, and that its former magnificence can only be imagined. Thus even as he imitates Virgil, Petrarch recognizes the gulf of radical discontinuity that separates them and locates in that gulf his own freedom, his alterity from both antiquity and the middle ages. Thus as we have already seen in Bembo, archaeology—whether literary or architectural—would become the model science of the Renaissance: like the robbing of tombs, it entails the violation of taboos, and sometimes a little necromancy as well, to achieve its ultimate goal of bringing the dead back to life (Greene, 88–93).

Yet if Petrarch was responsible for the tripartite view of history through a self-representation as the one who began the revival of antiquity, subsequent generations often denied him that honor. As Ferguson shows (22–24), a succession of later humanists excluded

Petrarch and Boccaccio from their ranks, relegating both of them to the benighted middle ages while fixing the beginning of the revival in their own generation. This continual, rhetorical postponement of the "renaissance" allows them comfortably to predict future achievements that will equal the ancients even as they emphasize their own attempts to begin to make up for the defects of the past. Ferguson's account of the history of humanist self-consciousness makes several important points. First, it recalls the connection established by Petrarch himself between politics and culture, which led later writers such as Bruni to remark on the lag between the rates of political and cultural development, and which was to have important consequences outside Italy. Second, it points out the overt sense of deficiency by comparison to antiquity, constantly cited as the standard; although there is contempt for what the humanists saw as the dark age that followed the collapse of Rome, there is also an implicit feeling of insecurity about their own age, only tenuously distinguished from that which preceded it. Third, it emphasizes that the beginning of the restoration of letters was variously dated, with the proclamation of a revival attaining the status of a trope. By constantly reappropriating Petrarch's idea of a renaissance as a defense against antiquity, the later humanists betray their chronic feeling of insecurity about the present when compared to the ancient past, and to the true pioneer humanists whom they attempt to ignore; by bringing forward the time of the rebirth, it is made to seem as if the moderns have had less time to catch up.[5] But why did the humanists feel a need to deprecate their own forebears? I argue that this tendency represented an attempt to excuse their own shortcomings, their own failure to achieve according to the antique standards that they themselves had reestablished, and the desire on the part of the later humanists for a degree of priority. How to account for the seeming inability to compose literary monuments on a par with those of antiquity? One way was to pretend continually that they lived at only the beginning of the revival, that they were the pioneers, and thus that they were only laying the groundwork for future generations.

Naïve attempts to recreate antique literature, however, were doomed to failure. Greene draws our attention to what he calls heuristic imitations that—like Petrarch's stroll through Rome—underline the gap between cultures, and he quotes extensively from Petrarch's letters on imitation, in which the poet emphasizes the need to process ancient texts and make them one's own. Borrowing from Cicero, Petrarch advises an imitator to be like a bee, tasting from various flowers but transforming the nectar into a honey all its own.[6] This apian model is then transformed into the famous digestive image, which has a prehistory going back to Seneca and which recurs throughout the Renaissance in discussions of imitation:

> I have read Virgil, Flaccus, Severinus, Tullius not once but countless times, nor was my reading rushed but leisurely, pondering them as I went with all the powers of my intellect; I ate in the morning what I would digest in the evening, I swallowed as a boy what I would ruminate upon as an older man. I have thoroughly absorbed these writings, implanting them not only in my memory but in my marrow, and they have so become one with my mind that were I never to read them for the remainder of my life, they would cling to me, having taken root in the innermost recesses of my mind.
>
> (3.212–13, *Familiares* 22.2; see Greene, 99)[7]

Here Petrarch stresses the transformatory aspect of imitation and the need to be true to one's personal style. Elsewhere, he warns against slavish imitation, comparing it with wearing someone else's clothing; in contrast, he claims to prefer his own "garment," however rude and ill-cut. To Greene this passage constitutes evidence of Petrarch's strong sense of the self, and of its expression through an individual style; the successful assimilation of models along these lines characterizes the best poetry of a humanist period that extends to the eighteenth century (97–99).

Summarizing Petrarch's contribution to the development of humanist inferiority as a cultural phenomenon, Greene argues that the "humanist poet is not a neurotic son crippled by a Freudian family romance, which is to say he is not in Harold Bloom's terms Romantic. He is rather like the son in a classical comedy who displaces the father at the moment of reconciliation" (41). But Greene takes too benevolent a view of father–son relationships when he offers the following letter to explain the connection between imitation and sonhood:

> An imitator must take care to write something similar yet not identical to the original, and that similarity must not be like the image to

its original in painting where the greater the similarity the greater the praise for the artist, but rather like that of the son to his father. While often very different in their individual features, they have a certain something our painters call an "air," especially noticeable about the face and eyes, that produces a resemblance; seeing the son's face, we are reminded of the father's. . . . We must thus see to it that if there is something similar, there is also a great deal that is dissimilar, and that the similar be elusive.

> (3.301–2, *Familiares* 23.19;
> see Greene, 95)

Although the father–son model of imitation is, like that of the bee, taken from Seneca, Petrarch's particular use of it here skirts close to the very family romance that Greene finds of no relevance. Like the earlier tropes emphasizing the imitator's divergence from models (his own suit of clothes, however ill-fitting; his own honey, made of the nectar gathered from many flowers), this one stresses both similarity and difference. Slavish imitation is likened to mimesis, but while the possibility of deviating from the prototype offers some comfort, the analogy between model and father, and imitation and son, suggests that the model poet engenders the imitator, and this relationship of direct dependency is closer to medieval notions of midgets on the shoulders of giants than to the humanist hermeneutic. Moreover, the reader's constant back-and-forth comparison between imitation and model, to Pigman a sign of competitive emulation (26), hardly eases the anxiety of poets attempting to compete with the great writers of the past.

The father–son model established in the letter on imitation underlies Petrarch's letter about Dante. There, Petrarch compares the Tuscan poet to his own father, both of whom were exiled from Florence at the same time: "[M]y father, compelled by other matters and by concern for his family, resigned himself to exile, while his friend resisted and began devoting himself all the more vigorously to his literary pursuits, neglecting all else and desirous only of glory" (3.203, *Familiares* 21.15). Because of Petrarch's own thirst for fame and his resentment about life in Avignon, he imagines Dante as a fantasy father, more appropriate than his own. Yet he then denies that relationship by asserting that he never imitated Dante. The purpose of the letter (which is addressed to Boccaccio) is to defend himself against the charge that he is jealous of the Florentine poet. Petrarch concedes that there are grounds for the allegation, but goes on to justify his behavior:

> While always passionately hunting for other books with little hope of finding them, I was strangely indifferent to this one, which was new and easily available. I admit this to be so, but deny that it was for the reasons that they give. At the time I too was devoted to the same kind of writing in the vernacular; I considered nothing more elegant and had yet to learn to look higher, but I did fear that, were I to immerse myself in his, or any other's, writings, being of an impressionable age so given to indiscriminate admiration, I could scarcely escape becoming an unwilling or unconscious imitator. . . . This one thing I do wish to make clear, for if any of my vernacular writings resembles, or is identical to, anything of his or anyone else's, it cannot be attributed to theft or imitation, which I have avoided like reefs, especially in vernacular works, but to pure chance or similarity of mind, as Tullius calls it, which caused me unwittingly to follow in another's footsteps.
>
> (3.203–4)

Like the romantic poets Harold Bloom studies, Petrarch here tries carefully to hide his debts, a task made harder by his clear dependence on the *Vita nuova* and the *Commedia* for the plan of his own *Rime sparse*.[8] Here, in the context of vernacular poetry, Petrarch abandons the combination of piety and independence with which he had characterized imitation of the classical authors. Instead, predecessors become dangerous and imitation an unavoidable snare for the unwary poet. In contrast to his earlier admission of casually reading minor authors and studying the major ones until they became part of him, he now denies ever being an imitator, and where similarity to a model was earlier explained on a genetic basis, Petrarch now resorts to the mimetic imitation of a similar reality, or even happenstance, to account for the resemblance of his works to Dante's.

In the same letter Petrarch also emphasizes his turn to Latin and away from the vernacular, attempting to elevate himself above Dante, who had followed just the opposite path in his career. Dismissing the notion that he is envious of Dante's popularity, Petrarch becomes shrill and unconvincing: "How can someone who does not envy Virgil envy anyone else, unless perhaps I envied him the applause and raucous acclaim of the fullers or tavern keepers or woolworkers who offend the ones they wish to praise, whom I, like Virgil and Homer, delight in doing without? I fully realize how little the esteem of the ignorant multitude carries weight with learned men" (3.205–6). Forgetting his republican principles, Petrarch here resorts to the tropes of *vituperatio*, portraying himself as a literary aristocrat appealing even in the vernacular to the more cultivated tastes of those who can appreciate Virgil and Homer (which is to say few indeed, as Petrarch himself probably did not know Greek). This letter, written at roughly the same time as his letters on imitation, gives us a very different image of Petrarch, struggling not with the ancients but with the living legacy of a more recent poet. The transparent defenses against Dante reveal the identity of his true poetic father and force Petrarch to employ every sort of reproach in his rhetorical warehouse. Just as his descriptions of the imitative process heuristically refer to both his Latin and his vernacular poetry, so too this letter reveals how even the strongest and most successful imitator can feel anxiety about his task.

Reviewing Petrarch's letters on imitation and the one on Dante, we can distinguish between two distinct reactions to his predecessors. The first is a sense of being inferior or deficient in comparison to the achievements of the ancients; this is what Harold Bloom calls "cultural belatedness" (*Map*, 77–80), and it became a defining feature of the Renaissance. Although Petrarch clearly looks up to their achievements and feels that his own culture as a whole has no comparable attainments, he is not ashamed to admit he has read their work. Indeed, he uses the digestive trope to emphasize how much labor he expended on study of the principal classical authors, to the point that they have been absorbed and transformed into a part of himself; in actuality, it is the very gulf between them that allows him the freedom to imitate these models in the fashion that Greene dubbed "heuristic." Dante poses a different set of problems, however, and Petrarch's clear retreat into the language of a Freudian family romance (the assertion and then denial of a fantasy father in the place of his own) cannot merely be accounted for in terms of the real acquaintance between Dante and Petrarch's biological father. Dante is threatening to Petrarch in a much more immediate way than were the classical authors because his works, however rough Petrarch may judge their language to be, are the towering accomplishment of Italian vernacular literature, and in textual, structural, and mythic terms they are a necessary model for Petrarch's own work. Thus his feelings about Dante constitute what

Bloom calls feelings of poetic belatedness, a nagging sense that the dead predecessor has formed oneself, and is even now speaking through one's own voice. Petrarch's shrillness regarding Dante is striking compared to his generosity about ancient authors; poetic belatedness is a much more emotional phenomenon than humanist belatedness, yet for that very reason, in a strong poet it produces greater results.

Shifting to Bembo, we can now appreciate the full implications of transfer to the vernacular of the tripartite model of history, and its attendant sense of humanist cultural belatedness. Bembo in the *Prose* explicates Petrarch's texts in terms of a rather idiosyncratic set of linguistic theories that were to have relatively little influence; what was influential was his designation of trecento Tuscan as the national literary language. Similarly, however much Bembo's theories of imitation may have been motivated by the need for well-trained writers in a papal chancery that was shifting its language of operation from Latin to Italian (see Donisotti's introduction to Bembo's *Prose e rime*, 36; and more recently Partner, 142–44), Bembo's argument is presented in terms of a myth of decline, and a proposal to stem the decline by reversing Petrarch's own self-proclaimed move from the vernacular into Latin. By using this myth, however, Bembo runs the risk of conflating the cultural belatedness of the humanists with the poetic belatedness Petrarch felt about his vernacular predecessor and rival. By crystallizing this union, Bembo transforms Petrarch from a mere linguistic model (one whose example is to be "followed," in Pigman's terms) into a classical model subject to transformation and competitive emulation. Yet if he burdens the Renaissance vernacular poet with Petrarch as a type of poetic father, he also provides that poet the freedom inherent in the humanist hermeneutic. This distance allows writers to make of Petrarch what they will; however much Bembo may have meant Petrarchism to be a sociolinguistic concept, Petrarchism—particularly outside Italy—can take on a variety of generic, stylistic, thematic, and even ethical dimensions. The freedom of the foreign imitator, however, is conditioned by the horizons offered by the national tradition; hence, we must turn our attention from Italy to the country that is the focus of this study, and examine the construction of a Castilian literary identity in the late fifteenth century.

SPANISH ALTERITY AND THE
LANGUAGE OF EMPIRE

Petrarchism outside Italy is necessarily different, for Bembo's linguistic prescription—that literary composition should employ the Tuscan dialect of the trecento—cannot be transferred where the adoption of Petrarch as a model necessarily involves a change of language, and where his influence is mediated through a different set of conditions on both literary and extraliterary levels. Spanish alterity arises from just such an interplay of social and literary factors: Spain, the first unified nation-state in Europe and for more than a century the most powerful, early on attained a self-conscious national literature. This process coincided with the completion of the so-called Reconquest of Granada, even as an intimate relationship with Italy brought a perception of Italian cultural superiority. Far from diminishing Petrarch's role as a model, alterity expands the ways in which he can be imitated, as imitators look beyond the linguistic surface that was Bembo's main concern: Petrarch was repeatedly a source of poetic renewal, as poets continuously reread, reinterpreted, and reappropriated his work. The new horizons led to imitations that at their worst fixated on the decorative aspects of Petrarch's style, but at their best looked to the organization of the *Rime sparse* as a macrotext and, in exceptional cases, tackled the profound issues of love, morality, and individuation that troubled Petrarch himself.

Humanist belatedness, while not unique to Italy, necessarily acquired different characteristics in other countries, resulting in the elevation of different *topoi* to the status of master tropes. Italians, for example, regarded the Romans as their ancestors, so the death and rebirth of ancient culture, while influenced by external invasions, were viewed as national concerns and expressed through the trope of the tripartite model of history. To scholars such as Curtius, the very idea of the "Middle Ages" is "a coinage of the Italian humanists and only comprehensible from their point of view" (20). The "Renaissance" was a strictly Italian affair, and "the concept that Spain, France, Germany, and so on, experienced 'Renaissances' is to be rejected. It is true, however, that these countries had one or more waves of 'Italianism'—which was the export form of the Italian Renaissance" (34 n. 44). Yet by acknowledging the existence of cultural rebirth as a trope in fifteenth-century Italy, and its subsequent dissemination abroad, he concedes that a notion of the Renaissance can be grounded in the self-concept of the period, and that as this movement spread it created a problem of priority for humanists outside Italy, where insecurity about the present was compounded by anxiety over national identity and its relation to the classical sources of Western culture.[9] Curtius illuminates the issue by examining one of the principal *topoi* used to counter the lack of priority, that of the *translatio studii*. According to this theory, the center of learning shifts periodically and moves gradually to the west: thus, the origin of civilization was in the ancient Near East, which gradually passed the torch to the Greeks and then to the Romans, and so on.[10] The trope was of little consequence to the Italian humanists (though, as we have seen, Bembo used it), but it was very important to those outside Italy who sought to show that their efforts were the most important. The Italian revival might be a continuation of Rome, but, viewed from abroad, a Renaissance in France or Spain indicates a new movement farther to the west, so French or Spanish humanists had to posit a *translatio studii* that lagged behind the *translatio imperii*, which had already been accomplished. Thus, like the trope of humanist belatedness, that of the *translatio* serves as much as a sign of hidden worries about the lack of priority, as an effective antidote. Moreover, it prompts an added degree of anxiety, for as a cyclical scheme of history it implies an eventual downfall for the very nations that use it to account for their rise. As Italian humanist ideas spread abroad, they carried with them, as Johan Nordstroem put it, Italian notions about the importance and superiority of Italian civilization, and a disdainful attitude regarding "barbarians" who lived beyond the Alps (15). The result of appropriating such Italian ideas may be termed "displacedness," a geographical sense of national inferiority parallel to the historical sense of belatedness.

In Spain a tradition of classical scholarship existed throughout the late medieval period, particularly in the wake of contacts fostered with Avignon during the reign of the Spaniard Pedro de Luna as Benedict XIII. Ottavio Di Camillo, adapting Ferguson's model to Spain, shows how these efforts remained largely "prehumanistic," for scholars did not conceive of themselves as renewers of antiquity; rather, they viewed the past ahistorically, minimizing the gap that separated them from ancient times. Only in the wake of Iñigo López de Mendoza, marqués de Santillana (1398–1458), did a more thoroughgoing, but still indigenous, form of humanist belatedness arise. In his "Proemio e carta"—the preface to an anthology of his poetic works, written in the late 1440s—Santillana presents a panoramic history of poetry from the ancients to his own day. The twelve-hundred-year gap he posits between the ancients and the moderns suggests the tripartite division of history that opens the way for the humanist hermeneutic, but by and large his is a chronologically and geographically inclusive list. Though deeply involved in the political events of his day, Santillana does not link the situation of Spanish poetry to military attainments, or view literary history in terms of a *translatio studii* that would set up an opposition between Spain and Italy. Similarly, Santillana's sonnets, though considerable poetical achievements in their own right, show an eclectic approach to imitation, and while permeated with Petrarchisms as decorative devices, they do not struggle to appropriate Petrarch as a single, privileged model.

Yet Santillana's importance to Spanish humanist self-consciousness stems as much from the posthumous praise of his followers as from his own accomplishments. In a letter written after Santillana's death, his nephew the poet Gómez Manrique pictures him as the first to join the cuirass to the gown, and as figuratively tearing ignorance from the fabric of Spain, while Pero Díaz de Toledo commented that more than anyone else in Spain this nobleman exercised himself so as to perpetuate his fame through both his wise writings and his extraordinary acts of chivalry (249–50). Even more interesting, as Di Camillo points out, are the comments of Diego de Burgos (in Schiff, 460–64). By attributing the revival of learning to Santillana, Burgos employs a trope already well established in Italian humanist circles; but Di Camillo is correct in underlining its significance, for Burgos uses it to set up an opposition between Italy and Spain. With language that anticipates later writers, he depicts Santillana as a warrior successfully looting that eloquence which was formerly the property of the Italians and bringing it to Castile, where now it begins to flourish.[11] His choice of words legitimizes Santillana's intellectual pursuits, for they result in the same aggrandizement of Castile as the other, more traditional and bellicose occupations of the nobility. Thus as Di Camillo concludes, with the development of a tripartite historical conscience, there grew both a sense of humanist belatedness and a turn toward Italy as the model country in which the literary recovery was furthest advanced.

Yet if fifteenth-century humanist belatedness was primarily indigenous, it was transcended at the end of the century by national developments that led to a more complex relationship with Italy. As Di Camillo observed, in humanist rhetoric Antonio de Nebrija (ca. 1441–1522) replaced Santillana as the instigator of the rebirth of learning in Spain; and while in part this move paralleled the Italian humanists' postponement of the Renaissance, with Nebrija's greater classical scholarship allowing him to eclipse Santillana, it also reflected the evolution of Spanish political and cultural institutions. By the end of the fifteenth century, the homogenization of Spain was clearly at hand, as the dynastic union of the crowns of Aragon and Castile presaged the imminent conquest of Granada and the expulsion of the Jews. With it came Castilian hegemony in linguistic as in political matters, but with it too came an internationalist attitude previously associated with Aragon. Late fifteenth-century concepts of Spanish cultural inferiority to Italy, and of the connection between literary achievement and the Spanish empire, can be glimpsed in the *Gramática de la lengua castellana* by Nebrija and the "Arte de poesía castellana" by his probable student Juan del Encina (1468–ca. 1529). To both Nebrija and Encina, literary history lags behind Spanish political and military achievements, and they contrast cultural shortcomings to Italian achievements. By casting both political and literary history in terms of a *translatio,* they seek to predict that literary accomplishments will eventually catch up with military ones. But in the process they reveal a rivalry with Italy for cultural legitimacy, based on feelings of belatedness and displacedness, and they burden Spanish culture with fear of eventual decline and extinction.

The year 1492 is a key one for the Spanish Renaissance, not only because of its political events, but also because the first grammar of a modern European vernacular was printed in Salamanca, the *Gramática de la lengua castellana* by Nebrija.[12] Although Nebrija had been engaged in its production since at least 1486, when he presented to the queen a sample of his proposed project, its appearance in that historic year was not entirely coincidental, as the conquest of Granada and the expulsion of the Jews only culminated longstanding policies designed to unify and pacify the Iberian peninsula. Castile seemed to be at its political and military peak, ready at last to look outside itself; and the most immediate opportunities lay in Africa and Italy, each in its own way symbolic of Spain's cultural heritage. Ferdinand's Italian policy was to yield, within a decade, the deposition of his Neapolitan cousins and the absorption of southern Italy by the Spanish crown. The new international prominence of Spain and its focus on Italy leave their mark on Nebrija's grammar, which emerges as the first document of Spanish cultural belatedness and thus of the Spanish Renaissance.

It is primarily in the prologue to the *Gramática* that Nebrija advances the concept of cultural belatedness, by linking the national language to a theory of empire, and presenting both in cyclical terms:

> Siempre la lengua fue compañera del imperio; y de tal manera lo siguió, que junta mente començaron, crecieron y florecieron, y después junta fue la caída de entrambos.
>
> (97)

> Language was always the companion of empire, and followed it such that together they began, together they grew and flourished, and later together they fell.

To substantiate this assertion of connection and cycle, Nebrija proceeds to a historical survey of the great political and linguistic powers of the past, combining military and literary accomplishments. Abraham spoke the Chaldean language of his birthplace, which, mixed with Egyptian, resulted in Hebrew at the same time that the Jews were constituted a nation. Moses was the first to philosophize and write in the language; from there it flourished, reaching its zenith during the peaceful reign of Solomon, after which, with the disintegration of the Jewish state, it declined. After the Jews the Greeks were the next to attain hegemony, a process that began with Orpheus and continued after the Trojan War with Homer and Hesiod, reaching its apogee at the time of Alexander the Great, when poets, orators, and philosophers gave the Greeks mastery of all the arts and sciences. With the dissolution of his empire, the Romans became their masters, and then simultaneously the Greek language began to dissipate and Latin to grow strong (98). Latin had its childhood with the city's foundation, and began to flourish at the time of

Livius Andronicus some five hundred years later. Thence it grew until the *pax romana* of Augustus, which was also the time of the birth of Christ, in a period of peace foretold by the prophets and prefigured by Solomon's own reign. Then flourished Cicero, Caesar, Lucretius, Virgil, Horace, Ovid, Livy, and all the others who followed until the time of Antoninus Pius, when the decline set in that ultimately resulted in the corrupt Latin of Nebrija's own day.

Nebrija employs these cycles from the past to establish a structure that he can apply to the situation of Spain. In view of that motive, the history he provides cannot be taken at face value, for it exists only to substantiate the pattern he wishes to defend. Thus, although his rhetoric is historical rather than metaphysical, the model he employs is essentially typological. He cites literary figures to support his argument of linguistic and cultural domination, and while avoiding theories of divine inspiration (Moses and Orpheus are merely the first writers in their respective traditions), he echoes the trope of the *translatio imperii* along with its accompanying *translatio studii.* This echo is particularly evident in his exposition of the transition from Greece to Rome, motivated by the dissipation of Alexander's empire, which in turn made possible the Roman conquest of Greece. At the same time, Nebrija extends the decline forward to his own day, so that the ancient traditions have not totally disappeared, though they have been corrupted. His portrait of contemporary Jews as completely ignorant of Hebrew ("ninguno sabe dar más razón de la lengua de su lei, que de cómo perdieron su reino, y del Ungido que en vano esperan" [none can explain the language of their laws, nor how they lost their kingdom, nor the Anointed One they vainly await], 98) plays an important rhetorical and typological function. On the one hand, as the first nation to decay, they have sunk the farthest, and thus they serve as a warning to the Castilians, appropriate in the year of the expulsion. On the other hand, Nebrija successfully privileges them: the reign of Solomon is the model for the reigns of Alexander and Augustus, and the Hebrew prophets are mentioned not at their pertinent historical moment but during his history of Rome. Contemporary Jews still awaiting a Messiah may not realize it, but the fulfillment of their history occurred precisely at the apogee of Roman military and cultural power.

That moment of universal peace "en que embió Dios a su Unigénito Hijo" (when God sent his Only-Begotten Son, 98) is also typologically related to present-day Castile, for the same organic pattern, with a childhood and then a maturity, is applicable to Castilian, as is the sometimes blurred combination of language, culture, and empire (see Sacks; Piedra). The language had its childhood, associated with the laws of León and Castile, and it showed its strength at the time of Alfonso the Wise, not only because of his *General estoria* and *Siete partidas* but also because he fostered the translation of works from Latin and Arabic into Castilian. This support gave it the strength to spread to Aragon and Navarre and even to Italy, "siguiendo la compañía de los infantes que embiamos a imperar en aquellos reinos" (following the company of the princes we sent to rule in those kingdoms, 100). It has reached its fullness in the reign of the present monarchs, through divine generosity but also because their diligent efforts have insured that the parts and members of Spain have been reunited. The subsequent religious purgation of Spain should guarantee its freedom from dissolution for hundreds of years; thus it is time for the arts of peace to flourish.

On this note Nebrija connects the current situation of Spain to the situation of those earlier empires at their apogee, with verbal echoes reinforcing the typology: "La monarchía y paz de que gozamos" (the monarchy and peace we enjoy, 100) is related to "aquella paz de que avían hablado los profetas" (that peace of which the prophets spoke [i.e., the time of Christ's birth], 98), and Solomon, in whose time "con la monarchía floreció la paz" (with the monarchy peace flourished, 98). Yet Nebrija also employs this connection to modulate from the history of the rise of Castile to its threatened decline. The first art of peace is language, yet Castilian remains "suelta y fuera de regla, y a esta causa a recebido en pocos siglos muchas mudanças; por que si la queremos cotejar con la de oi a quinientos años, hallaremos tanta diferencia y diversidad cuanta puede ser maior entre dos lenguas" (loose and unregulated, and for this reason it has changed a great deal in just a few centuries; thus if we compare the language of today to that of five hundred years hence, we will see as many differences as exist between two languages, 100). Time is thus spatialized: the language of his Spanish contemporaries could be a foreign tongue to their descendants, and just as the decline of earlier empires had led to linguistic corruption and oblivion, the same thing could happen to Spain if the cycle were to be repeated. Their majesties' chronicles and histories, written to ensure their immortality, would eventually expire along with the language, or survive weakened in translations.

Yet this decline need not occur, for the language has a champion in Nebrija, who has decided to regulate the Castilian tongue, so that whatever is written from then on may be of one kind, which can extend itself through time. This is how Latin and Greek survived; "fue aquella su gloria" (that was the glory [of the classical grammarians]) "y será nuestra" (and it will be ours [both the monarchs' and Nebrija's], 101) to do the same. The time is right for this endeavor, "por estar ia nuestra lengua tanto en la cumbre, que más se puede temer el decendimiento della que esperar la subida" (for our language is already at its height, so that its decline is to be more feared than its growth to be expected, 101). The grammar will also help those wanting to learn Latin and, more importantly, foreigners wanting to learn Castilian. Nebrija recalls how, when he presented a sample to the queen and she inquired about its utility, the bishop of Avila (Hernando de Talavera, later first archbishop of Granada) answered for him that as she subjected new lands to her yoke, foreigners would need to be able to read the laws she decreed. The extent of the empire Nebrija envisions is clear: not only Muslims in Africa will have to learn the language but also Basques, Navarrese, Frenchmen, and Italians. Thus in imitation of those ancients who dedicated their works to august patrons, Nebrija dedicates his grammar to the sovereigns, removing it from "la sombra y tinieblas escolásticas a la luz de vuestra corte" (the shadow and darkness of the schools to the light of your court, 102).

The key to Nebrija's concept of history is his notion that Castile is at a pivotal instant, which he links typologically to the rule of Solomon in Israel, Alexander in Greece, and Augustus in Rome. Not all nations achieve this moment, and it has literally moved westward and arrived in Spain. It is the time when great empires come into their own, but also when they begin to decline; and while ordinarily political dominance is accompanied by cultural hegemony, in Spain's case the latter feature is lagging. Nebrija's grammar will facilitate the extension of the Spanish empire by allowing foreigners to learn the language, and its perpetuation by insuring that future generations will always be able to read it. Yet although the thrust of Nebrija's argument is clear, his method is subtle in its equivocations.

The nature and the workings of the cycle are ambiguous, for the argument is mythological rather than scientific, and only in the case of Rome's conquest of Greece does he suggest how dominance is passed on. Language change is invoked only in terms of decline, and Nebrija's philological explanation of how Spanish evolved from Latin, present in other parts of the grammar, is absent from the prologue. Moreover, in contrast to the quick succession of Greece and Rome, the fourteen-hundred-year lag between the latter and Spain begs a question about the regularity of the cycle, and the sense of belatedness is implicit in that Spain, supposedly at its peak, has nothing to rival classical and biblical literature.[13] Indeed, the grammar is intended to jump-start the process of cultural development. Yet while a decline in Spanish fortunes would seem an imminent and inevitable feature of the cycle, Nebrija holds out an uncertain promise for the sovereigns: perhaps his grammar will assure their immortality by allowing future generations to read their history; perhaps it will possess an efficacy allowing the further extension of the Spanish empire, at the cost of the peace that marks the apogee. Although Nebrija never invokes the argument over arms and letters, he implies an ambiguous role for the aristocracy, on the one hand continuing to extend Spain's rule over neighboring countries, on the other, wasting their precious leisure reading novels and stories for lack of better alternatives. The empire can be extended only if Nebrija is successful in regulating the language of all Spaniards, so his function as grammarian will parallel that of the nobility as warriors.

In rhetoric, style, and ideology the prologue stands apart from the rest of the grammar, for there is something nearly apocalyptic in Nebrija's attitude regarding the *translatio,* a suggestion that Spain may—perhaps because it is the westernmost European country— be its fulfillment and thus escape the fated decline. It is this suggestion that led Américo Castro to infer a Semitic background for Nebrija's prologue, asserting that "the Hebraico-Islamic . . . lived in the *will-be* of his hope, in prophecy, in messianism, in a temporal and spatial beyond" (593). Nebrija, instrumental in bringing the press to Salamanca, was surely aware of its capabilities for aiding the exercise of control over the national language. Yet such messianism is absent from the rest of the grammar, even from the special prologue to book 5, devoted to the teaching of Spanish to foreigners. Moreover, throughout the grammar, but particularly in the chapter devoted to rhetorical figures, Nebrija cites as examples quotations from earlier fifteenth-century writers without any of the reservations expressed in the opening prologue.[14] Nebrija's cyclical view of the *translatio* is problematic, for behind his optimistic view of Spain as the heir to Greece and Rome there lurks the threat of a Spanish decline (see Buceta), while the fourteen-hundred-year gap between Rome and Spain raises the question of modern Italian culture as either a successor to or a continuation of Rome. These issues are taken up and given a more specifically literary refraction in the "Arte de poesía castellana" by Nebrija's probable student Juan del Encina, first printed in Encina's *Cancionero* (published in Salamanca by the printer of Nebrija's grammar in 1496).[15]

Encina's 1496 *Cancionero* is notable in Spanish literary history as the first major published collection of secular poetry by a living author; his close links with Nebrija's circle in Salamanca suggest that Encina himself may have supervised the edition.[16] In addition to the "Arte," it contains translations of Virgil's eclogues, considerable amounts of religious and secular poetry, and some of the earliest surviving dramatic texts in Spanish. The general prologue dedicates the entire book to the Catholic monarchs:

> Dizen los antiguos y fabulosos poetas, que Prometeo, hijo de Japeto, acostumbrado a fabricar cuerpos umanos de barro, subió al cielo con ayuda y favor de Minerva y traxo de una rueda del sol un poco de fuego con que después introduzía vida y ánima en aquellos cuerpos. Y assí yo, desta manera, viéndome con favor del duque y duquesa de Alva, mis señores, subí a la gran altura de la contemplación de vuestras ecelencias por alcançar siquiera una centella de su resplandor, para poder, en mi muerta labor y de barro, introduzir espíritus vitales.
>
> (1.2)

> The ancient mythological poets say that Prometheus son of Iapetus, accustomed to making human bodies out of mud, rose to heaven with Minerva's help and took from the wheel of the sun some fire with which he gave life and soul to those bodies. And so I, in this way, seeing myself in favor with the duke and duchess of Alba, my lords, rose to the heights of contemplating your excellencies by reaching just a spark of your splendor, so as to introduce vital spirits into my dead labor of mud.

In this opening image, masterfully analyzed by Andrews (85–91), Encina exhibits the combination of obsequiousness and arrogance, humility and pride, typical of his prose style. The *amplificatio*, often achieved through doublings ("antiguos y fabulosos," "ayuda y favor"), fails to obscure the keystone of the analogy ("assí yo"), through which Encina identifies himself with Prometheus. By the repetition of the word "favor," his current patrons are reduced to types of Minerva, boosting him up to heaven, with which the monarchs are identified, while he associates his work of poetic creation with Prometheus's divine creation of life. As Andrews notes, "The exaltation of the King and Queen is not 'free,' but is intermeshed with considerations of personal import. As one who has contemplated their excellence, who has tapped the moving force of their effective virtue and who has handled a flash of their brightness, Encina enters the realm of the select servants of their divine magnificence" (87). The message is clear: if they patronize him, only greater glory both for him and for them will ensue. Yet the prologue is also permeated with a fear of rejection, expressed in what Andrews called "a humility almost without modesty" (90), and in warnings about "detratores y maldizientes" (detractors and gossips, 1.3) out to blacken his reputation.

These psychological themes, in particular a love–hate relationship with the nobility coupled with a fear of slanderers, pervade many of the works in the 1496 volume. Nebrija, despite a reliance on aristocratic patronage, was ultimately a technocrat, offering philological skills to the monarchs whom he proposed to serve. Encina, by the nature of his artistic talents, was more directly dependent on patronage, so he attempts from the start to coopt the nobility with a theory of *ocio*, or aristocratic leisure (see Andrews, 71–72; López Estrada). Like Nebrija, Encina proposes to ameliorate the quality of Spanish literature; but while the former had aimed to improve what was available for the nobility's consumption during its moments of leisure, the latter proposes to make poetry an aristocratic activity by regulating that leisure. He opens the "Arte" by providing himself with a classical antecedent, Cicero's description of Scipio the Elder, "que dezía nunca estar menos ocioso que cuando estava ocioso" (who declared he was never less leisured than when he was at leisure, 1.6), and thereby confronts a double paradox: poetry requires *otium*, an aristocratic neglect of the very duties associated with the position of a nobleman, particularly in Spain, while leisure must be used constructively and in a disciplined way, which negates its status as leisure. Poetry requires not just talent but also skills that must be mastered, and which Encina proposes to teach, claiming to have written the treatise "por donde se pueda sentir lo bien o mal trobado, y para enseñar a trobar en nuestra lengua, si enseñar se puede, porque es muy gentil exercicio en el tiempo de ociosidad" (so that good verse may be told from the bad, and to teach how to write verse in our language, if such a thing may be taught, for it is a very gentle exercise for moments of leisure, 1.7). Thus the aristocratic poet must embrace poetic work instead of military and governmental tasks. Yet Encina does not picture this departure as a radical one, for he describes Prince John, the son of the Catholic monarchs to whom the "Arte" is dedicated, as raised in the lap of sweet philosophy, favoring the ingenuity of his subjects, and inciting them to knowledge with himself as the example (1.7). These accomplishments in turn are traced back to the monarchs, "tan poderosos y cristianíssimos príncipes, que assí artes bélicas como de paz están ya tan puestas en perfeción en estos reynos por su buena governación" (such powerful and Christian princes, that the arts of war as well as of peace are perfected throughout these realms, by their good government, 1.6). Thus Encina links the abundance of *ocio* back to the typological role of the kings, earlier exploited by Nebrija. With false modesty, Encina promises the prince that if he desires,

> estando desocupado de sus arduos negocios, exercitarse en cosas poéticas y trobadas en nuestro castellano estilo, porque lo que ya su bivo juyzio por natural razón conoce, lo pueda ver puesto en arte, según lo que mi flaco saber alcança.
>
> (1.7)

> when not occupied in his arduous affairs, [he] can exercise himself in poetry composed in our Castilian style, so that what his lively judgment through natural reason recognizes, he may see regulated, insofar as my slender knowledge allows.[17]

Having established this didactic aim and connected it to the historical moment, Encina describes yet another reason for writing the work. Specifically recalling Nebrija's attempts to reform the language through a printed set of rules, he presents his own efforts as a parallel:

> Creyendo nunca aver estado tan puesta en la cumbre nuestra poesía y manera de trobar, parecióme ser cosa muy provechosa ponerla en

arte y encerrarla debaxo de ciertas leyes y reglas, porque ninguna
antigüedad de tiempos le pueda traer olvido.

(1.8)

Believing our poetry and manner of verse never to have been at such
a height, it seemed to me a useful thing to codify it and place it under
rules and laws, so that no passage of time can cause it to be forgotten.

To reinforce the danger of oblivion, Encina declares that while pre-
vious Spanish poets may have surpassed his contemporaries, he is
ignorant of their work. Instead he offers a history of poetry, begin-
ning with its divine origin as understood by the Greeks and as evi-
denced in the Bible. The former attributed its origins to Apollo,
Mercury, Bacchus, and the Muses, while much of the Old Testament
was written in verse, and in view of the anteriority of the Hebrews
to the Greeks, Moses can rightly be called the first poet (see Curtius,
241–46, 446–58). Encina also cites generals who exhorted their
troops by means of speeches in verse and recalls how Orpheus
moved stones with his poetry, how other poets had their lives
spared because of their verses, and the high esteem both Greeks
and Romans had for their poets.

This historical discussion of the origins of ancient poetry ends
with an account of meter and rhyme in ancient Christian hymnody,
which Encina sees as the genesis of modern vernacular poetry; but
he asserts that the Spanish received it only through the mediation
of the Italians:

> Quanto más que claramente parece, en la lengua ytaliana aver avido
> muy más antiguos poetas que en la nuestra, assí como el Dante y
> Francisco Petrarca y otros notables varones que fueron antes y
> después, de donde muchos de los nuestros hurtaron gran copia de
> singulares sentencias, el cual hurto, como dize Virgilio, no deve ser
> vituperado, mas dino de mucho loor, quando de una lengua en otra
> se sabe galanamente cometer. . . . Assí que, concluyamos luego el tro-
> bar aver cobrado sus fuerças en Ytalia, y de allí esparzídolas por nues-
> tra España, adonde creo que ya florece más que en otra ninguna
> parte.
>
> (1.14–15)

Moreover, it seems clear that in the Italian language were poets much
more ancient than those in our own, such as Dante and Francis Pe-
trarch and other notable men who came before and after, from whom
many of ours took a great quantity of singular ideas, which theft, as

Virgil says, should not be criticized but is worthy of much praise, when it is gallantly made from one language into another. . . . Thus we may conclude that verse drew its strength in Italy, and from there was broadcast and sown in Spain, where I now believe it flourishes more than in any other place.

With this transition to the modern Italians, who pass the art of poetizing on to the Spanish, Encina also modulates into the notions of belatedness and of the *translatio*. Once again there is a gap between ancient Rome and Spain, only this time it is partly filled with Christian hymns and with Dante and Petrarch. As in Nebrija, culture is linked to empire, and to effect the *translatio* Spanish poets literally have to sack or rob their Italian predecessors, carrying the booty back to Spain. This action is justified with an indirect (and pseudo-) Virgilian quotation, which also reinforces the link between Rome and Spain first established through the allusion to Cicero that opened the "Arte." By citing only Romans and Italians, Encina preserves the westward movement dictated by the *translatio*, but at the cost of ignoring not only the Provençal troubadours and the eastward movement of poetry into Italy (recognized by Santillana and other fifteenth-century writers; see Andrews, 75–76) but all Spanish poetry before his own day (see Weiss, 237); only Nebrija is praised for his earlier effort at codification of the Spanish language. This selectivity allows Encina to employ the same historical scheme as Nebrija and to present Spain as the true heir of Greece and Rome, an aspect he highlights by referring to Quintilian as "nuestro Quintiliano" because of his birth on the Iberian peninsula, and by emphasizing that the Spanish language is descended from Latin (see López Estrada, 157).[18] Yet Encina's use of the *translatio* has its inescapable drawbacks, for it polarizes literary history into a decline/ascent dichotomy. Italy was the source of Spanish poetry, but by fertilizing Spain, Italy lost potency. Now it is the Spanish who are on the ascent, but they must compete with the prior Italian achievement in order to surpass it and at the same time regulate their own art in order to assure its comprehension by future generations.[19]

Having justified the work in terms of a larger historical vision, Encina now turns to more immediate didactic ends, and here the discussion of poetry changes from the mythical accounts of its origin to more familiar Horatian precepts. He defends, by appealing to the examples of Horace and Quintilian, the need for an *arte*, a technical handbook to instruct poets, for natural talent is not enough. Indeed, drawing on the contrast between composer and performer, geometer and stonemason, he argues for a distinction between the *poeta* and the *trobador:* the former term is reserved only for those who have studied and are conscious of the quantitative rules of poetry (on this distinction see Weiss, 190). Ever aware of his royal audience, Encina even here attempts to couch his argument in ways that would appeal to the nobility, extending the analogy to include lord and slave, captain and soldier. He warns that the distinction is not much observed in Spain, and while he himself sometimes neglects it, the point is an important one, for in contrast to the confidence in the opening chapter about the position of Spanish letters, we now get a sense of confusion, of the need for rules and, even more, for the public recognition of rules. They must be acknowledged by the talented, and are best nurtured by reading:

> Deve exercitarse en leer no solamente poetas y estorias en nuestra lengua, mas tan bien en lengua latina; y no solamente leerlos como dize Quintiliano, mas discutirlos en los estilos y sentencias y en las licencias, que no leerá cosa el poeta en ninguna facultad de que no se aproveche para la copia que le es muy necessaria.
>
> (1.20)

> He should exercise himself by reading poets and historians not only in our language but also in Latin; and, as Quintilian says, not only read them but discuss their style and ideas and figures, for there is nothing the poet will read that he will not take advantage of for that abundance which is necessary to him.

These passages reinforce the earlier ones asserting the need for poetic work.

Most of the rest of the treatise is taken up with technical matters, such as meter, line lengths, and the like. The fundamental unit of verse is the line, or *pie*, composed of either eight or twelve syllables (respectively, *arte real* and *arte mayor*). Encina also discusses the division of *arte mayor* into hemistichs, the use of *pies quebrados* (four-syllable half-lines), and the rules for consonant and assonant rhyme. He admits the possibility of rhyming *proverbio* with *sobervio* (rhyme is based on sound, not orthography), and advises against internal and repetitious rhymes. Lines of verse may be gathered into units of two, three, or more; only those units with at least four lines may properly be called *coplas*.[20] Throughout this section of the "Arte," Encina cites poems by earlier fifteenth-century poets, particularly Juan de Mena. Thus here, as in Nebrija's grammar, there is a distinction between the visionary rhetoric of the preface and the body of the work itself. Encina's rules, centered on syllable count, reflect an aural conception of poetry, but also an attempt to apply to poetry those mathematical forms of analysis which make music and geometry part of the quadrivium. The examples from Mena justify Encina's rules (see Andrews, 172–73, nn. 12–13), but those rules more accurately reflect Encina's own poetic practice (see Clarke, "On Juan"). As such, study of the "Arte" trains not only poets but also readers who will be properly appreciative of Encina's own work. The chapter on poetic colors is mostly concerned with rules for adapting words to fit the meter, and with complex rhyme schemes. Encina thus emphasizes melopoeic devices, while figures such as metonymy and metaphor are scarcely mentioned, for as they are not unique to poetry, they belong to the more general fields of rhetoric and grammar.[21] The last, brief chapter includes instructions on breathing during oral performance, perhaps a reflection of Encina's double role as musician and poet; but it concludes with a discussion of how a poem should look on a page, reflecting the luxuries introduced by the mass production of paper and printing.

Encina is not ambivalent about the social status of poetry: he regards it as an aristocratic activity, a talent that only the man of leisure can afford to cultivate. Yet the very notion of devoting leisure time exclusively to literary pursuits reflects Encina's professional situation and is antithetical to the Spanish nobleman's concept of himself. Moreover, he never seems quite convinced of the superiority of Spanish letters. Spaniards may be, via the Italians, the heirs to Greece and Rome, but they are not really as accomplished; and just as the Romans, at the height of their powers, needed handbooks of poetry and rhetoric, so too the Spanish must have them. In the treatise Encina attempts to come to terms with the legacy of the past, both antiquity and, more immediately, the Italians. He thus stands at a crux, on the one hand ignoring (save for Juan de Mena) the poetical accomplishments of medieval Spain, much of them already in print, on the other hand citing Dante and Petrarch as poets from whom the Spanish have learned a great deal. Yet Encina does not slight traditional Spanish forms, and whatever the influence of Dante and Petrarch may have been, he makes no mention of sonnets or hendecasyllabic verse. Indeed, as Rico has shown, the traces of Petrarch in fifteenth-century Spanish poetry are primarily linguistic and decorative, while only Santillana wrote sonnets.

Spanish belatedness as a national cultural problem thus arises toward the end of the fifteenth century, and its appearance at that time is related to a number of roughly coinciding developments, including the introduction of printing, national unification and purgation, and greater Spanish intervention in Italy. The basic text for Spanish belatedness and alterity is the prologue to Nebrija's Spanish grammar; employing the trope of the *translatio*, Nebrija demonstrates how the great civilizations of the past attained their apogee at a moment of peace, when culture also flourished. He finds contemporary Spain at that point in its military history, but culture lags and deterioration threatens to set in: if it does, the achievements of his day will be forgotten. With his grammar he hopes to redress that lag and perhaps even deliver Spain from the previously inevitable decline. Nebrija's program is refracted in Encina's "Arte de poesía castellana," in which Encina makes the *translatio* more pointed by combining it with Greco-Roman and Christian poetics: poetry began with the Jews and was practiced successively by the Greeks, the Romans, and their latter-day descendants Dante and Petrarch. By responding to the formation of the nation-state and identifying the fate of the empire with that of its poetry, Nebrija and Encina codify Spanish belatedness and alterity, and ultimately prepare the way for the poetical innovations of Boscán and Garcilaso forty years later. As each successive generation continues to perceive a cultural inferiority to Italy, the *translatio*, which Encina saw occurring in his own day, is successively postponed, and Petrarch's status—for Encina merely proverbial—becomes ever more significant. Encina tries to elevate the status of poetry by tying it to a theory of aristocratic leisure and associating it with the quantitative study of the quadrivium; while his rules for poets are primarily melopoeic, his conception of literary history opens the way for the transformations of the next 150 years.

SOME QUESTIONS OF METHOD

My approach to Spanish Renaissance lyric is based on an understanding of Renaissance cultural belatedness as elaborated by examining Petrarch and Bembo, and then contextualized by reference to

Spain. These strictly literary determinations are leavened with a consideration of the social and historical environment in which the poetry was written and read. The significance of the social context is strongest in the earlier chapters, which cover the time during which the link between Petrarchism and the Spanish empire is being forged; it diminishes later as that link becomes more and more residual. My emphasis is on those poets who were most self-conscious of the conflicts between their roles as imitators of Petrarch and their desire for national and individual priority. The collective judgment of history has in fact identified them as the principal Petrarchist poets of the Spanish Renaissance; consequently, this study focuses on the most canonic poets of the period, from both the first rank (Garcilaso, Góngora, Quevedo) and the second (Boscán, Herrera). The historical and theoretical importance of less-canonized poets such as Gutierre de Cetina and Francisco de la Torre is an interesting problem in its own right, but not one that concerns us here.[22] Similarly, I do not discuss the continuing popularity of verse in traditional Castilian forms; Boscán, Garcilaso, and Herrera conscientiously turned their backs on these genres, differentiating Italianate poetry as a separate discourse, a status it retained into the seventeenth century. Other historical and theoretical issues worthy of further discussion but excluded because of their relatively tangential relation to this study are the role of primarily Portuguese poets such as Camoens in the fuller Iberian polysystem; the mystic poets, Fray Luis de León and St. John of the Cross, on whom Petrarchism was an important but secondary influence; and Lope de Vega, whose Petrarchist lyric is not at the center of his literary production. My approach does however entail a consideration of poetic theory along with poetic texts. Not until the end of the Renaissance did poetic theory attain in Spain the status of an autonomous discourse (see Terracini, *Lingua,* 122–25), and systematic preceptive poetics were antithetical to the courtly aesthetics associated with Petrarchism in Spain (see Elias Rivers, "L'humanisme linguistique" and chapter 2, below). Most often, Petrarchist poetic theory was expressed in the form of paratexts on the poetry itself, particularly prefaces and commentaries, and nearly all of the poets I consider either wrote such paratexts or were the objects of others' paratextual production.

By using Curtius and Bloom to elaborate a theory of cultural belatedness, we not only apply twentieth-century theory to early modern Spanish texts but also use those texts to historicize the theory and explore its specifically Renaissance applications. Bloom, a close reader of Curtius, whose work he calls "the best study of literary tradition I have ever read" (*Map*, 32), considers belatedness a "recurrent malaise of Western consciousness" (77) and distinguishes psychopoetic belatedness from the cultural belatedness of the Renaissance (77–80). To Bloom, "reading, when active and interesting, is not less aggressive than sexual desire, or than social ambition, or professional drive" (*Breaking*, 13), as the act of reading forces a confrontation over the lack of priority, particularly on poets who are in competition with their predecessors. Yet while the romantic poets on whom Bloom concentrates could attempt to disguise their predecessors, Renaissance poets had canons that determined their models, and as a result compounded their psychopoetic and cultural belatedness. The applicability of Bloom's theory to Renaissance literature is controversial; the Freudian terms of his analysis are often rejected on grounds resembling Greene's, that the humanist poet is not a neurotic son in an Oedipal struggle with predecessors (41; for comment on Greene see Cruz, *Imitación*, 7–9).[23] However, Bloom's use of Freud (along with Lucretius and the cabala) is heuristic, serving more to explain a theory than to construct it, and the poets he studies, ranging from Milton to Wallace Stevens, were hardly crippled by their relationships with their predecessors. Bloom's triad (sexual desire/social ambition/professional advancement), meant as a catalog of what his audience might recognize as their strongest drives, is also an appropriate delineation of the passions that motivated Renaissance poets, who often composed poems about love in order to obtain not just a woman's favor but also recognition at court and its tangible benefits.

For me Bloom himself serves a heuristic purpose, which brings several advantages. The first is that his once-exotic critical terms have passed into common use, allowing one to describe Petrarch's belatedness (the section on Bembo and Petrarch, above), Garcilaso's metalepsis (chapter 3), Quevedo's clinamen (chapter 5), and the like by analogy, without positing a pathological diagnosis. Second, Bloom's theory of poetic agon resonates in two important directions. One of them is what Pigman calls eristic imitation or emulation, in which "the model, without whose help any progress is impossible . . . has become an adversary engaging the young author in a fight to the death" (Pigman, 18). While Pigman makes a good case for the presence of three kinds of imitation in the theorists he studies, only agonistic emulation held out, for Spaniards, the possibility of surpassing Italian hegemony. Bloom's theory also resonates with Bakhtin's investigation of the relation between imitation and polyphony. Development of a Bakhtinian approach to the lyric has been somewhat stymied by the Russian theorist's conception of lyric poetry as a "straightforward" genre, incapable of being truly polyphonic (*Dialogic Imagination*, 49–50; see also Todorov, 63–67). But in *Problems of Dostoevsky's Poetics*, Bakhtin, while not specifically addressing the question of lyric poetry, takes up the question of how imitation can lead to polyphony or intertextuality. To Bakhtin, mere stylization or nonagonistic imitation of the type recognizable by a specialist does not make a discourse polyphonic (*Problems*, 186–87).[24] But in imitation of the type that Bakhtin calls parodic, polyphony does occur because there is a clash between the original and the later discourse, in which the latter is given a new orientation (ibid., 189). Bakhtin goes on to explain how this is different from ordinary imitation, wherein the other's voice, while taken seriously, is not heard as an other but is merged with the author's own voice. In parody,

> as in stylization, the author again speaks in someone else's discourse, but in contrast to stylization parody introduces into that discourse a semantic intention that is directly opposed to the original one. The second voice, once having made its home in the other's discourse, clashes hostilely with its primordial host and forces him to serve directly opposing aims. In parody therefore, there cannot be that fusion of voices possible in stylization . . . the voices are not only isolated from one another but also hostilely opposed.
>
> (ibid., 193)

Bakhtin limits polyphony to what he calls parody, but as Linda Hutcheon notes, the historical phenomenon that most closely and most consistently approximates theoretical parody is Renaissance imitation, which, like parody, "offered a workable and effective stance toward the past in its paradoxical strategy of repetition as a source of freedom. Its incorporation of another work as a deliberate and acknowledged construct is structurally similar to parody's formal organization" (10). Admittedly, the relationship among Bloom's notion of poetic agon, Renaissance ideas about emulation, and the

Bakhtinian theory of parody is not one of identity but one of affinity. Still, consideration of these related phenomena allows us to qualify and to historicize Bloom's model, better adapting it to our own purpose.

In her discussion of parody, Hutcheon also cautions against a shallow approach that remains on the level of merely noting the structural or formal relations between texts (exemplified for us by Herrera's laconic introductions, "la imitación es de" [it is an imitation of], *Anotaciones*, 334; but see chapter 4). Rather, she argues for a pragmatic approach that considers both the encoder and the interpreter (22–23), as well as the parodists' double role as both interpreter of the original and encoder of the new sign. Here again there is a family resemblance with Bloom's notion of poetic misprision. Intertextuality can then become, as for Maria Corti, "un avvicente forma di ermeneutica testuale" (a prospective form of textual hermeneutics: *La felicità mentale*, quoted in Gargano, 9). For us to cast an imitation/parody in terms of Bloom's revisionary strategies, then, is not to make an aesthetic judgment about a work but to interpret the way that the author of the imitation has encoded within that text his own relationship with the original. Furthermore, by emphasizing the historical process of reading and writing, Bloom also enables us to write something approximating a narrative history, albeit an idiosyncratic one.[25] Spanish literary studies, particularly of Golden Age poetry, have long labored under the shadow of Dámaso Alonso's approach, which—drawing on Saussure—viewed a poem as an accumulation of signifiers crafted to affect a reader.[26] On practical and theoretical levels, Alonso made important contributions to literary history, but by privileging Saussure he also privileged synchronicity and thus a method that, like *Poesía española*, results in a series of chronologically arranged essays on various poets, rather than a diachronically developed argument.[27] I acknowledge a debt to Alonso, whose historical contributions and stylistic analyses, along with those of his intellectual progeny, are used throughout this book in the discussion of particular poets, particularly the later ones whose rhetorical complexity demands a traditional "close reading"; but in the end, mine is a different approach.

In addition to the ones already described, there are further points of contact between Renaissance and modern theory, and between formalism and historicism; one, as Kennedy argued (*Rhetorical*

Norms, 1–3, 16–18), is the reader as an implied, fictionalized entity (Ong), as a hermeneutic principle (Gadamer, Jauss), and as a phenomenological reality (Ingarden). Kennedy argues against a strict adherence to formalist and structuralist notions of literature as a closed system, but agrees that it is only within the context of historically specific horizons of expectations that readers and poets appropriate other texts. Thus I prefer, as a model for synchronic characterization, Even-Zohar's nuanced formulation of a literary and cultural polysystem, creating multiple opportunities and constraints, multiple ways of approaching and rewriting a predecessor text.[28] Three further theorists have also contributed to my understanding of Renaissance poetry. The first is Ezra Pound, whose distinction between the phanopoeic and melopoeic aspects of a poem is particularly useful for understanding the aesthetic transformation that accompanied the shift from medieval Castilian octosyllabic poetry to genres employing the hendecasyllabic line (see chapters 2 and 4, below). Second, there is Maria Corti's notion of a macrotext, an organized collection that is a sign in its own right and whose meaning thus exceeds the sum of its parts (see chapters 3, 4, and 5). Finally, I use Bakhtin's discussion of imitation and parody to analyze the breakdown of Petrarchism through the overabundant intertextuality of seventeenth-century poetry (see chapter 5).

The lyric potency of the Petrarchist myth cannot be explained by exclusive recourse to formalism or literary history, however. Belatedness played an important part, but so did artistic ambition. As Kerrigan and Braden expressed it, "Artistic and sexual ambitions are interchangeable; they can be substituted for each other in the course of reaching countless bargains. A solitude stocked with images may be preferable to having an amorous partner. The value of postponement, hedonistic as well as moral, is considerable" (188). Petrarchism is thus best understood as a synecdoche for the broader yearning for fulfillment and autodetermination. As such, it is always slightly subversive, even when most established and canonical. At a time when legitimate expressions of sexuality were tightly controlled (by family, by royal decree, by rules of celibacy, by economics), every time a Petrarchist lover complains, he suggests that sexual relations ought to be freer, without recourse to the burlesque world of prostitution. Every poem about powerlessness and imprisonment spoke to a real and ever-present danger for the religiously searching and the politically active; every poem about bodies and wealth spoke to the unbalanced economy of Renaissance Spain, and even to the slave labor of the Americas. There is relatively little of Petrarch's moral questioning in this poetry, which depends on the fantasy that the impossible should be possible, without asking whether it is deserved. Such questions could bring down the system (and, in Quevedo's case, possibly did), by destroying both the fantasy and its capacity to generate new avatars of the myth. I will touch on these issues now and then in the course of this study, and return to them in the conclusion.

2

Poetic Theory in
the Reign of Charles V

Castiglione and the Spanish Renaissance

The poets and courtiers Juan Boscán (ca. 1490–1542) and Garcilaso de la Vega (ca. 1501–1536) transformed the nature of Spanish lyric in the second quarter of the sixteenth century, in part through the example of their poetic works, but also through their dissemination and appropriation of Italian courtly aesthetics. The impressive body of lyric that Boscán and Garcilaso produced, published in 1543, is examined in the next chapter; here I focus on their role as translators of Baldesar Castiglione's *Il libro del Cortegiano*. Published only six years after the first Italian edition, the Spanish version, done by Boscán at Garcilaso's instigation, set the terms for Spanish Petrarchist literary theory; although the *Cortegiano* does not expound any particular theory of poetry, such a theory can be construed from its discussion of linguistic, aesthetic, and social issues. This theory was highly inimical to the kind of poetry represented in the fifteenth- and early sixteenth-century poetic anthologies (*cancioneros*), which was based on strict observance of complex prosodic rules. The theory also has important political and linguistic ramifications, for by associating such poetry with the cultural tastes of unaristocratic Castilian nativists, Boscán uses Castiglionian principles to identify his own Petrarchist poetry as a cosmopolitan cultural form more in keeping with the transnational empire of Charles V. The indirect manner—the translation of a dialogue on courtiership—through which Boscán and Garcilaso advance their views is itself an embodiment of the aesthetics of indirection and *sprezzatura* that they espouse. Consequently, Spanish poetic theory of this period must be gleaned from a variety of sources. Of particular importance is Boscán's preface to his poetic works; this, the major theoretical statement of the period, employs indirect courtly rhetoric to disguise a presentation of aesthetic principles and a theory of literary history.

THE SPANISH APPROPRIATION OF
IL CORTEGIANO

Traditional Spanish historiography emphasizes the importance of the Castilian–Netherlandic connection: the unexpected inheritance of Castile by Joan the Mad and her Flemish husband Philip the Handsome, and his premature death, leaving the Belgian-bred future Charles V as his heir. When the latter duly claimed his inheritance in 1517, his northern upbringing, and the many Flemish and Burgundian ministers and courtiers who accompanied him to Spain, were widely resisted, and his departure in 1520 to claim the imperial crown led to a widespread rebellion known as the revolt of the *comuneros*, in which the leading cities and much of the lower nobility took part. The repression of this movement discredited narrowly focused Castilian nationalism and its cultural manifestations, leaving the way open for new forms with the potential for expressing an international culture that befitted the transnational empire. Italian culture and manners presented just such an alternative, for Italy was not an entirely foreign country, but another part of Charles's far-flung realm. Yet the relationship to conquered Italy was psychologically complex; as Croce put it,

> España e Italia tuvieron más de dos siglos de vida casi común a consecuencia de la dominación territorial y de la hegemonía española de nuestro país. El centro cultural de los italianos, o como se decía entonces, 'la corte', era Madrid; muchísimas familias españolas se habían establecido definitivamente en Italia; nobles y plebeyos italianos engrosaban las filas de los ejércitos de los Reyes Católicos; políticos y magistrados italianos figuraban en sus consejos; lengua, costumbres, y algunos de los monumentos de la literatura española, tenían vigencia entre nosotros de la misma manera que nuestra lengua, literatura, y costumbres imponíanse en España.

(11)

Spain and Italy had more than two centuries of almost conjugal life as a result of Spanish territorial domination and hegemony over our country. The cultural center for Italians, or as they then said, the "court," was Madrid; many Spanish families established themselves definitively in Italy; both noble and plebeian Italians fattened the ranks of the Catholic monarchs' armies; Italian politicians and magistrates figured in their councils; the language, customs, and some of the monuments of Spanish literature ruled among us just as our language, literature, and customs imposed themselves on Spain.

From 1492 to 1503 the Spaniard Rodrigo Borgia presided over the church as Pope Alexander VI, while Ferdinand of Aragon, after twice intervening to foil the Neapolitan ambitions of the French monarchy, assumed direct rule over Naples in 1504, residing there for two years. Together these developments provided enormous opportunities to Spaniards for patronage in Italy, and these opportunities did not diminish in the succeeding years. As Croce showed, the presence of so many Spaniards in Italy and Italians in Spain had a profound effect on many areas of life, particularly in the cultural and linguistic realms.

The exchange of people and the transformation of cultures only increased after Charles's ascension to the joint thrones of Castile, Aragon, and Naples. From the beginning of his reign, his major foreign preoccupation was a rivalry with the French king, Francis I; after Charles secured the imperial election in 1519, that rivalry was principally played out in Italy. Francis repeatedly invaded the peninsula, but after his capture at the Battle of Pavia in 1525, Milan became yet another of Charles's possessions. On a symbolic plane, the Spanish domination over Italy was represented by the sack of Rome in 1527; though carried out by predominantly German troops under the command of a renegade Frenchman, the army was at least nominally the emperor's, and the attack left Charles, and thus Spain, the undisputed major player in Italian affairs. The sack both shocked and amazed contemporaries; over the years it was followed by other signs of Spanish hegemony, such as the imperial coronation in Bologna (1530) and Charles's speech, in Spanish, to the Roman curia (1536; see Fernández Alvarez, 65–67, 83–88, 106–7). To contemporary observers, these events could only mark the eventual ascendancy of Spain in the cultural as well as the military spheres.

The pope's nuncio in Spain at the time of the sack was Count Baldesar Castiglione (1478–1529), whose *Libro del Cortegiano,* a work steadily elaborated and revised for nearly twenty years (see Guidi, "Reformulations"), was first printed in 1528. Castiglione had been negotiating with Venetian printers before the sack, and his motivation for publishing it may well have been, as he claims in his dedication to Michel de Silva, to counter the unauthorized circulation of a manuscript copy by Vittoria Colonna, marchioness of Pescara. Yet his publication, at this time, of a nostalgic and fictionalized evocation of Italian court life from a generation before may have had an added significance as well. The elaboration of the text took place over the backdrop of growing Spanish domination of Italian affairs; Castiglione, who was shortly to write of himself, "non mi riputarò giammai di essere meno spagnuolo che italiano" (I will never again consider myself less Spanish than Italian, quoted in Guidi, "L'Espagne," 201 n. 399), was both fixing for eternity an idealization of Italian culture and asserting its superiority over that of the nation he now called home.

In 1534, the *Cortegiano* was translated into Spanish by Boscán at the instigation of Garcilaso de la Vega, who also revised the translation. Just as in the sack of Rome Spanish troops had made off with the cultural artifacts of the premier Italian city, so by translating Castiglione's work the poets appropriated the book's teaching, making it available to Spaniards and thereby transferring the locus of its reception and influence. For if the book proclaims Italian culture of a certain time as a model, the translation asserts that the relevant audience for that model, the place where the imitation is to be realized, is Spain. That the Castiglione-Boscán *Libro del cortesano* should be a major document for the development of Spanish Petrarchist poetic theory may seem surprising; the book was translated into other European languages, and Petrarchism spread throughout Europe, but the two developments are not usually linked, other than as marking the general spread of Italian influence.[1] Most criticism of Castiglione is concerned with divining his intended meaning; those who consider *Il Cortegiano* primarily in an Italian context see the work as hostile to the Bembist conception of Petrarchism as a vernacular analogue to Ciceronianism and as a linguistic determination that writers should use only the idiom that had been used by Petrarch and Boccaccio. But consideration of the work's reception in the Spanish cultural context is a different matter. Boscán's translation of Castiglione's text must naturally be the point of departure, but to gauge its importance for Spanish poetic theory, one must also perform a purposeful misreading of the text, emphasizing how it would have been read in Spain, and how it was appropriated by

Boscán and Garcilaso in support of the generic transformations they were effecting in Spanish poetry.[2]

Surprisingly, Castiglione's book is not overly concerned with poetry, a topic about which the speakers have little to say directly. But from scattered comments, primarily but not exclusively in book 1, a theory of poetry can be construed. As already noted, the author is hostile to Petrarchism as a literary idiom. In the preface dedicated to de Silva, written shortly before the book's publication in 1528, the author rejects the use of a Tuscan norm:

> No convenía usar yo muchas [palabras] de las del Bocacio, las cuales en su tiempo se usaban, mas agora ya andan desechadas aún por los mismos toscanos. Tampoco he querido obligarme a la costumbre del hablar toscano de nuestros tiempos.
>
> (16)

> I did not find it desirable to use many of Boccaccio's [words], which in his day were used but now are abandoned even by the Tuscans themselves. Nor have I wanted to force on myself the usage of the Tuscan spoken in our time.

Castiglione protests too much, for in fact he submitted his text to revision and Tuscanization by none other than Bembo himself. Yet ordinarily one need not describe one's choice of language, for its very use demonstrates the choice that has been made; thus this statement is an example of how Castiglione means his book to be both didactic and exemplary—as Kinney put it, "it *is* what it is about" (134). These remarks sum up an extended discussion in book 1, written ten years earlier, in which Count Ludovico de Canossa and Federico Fregoso debate the issue of literary idiom. The identity of these speakers is important, for both are central contributors to the dialogue. Canossa is entrusted by Emilia Pia, in book 1, to form the verbal portrait of the ideal courtier, while Federico was the original proponent of the game of defining the courtier, and in book 2 he takes Canossa's place as the principal speaker. The comments of both speakers should thus be taken seriously, for neither is ordinarily a straw figure making arguments to be defeated.

Yet here Federico seems to be on the losing end of the discussion. The count recommends to the ideal courtier a literary idiom based on his actual speech, counseling the avoidance of affectation in the form of ancient Tuscan words that have fallen into disuse. But Federico holds out for a certain acuity (Boscán, "una cierta agudeza sustancial," 65; Castiglione, "acutezza recondita," 1.30) in writing attainable by using a distinctive vocabulary, and criticizes any reader unable to understand it. We should follow Petrarch and Boccaccio, he declares; Virgil himself did not hesitate to imitate Homer (66–67). But the count maintains that Petrarch and Boccaccio did not use words that were outdated in their own day, and as only rustics use them now, such words are no longer part of sophisticated speech.

There follows a defense of modernity based on the concept of linguistic mutability, the growth and decay of words, and the pleasure of neologisms.[3] The resulting language would be common to all Italy, yet heterogeneous, like a garden full of different flowers. But Federico continues to argue for a vernacular Ciceronianism:

[A] mí no me cabe que en una lengua particular, la cual no es universalmente a todos los hombres así propria, . . . sino una invinción contenida debaxo de ciertos términos, no sea más razón tener fin a seguir aquellos que hablan mejor, que hablar a caso; y que, como en el latín el hombre se debe esforzar a parecer a Virgilio o a Cicerón más aína que a Silio o a Cornelio Tácito; así también en el vulgar no se haya de tener por mejor seguir la manera de hablar de Petrarca y de Bocacio que la de los otros.

(78–79)

I do not see why in a particular language, which is not the universal property of all . . . but is an invention ruled by certain conventions, it would not be more reasonable to follow those who speak better, than to speak randomly; and just as in Latin we should make the effort to resemble Virgil and Cicero more than Silius or Cornelius Tacitus, should it not be better also in the vernacular to follow the speech of Petrarch and Boccaccio than that of others.

To Federico, language is not idiolectical but diachronically social; its beauty consists in observing the propriety of words and using them in the same way as did those who wrote best, in following their style. But the count retorts that many praise Cicero and Virgil only because they have heard them praised, without knowing why; in reality Caesar, Varro, and others, though using different words, are just as good.

Here Emilia Pia ends the discussion; by her interruption Castiglione grants the count the final word, rejecting linguistic Petrarchism as he declares his objections to a vocabulary limited to old Tuscan words, in favor of a more contemporary and cosmopolitan idiom; as Guidi notes ("L'Espagne," 164), Castiglione, perhaps to avoid insulting an old friend, never has the Bembo in the dialogue speak in defense of his eponym's linguistic theories. Thus, while alluding to the *questione della lingua*, Castiglione also implicitly rejects it; Emilia Pia's repeated attempts at interrupting the debate indicate both that the issue cannot be resolved and, worse, that it is essentially tiresome.[4] Instead of an absolute linguistic standard, Castiglione prefers an aesthetic one; deconstructing the example of Virgil imitating Homer, Canossa points out that they wrote in different languages. The issue thus is not linguistic purity, but stylistic—and thus aesthetic—borrowing. To privilege words as the Petrarchists do is to separate them from their meaning. Going against the book's general preference for manner over substance, Canossa asserts that "lo que más importa y es más necesario al Cortesano para hablar y escribir bien, es saber mucho" (what is most important and most necessary for the Courtier, if he is to speak and write well, is to know much, 70), and to a question about whether such refined speech would be intelligible, the count replies that "la facilidad y la llaneza siempre andan con la elegancia" (ease and plainness always accompany elegance, 71). That aesthetic standard is all-pervasive in Castiglione's book, and it is here that one finds a key to his influence on Spanish poetic theory. By appropriating, even as he rejects them, the terms of the *questione*, Castiglione prepares the way for a new standard of literary evaluation that is potentially applicable in any national or linguistic context.[5]

Related to the aesthetization of life is Castiglione's transformation of the nature of the ludic, which comes to include former nonludic areas of life. This is underlined at the beginning of the book when the courtiers are choosing the game that is to be the night's activity. After the feasting and music are over, the duchess, herself a substitute for the crippled and absent duke, delegates to Emilia Pia the task of devising a game for the evening's entertainment; she in turn decrees that each person should propose a new game until one emerges that strikes her fancy. Thomas Greene ("*Il Cortegiano* and the Choice of a Game," in Hanning and Rosand, 1–16) notes how the other games rejected by Emilia Pia also emphasize the importance of play, as do the enclosed space, the circle of participants, etc. Yet this echo of the *Decameron* is also a ludic *mise en abîme* that transforms all life into a game; as Regosin put it, "the courtier is thus that which forms itself through its art—with words or with other signs, as we shall see—and that which performs itself to earn the name of courtier. Courtiership is not a state or a mode of being but an attribution, a name given—and taken away—by a public which judges the performance; it is not a signified but a signifier" (24). Like Greene, Regosin notes that the proposed and rejected games are important examples of rules of the larger game that is courtiership (33–36), and that they demonstrate the unlimited amplitude required if the discussion is to perform its role of a pastime (30–31).

The key to all this ludic activity is *sprezzatura*, which "signifies that i) there is no art; ii) there is art but it is so well-hidden that it does not show; iii) if there were art the actor could do even better than he has done" (Regosin, 37). Yet the fact that all activity is ludic and aesthetic permits a kind of synesthesia; as already noted, Castiglione has relatively little to say about verbal art, but the principles for such art, and specifically for poetry, can be induced on the basis of his comments about other arts.[6] *Sprezzatura* (generally translated by Boscán as *descuido*; see Morreale, 163–64; Terracini, *Lingua come problema*, 55–70), as described by the count, is not only an aesthetic principle but also a universal one:

> Pero pensando yo mucho tiempo entre mí, de dónde pueda proceder la gracia, no curando agora de aquella que viene de la influencia de las estrellas, hallo una regla generalísima, la cual pienso que más que otra ninguna aprovecha acerca desto en todas las cosas humanas que se hagan o se digan; y es huir cuanto sea posible el vicio que de los latinos es llamado afetación; nosotros, aunque en esto no tenemos vocablo proprio, podremos llamarle curiosidad o demasiada diligencia y codicia de parecer mejor que todos . . . usando en toda cosa un cierto desprecio o descuido, con el cual se encubra el arte y se muestre que todo lo que se hace y se dice, se viene hecho de suyo sin fatiga y casi sin habello pensado.
>
> (59)

> But after myself considering for a long time where grace comes from, excluding for now that which comes from the influence of the stars, I arrived at a general rule which I believe more than any other will enable one to employ it in all things done or said; and that is to flee as much as possible from the vice the Romans called affectation, and

which we who have no proper word for it might call curiosity or ex-
cessive diligence and a desire to seem better than anyone else . . .
employing in all things a certain disdain or carelessness that hides
skill, and shows that all things one does or says, are done for them-
selves without effort and almost without thought.

Sprezzatura is thus applicable to all human actions, of word or deed.
This view is borne out by the succeeding examples the count gives
of *sprezzatura* in action: while the first, of ancient orators who pre-
tended to be unlearned so that their speeches might be more per-
suasive, is a literary one, it is quickly followed by examples from
other arts. First come the two courtiers, one who dances affectedly
on tiptoe, one who pretends such negligence that he allows his cape
to fall off. This example is followed by a discussion of music, in
which too many consonances are unbearable, and excessive har-
mony should be moderated, so that "lo bueno puesto cabe lo malo
parece muy mejor" (the good placed next to the bad appears even
better, 61). In painting, Apelles reproached Prothogenes for never
knowing when to stop; even the application of cosmetics has some-
thing to teach about the nature of *sprezzatura*.

Just as the other arts provide lessons applicable to literature, so
too the inverse, as the traditional literary precept of *imitatio* is ap-
plied to the development of a personal, graceful style of comport-
ment, and just as linguistic Petrarchism is abandoned, so too its
methodological underpinnings are also implicitly discarded. The
count rejects specific rules for gracefulness, but recommends choos-
ing as a model one who has already achieved it, and instructs the
hopeful first to imitate closely, seeking almost to transform them-
selves into the object of imitation, and then to move on to the imita-
tion of other models, concluding with the famous image of the bee
going from flower to flower, "tomando, ora del uno y ora del otro,
diversas cosas" (taking, first from one, then from another, diverse
things, 58), but ultimately making its own honey. This figure is in
turn followed by an account of a failed attempt at imitation, that of
the courtier who picked up only King Ferdinand's mannerisms and
not his essential grace, and thus became an object of derision (see
Kinney, 101). The technique of inductively defining *sprezzatura* by
repeated example rather than by precept is consistent with Castig-
lione's general rejection of absolute rules. The adduced examples,
from every field of human activity, lead ultimately to a complete

breakdown in any workable distinction between life and art, reality and game; and while this results in the aesthetization and ludicization of everyday lives, it also rejects art as an activity that stands in some kind of opposition to reality. Artistic accomplishment is no longer to be defined by a specific set of rules, but by the good taste that the courtier must take pains to develop:

> La buena costumbre de hablar no es ésa, sino la que nace de los hombres de ingenio, los cuales con la dotrina y esperiencia han alcanzado a tener buen juicio. . . . ¿No sabéis vos que las figuras del hablar, las cuales dan mucha gracia y lustre a la habla, todas son abusiones de la reglas gramaticales? Pero son admitidas y confirmadas por el uso, sin poderse dar otra razón dello sino solamente porque agradan y suenan bien al oído y traen suavidad y dulzura.
>
> (74)

> Good usage in speech is none other than that which springs from men of talent, who with knowledge and experience have attained good judgment. . . . Don't you know that figures of speech, which give it such grace and luster, are all violations of grammatical rules? But they are permitted and confirmed by their use, with no other justification than that they give pleasure, sound good to the ear, and bring gravity and sweetness.

This pleasantness in speech is the governing virtue of linguistic discourse, an attitude concordant with the earlier recollection of ancient orators who strove to make their speech as natural as possible; the full impact of this recommendation is evident when it is juxtaposed to the requirement that writing be like recorded speech, and thus not subject to any particular rules or entitled to any licenses. Once again the line between ludic and nonludic activities is blurred.

We can now analyze how this breakdown of the distinction between art and life, ludic and nonludic, augurs a new kind of poetry for Spain. Castiglione's conception of poetry (and, by extension, Boscán's and Garcilaso's), and of artistic activity in general, is antithetical to that of Encina and the other fifteenth-century Spanish theorists. In their view, poetry was a distinct activity, separated in terms of social function and time from everyday life. The poet might aspire to be the equal of the patron, but by that very aspiration he revealed his difference and inferiority; his occupation, or *negocio*, is what the nobleman practiced only in his moments of leisure, or *ocio*. Castiglione expressly extends aesthetization to the activities of everyday life (or at least, the everyday life of the courtier), breaking down the general *ocio/negocio* dichotomy. Life itself becomes aesthetic, and aesthetics (a guide to conduct in the dangerous world of the courtier; see Javitch, "*Il Cortegiano*," in Hanning and Rosand, 17–28) is life. The new kind of poetry must be one that conforms to the principle of *sprezzatura*, that permits itself to hide its own artfulness; the new poet is not the man of letters, but the professional dilettante.

If this breakdown is implicit in Castiglione, it becomes explicit in Boscán, who in his translation emphasizes the point by using the Latinism *ocio* only once, in a pejorative context in book 4. Otherwise he uses the more colloquial *sosiego*, which, while generally synonymous, is not the specific Latinate lexeme preferred by fifteenth-century theorists such as Santillana and Encina.[7] The old poetry depended on the distinction between *ocio* and *negocio*, for it was obviously artistic; by abandoning the principle of *ocio*, Boscán and Garcilaso appropriate *Il Cortegiano*, for three purposes. First and most obviously, Castiglione values the practice of art by the nobility, and indeed insists that the ideal courtier do so as well. In the context of continuing Spanish resistance to the commingling of arms and letters, this assertion of superior Italian manners can only be helpful. But for letters to be made fully aristocratic, the nonnoble, educated *letrado* must be excluded from the ludic world of the court. This is the Spanish poets' second purpose: to assert that poetry is not only an aristocratic activity, but an exclusively aristocratic activity from which those not graced with courtly *sprezzatura*, those who must labor to learn rules, are excluded. Third, the nature of poetry is transformed so that it may properly screen courtier from noncourtier, the latter a category that includes both *letrados* and the lower nobility, two groups seriously implicated in the *comunero* rebellion (see Lynch, 1.45). The circle of the court is to be a special ground between the literate world of the chancery and the military world of the nobility, with its own criteria for admission.

Both Castiglione and his Spanish translators reject the notion of an *arte*, a systematic set of rules defining acceptable conduct. The old poetry was predicated on the mastery of just such a set of prosodic rules; the new poetry will not only violate those rules, but also privilege completely different facets of lyric poetry. Aspects of Castiglione's new theory of poetry can be ascertained by examining remarks, scattered throughout the book, about the nature of verbal art. Written language should approximate spoken language, for "lo escrito no es otra cosa sino una forma de hablar que queda después que el hombre ha hablado" (writing is nothing more than a form of speech that remains after one has spoken, 64); the proximity of spoken language to written language by extension approximates verse to prose.[8] Apparent spontaneity is also a virtue, even if it involves a certain amount of duplicity. Yet the ability to compose poetry is important for the courtier, for the count requires that he be "en las letras más que medianamente instruído . . . y tuviese noticia, no sólo de la lengua latina, mas aun de la griega" (in letters more than passably educated . . . with knowledge, not only of Latin, but even of Greek, 87). Poetry and oratory, as well as history, should be part of his reading matter, and he should practice writing in meter and prose, especially in the vernacular, "porque demás de lo que él gustará dello, terná en esto un buen pasatiempo para entre mujeres, las cuales ordinariamente huelgan con semejantes cosas" (because in addition to his personal enjoyment, he will have in this a good pastime for women, who often entertain themselves with such things, 87). If not worthy of praise, the courtier should keep the poems quiet, but he should still write, for it will help him appraise the writing of others.

I have already noted how, in contrast to the count's preference for a written style that approximates speech, Federico Fregoso prefers a more piquant manner, which he would achieve through the use of old Tuscan words. Federico becomes the chief speaker in book 2, much of which is also important for a theory of lyric. Like the count, he values above all the avoidance of affectation, and links this to a theory of decorum:

> La primera y más importante [regla] es que huya (como muy bien trató ayer el señor Conde) sobre todo el vicio de la afetación. Tras esto, considere atentamente la calidad de lo que hace o dice, el lugar, en presencia de quién, a qué tiempo, la causa por que lo hace, la edad y profesión suya, el fin donde tiene ojo y los medios con que puede llegar allá.
>
> (117)

> The first and most important [rule] is that he above all flee (as the count very well explained yesterday) the vice of affectation. After this, let him pay attention to the nature of what he does or says, the place, in whose presence, the time, the reason he does it, his age and profes-

sion, the end on which he has his sights and the means through which he can attain it.

The result is not a uniformity of style but the selection of an appropriate tone, depending on the circumstances and the addressee. Thus Castiglione demonstrates an openness to different stylistic registers, exemplified by the varying levels of the discussion and in particular of the contributors. The *mediocrità* of the dialogue is achieved not through a monotone but through the collective speech of the contributors.

The balance of book 2 is devoted to a discussion of joking, important because of the value Castiglione places on wit. Federico, who earlier had argued for acuity in the courtier's written style, here employs related terms to describe the function of humor. Verbal humor is subdivided into funny stories and witty remarks; while the gift of telling the former is inborn, the latter are the result of "festividad o urbanidad" (festivity or urbanity, 161; see Morreale, 209–10). He proceeds:

> La otra suerte de donaires es breve, y está solamente en los dichos prestos y agudos [Castiglione: *pronti e acuti*, 2.43], y que alguna vez pican . . . y aun parece que no tienen gracia si no muerden.
>
> (161–62)

> The other kind of pleasantry is brief, and just consists of quick, sharp remarks that sometimes even sting . . . it even seems that they have no grace if they do not bite.

The phrase "agudos y que alguna vez pican" recalls the vocabulary Federico himself had used in book 1 to describe the desired effect of Tuscanisms on the courtier's written style, and thus serves to connect that linguistic and stylistic discussion to this one. When Bibbiena takes over the lead in the discussion of humor, he again employs Federico's terms. Jokes occupy a special place in the heavily regimented world of the courtier; laughter is provoked by something that, like *sprezzatura*, "en sí no conviene, y con todo esto no está mal" (in itself doesn't conform, and yet is not all bad, 166). The rhetoric of provoking laughter is closely related to that of serious praise and blame, and often the same words can produce opposite effects; for this reason, observing the rules of decorum is even more important in witticisms than in everyday speech. Joking thus assumes a hyperludic function in the world of the courtier. Special acuity (Boscán: "presta agudeza," 178; Castiglione: "pronta acutezza," 2.57) can be attained by using words or expressions with two meanings, by saying the unexpected, or by appropriating a proverb or well-known verse to different circumstances. Thus, ultimately, humor too is subject to the rules of *sprezzatura*.

The connection between joking and poetry is enhanced in Boscán's translation, as he provides extended glosses to those principles cited by Bibbiena which promote wit, but which also have literary applications (see Morreale, 211). Thus, for example, ambiguity— "facezie che nascono dalla ambiguità" (pleasantries born from ambiguity, 2.58)—becomes "aquellas [gracias] . . . que nacen de una palabra o razón que se puede echar a dos sentidos, lo cual entre los latinos, especialmente en este caso, se llama ambigüidad" (those graceful remarks . . . which are born from a word or phrase that can be taken in two senses, which among the Romans, especially in cases such as this, was called ambiguity, 178); and paronomasia—"bischizzi" (2.61)—becomes "una suerte . . . de dichos, la cual vulgarmente llamamos derivar" (a type of remark that we in the vernacular call *to derive*, 181). Among the other principles that receive extended glossing are metaphor, irony, and incongruity.

The discussion of humor takes on additional importance because wit is singled out by Castiglione as one of the special virtues of the Spanish (161); this is only one of the many times, particularly in book 2, that Castiglione celebrates Spanish courtiership.[9] They are better courtiers than the French (134), and even their dress is superior:

> Verdad es que yo querría que no siguiesen los estremos, echando demasiadamente a la una parte o a la otra, como el hábito francés que ecede en ser muy ancho, y el tudesco en ser muy angosto, sino que fuesen como los que, tomando del uno y del otro, son corregidos y reducidos en mejor forma. . . . pero en lo demás, querría que mostrasen el sosiego y la gravedad de la nación española; porque lo de fuera muchas veces da señal de lo de dentro.
>
> (141)

> I would prefer them not to go to extremes, tending too much to one part or another, as is the French way of dressing which is excessively loose and the German in being very tight, but rather that, taking from

one and the other, they be corrected and reduced to the best form. . . . But as to the rest, I would wish them to show the sobriety and gravity of the Spanish, for externals are often signs of the internal.

This passage is significant, not only for appropriating a standard trope of literary criticism already used in book 1 (like the bees going from flower to flower, etc.) and applying it to yet another realm of experience. The context for the passage is a discussion of how Italians no longer have a distinctive manner of dress, but instead copy Frenchmen, Germans, and even Turks, and the fear that this imitation augurs their eventual domination by outsiders. Castiglione's Italian readers, looking back in the late 1520s to 1506 (the fictitious date of the conversation in Urbino), see here a melancholy warning of the extinction of the independent Italian courts and a preferential option for the Spanish, ultimate victors in the struggle for the peninsula. But for Boscán's Spanish audience, these remarks herald the extension of Spanish hegemony over Italy, their mode of dress anticipating, on one plane, the sack of Rome and, on another, the translated text in their hands.

Yet for the *translatio* to be fully realized, Spanish cultural life needed to be transformed. The old poetry, which could be judged good or bad on the basis of established rules, would no longer do, for a poetic meritocracy could exclude aristocrats from the tenuous world of acceptable courtiership, or even admit educated commoners like Encina; as Whigham has argued, it is important to Castiglione that he replace a meritocracy of achievement with an aristocracy based on manner. Similarly, the old poetry must be replaced with a new kind to be evaluated on the basis of new aesthetic criteria, for its facility, its wit, its artificial naturalness. No longer can it be marginalized as a pastime for women and an occupation for lettered servants; the latter are now definitively excluded, while the former are elevated and at the same time judged by many of the same standards as men:

Quiero que esta Dama tenga noticia de letras, de música, de pinturas, y sepa danzar bien, y traer, como es razón, a los que andan con ella de amores, acompañando siempre con una discreta templanza, y con dar buena opinión de sí, todas aquellas otras consideraciones que han sido enseñadas al Cortesano.

(234)

I wish the Lady to have a knowledge of letters, of music, of painting, and to know how to dance well and to bring along, as is reasonable, those who are in love with her, always accompanying all those other considerations that have been taught to the Courtier with a discreet restraint and creating a good opinion of herself.

These remarks lead the misogynist Gaspar Pallavicino to grumble, "pues dais a las mujeres las letras . . . no queráis también que ellas gobiernen las ciudades, y hagan las leyes, y traigan los exércitos, y que los hombres se estén quedos hilando, o en la cocina" (for as you give women letters . . . won't you also want them to govern cities, make laws, and lead armies, while men remain quiet, spinning or in the kitchen, 235). To the threatened traditionalist, Castiglione's rules are tantamount to a complete social inversion, a world turned upside down.

As noted at the beginning, there is nothing inherent in the Italian text, or even in Boscán's translation, that specifically heralds a revolution in lyric poetry, an idea alien to the conservative Castiglione. As Javitch conceded, "Poetry had always possessed and been seen to possess the ornamental, deceptive, and playful properties that proper court conduct eventually shared with it. In fact, the Renaissance courtly code, as Castiglione defines it, drew many of its rules for beautifying the self from traditional procedures in verbal and pictorial art. . . . I do not mean to suggest, therefore, that the art of poetry needed the example of beautiful manners to come of age" (*Poetry*, 105). It is only the application of Castiglione's doctrine to Spain, its appropriation and grafting by Boscán and Garcilaso into the Spanish cultural polysystem, and its reception by a different audience that suggest these results. Only in Italy, and only to readers familiar with the *questione*, is there an inherent contradiction between the linguistic positions espoused by Canossa and those articulated by Federico Fregoso. In Spain a synthesis is possible, one suggested by the fact that Virgil could write in Latin and still borrow from Homer. If such interlinguistic imitation was possible in ancient times, and indeed was instrumental in the transfer of cultural dominance from Greece to Rome, the same procedure could again be used in their own day: Spanish poets need only adopt an urbane courtly idiom, while imitating Petrarch's style.[10] Such a procedure would allow the devolution to Spain of Petrarch's *agudeza*, the very same quality identified in book 2 as a particularly Spanish talent.

Furthermore, by translating *Il Cortegiano,* Boscán and Garcilaso produce a text that is revolutionary in a uniquely courtly manner: indirect rather than tendentious, suggestive rather than didactic.[11] Their successful adherence to these aesthetic values, in prologues scattered throughout their various works, has led to a depreciation of early sixteenth-century Spanish poetic theory: there seems to be a gap between Encina and Herrera, there is nothing comparable to Du Bellay's 1549 *Deffence et illustration de la langue francoyse.* That text, however, would have seemed to partisans of Castiglione's aesthetic a terrible throwback to the days of specific rules for specific genres, and of the Horatian isolation of the poet in his studies. Castiglione prefers to teach by example rather than by systematic pronouncement. Repeatedly the main speakers in *Il Cortegiano* reject attempts to pressure them into pronouncing a set of rules for speaking, writing, dressing, joking, and so on. Instead they provide examples, analogies, comparisons, and general principles, such as the avoidance of affectation, that are meant to provoke in the quick recipient a development of his or her own individualized style. Castiglione's hostility to established and objective rules pervades Spanish poetic theory for the next century. The more seriously we take Castiglione's rejection of specific rules and lists of rules, and the more we are attuned to his aesthetic preference for manner, example, and *disinvoltura,* the more we will perceive his influence on Spanish poetic theory, both in method and in substance, and the more we will recognize the sophistication of the Spanish texts.

Not surprisingly, Castiglione's influence is evident in the prefaces by Boscán and Garcilaso to the translation. Touching on many of the topics associated with lyric theory, the prefaces are exemplars of courtly prose, combining a formal dedication to Gerónima Palova de Almogávar with a theory of intervernacular translation, a defense of women, and an evaluation of the contemporary situation of Castilian literature. Boscán attempts to display *sprezzatura* by belittling his own talent and effort, and by crediting all his success to the inspiration of Garcilaso and Doña Gerónima. He ascribes his interest in the book to Garcilaso's having sent it: both the title and the identity of the sender moved him to read it right away, and he immediately wanted to translate it so that "los hombres de nuestra nación participasen de tan buen libro y que no dexasen de enten-delle por falta de entender la lengua" (the men of our nation could benefit from such a good book and not fail to understand it for lack of knowledge of the language, 5). He initially held back, however, because of a general distaste for translation, to him a vain task that even when well done is worth little. Fortunately, Doña Gerónima overruled his doubts by commanding him to translate it, so the book is truly hers, to correct or to censure. The book is about the perfect courtier and lady, a topic so important that his little shortcomings should be forgiven, and while the author touches on many grave themes that some would consider inappropriate for women, science is so intermingled with pleasure, and even the most severe philoso-phy is handled with such artifice, that only the most foolish would find the book objectionable. Doña Gerónima has never sealed her-self off from such topics, and by favoring the book she can put a stop to the complaints.

Courtly indirection, as typified by the triple negatives of the statement quoted above (no/dexasen/por falta), determines Bos-cán's pose of ambivalence about the value of translation. As Mor-reale has shown (15–26), his declaration of principles, with its rejec-tion of word-for-word translation in favor of translating the general sense, fits into a long tradition dating back to St. Jerome. Equally important however is Boscán's distinction between translation of the classics, with attendant problems about the possible insufficiency of Castilian, and translation between vernacular languages. Boscán uses two different words for the two types: the former is *romancear*, meaning to make vernacular, while the latter is *traducir*, with the implication of leading the text across linguistic boundaries: "tra-ducir este libro no es propriamente romanzalle, sino mudalle de una lengua vulgar en otra quizá tan buena" (translating this book is not, properly speaking, making it vernacular but moving it from one vernacular language to another perhaps as good, 5). Boscán is will-ing to accept the possible inferiority of Castilian to the classical lan-guages, as suggested by the homely *romancear;* but *traducir* is a Latinism, reflecting a more sophisticated awareness of the plurality and equality of vernaculars.[12] As Morreale (22–23) and Terracini (*Lingua come problema,* 70) both note, Boscán attempts to prove the capacity of Castilian by avoiding neologisms, but with the result that words become imprecise and polyvalent as they acquire new meanings. Yet the element of personal taste in Boscán's linguistic choices is itself, in Castiglione's terms, a virtue. Boscán, forced to confront discrepancies in the languages—particularly in those sections most closely associated with Italian court life—rather than adhere to a vocabulary that would highlight its foreignness, appropriates the text, both in order to make the original more Spanish, and to advance his and Garcilaso's aesthetic agenda. The struggle to conquer Italy is an analogue to the struggle to hispanize the original text, as suggested by the etymological roots of *traducir*, with its implication of leading away, and overtones of wartime booty, of the enslavement of foreigners, and of the sacking of Italy.[13] The word emphasizes the materiality of the book's contents, as does the phrase "por ser de cosa que traemos siempre entre las manos" (it being about things we always have in our hands, 5), as well as the particularity of that subject matter which will be useful for Spaniards to have, in order that the *translatio* take place.[14]

Garcilaso's preface, while rather more gallant, touches on many of the same themes. After declaring that Doña Gerónima's approval of the book is its greatest virtue, he too moves on to issues of translation theory, echoing Boscán's distinction between *romancear* and *traducir*. The terms of his praise for the fidelity of Boscán's version recall longstanding theories of translation and interpretation: Boscán was a very faithful translator, for he tied himself not to the rigors of the letter, but to the truth of the sentences, and through different paths he put in Castilian all the strength and ornament of the Italian, and thus left everything as he found it. It being as difficult to translate as to write anew, Boscán did well, for the book does not seem to have been written in another language. Echoing Castiglione, Garcilaso explains that he urged Boscán to publish it before someone else printed an inferior text, and even undertook the Horatian task of polishing his friend's work.

Even more interesting than Garcilaso's comments on translation theory are the specific terms in which he praises this particular work. As Terracini noted (150), his praise is based on both its subject matter, preserved by Boscán's exemplary fidelity, and its style, characterized by "naturaleza" (naturalness), "limpieza" (cleanness), and other formal qualities. Men and women must not only try to do the best, but also to avoid what might degrade, and this book treats of both. Therefore it was important to have it available in the Castilian language, "porque ... apenas ha nadie escrito en nuestra lengua sino lo que se pudiera muy bien escusar, aunque esto sería malo de probar con los que traen entre las manos estos libros que matan hombres" (because ... almost no one has written in our language anything save that which we could well have done without, although this would be difficult to prove to those who go about with lethal books in their hands, 10). In these comments about other works in Castilian, Garcilaso goes beyond Boscán's critique of earlier translations, to find no other prose works worthy of praise; Terracini correctly interprets "estos libros que matan" as an aesthetic rather than a moral evaluation. Boscán thus accomplished in Castilian something few others have, "que fué huir del afetación sin dar consigo en ninguna sequedad, y con gran limpieza de estilo usó de términos muy cortesanos y muy admitidos de los buenos oídos, y no nuevos ni al parecer desusados de la gente" (that is, to flee affectation without becoming dry, and with great cleanness of style he used very courtly terms that are accepted by the best ears, rather than those which are new or apparently neglected by people, 10). Here, as Terracini noted (*Lingua come problema*, 151–52), Garcilaso comes closest to appropriating Castiglione's aesthetic terms in order to praise Boscán. Variations in style are due to the desire that not all characters speak equally well, for he was trying to show all of the different manners of speech; this emphasis recalls Castiglione's own contention that *mediocrità* can best be realized through a balance in stylistic registers, and that ugliness is sometimes necessary in order to set off the beautiful better.

While Boscán's preface focuses more on specific issues of translation theory and the translatability of this particular book, Garcilaso amplifies the issues. The general poverty and dependence of Spanish literature become more evident in the stylistic inferiority of other contemporary texts, and in the need for Boscán's translation as a model. This translation is praised in courtly terms, showing how for Garcilaso it will function in a double way: first, as the exposition of certain aesthetic principles and, second, as the fulfillment of those principles, attaining an exemplary role for future writers of Castilian prose. The fact that the original already exists in Italian shows the belatedness of Spanish letters, but the translation will serve in its new context just as the original did in its; to paraphrase the earlier quotation from Kinney, it will be what it is about. Boscán's preface, written at the conclusion of a possibly thankless task that must have consumed a considerable amount of time, shows him attempting to justify that task in terms of its accomplishment. Garcilaso's preface, written from Italy just as the poet is beginning to produce his greatest poems, shows his consciousness of the gap between the countries, and at the same time of the possibility that it can be overcome.

BOSCÁN AND THE AESTHETICS OF THE HENDECASYLLABIC LINE

The impact of Castiglione's book on Spanish poetic theory, and the heightened sense of belatedness and displacedness essential for a truly Renaissance Petrarchism, all become manifest only in Boscán's preface, "A la Duquesa de Soma," published in the volume *Las obras de Boscán y algvnas de Garcilasso de la Vega repartidas en quatro libros* (1543); there he proclaims that the adoption of Italian forms will lead to the transfer of learning to Spain, yet worries about whether the latter can truly be accomplished. In the first chapter we saw Nebrija and Encina, at the end of the fifteenth century, attempting to introduce reforms that would allow Spain, now that it had (so they thought) attained its political and military apogee, to make up for its cultural backwardness. Similarly, Juan de Valdés praised Petrarch and Boccaccio and lamented that writers in Castilian had failed to take similar care in developing their language, so that they could perform a similar role as stylistic models (44). All three writers reveal a growing sense of the inadequacy of Spanish literature, particularly in comparison with Italian, expressed through the trope of the superiority of Petrarch and Boccaccio. The Italy to which they refer, therefore, draws on the greatness of its fourteenth-century writers. Implicit in their expressions of national inferiority is a sense of belatedness, of the need to measure up to the great achievements of the past; and they offer advice for improving Spanish letters. Unlike his predecessors, however, Boscán is ready to take radical steps to reform Spanish poetry: he transforms the trope about the superiority of Petrarch into a plan, for to him it is only by adopting the hendecasyllable and other Italian forms and by breaking with the traditional genres that the Spanish will ever be able to catch up with the Italians. But the arguments are presented indirectly, for the preface is written in a courtly discursive mode that identifies the new poetry with Charles V's transnational empire, and weaves a serious discussion of aesthetic principles and a theory of literary history with courtly rhetoric where the topics of aristocratic superiority predominate.

The theme of social superiority begins in the opening lines of the preface: Boscán, in offering his book to the duchess, claims for it the approbation of Garcilaso, whose own verses constitute the fourth section of the volume, and of Diego Hurtado de Mendoza, who used to take pleasure in Boscán's *coplas*, or poems in the traditional Castilian genres, which take up book 1. With this double sanction, Boscán asserts for his poetry company of the highest caliber that will only be enhanced with the eventual approval of the duchess herself.[15] Their approval is contrasted to the complaints of Boscán's detractors, characterized as "hombres que me cansaron" (men who bored me, 87):

> Los unos se quexavan que en las trobas d'esta arte los consonantes no andavan tan descubiertos ni sonavan tanto como en las castellanas. Otros dezían que este verso no sabían si era verso o si era prosa. Otros argüían diziendo que esto principalmente havía de ser para mugeres y que ellas no curavan de cosas de sustancia sino del son de las palabras y de la dulçura del consonante.
>
> (87–88)

> Some complained that in poems of this type the rhyme was not as discernible as in the Castilian ones. Others said that they could not tell if this was verse or prose. Others argued that this was primarily for women who do not care for matters of substance, but only for the sound of the words and the sweetness of the rhymes.

The final accusation recalls the notion that literature is not a suitable occupation for gentlemen; through this statement of objections, Boscán would seem to prepare readers for a dialectical refutation that will in turn advance his thesis. Yet instead he chooses, as Bianchini put it, "to elude their criticism with a rhetorical strategy aimed at belittling their accusations" ("A Note on Boscán," 2), essentially by impugning their nobility. This is already implicit in the fact that they, unlike Garcilaso, do not appreciate the new poetry; it becomes explicit in their attitude to women, reminiscent of Pallavicino's in the *Cortegiano*. By alluding to their misogyny, Boscán performs the same maneuver as in the preface to his translation, putting his critics outside the pale of those worthy of a response. He also associates their literary taste with their supposedly plebeian background, by a play on words: those who want poetry full of rhyme, he says, can look in that *cancionero* "que acordó de llamarse general para que todos ellos bivan y descansen con él generalmente" (which is by agreement called general so that they can all in general live and take pleasure there, 88).

His opponents have one more complaint, however: that Boscán has adopted Italian forms only in the pursuit of novelty. To deflect this charge, Boscán separates himself from the socially lower class of literate servants, making it clear that writing is for him a pastime, "quiero que sepan que ni yo jamás he hecho professión de escrivir esto ni otra cosa" (I wish them to know that I have never made a profession of writing, neither this nor anything else, 88). He then tells the story of his meeting Andrea Navagero in Granada, of their subsequent discussion about literary matters, and of the Italian asking and even begging him to try to write sonnets in Castilian. Shortly thereafter, on the long trip home, Boscán took up Navagero's suggestion, and although it seemed difficult at first because of the many differences between these forms and the Spanish ones, he eventually found it easier. Even then he would not have continued to compose these poems but for the influence of Garcilaso's judgment, "el qual no solamente en mi opinión, mas en la de todo el mundo, ha sido tenido por regla cierta" (which not only in my opinion, but in everyone's, has been regarded as a sure arbiter, 89).[16] He not only approved of Boscán's efforts and encouraged him to continue, but served as a model in following the same path and writing sonnets himself. Here Boscán's strategy again resembles that in the *Cortegiano* preface, with Garcilaso replacing Doña Gerónima and in turn being replaced by Navagero, yet the purpose is the same: to assert an approving, aristocratic readership for his work that counteracts the negative reaction of his detractors. The locus of the meeting is also important, because it links the new forms, indirectly, to the emperor himself: Boscán and Navagero were in Granada as part of the court, attending the festivities surrounding Charles's wedding (see Menéndez y Pelayo, 67–72; Fernández Alvarez, 62–65), and this information in turn dates Boscán's first attempts at the new forms back to 1526. The anecdote thus serves the same function as the short narratives used by the speakers in Castiglione's book, advancing a position through indirect association rather than through direct argument.

Boscán's assertions of nobility culminate in the claims he makes for the genres themselves. The Italian verse-forms are inherently superior—a point to which we shall return—but they can also claim a better pedigree than the Spanish. This assertion strikes the modern reader as somewhat anticlimactic; after the earlier assertion of aesthetic superiority, it seems odd that Boscán would devote so much attention to the question of genealogy. Here too, however, it is a matter of courtly rhetoric at work, for in a sixteenth-century context lineage is very important indeed. While the origin of the Castilian forms, like that of suspect New Christians, is unknown, the Italian verse forms can be traced back to Petrarch, before that to Dante, and before him to the Provençal poets, whose works, because of the passage of time, have been largely forgotten even though they were also the source of the Catalan poets, including Ausías March. One can even go farther back than the Provençals and find that the Romans used the same hendecasyllables (insomuch as the difference in languages can allow one to speak of the same meter), and that they in turn took it from the Greeks. Thus the genealogy asserts for the hendecasyllable an ancestry in Greco-Roman antiquity not unlike that of knights in romances, while the origin of the Castilian forms, like that of people hiding their Jewish ancestry, cannot be traced.[17] Paradoxically, only the Italian, by being foreign, can be ascertained to be truly noble, fully acceptable. Moreover, in his history of its origins Boscán includes not only the necessary Italian and classical antecedents, but the Provençal ones as well, which permits a digression in praise of Boscán's fellow Catalan poets and particularly Ausías March. In contrast, all medieval Castilian poetry, a well-established canon that includes works by noblemen such as Santillana and Manrique, is ignored, and by implication marginalized with the *Cancionero general* into the category of works fit only for plebeians.

The repeated assertions of nobility for the new genres and their practitioners constitute one of the principal recurrent themes in Boscán's preface. In the context of Castiglione's book, it is understandable, for there too aristocratic origins had been favored, if only for the sake of a better first impression. The point becomes even more important in the Spanish context because Boscán, from the time of

the *Cortegiano* translation, has been trying to impose a new and com-
peting notion of just what constitutes acceptable courtly behavior;
thus his recourse to authorities like the duchess, Diego Hurtado de
Mendoza, Navagero, and above all Garcilaso himself, cited here, as
in Valdés, as an authority on courtiership. Even more pointedly than
in the translation, Boscán here attempts to distinguish between the
general class of the merely literate (that is, the detractors) and those
who can claim to belong to the inner circle of imperial courtiers.[18]
Yet Boscán also has serious aesthetic reasons for preferring the new
mode, which are again in line with the aesthetic principles in Castig-
lione. From the very beginning of the preface, beneath an overlay of
courtly and religious associations, Boscán asserts the inherent supe-
riority of the new forms: "Este segundo libro terná otras cosas
hechas al modo italiano. . . . La manera d'éstas es más grave y de
más artificio y (si yo no me engaño) mucho mejor que la de las
otras" (This second book will contain other things in the Italian
mode. . . . Their manner is graver and of greater artifice and [if I am
not mistaken] much better than that of the others, 87). This is in
fact his thesis, but it is tempered by the indirect presentation and
qualifications. Much of the preface is taken up with explicating the
precise nature of the Italian forms' superiority, a theme to which he
returns again and again; but while this theme forms the aesthetic
core of his argument, he presents it in bits and pieces, never
allowing it to overwhelm the courtly, disinterested tenor of his pre-
sentation.

The initial complaint of the detractors, that the new poetry is
lacking in rhyme and is generally indistinguishable from prose, is
never refuted:

> ¿Quién ha de responder a hombres que no se mueven sino al son de
> los consonantes? ¿Y quién se ha de poner en pláticas con gente que
> no sabe qué cosa es verso, sino aquél que calçado y vestido con el
> consonante os entra de un golpe por el un oído y os sale por el otro?
> Pues a los otros que dizen que estas cosas no siendo sino para mu-
> geres no han de ser muy fundadas, ¿quién ha de gastar tiempo en
> respondelles? Tengo yo a las mugeres por tan sustanciales . . .
>
> (88)

> Who can answer those men who are moved only by the sound of
> rhyme? And who can discuss things with people who don't know
> what a verse is, save that which shod and dressed in rhyme enters

you with a blow through one ear and leaves you through the other? And as to those others who say that as these are women's things, they do not need a good foundation: Who will waste time in answering them? I hold women to be so substantial . . .

At first Boscán's response here—mostly limited, as Terracini noted (*Lingua come problema*, 155), to a restatement of the *defensa de mujeres*—seems inadequate. In fact, it is a courtly move that allows Boscán to dismiss his detractors while appropriating their criticisms to show that the new poetry is substantially in accord with the precepts in Castiglione and Valdés: that writing should be like speech and poetry, like prose. Boscán uses the detractors' complaints to explore, in a more specific way than in the translation, the ways in which Castiglione's courtly principles can transform the Spanish lyric. In comparison to the traditional genres, the hendecasyllable does seem less melopoeic; although there are many stylistic and thematic similarities, in medieval Spanish poetry, rooted in the oral tradition, the reader—and even more the listener—is borne along by the regular rhythms and patterns of sound. These are the *consonantes* that the detractors found wanting; the word means rhyme, but with etymological overtones of euphony as well. Italian-style poetry would strike someone familiar only with the traditional Spanish forms as totally lacking in sound patterns, nearly prose. Of course, this is not true; Italian poetry is in fact characterized by elaborate sound patterns, such as the complicated rhyme schemes of the sonnet, *canzone*, and *sestina*, as well as the subtle stress patterns of the hendecasyllable.[19] But as these are not the kind of pattern with which the Spaniard is familiar, they are not recognized, and the long line obscures in particular the presence of rhyme (see Lázaro Carreter, "Poética"). Just as Castiglione used Pallavicino, so too Boscán uses his critics to make a point that must be accommodated, embedding it in an indirect, dialogic discourse.

Similarly, the detractors' further complaint, that Boscán is pursuing novelties, has a serious dimension, for it amounts to a charge of affectation, the gravest aesthetic fault. As already noted, Boscán attempts to avoid the issue by registering his status as an amateur writer, with no ambitions. Yet he acknowledges a contradiction between these words and the publication of his poetry, one that he can resolve only by an assertion of *sprezzatura*:

Pues si ... he querido ser el primero que ha juntado la lengua castellana con el modo de escrivir italiano ... nunca tuve fin a escrivir, sino a andarme descansando con mi spíritu ... [y] nunca pensé que inventava ni hazía cosa que huviesse de quedar en el mundo, sino que entré en ello descuydadamente como en cosa que iva tan poco en hazella, que no havía para qué dexalla de hazer haviéndola gana.

(89)

For even if ... I have wanted to be the first to join the Castilian language with the Italian way of writing ... I never had any purpose for writing, other than to rest with my spirit ... [and] I never thought I was inventing or doing something that would remain in the world, so I entered upon it carelessly as with an occupation so insignificant that there was no reason for not doing it if I so desired.

The key word here is *descuydadamente*, reminiscent of *descuido* in the *Cortegiano* translation. There is no reason for him not to have tried his hand at the new forms because, unlike those for whom writing is a profession, he sought no benefit from it. Thus, echoing the very language that he had earlier used to render Castiglione's introduction of the concept of *sprezzatura*, he underlines his poetry's ludic function as a pastime so inconsequential that there could be no stricture of affectation held against it. But just as he had earlier appropriated the detractors' argument, so too here this defense allows him indirectly to incorporate the charge he is refuting, modestly minimizing his actions even as he lays a claim to being the first to practice the Italian forms in Castilian, one he substantiates with that early *terminus a quo* for his efforts implicit in the meeting with Navagero.

Sprezzatura/descuido is an ambiguous concept, part aesthetic principle, part social precept, and one better illustrated through example than defined through precepts. Thus this passage is also important because it leads into the story of the meeting with Navagero, which has entered Spanish literary history as a description of the origins of Petrarchism in Spain.[20] While it is possible that the conversation took place as Boscán described it, the story must be read in the context of the *sprezzatura* alluded to in the preceding passage. Consequently, Boscán presents himself being begged by Navagero to try the new forms, taking them up to pass the time on the journey, quickly mastering the requirements, but persevering only at Garcilaso's insistence. At the same time, the account subtly undermines the notion of poetry as the product of *ocio* in its paradoxical sense of free time that can be devoted to poetic work. Instead Boscán presents his poems as a pastime, something to be done during a journey when his mind was not fully occupied, which explains why they may strike readers as lacking in poetic interest. As with the charge that the new poetry is prosaic, Boscán does not so much refute the accusation of novelty as appropriate it, countering the implication of affectation with the virtues of *sprezzatura* and his ultimate success exemplified through Garcilaso's work. The assertion of *sprezzatura* is all the more evident because the poetry in book 2 shows Boscán to be much too careful and self-conscious a poet for writing verse to have been just a diversion.

Having dealt with the accusations against him, Boscán is finally free to take up the virtues of the new genres:

> En él vemos dondequiera que se nos muestra una disposición muy capaz para recibir qualquier materia: o grave o sotil o dificultosa o fácil, y assimismo para ayuntarse con qualquier estilo de los que hallamos entre los autores antiguos aprovados.
>
> (90)

> We see that it shows itself everywhere capable of receiving any subject matter, whether grave or subtle, difficult or simple, which can thus be joined to any style that can be found among the approved ancient authors.

Here Boscán finally explicates the assertion of superiority first made at the beginning of the dialogue, when he contended that the new poetry was "mucho mejor." Its superiority lies in its capacity for adornment, its susceptibility to variety, and its adaptability to any subject matter and any stylistic register. This virtue is particularly important in terms of Castiglione's ideals of decorum and of *mediocrità*, achieved through the balance of stylistic levels. Traditional poetry, drummed in one ear and out the other, limited the appreciation of these virtues; freed from the tyranny of sound and the preoccupation with prosodic "galas" and "licencias," the new poetry places the emphasis instead on stylistic features such as metaphor and wit, allowing the poet to adapt his writing to any mood or style.

As we have seen, Boscán's aesthetic arguments are not entirely

distinguishable from his courtly rhetoric. Both are based on prin-
ciples derived from Castiglione, and, like *sprezzatura* itself, they
straddle the line between aesthetics and social convention. Boscán's
mode of argumentation, too, is like Castiglione's in incorporating
the critics' voices and ideas even as the proponents are themselves
dismissed, and in teaching by example rather than by precept. In
the course of the preface, Boscán considers the effect of his poetry
on two audiences, a courtly and appreciative one, symbolized by
Garcilaso and Diego Hurtado de Mendoza, and the "tiresome men."
Yet Boscán is also conscious of another audience: posterity. To him,
the Italian forms are not only worthy of adoption, but indeed should
supersede all the vernacular forms; then some day the Castilian
poets may actually surpass the Italians in fame. Once again the
grounds for this implicit theory of literary history are carefully pre-
pared; from the very beginning of the preface, there is a fixation on
the theme of transition.

Indeed this preoccupation arises from the very location of the
text. Boscán's epistle is generically a dedicatory preface, analogous
to the earlier one dedicating the Castiglione translation to Doña
Gerónima. Yet instead of being conventionally placed at the begin-
ning of the volume of his and Garcilaso's verses, it is strategically
shifted to a position between the first and second books. Boscán
displaces it in order to mark the transition from what he calls his
early verses in Castilian genres to works written in hendecasyllabic
lines, particularly book 2, a macrotextual collection of sonnets and
canciones. The insertion of a dedicatory epistle in this odd location
underlines the break between the first and the rest of the books; at
the same time, it thematizes its transitional function, explaining the
need for the change in poetic genres.[21] As such it marks the passage
from one book to another, and symbolizes the national movement
from the old genres to the new and the ensuing transfer of learning
from Italy to Spain. In the opening lines of the preface, Boscán as-
serts a transitional role for his Italianate poetic production, brack-
eting it between, on the one hand, the final book, containing the
works of Garcilaso, "éste . . . que no cansará a nadie, mas aún dará
muy gran alivio al cansancio de los otros" (he . . . who will tire out
no one, but rather grant relief from the exhaustion of others), and,
on the other hand, the poetry in the first book, which is in Castil-
ian forms:

En el primero avrá vuestra señoría visto essas coplas (quiero dezillo assí) hechas a la castellana. Solía holgarse con ellas un hombre muy avisado y a quien vuestra señoría deve de conocer muy bien, que es don Diego de Mendoça. Mas paréceme que se holgava con ellas como con niños, y assí las llamava las redondillas.

(87)

In the first your ladyship would have seen those ditties (I want to call them that) done in the Castilian style. A very discreet man your lady-ship must know well, namely, Don Diego [Hurtado] de Mendoza, used to enjoy them. But it seems he enjoyed them as one enjoys children, and so he called them quatrains/little round ones.

The pun in the final word emphasizes the infantile nature of the early poems, while, with the double sanction of Diego Hurtado de Mendoza and Garcilaso, Boscán asserts for his poetry company of the highest caliber. Yet although the Castilian poetry was pleasing to Diego Hurtado de Mendoza, and thus is worthy of publication, this was only as a trifle, a childish accomplishment to be outgrown and put behind him. The passage echoes St. Paul's First Letter to the Corinthians: "Cuando yo era niño, hablaba como niño, sentía como niño, pensaba como niño. Mas cuando fuí ya hecho hombre, dí de mano a las cosas de niño" (When I was a child, I spoke as a child, felt as a child, thought as a child; but when I became a man, I left behind childish things, 13:11). By equating his conversion, from one type of poetry to another, to St. Paul's, Boscán makes the argument rhetorically stronger.

The process of conversion is itself narrated in personal terms; that essentially is what the Navagero story is about. Yet from the very opening lines Boscán also extends the conversion to a collective level by justifying its value in terms of Garcilaso's poetry. This is an argument to which he returns near the end of the preface, where he predicts the effects of the widespread adoption of the hendeca-syllable:

Porque ya los buenos ingenios de Castilla, que van fuera de la vulgar cuenta, le aman y le siguen y se exercitan en él tanto, que si los tiempos con sus desasossiegos no lo estorvan, podrá ser que antes de mucho se duelan los italianos de ver lo bueno de su poesía transferido en España. Pero aún está lexos, y no es bien que nos fundemos en estas esperanças hasta vellas más çerca.

(91)

For already the best minds of Castile, whom the vulgar do not take
into account, love it and follow it and so exert themselves that, if time
with its disappointments does not intervene, it may be that before
long the Italians will complain about seeing the best of their poetry
transferred to Spain. But this is still far away, and it is best not to
ground ourselves in such hopes until we see them up close.

The "buenos ingenios" include above all Garcilaso, who joins Bos-
cán in the project of effectuating the *translatio*, and bringing the seat
of poetic glory from Italy to Spain. Although his account of the his-
tory of the hendecasyllable does not strictly delineate a westward
course of *translatio*, the phrase "se duelan los italianos de ver lo
mejor de su poesía transferido en España" makes direct reference
to the trope. Thus the theme of transition is shifted to a third level:
when all poets make the transition that Boscán has already made,
then poetry will transfer itself from Italy to Spain. No longer will
the Spanish language need to extend itself abroad, but rather the
richness of culture will be making the journey; significantly, Boscán
here abandons the more limited concept of Castile to invoke that
grander entity, Spain. He also considers the effect of his efforts on
the republic of readers, and locates his adoption of the new genres,
whatever the merits of his own poetry, in the larger context of a
universal literary history. Boscán is thus himself the author of the
position in the canon that he holds to this day, the innovator who
brought the Italian forms to Spain, and the teacher of the great poet
Garcilaso whose own works are the fourth book, the ultimate prod-
uct, of Boscán's volume.

Yet there remains a lingering element of doubt in this triumphal
projection. If the duchess should find his book in any way wanting,
she should remember that he is only the instigator of the process,
and "los primeros hazen harto en empeçar y los otros que después
vienen quedan obligados a mejorarse" (the first do enough by ini-
tiating and those who follow are obliged to improve, 91); in this
way, Boscán excuses his shortcomings and takes indirect credit for
Garcilaso's achievements. Similarly, the *translatio* is still far away; in
spite of his efforts, in spite even of Garcilaso, the shift has not yet
occurred, so the duchess is reminded that he is only initiating a
movement in which others will be obliged to succeed. With this
closing, Boscán reverts to the trope of the recent restoration of let-

ters, employed by Bembo (whose *Prose* was the source for much of Boscán's poetic genealogy) when he portrayed himself beginning the task of restoring Italian to its trecento greatness, and adopted by him from the Latin humanists. Like Bembo, Boscán privileges Petrarch, "Petrarcha fué el primero que en aquella provincia le acabó de poner en su punto, y en éste se ha quedado y quedará, creo yo, para siempre" (Petrarch was the first in that land to have perfected them, and so they have remained and, I believe, always will remain, 90) and, as Reichenberger noted, attempts to fully classicize him by linking him to the Greeks (see "Boscán and the Classics," 99). Thus he introduces, at the end of the preface, a somewhat discordant and uncourtly note, transforming the trope about Petrarch and Boccaccio from a general recognition of their excellence and care (as it was for Encina and Valdés, who wrote "tengo [la lengua castellana] por más vulgar, porque veo que la toscana stá ilustrada y enriquezida por un Bocacio y un Petrarca" [I hold (the Castilian language) to be inferior, for I see that Italian is illustrated and enriched by a Boccaccio and a Petrarch, 44]) to a singling out of Petrarch as the greatest modern poet, with whom Spanish poets must struggle if poetic glory is ever to be brought to Spain. At the same time Boscán eliminates from his preface the references to military glory that had been the basis of Nebrija's and Encina's arguments, and implicit in Valdés's. The result is a psychologically much more complex relationship with Italy and in particular with Petrarch, one laden with anxiety. The introduction of the Bembist note imbues the closing of the preface with pessimism, and carries latent within it a host of ideological and aesthetic preoccupations with the imitation of a single canonical model, which are at odds with Boscán's primarily courtly orientation.

Writing of Boscán's epistle, Menéndez y Pelayo recognized that in spite of its simple form, it has all the importance of a manifesto (106), and Martí viewed the letter as an attempt at an art of poetry (38–40). To the degree that it is a serious exposition of the aesthetic shifts involved in the transition from traditional Castilian verse to the hendecasyllabic line, they are right. Bianchini on the other hand regretted that it "confounds rather than clarifies the issues and ideological shifts associated with the adaptation of the hendecasyllable to Spanish verse" ("A Note," 1).[22] She too is right, for the letter is in effect an anti-*arte*, in its rejection of systematic exposition of metrical and aesthetic issues. Boscán's pronouncements are truly radical, for they do not follow from the fifteenth-century Spanish tradition of systematizing poetic theory. He thus emerges for the careful reader of the letter as not just the almost inadvertent introducer of the sonnet into Spain, but as an important theorist, critic, and enthusiastic supporter of the new poetry. Written with Castiglione's indirection, its primary purpose is to secure the composition of Italianate poetry as an aristocratic activity, and the only fitting mode for a courtier. It does so by associating the old poetry, and its proponents, with lower social classes of unknown origins, while the new poetry is wrapped in the mantle of its Greco-Roman-Italian heritage, and in the social prestige of known members of the imperial court. Then he carefully lays the groundwork for change, as he considers the effect of his poetry on an expanding circle of readers, from courtiers who would have read it in manuscript, to the tiresome men who will have access to the book, to the republic of letters, both present and in the future, that will recognize his role in literary history. Boscán also succeeds at appropriating, even as he discredits them, the arguments of his critics to underline the real aesthetic differences between the forms. The obvious danger of affectation that such a novelty might pose is deflected, by arguing instead that adoption of the new modes was an act of *sprezzatura* on the poet's part.

The terms set by Boscán in his preface were to govern Spanish Petrarchism for the succeeding century. Through his appropriation of Castiglione and his use of an indirect, courtly manner to advance an argument, he privileges nonsystematic, circumstantial means of elucidating literary ideas. These instruments include self-styled "orations" on the Castilian language (see the first section of chapter 4), and in particular paratexts such as prefaces and commentaries. By identifying Petrarchism with the emperor's court, Boscán also transforms it into a metonymy for the empire, so that the practice of Petrarchism takes on a political dimension. Conversely, anyone opposed to the new forms is by implication opposed to the emperor, and to Spain's attainment of much-deserved literary glory. The strength of Spanish Petrarchism, however, is more than just political, for Boscán imported from his Italian sources the belatedness of the humanists. Bembo, in canonizing Petrarch as the only fitting model for lyric poets, had transferred this belatedness to the vernacular, and Boscán brings to Spain the challenge of surpassing the achievements of a long-dead predecessor. No matter how eclectic a successor poet's sources, competition with Petrarch—and to a lesser degree with Garcilaso—will be the standard used for literary evaluation. Yet in the very act of canonizing the new forms in Spain, Boscán's recourse to the trope of the *translatio* shows him, half a century after Encina, still susceptible to feelings of inferiority to Italy, and still unsure about when the long-delayed ascendancy of Spain would finally occur. By seeking a legitimate Greco-Roman ancestry for Spanish poetry, he betrays the ethnic preoccupations that lay behind Spanish alterity and exacerbates the indigenous belatedness that had been present in Nebrija and Encina. For him, Spanish literature is not only inferior to Italian; it will remain so until Spanish poets forsake their native tradition and adopt the new, imported genres.

These however are superior not only because of their history, going back to Petrarch, Dante, and the Provençal poets, but also because, instead of confining the poet with rigid phonetic demands, they open up wider possibilities and are adaptable to a variety of circumstances. That Boscán makes these judgments shows that he had shifted the basis for judging poetry away from the received criteria employed by Encina and his predecessors to a new position more open to innovation and one that values different aspects of the lyric; such a judgment could not have been made without this shift first having taken place. Clearly, too, Boscán's contemporaries have not all made the same shift; so while the letter is aggressive in tone, it is defensive in nature. By 1543 the optimism of the Castiglione translation was gone. There are many possible reasons for this change: the heady days between the sack of Rome and the emperor's coronation had passed, and Spain, mired in continuous war, seemed no closer to its apogee. Nine years had elapsed, Garcilaso was dead, and Boscán himself was to be dead by the time the book was published. Italy itself had recovered from the sack, it remained culturally superior, and the cultural *translatio* had still not taken place. Yet poets like Garcilaso and Boscán are so imbued with Italian culture that they appropriated the Italians' own anxiety about their fourteenth-century predecessors, and their poetry was quickened by the personal struggle with Petrarch. The appropriation is very evident in Boscán, whose attempt to rewrite the *Rime sparse* follows immediately after the prefatory letter; it can also be seen in Garcilaso, who succeeds in finally absorbing and withstanding Petrarch's influence, and in attaining the status of an equal.

3

Boscán, Garcilaso,
and the Codes of Erotic Poetry

Boscán was the first poet in Spain to propose a radical plan for the rehabilitation of Spanish letters through the adoption of Italian verse forms. Specifically singling out Petrarch as a model for his contemporaries, he took up that challenge himself in book 2 of *Las obras de Boscán y algvnas de Garcilasso de la Vega* (first ed., 1543), through the composition of sonnets and *canciones* and their organization into a macrotextual collection. Although he pretends in these poems to address ignorant readers in need of instruction about the dangers of love, the poems are also directed at more knowledgeable readers, for they present, in the opening and closing sequences, a critique first of earlier Spanish poetry, and then of the Italian model itself. The result is constant intertextual tensions (with predecessor texts) as well as intratextual tensions (between the implied and intended readers).

While Garcilaso does not imitate Petrarch's organizational strategy, his sonnets reveal a close reading of Petrarch's poetry, as many of his poems take as a point of departure a line, a phrase, or an image sometimes deeply embedded in a Petrarchan text. To meet the challenge of this borrowing, Garcilaso marshals poetic resources drawn from a variety of different sources, including Ausías March, the *cancionero* tradition, and other Italian and classical poets; often this eclectic imitation brings with it erotic codes at odds with the initial model text. In the larger poems this play of erotic codes is amplified, as Garcilaso distances himself from the Petrarchan code, which is relegated to an alienated character. Finally, an allegorical reading of the third eclogue shows Garcilaso performing a metalepsis, reducing Petrarch to the status of one among many predecessor poets, and presenting himself as the fulfillment of all preceding traditions.

BOSCÁN'S REWRITING OF THE
RIME SPARSE

The *translatio studii*, as we saw in the last chapter, was a persistent topic in the Spanish Renaissance. Although earlier commentators such as Encina and Valdés cited the accomplishments of Boccaccio and Petrarch as models for the Spanish, they did so in terms of the Italians' efforts at improving their language. Juan Boscán was the first to assert that Petrarch should be a textual model, explaining, in the dedication that precedes book 2, his preference for the Italian forms because of their better antecedents (having been employed by Petrarch, Dante, and the Provençal poets), and because the longer hendecasyllabic line is aesthetically superior to the short, sound-oriented lines of medieval Castilian poetry. By ignoring fifteenth-century imitators of Petrarch, Boscán posed as the first Spanish Petrarchist poet, translating, as if in a vacuum, the Italian forms to Spain.[1] Although the preface is imbued with the spirit of courtly *sprezzatura*, Boscán's sonnets are not mere exercises, but an ambitious set of Petrarchan imitations both individually and in their macrotextual arrangement.

The arrangement of the poems in Boscán's second book is canonical: although he died shortly before their publication, his wife, Doña Ana Girón de Rebolledo, declares in her unsigned preface that as the task was nearly completed, "á parescido passar adelante lo que él dexava enpeçado, digo la impresión" (it has seemed best to proceed with what he had begun, by which I mean the printing, 3). Yet this organizational aspect to the poems in book 2 was insufficiently appreciated by the early editors and critics of Boscán's works. In the first modern edition of Boscán's poetry (1875), William I. Knapp separated the *canciones* that the poet had intercalated among the sonnets, gathering them at the end. This rearrangement had a significant effect on subsequent readers of the poetry, who tended to emphasize, on a microtextual level, Boscán's borrowings from Petrarch, Ausías March, and other sources.[2] Thus although sixteenth-century editions of Boscán are by no means rare, and in 1936 there appeared a facsimile of the 1543 *princeps*, only the publication of the critical edition by Martín de Riquer in 1957 rectified the situation.[3] Recognition that the poems in book 2 constitute a macrotext is important because Boscán has suffered from the reputation of being a mediocre poet at best; he has been criticized for using forced rhymes (Parducci, 48–51), for having very little imagery (Morreale, 251–53, 261–63), and for following Petrarch both too closely (Menéndez y Pelayo, 282) and not closely enough (286–87). These judgments are all based on notions of originality and poetic language as applied to individual poems; examination of the collection as such places Boscán in a better light, for as a collection the group of poems functions very well indeed. It is also historically notable that he chose to present his poems to us in this way, for macrotextual collections never became the rule in sixteenth-century Spain.[4]

Book 2 consists of ninety-two sonnets and ten *canciones*. Like Petrarch, Boscán uses the *canciones* to focus the collection, recapitulating the preceding sonnets and sending the subsequent poems off in a different direction. Yet the total lack of autobiographical detail is a surprise, for where Petrarch localized Laura in time and space and used her name as one of the symbolic underpinnings of the collection (*laura* as the laurel tree and thus a symbol for poetry, as well as a reminder of the myth of Daphne and Apollo; *l'aura* as the dawn; etc.), Boscán refuses to name his beloved or give any information about her. Thus there is no sonnet parallel to Petrarch's "Era il giorno ch' al sol si scoloraro" (where Petrarch falls in love) or "Quando io muovo i sospiri a chiamar voi" (where Petrarch tells us Laura's name). Because otherwise Boscán follows the Italian poet's example very closely, this reticence shows him not only imitating Petrarch, but trying to rival him as well by doing something different. By not tying himself down to the specific circumstances of a particular love affair, Boscán attempts to write a sonnet collection that is both more universal and more abstract.[5] The departure is immediately felt by the reader, whose expectations of Petrarchan detail are continuously frustrated.

The knowledgeable reader recognizes that Boscán is imitating Petrarch, for the very pretense of addressing an innocent reader is only the first of Boscán's Petrarchan imitations. The first four poems in the collection develop the theme established by Petrarch in his first poem: the poet addresses a reader and warns about the travails of love, and the very first line of Petrarch's first sonnet, "Voi ch' ascoltate in rime sparse il suono" (you who hear in scattered rhymes the sound) is echoed in line 9 of Boscán's "¡O! vosotros que andáys tras mis escritos" (Oh! you who wander after my writings, XXIX;

but note the transformation from an oral context, *ascoltate*, to a written one, *escritos*, important in terms of the critique of sound-oriented poetry in Boscán's preface).[6] Like Petrarch, Boscán appears concerned that readers draw a moral lesson from his sorrows, a point he repeatedly makes in the first few poems. In the initial sonnets, he employs an almost semiotic vocabulary to mark the shift from hearing to reading and to underscore his concern that, by presenting signs of his wounds and pains (that is, by writing them up in these poems), the poet will be able to teach his readers a moral lesson. Thus in the opening lines of sonnet 2 he expresses the desire that his invisible (because they are interior and emotional) wounds become visible signs capable of instructing others, and he refers to them as an "istoria," a history or narrative available to those who know how to decipher it. Yet he hesitates, for the wounds are "señales tan feas, que é vergüença de mostrallas" (such ugly signs, that I am ashamed to show them, 2, XXX.13–14). The verb *mostrar* leads directly into the next poem, in which he resolves to show them because the potential benefits to others outweigh his shame, and in which he envisions the wounds as a broadsheet, "de mi muerte'l gran letrero" (of my death a great announcement, 3, XXXI.11). This textualizing of his suffering takes a further step in the next sonnet, in which knowledge of his suffering precedes him, "dando nuevas de mi desasossiego" (giving news of my distress, 4, XXXII.6); those who follow him will have no excuse for their ignorance. The semiotic theme continues in the ninth poem: there the poet compares himself to an astronomical sign in need of interpretation, and in sonnet 10, a meditation on his failure to assess correctly the beloved's attitude, in which he uses the word "vi" (I saw) to mark his enlightenment. It culminates in the last line of the eighteenth sonnet (XLVI), where he certifies himself as an interpreter, "ya no soy sabidor, sino adevino" (I am no longer knowledgeable but clairvoyant), and thus takes on the ancient mantle of the *vates*.

In sonnet 5 Boscán hyperbolically develops Petrarch's sonnet 2 ("Per fare una leggiadra sua vendetta / . . . / celatamente Amor l'arco riprese" [To take a graceful revenge . . . Love took up his bow again secretly], *Rime sparse* 2.1, 3); he too is enslaved by love, only it happened to him when he was still an infant, "aún bien no fuý salido de la cuna, / . . . / quando el amor me tuvo condenado" (I had not yet emerged from my crib . . . when love seized and condemned me). The poem concludes with a set of questions:

> ¡O coraçón!, que siempre has padecido
> dime: tan fuerte mal, ¿cómo es tan largo?
> Y mal tan largo—di—, ¿cómo es tan fuerte?
> (XXXIII.1, 3, 12–14)

Oh heart, you who have always suffered tell me: such a strong pain, how can it last so long? And such a long pain—say—how can it be so strong?

These questions also become a motif of the early sonnets, as the poet struggles to understand what has happened to him. Thus in sonnet 6 (whose astrological imagery parallels that in Petrarch's third sonnet), he is caught in an everlasting night; while in sonnet 7 ("Solo y pensoso en páramos desiertos," an echo of "Solo et pensoso i piú deserti campi") his senses have fled from him. In sonnet 8 he recalls desiring to express his love to his beloved; this frustrated desire is balanced by the comet in sonnet 9 that makes men prophets, which is compared to the effect that his suffering will have on others who can interpret it. In the twelfth poem the Petrarchan landscape—wild and unknown, an echo of poem 7—in which the poet finds himself stands metaphorically for his emotional condition, which resists understanding. The image of the poet as a wanderer reappears in the next two poems as well, where he trembles at seeing where his footsteps have brought him and longs to stop moving. Increasingly, he is alienated from himself: "Traygo este cuerpo" (I carry this body, 14, XLII.5) becomes, a couple of poems later, the Quevedesque "llevo tras mí mis años arrastrando" (I drag my years behind me, 17, XLV.2).

The twin themes of his failure to understand his condition, together with his suffering as a sign to others, continue to preoccupy him through the subsequent sonnets. They culminate in sonnet 18, the last before the first *canción:*

> Oíd, oíd, los hombres y las gentes,
> un caso nuevo que'n amar s'offrece:
> amor en mí con su deleyte creçe,
> mientras más males tengo, y más presentes
> (XLVI.1–4)

Hear hear, men and peoples, a new instance of love offers itself: love
with his delights in me grows, the more sufferings I have, and the
more present

and in the *canción* itself, "Quiero hablar un poco, / mas teme'l cora-
çón de fatigarse" (I wish to speak some but my heart fears exhaus-
tion, XLVII.1–2). When one considers that this is the first Petrarchist
poem collection written in Spain, Boscán's torments, his incompre-
hension, and at the same time his desire to be a sign for others take
on a new aspect. Like the preface, these first few poems serve as a
platform for a critique of earlier Spanish poetry. Boscán was unable
to understand what had happened to him because he had no mod-
els, no literary forerunners who could enlighten him about the na-
ture of Petrarchan love, which he presents as in some crucial way
different from the kind of love present in earlier poetry. Had other
Spanish poets written about Petrarchan love before him, he would
have been able to understand it. He thus draws a connection be-
tween the new meters and genres, and a new thematics of love.[7]
Similarly, he asserts for himself a role in literary history, instructing
others who read him in the new ways of love and poetry; those who
read his poems but fail to learn their lesson will no longer have an
excuse. In sonnet 18 he receives some encouragement and it enables
him to address the reader directly. Instead of having the reader
draw conclusions from his sufferings and interpreting them as signs
and comets are interpreted, Boscán can now tell us directly about
his love; in semiotic terms, this change presents a shift from visual
showing to oral saying. It is consequently no coincidence that both
sonnet 18 and the first *canción* start with addresses to the reader:
"listen" and "I want to speak."

Thus, there is a double didacticism at work in these early poems.
On the amatory, thematic level, they are meant to admonish people
not to make Boscán's mistake, not to fall in love as he has done; this
aim will ultimately be inverted at the end of the collection. But on
a metapoetic level, Boscán provides instruction both in Petrarchan
love and in writing Petrarchan sonnets, so that in spite of the stated
aim of warning people away, he actually seeks to be imitated. Bos-
cán builds his collection consciously around the model provided by
Petrarch, and it should be read in the same way, so that the decisions
he makes exist in tension with Petrarch's collection and with the

reader's own ability to understand the love that afflicts the poet even as he himself does not. He obliges readers to "fictionalize" themselves (see Ong, 62–69) twice over, as erotic naïfs in need of instruction, but also as literary connoisseurs who recognize his models.[8] The awareness of Petrarch's text creates a split, with the historical Juan Boscán and the reader, both familiar with Petrarch, on one side, and the implied reader as well as the poet-lover on the other. The latter figure is in turn fragmented even more: there is the lover's past history, which he did not understand, and which is narrated by the poet recollecting it in something less than tranquility and with greater or lesser degrees of understanding.[9]

This division becomes particularly apparent in the first *canción* (poem 19, XLVII). As Parducci suggests (67–69), its basis is in Petrarch's famous *canzone* of metamorphosis, "Nel dolce tempo," save that for Boscán stasis triumphs over transformation. Yet stasis must give way to mutation so that a narrative can get started, or else the entire work might come to a halt. The need to narrate in order to organize a poem collection is the underlying theme of the 453-line poem, in which, as noted before, the poet finally gets to speak; and in contrast to his earlier tongue-tied and paralyzed state, he is at first unable to restrain himself:

> hablaré, por no starme como stoy,
> pues no puedo star quedo,
> . . .
> Si parto, sólo por irme, me voy;
> mudanças hago por no ser quien soy.
> (18–19, 21–22)

I will speak, so as not to be as I am, for I cannot remain quiet. . . . If I depart, only to leave, I go; I transform myself so as not to be who I am.

The disjunction between lover and poet in this poem becomes particularly clear when one examines the use of grammatical tenses. The frame of the poem, "quiero hablar," is in the present, but the subject of this discourse is the history of his love.[10] Speaking of it should serve as an instructional sign for others, as in the sonnets, and it may also have a therapeutic effect, "escójolo por menos peligroso" (I choose it because it is less dangerous, 9). Yet it might also bring him shame and, by forcing him to relive the experience, cast

him back into its turbulence, a possibility both frightening and irre-
sistible:

> Oyo llamar de lexos mis gemidos,
> y é lástima de ver que van perdidos.
> ¡O mis crudos dolores,
> dadme un poco d'alivio porque pueda
> provar a ver si diré lo que digo!
> (59–63)

I hear my cries call from afar, and I grieve to see they are lost. Oh my
cruel pains, give me some relief so that I might attempt to see if I will
say what I say!

The future tense here and at other key points throughout the poem
suggests that once the discourse is started, the poet himself does
not know where it will take him. Still it is not easy for him to get
started, and so much of his speech becomes a metadiscourse on the
difficulties of narration. His memory fails him, and "olvidando el
comienço, el fin no hallo" (forgetting the beginning, I cannot find
the end, 53). Whatever he says he must unsay, and everything comes
out disorganized. Recalling the sonnets, he once again stresses the
unprecedented nature of his love experience, but his attempt to nar-
rate flounders in a series of imperfects that describe a recurring
condition: *hazía, spantava, osava, tentava, scapava, dexava, crecía, oco-
rríame,* and so on—two and a half fourteen-line stanzas of almost
exclusively imperfect verbs. When he does break into preterits, it
is only to admit the hopelessness of his situation: "Quando pude
curarme, no lo vi; / agora que no puedo, lo entendí" (When I could
cure myself, I did not see it; now that I cannot, I understand, 149–
50). Although these struggles with narration continue, he eventually
succeeds in describing what happened to him, in a series of terse
and halting independent clauses:

> El mal se declaró,
> señaló y encontró todo en un punto;
> mató después por términos, y largos;
> salióme el dolor junto;
> dizen que'l alma del golpe cayó.
> (211–15)

Suffering declared itself, signaled and found everything ready; later
it killed in long measures; pain appeared along with it; they say my
soul fell from the blow.

From this point on he can describe his love in terms of the familiar
(to the reader) Petrarchan paradigm: he loved in secret and enjoyed
the beloved's favors, but when he confessed ("Assí osando y
temiendo, / díxeos no sé qué; no sé si os lo dixe" [thus daring and
fearing, I don't know what I said to you; I don't know if I said it to
you], 86–87), she spurned him.[11] Eventually, however, he becomes
trapped in stasis once again: the wheel of fortune turns but his situa-
tion remains always the same, and this new cycle of recurring situa-
tions, in the present tense, recalls the earlier one in the imperfect.
Love keeps bringing back the same fantasy of hope even as he real-
izes that he can never attain it; once again he is unable to understand
his situation ("Mas ¿dónde stoy? ¿Qué hago? / ¿Do tan allá el tor-
mento me desvía?" [But where am I? What am I doing? To what
beyond is torment diverting me?], 439–40), and finally his discourse
breaks down completely ("No quiero más con quexas encenderme"
[I no longer wish to burn with complaints], 443).

Still, this first *canción* has not been a total failure, for it has moved
the lover away from his initial state of ignorance, and with him the
putatively innocent reader, bringing them both closer to the actual
poet and reader. It is followed by Boscán's most famous poem, the
canción "Claros y frescos ríos" (XLVIII), an imitation of Petrarch's
"Chiare fresche et dolci acque" (*Rime sparse* 126), which was itself
also preceded by a poem devoted to the difficulty of speaking, "Se
'l pensier che mi strugge" (*Rime sparse* 125; see Durling, *The Figure*,
68–72). Yet the landscape that for Petrarch was so suggestive of
Laura's body here becomes harsh and psychologically symbolic: as
Cruz points out, the departures from the model stress the poet's
isolation from his beloved and at the same time reduce the element
of erotic idolatry present in the original, with the result that Boscán
effects a disjunctive imitation of his model, recognizing its origin in
order to hide it in his own poem (55).[12] In contrast to the preceding
canción, the smoothly flowing hepta- and hendecasyllables exem-
plify the virtues Boscán asserted in the preface, without the paralyz-
ing, fractured syntax that reflected the first *canción's* concern with

the difficulties of narration. In the third stanza, Boscán finally presents what is to be the somewhat obsessive theme of the poem, the continuing appeal of fantasy over harsh reality:

> He de querer la vida,
> fingiéndome sperança,
> y engañar mal que tanto desengaña.
> (27–29)

I ought to love life, feigning hope, and deceive that suffering that so undeceives.

As this conflict is one he shares with both Petrarch and the native tradition, Boscán here is not so much declaring his independence as asserting his continuity with his predecessors. Like his Italian model, in successive stanzas he imagines himself speaking with the beloved, pictures her laughter, and returns in his mind compulsively to the place where they first met:

> Viéneme a la memoria
> dónde la vi primero,
> y aquel lugar do comencé d'amalla.
> (79–81)

There comes to my memory the place I first saw her and where I began to love her.

Parducci (57) sees in the appeal to memory an echo of Petrarch's "dolce ne la memoria" (sweetly in memory, *Rime sparse* 126.41); more generically, one can note throughout Petrarch a similar return to the time and place of his meeting with Laura (e.g., "Benedetto sia . . . e 'l loco ov' io fui giunto" [Blessed be . . . the place where I was struck], *Rime sparse* 61.1–4; "la memoria . . . mi mostra e 'l loco e 'l tempo" [memory . . . points out to me the place and the time], ibid., 175.13–14). Recalling the opening sonnets, Boscán repeatedly stresses the visual nature of his fantasy, but as Cruz observed (*Imitación*, 58) he shies away from actual physical description in favor of a catalog of her virtues. The cycles of encouragement and discouragement recall the preceding *canción* (and are a theme in Garcilaso as well), yet working against the alternation, as Cruz points out, Boscán's poem emphasizes the lovers' sure reconciliation, indicated by the future tense in the lines just before the envoi, "que yo la veré presto, / y miraré aquel cuerpo y aquel gesto" (for I will see her soon, and gaze on that body and on that face, 168–69). As these lines are spoken by the poet to his heart in an attempt to encourage it, they do not have an objectively prophetic value, yet they do suggest an outcome different from Petrarch's, and implicate this poem in a linear narrative that will be achieved in the final poems of the collection. The theme of vision is playfully turned in on itself in the closing lines:

> Canción; bien sé dónde bolver querrías,
>   y la que ver desseas,
> pero no quiero que sin mí la veas.
>   (170–72)

Song, I know where you wished to return, and her whom you desire to see, but I don't want you to see her without me.

The envoi echoes Petrarch's "Ben sai, canzon" (*Rime sparse* 127.99), but, in contrast to Petrarch's fantasy about his song orally (and thus together with him) presenting a message to Laura, Boscán emphasizes that a written poem can make a journey, and "see" the beloved as she reads it (a point Petrarch exploits in other poems).

Boscán's second *canción* opens the main body of the collection. It consists of a mixture of sonnets and *canciones* in a combination of Petrarchan and traditional Castilian styles, in which the poet continues his struggle to narrate and to attain permanent rather than cyclical change. Particularly interesting, as Armisén has pointed out (391–95), is the sequence surrounding the forty-ninth poem (LXXVII), a sonnet at the very center of the collection. Its centrality is itself thematized within the poem, as Boscán recalls his position in the middle of fortune's wheel and recapitulates the cycles of hope and despair that have preoccupied him since the first *canción*, particularly in the two preceding sonnets; the metatextual concern with centering at the very center of the collection shows Boscán's strict sense of architectural organization. The central sonnet in turn is framed on the other side by a series recapitulating the beloved's birth in astrological terms, his falling in love, and their separation— the very subject matter of those early, halting poems, but now with greater self-understanding. The opening lines of the fiftieth poem, "Mueve'l querer las alas con gran fuerça / tras el loor d'aquella que

yo canto" (Desire moves its wings with great strength in praise of
her whom I sing, LXXVIII.1–2), are ambiguous as to which—desire
or the poet's song—is responsible for the other. The same suggestion
that art precedes reality recurs in the following poem, where heaven
and earth, pictured as artists, pool their skill to create his beloved;
these masters, pleased with their creation, see that "acudía / la
mano al punto de la fantasía" (their hands were capable of the fan-
tasy, 51, LXXIX.6–7). The emphasis on visual image recalls the sec-
ond *canción*, as does the restatement of Petrarch's "Benedetto sia"
(*Rime sparse* 61):

> Dichoso el día, dichosa la hora,
> también la tierra donde naçer quiso
> ésta del mundo general señora.
> Dichosa edad, que tanto se mejora,
> pues entre sí ya tienen paraýso
> los que infierno tuvieron hasta'gora.
> (51, LXXIX.9–14)

Happy the day, happy the hour, also the land where she chose to be
born, this lady commander of the world. Happy the age that so im-
proves, for they have among themselves a paradise who until now
had only a hell.

But while in sonnet 61 Petrarch praises not where Laura was born
but where he met her and how the experience transformed him into
a poet, Boscán in these closing lines veers from mythological enco-
mium to sacred hyperbole (associating her birth with Jesus's), a di-
rection carried farther in the next sonnet, where the poet asks him-
self how her birth could have gone unnoticed, and asserts that she
is not given but merely lent by God in order to show his capabilities.
Whereas two poems earlier Boscán had sublimated himself in her,
"vean a mí, y entenderán a ella" (look at me, and you will under-
stand her, 49, LXXVII.10), now he affirms that "en ella él se viesse"
(he could be seen in her, 52, LXXX.13).[13] This assertion of the saving
power of the beloved again underlines the linearity of the collection
by pointing to its conclusion. Just as the opening set of sonnets in
the collection constituted a defined set, so too do the closing group
of poems. The transition to this final group is an abrupt one; in
sonnet 85 (CXIII), Boscán declares that the thought of perishing was
so welcome to him that it gave him the very strength that led to his

inadvertent survival. This concept, emblematic of the vicious circle in which he has been caught since the first *canción*, is common in Petrarch and the *cancionero*, and by using it at this point in the collection Boscán reasserts his connection to the preceding traditions, highlighting the degree to which he will depart from it in the concluding poems.

In sonnet 18 Boscán referred to himself as "un caso nuevo" (a new case). This line is echoed in the eighty-sixth poem (CXIV), which occupies an almost symmetrical position in relation to the end of the collection, and in which Boscán describes a sudden change of state:

> Otro tiempo lloré y agora canto,
> canto d'amor mis bienes sossegados;
> d'amor lloré mis males tan penados,
> que por necessidad era mi llanto.
> Agora empieça Amor un nuevo canto.
>   (1–5)

Once I wept and now I sing, I sing of the wealth my love secured; I wept my painful love sufferings, that made weeping necessary. Now Love begins a new song.

The phrase *nuevo canto* echoes Petrarch's "Io canterei d'Amor sì novamente" (I would sing of love in so rare a way, *Rime sparse* 131.1), but also Psalm 149:1, "Entonad al Señor un canto nuevo, su voz suene en el concejo de los altos" (Sing to the Lord a new song, let his voice ring in the councils of the high); throughout this last section of the poem collection, both Petrarchan and biblical allusions tie the poems together as Boscán celebrates his conversion from a passionate love which brought him only unhappiness, a conversion that recalls the one experienced by Petrarch after Laura's death (although of course Boscán gives us no such biographical fact to explain or motivate it).[14] Yet, in addition to these references, two other features unite the closing poems: specific recollections of earlier poems in the collection, particularly the opening sequence of sonnets and the first *canción*, and a growing assertion of the poet's role as a rival to Petrarch.

Indeed the very biblical allusions that Boscán uses serve in part to assert this rivalry, for just as Petrarch used as an organizing principle allusions to the Passion, Boscán selects passages typologically associated with the Resurrection. Thus in sonnet 88 (CXVI) he speaks of being resurrected by love; in 90 (CXVIII) he recalls the plagues in Exodus, from which he is spared; and in 91 (CXIX) he is in Paradise. In 92 (CXX) God is responsible for the change in him, while in 96 (CXXIV) he compares himself to both the blind man whose sight was restored and the Jews marveling at his recovery. In 99 chaste love, sent by God, speaks to him the words spoken by Jesus to the cripple, "¡toma tu lecho a cuestas y haz tu vía!" (take up your bedding and go on your way! CXXVII.8; cf. John 5:8, etc.).

In addition to these biblical and religious allusions, the closing sonnets also contain a great many references to the opening poems. The new love introduced in sonnet 86 allows him to sing, that is, to compose poetry, the very activity that the old love made so difficult in the first *canción*. That poem is also specifically recalled in the next sonnet:

> Demás del gran milagro que Amor hizo,
> haziéndome, después de star deshecho,
> fué muy maravilloso y nuevo hecho
> ver que un Amor me hizo y me deshizo.
>
> (87, CXV.1–4)

> In addition to the great miracle Love performed, making me after I had been unmade, it was a new and marvelous deed to see how Love could make and unmake me.

The earlier cycle of *hacer* and *deshacer* is now cast in the preterit, as something finished, while a new cycle that remakes him has replaced it. In light of this transformation, he learns that he can both love and be loved, and "que'n Amor no es término forçado / sólo scrivir aquél que dolor siente" (in love it is not obligatory that only he who is in pain can write, 89, CXVII.3–4). Poetry can thus free itself from the ancient paradigms of suffering. Two poems later, love can provide him a "dulce . . . un no sé qué" (a sweet . . . I know not what, 91, CXIX.9), a phrase that recalls his barely comprehensible confession in the *canción*. Above all, no longer is his poetry, like Petrarch's, a warning against love: now it is an encouragement to love, to take heart from his example. Whereas earlier he had been a sign warning of sterility, in 94 the fire with which he burns is "puro y simple" (pure and simple, CXXII.2); and in contrast to the desolate landscape portrayed in the second *canción*, he brings spring wherever he goes. Thus the breach between his functions as model lover and model poet is healed.

The closing sonnets also contain a number of navigation images, in which the poet speaks of being safely in a harbor and of being saved from a shipwreck. In part they refer to a series of sonnets in the middle of the collection (71, XCIX; 72, C; 79, CVII; 84, CXII) in which the opposite was the case. The *topos* is Horatian in origin, and while it has some biblical resonances as well, they are relatively weak. Why then does Boscán repeatedly employ it in this final section of his collection? To find the answer one must turn back to Petrarch and examine the nature of his conversion in the final poems of the *Rime sparse* (see Kennedy, 40). After Laura's death, Petrarch does indeed change his attitude about love, but his initial reaction is to despair: her death has left him totally disconsolate, and he compares himself several times to a ship out of control in a storm. As Parducci noted (65–66), Boscán picks up the image from Petrarch, but he turns it around: whereas Petrarch is lost on stormy seas, Boscán is safe and sound. Indeed, several times in these final poems Boscán sets himself up as a direct rival to Petrarch; sonnet 89, for example, contains the only overt allusion to the laurel in the entire collection:

> Celebrado seré en toda la gente,
> llevando en mi triunpho para'l cielo,
> con el verde laurel la blanca palma.
> (CXVI.11–14)

I will be celebrated by all peoples, taking my triumph to heaven, the white palm together with the green laurel.

Boscán's conception of love, at the end of the collection, is likewise very different from the Petrarchan love that at first he could not understand. As already noted, at the end of the collection Love is specifically associated with the poet's salvation; he is the one who speaks God's words, and it is only because Boscán has experienced "un nuevo Amor" (a new Love, 90, CXVIII.1) that he can sing his "nuevo canto." He sums up this lesson in sonnet 93:

> Amor es bueno en sí naturalmente,
> y si por causa d'él males tenemos,

será porque seguimos los estremos,
y assí es culpa de quien sus penas siente.
(CXXI.1–4)

Love is good in itself by its nature, and if because of him we have
sufferings, it is only because we exceed his limits and so the fault
belongs to him who suffers.

For Petrarch, Love always remained a trickster who had enslaved
him, and while once Laura was dead he came to value chastity, it
was only because it increased the chances of their being reunited in
Paradise. Boscán by contrast transforms the notion of love in this
world, and with this new conception of love, he is already in Para-
dise. Petrarch looks forward to death, while Boscán is already resur-
rected.[15]

These themes are all brought together in the final poem of the
collection—a *canción*—which, in contrast to the first one, opens with
a relatively simple and direct autobiographical narration of his early
errors. He concedes that love had brought him both pleasure and
pain, but both were equally the misguided results of his delusions.
Only the direct intervention of God, "que derramó su sangre por
nosotros" (who spilled his blood for us, 102, CXXX.62), has broken
this cycle, and the implied biblical comparisons of the closing son-
nets are finally resolved by the poet when he overtly compares him-
self to Lazarus,

> Tú, Dios, con tu sentencia
> m'enterraste'n dolores tan continos,
> porque después me diesse tu clemencia
> que otro Lázaro fuesse'n tu presencia
> (73–75)

You, God, with your sentence buried me in continual pain, so that
later you could give me your clemency that I might be another Laza-
rus in your presence

as well as to the victim rescued by the good Samaritan (see Darst,
Juan Boscán, 77–80 and Cruz, *Imitación*, 61).

The overall result is to give the implicit narrative a stronger end-
ing than that of Petrarch's *Rime sparse*. Instead of the weak lover
gradually finding solace in the notion of a world to come, we have
a strong one who has already managed to find his salvation. When

discussing the end of the collection, traditional Boscán scholarship has focused on interpreting just what this new love of Boscán's is meant to represent. Cruz (ibid., 62) is closer to the mark when she asserts that the autobiographical implications of the last poems derive from Boscán's imitation of Bembo and Petrarch, and that a literary appreciation of their function need not be based on any particular interpretation of these poems. Thus the final poems are important not only for our understanding of Boscán's notions of love, but even more for our appreciation of what he, as a latter-day rival of Petrarch, was trying to do. He began the collection by obviously imitating Petrarch, leading the reader to expect the same kind of thing. He concludes it by challenging Petrarch and setting up an alternate vision of love, and an immanent rather than a transcendental closing to the collection. Whereas the first poems in the collection offer us a paraphrase of Petrarch, frustrating to the reader familiar with the *Rime sparse* in their lack of personal detail, the last poems present a rewriting of the sonnet collection in which the poet frees himself from the limits imposed by Petrarch's conception of love.[16] Only by reading the collection as a whole and in comparison with Petrarch's can Boscán's achievement be appreciated on its own terms; reading them together illuminates Boscán's choices and casts a critical light on the original.

As noted at the beginning of this section, the collection contains a double narrative, that of the lover learning about love, presented in a series of present-tense "snapshots," but also the somewhat later recollections of the poet. The key event both in the fiction of his life and in his struggle to narrate is the conversion that occurs at the eighty-sixth poem, which is presented by means of Christian imagery. Yet this is not Boscán's only conversion; it depends, in fact, on that earlier conversion, before the poem collection even began, to Petrarchism and away from the composition of traditional Spanish poetry. It is the subject of the preface to the collection, and in that preface it too is described via biblical allusions. Thus in addition to the fictional love-narrative and the narrative of the poet writing about his love, we have a third narrative, perhaps also fictional, of Boscán learning to write like Petrarch and then gradually outdoing him.

Yet a fourth narrative can be construed, that of our reading of the collection. For Corti, one of the keys to macrotextuality is the arrangement of the texts. Most of these features, particularly the carrying over of images and allusions, can only be ascertained through a process of reading through a collection that is at least somewhat extensive. Reading implies time, and time in turn begets narration; that makes reading any macrotext somewhat akin to reading fiction. Narrativity, in imitation of Petrarch, is a key feature of Boscán's work, both formally (because he is imitating Petrarch and Bembo in writing an *imitatio vitae*) and thematically (the many poems that reflect on the difficulty of narration). In this fourth narrative the break between the doubly fictionalized readers is healed, and it is we as readers who are converted, minimally into admirers of Boscán, maximally into his imitators.[17] Corti, by singling out the macrotext as a special kind of sign and providing terms for its evaluation that take into account the special modes of signification that it employs, gives us another way to approach Boscán's literary accomplishment. Applying the criteria of macrotextuality to book 2 gives us a very different view of Boscán's poetic abilities, albeit one that resists the kind of anthologizing that earns a place in the canon. Boscán's techniques—a careful web of literary allusion, themes carried over from sonnet to sonnet, and images recalled across the space of many poems—are borrowed from Petrarch, but they must be examined with a literary theory that has a place for them. When this is done, Boscán's collection as a whole is seen not as a weak copy of Petrarch, but instead as a strong work that stands not only on its own, but in tension with the original.

GARCILASO AND THE CODES OF
EROTIC POETRY

The arrangement of Garcilaso's poetry does not permit the poem-by-poem analysis one can perform on Boscán's; Garcilaso's response to the challenge of Petrarch's canonicity is not articulated in macro-textual arrangement but in a marshaling of resources to address a particular poetic problem, often derived from the careful reading of the source text. Many of the sonnets take as their point of departure a line, image, or trope with specific Petrarchan resonances; Garcilaso's successful struggle to incorporate the allusion in his own poem often casts a critical light on the original. In the longer fifth *canción* and in the eclogues, the Petrarchism is even more revisionary as it is alienated away from the poet's own voice and relegated to a distanced character. Garcilaso's relationship with Petrarch can be explored through an allegorical reading of the sonnets and the third eclogue: in the former the overwhelming exposure to a poetic father, in the latter his metaleptic reduction to the status of a predecessor.

As noted in the preceding chapter, Boscán in his preface presents himself as the one who taught Garcilaso to write sonnets, and thus his friend's poetry may be seen as the culmination of his own. Boscán is also responsible for the preservation of that poetry, having acted as the Castilian's literary executor: Doña Ana, in her preface, recounts that because of their great friendship Boscán was entrusted with Garcilaso's works, and that Boscán agreed "que las dexasse como devían de estar" (to leave them as they should be, 3). The function of Garcilaso's poetry as culmination of the book was recognized by the privilege that the emperor granted Doña Ana to publish a volume to include "ciertos sonetos y canciones del dicho Garcilasso" (certain sonnets and songs of the said Garcilaso, 5). We know, however, from the existence of texts left out of this first edition, that in his exercise of direct control over the contents of the volume, Boscán did not include all of Garcilaso's poems—because he did not have a copy of the others, or because he did not like them, or, as Armisén has argued (424), because they did not fit the aesthetic and ideological aims of the 1543 edition. While it is clear from that edition that Boscán (or conceivably Doña Ana) attempted to impose an order on the poems, in our terms to structure their reading, by placing the first *canción* between sonnets 16 and 17, the effort is dropped and the rest of the *canciones* appear after the sonnets (see Cruz, *Imitación*, 64). Subsequent editors who corrected this effort and reunited the *canciones* have also differed on the order in which to arrange the additional sonnets by Garcilaso that have since come to light.

The lack of an overriding architecture governing the arrangement of the poems is not a grievous loss, however, for Garcilaso's response to the challenge posed by Petrarch's hypercanonicity is quite different from Boscán's. The latter attempts, through echoes of Petrarch's poems and through the ordering of his own, to elaborate an alternative macrotext that will lead the reader to new understandings of both love and poetry. Garcilaso's approach is to marshal his poetic

resources so as to meet the challenge of specific problems often de-
rived from his careful reading of Petrarch. Among those poetic re-
sources are the language and techniques of *cancionero* poetry, the
Catalan legacy of Ausías March, and the imitation of classical and
secondary Italian poets. As Cruz argues (ibid., 71–72), Garcilaso's
imitative technique involves an eclectic group of models, but while
details may come from here or there, the overall conception of the
poem is often, and often explicitly, taken from Petrarch. By manipu-
lating diverse sources and traditions within a constant Petrarchist
generic context, Garcilaso weaves his way through the boundaries
demarcating various erotic codes.

   Yet it is also possible to investigate how Garcilaso structured the
reading experience of individual poems, for we have an invaluable
resource in the Renaissance commentaries by Francisco Sánchez de
las Brozas ("El Brocense," 1574), Fernando de Herrera (1580), and
Tomás Tamayo de Vargas (1622) that document the way in which
near contemporaries read and attempted to shape others' readings
of his works.[18] In addition, Rafael Lapesa, in his magisterial *Trayec-
toria poética de Garcilaso*, attempted a structured reading through a
systematic, chronological examination of the texts. Lapesa's book
held sway as the dominant interpretation of Garcilaso's poetry for
nearly forty years, but in spite of the sensitivity of his readings and
the degree of his erudition, as a global interpretation of Garcilaso it
depends on some crucial assumptions: that the few poems we pos-
sess today are a large enough sample of his poetry to be considered
representative; that a chronological sequence can be established;
and that the keys to this chronology are Garcilaso's love for Isabel
Freire and a set of phases in his career in which Petrarch replaced
the *cancionero* as the primary source of influence, only to be sup-
planted in turn by Sannazaro and Virgil. Yet a series of recent ar-
ticles has shown that Garcilaso and Freire may never have met, and
that the myth of their love dates from more than a century after
his death (see Goodwyn; Darst, "Garcilaso's Love"; and Waley).[19]
Without Freire there are no grounds for Lapesa's chronology and
hence for his trajectory, or for the structure of his reading. Moreover,
as we shall see, the concept of phases in Garcilaso's career has been
exaggerated. Lapesa's book is invaluable for the insights about indi-
vidual poems and their relations to their sources (hence Nadine Ly's
attempt to rehabilitate part of the trajectory on purely stylistic

grounds). Freed of the trajectory, post-Lapesan Garcilaso criticism can open up new issues in both source scholarship and interpretation.

Traditional Garcilaso criticism has tended to discount the most clearly imitative poems as literary exercises difficult to accommodate in a biographically centered trajectory. One such poem, troubling to the dominant interpretation of Garcilaso, is sonnet 22, in which the poet expresses, with Ovidian wit, a desire to look through the beloved's dress to see her breasts; the poem ends with a quotation from Petrarch's *canzone* 23:

> Con ansia estrema de mirar qué tiene
> vuestro pecho escondido allá en su centro
> y ver si a lo de fuera lo de dentro
> en aparencia y ser igual conviene,
>   en él puse la vista, mas detiene
> de vuestra hermosura el duro encuentro
> mis ojos, y no passan tan adentro
> que miren lo que'l alma en sí contiene.
>   Y assí se quedan tristes en la puerta
> hecha, por mi dolor, con essa mano,
> que aun a su mismo pecho no perdona;
>   donde vi claro mi esperança muerta
> y el golpe, que en vos hizo amor en vano,
> *non esservi passato oltra la gona.*

With great desire to see what your chest holds there hidden in its center, and to see whether the inside is equal to the outside in appearance and being, I put my eyesight to it, but your beauty detains my eyes from a stiff encounter, and they do not penetrate enough to see what the soul in itself contains.

And so they remain joyless at the door made, for my suffering, by that hand which does not forgive its own breast; thus I saw clearly the death of my hope, and the blow love gave you in vain, *never having passed beneath your gown.*

The seed for the poem is its final line, which Garcilaso filches—an action that itself imitates Petrarch's *canzone* 70, in which the concluding lines of the stanzas are taken from other poets.[20] Garcilaso also turns Petrarch's own meaning on its head, thus performing one of the verbal tricks most praised by Castiglione, that of taking a well-known phrase but subverting its intent. The choice of this phrase shows Garcilaso to have been a careful and imaginative reader of

Petrarch; here as elsewhere, he develops the source in an original way that also comments on the underlying text. In the *canzone*, the line referred to Petrarch's own gown, not yet penetrated by the arrows of love. Garcilaso seizes on the full erotic potential of the unpenetrated gown, appropriate as neither he nor love has gotten under the dress of the woman in question. Yet that the quote is from *canzone* 23 is itself significant, because that poem ends with Petrarch, like Actaeon happening upon the naked Diana, transformed into a stag and torn apart by hounds. Garcilaso's sonnet too is ultimately about a frustrated act of voyeurism, and the woman quickly covering her body recalls this myth and thus underscores the degree of violation implicit in the poet's ocular desire. In Petrarch, the Diana myth serves as the basis for a visual fetishism that extends throughout the collection (see Nancy Vickers); Garcilaso for his part gives the poet's eye an odd will of its own; it desires a "duro encuentro" and hopes to pass literally into the beloved's body.

Consequently it is not surprising that the poem has been very troubling to the commentators. El Brocense remarks,

> Más fácil sería en este Soneto refutar lo que otros han dicho, que decir cosa cierta: porque no se sabe el intento a que fue hecho. Parece que él la topó algún día descompuesta, y descubierto el pecho, y ella pesándole dello, acudió con la mano a cubrillo, y hirióse con algún alfiler de la beatilla en él, de lo cual el Poeta se duele.
>
> (269)

> It would be easier to refute what others have said about this sonnet, than to say anything certain; for the purpose for which it was made is unknown. It seems that he found her undressed one day, with her breast uncovered, and she, regretting this, attempted to cover it with her hand, and hurt herself with a pin from the linen, causing the poet's distress.

El Brocense diverts the reader's attention with an anecdote about an accidental injury that has no basis in the text: the note implies that others have found the poem objectionable, and it attempts to rescue Garcilaso by inventing an elaborate story about how he happened to see his beloved uncovered. Herrera takes a different tack but also tries to distract; his explanation centers on the word "hermosura" in the second line, giving it an extended Neoplatonic gloss and using it as the basis for an interpretative reading, such that Garcilaso "paró en la belleza exterior, yendo a la contemplación de la celestial del espíritu" (stopped at exterior beauty, while on his way to contemplate that celestial [beauty] of the spirit, 368). He also severely criticizes Garcilaso for incorporating into his poetry another poet's words in another language, though acknowledging Petrarch's own example in this regard. Tamayo ignores El Brocense's anecdote and rejects Herrera's spiritual reading, instead interpreting "la puerta / hecha . . . con esa mano" to mean a collar that she herself had made, and concentrating his attention on the issue of interlinguistic borrowing (603). José Nicolás de Azara (1765) merely declares that the previous interpretations are not satisfactory (668); and Lapesa largely ignores the poem, commenting only that, with its last line in Italian, it was most probably written in Italy (193).

The commentators may be right in seeing an anecdotal basis for this sonnet, but it is important for us in that it exemplifies how Garcilaso misreads Petrarch by playing with the codes of erotic poetry. What is troubling about this poem is its expression of erotic desire not through the canonized medium of *cancionero* erotic poetry (see Whinnom, 374–81), but within the confines of a self-conscious (and self-signaled) Petrarchan tradition. Interpreters feel that they are faced with the necessity of either spiritualizing its intent or dismissing it as a decadent Italianism, in order to preserve intact their horizons of expectations. Yet what Garcilaso has done is to remotivate a highly suggestive line of Petrarch's, wasted, as it were, in its original context, by plundering *canzone* 23 and making the spoils unmistakably his own. The procedure, moreover, is a typical one for him; this poem is only the most obvious instance of Garcilaso's appropriation of a Petrarchan motif.

The sonnet is also important in building a bridge to *canzone* 23, a poem that underlies, covertly or overtly, much of Garcilaso's work. In poem 23, the first *canzone* of the *Rime sparse*, Petrarch narrates his youthful imperviousness to Love until the latter, with the aid of a powerful lady, transformed him into a green laurel: his hair turned into the leaves "di che sperato avea già lor corona" (I had formerly hoped would be my crown, 44), and his feet "diventar due radici sovra l'onde / non di Peneo ma d'un più altero fiume" (becoming two roots beside the waves not of Peneus but of a prouder river, 48–49). The details of his metamorphosis look back to the myth of Apollo and Daphne as told by Ovid; Petrarch, by means such as the leaves and the name of the river, specifically recalls the myth, yet he also represses the connection. As Barnard argued (*The Myth*, 83), because Daphne prefigures Laura, one expects her to be the transformed; but then by extension Apollo, in his erotic pursuit, would be a prototype of the poet, an admission of sexual desire too direct for Petrarch, whose entire collection is predicated on defenses against his sexuality. Thus by transforming himself, rather than Laura, Petrarch attempts to allude to and at the same time evade the erotic passion that was the basis of the myth. Moreover, although this metamorphosis is crucial to the collection, it is not the poet's only transformation in the poem. Like Cygnus lamenting the loss of Phaeton, he is turned into a swan; confessing his love, Laura transforms him, through her continuing disdain, first into stone and then, like Byblis, into a fountain of tears. Moved by pity, she restores him, only to have him offend again and be reduced, like Echo, into rock; released yet again, he sees her bathing and is changed, like Actaeon, into a stag. Like the Daphne myth, each of these others has a specifically erotic dimension that Petrarch tries simultaneously to recall and avoid, and with each transformation the tension grows as the "innocent" poet violates the sexual taboo even more. Like the myth of Daphne, the others too have to do with water, which thus acquires a symbolic association with a sexuality that lurks beneath the surface.

Expanding on *canzone* 23, Durling, Freccero, and Sturm-Maddox, among others, remind us of the nature and importance of Petrarch's love experience. Unlike Dante, for whom Beatrice became a means to salvation, Petrarch never fully overcomes his love for Laura, a love that is in its essence sinful because it is founded on his sexual desire for her beauty. The very symbol he assigns to her—the eponymous laurel tree—stands for poetic glory but at the same time reminds us, through a contrasting typological relationship with the fig in Augustine's *Confessions*, of his idolatry. Whatever else she may represent she remains, at least within the fiction of the poem collection, a woman he loves, and beneath many of the poems there is a strong undercurrent of eroticism. It is precisely this undercurrent that Garcilaso brings to the surface, not only by realizing the ambiguous potential of the line he directly quotes, but also by alluding to one of the principal myths in Petrarch's poem. The result is to reinvest the Petrarchan imitation with an Ovidian wit that is both antithetical to and necessary for the original. To perform this operation Garcilaso must take Petrarch apart, both psychologically and literarily, and then reconstruct the remains.

Another example of the use of Ovidian style within a Petrarchist context can be found in Garcilaso's thirteenth sonnet, which retells the crucial Daphne and Apollo myth. As noted, while using the myth as the cornerstone of his collection, Petrarch in *canzone* 23 is evasive about its direct significance, merely alluding to the violent passion that caused the pursued nymph's transformation into a tree. Garcilaso by contrast identifies directly with Apollo:

> A Dafne ya los braços le crecían
> y en luengos ramos bueltos se mostravan;
> en verdes hojas vi que se tornavan
> los cabellos quel oro escurecían;
>   de áspera corteza se cubrían
> los tiernos miembros que aun bullendo 'stavan;
> los blancos pies en tierra se hincavan
> y en torcidas raýzes se bolvían.
>
>   (13.1–8)

Daphne's arms were already growing and showing themselves changed into long branches; into green leaves I saw that hair turn that had once made gold dim: with a harsh bark were covered those members that still moved, and the white feet sank into the earth and into twisted roots were transformed.

The key here is the word "saw," "en verdes hojas *vi* que se tornavan." Herrera, the only one of Garcilaso's Renaissance annotators to comment on the word, thought its only purpose was to fill out the line (349). Yet its use also recalls several key lines of Petrarch's, including the idolatrous *sestina* 30 "Giovane donna sotto un verde lauro / *vidi*" (A young woman beneath a green laurel / I *saw*, *Rime sparse* 30.1–2), and *canzone* 23 itself, "e i capei *vidi* far di quella fronde" (and hair I *saw* turned into those leaves, 43). But in the *canzone* Petrarch sees his own transformation, while in Garcilaso's sonnet the object of his vision is not the poet himself. He may be describing a painting, which would link this poem to his many ekphrastic compositions, particularly the third eclogue (see Lapesa, 164–65). But he also figures himself as Apollo the pursuer (see Barnard, *The Myth*, 115–16), putting the poet—and by extension the reader—directly in Apollo's place, seeing the transformation as he saw it and feeling his frustration. Like Ovid, Garcilaso presents Apollo's loss of Daphne's beauty in terms of synecdoches: arms become branches; hair, leaves; and feet, roots; while her still-heaving body is not so much transformed as covered by the bark, eternally denied to the pursuing lover. Lapesa, unable to fit this poem in a trajectory centered on Garcilaso's relationship with Freire, correctly places it in the class of the poet's "plastic" compositions, but emphasizes the connection to Ovid, going so far as to link it with other late poems in which Garcilaso abandons subjective inspiration and Petrarch's influence is either weak or completely absent (182). Yet subjective vision is what this sonnet is about, and considering the role of this myth in Petrarch, El Brocense is surely correct in asserting that Garcilaso imitates Petrarch (268), an assertion unchallenged by Herrera (see also Barnard, *The Myth*, 110–15).

In the tercets, however, the poet steps back and comments on what he sees, employing what Rivers in his notes characterizes as "una agudeza . . . conceptista" (metaphysical wit, 101):

> Aquel que fue la causa de tal daño,
> a fuerça de llorar, crecer hazía
> este árbol, que con lágrimas regava.
> ¡Oh miserable 'stado, o mal tamaño,
> que con llorarla crezca cada día
> la causa y la razón por que llorava!
> (13.9–14)

He who was the cause of so much damage, by the force of his weeping made this tree grow, as with tears he watered it. Oh miserable state, oh great suffering, for by sobbing over her every day, he causes the reason for his weeping to grow.

Through this remark the situation is transformed, as Garcilaso finds a way for Apollo's bodily effusions nonetheless to fertilize the elusive nymph and to make her "hojas" (leaves/pages) grow; on an allegorical level, to make poetry divine. By emphasizing Apollo's continuing ability to inseminate, Garcilaso distances himself from Petrarch's insistence on his own sterility ("i' non fu' mai quel nuvol d'oro / che poi discese in preziosa pioggia / sì che 'l foco di Giove in parte spense" [I was never the cloud of gold that once descended in a precious rain so that it partly quenched the fire of Jove], *Rime sparse* 23.161–63; see Nancy Vickers, 267). At the same time, by acknowledging Apollo's responsibility for the alteration, Garcilaso also recalls and critiques Petrarch's evasions in the original *canzone*. The closing witticism is based on a combination of sources: as Barnard points out (*The Myth*, 127), in Ovid Apollo designates the laurel as the tree of poetry, while in sonnet 228 Petrarch feeds it with his tears. Garcilaso draws on both sources, exacerbating the implications of the latter's image by combining the two: the tree prompts the *agudeza* which is emblematic of poetry itself.[21] Far from being, as for Petrarch, a rival, Apollo here becomes the poet's accomplice and alter ego, as together they (and the reader) mouth the closing witticism. Hence the loss of the nymph Daphne is poetically empowering, for had he had his way with her, there would have been no need for the remark, and no opportunity for the poem. In this way Garcilaso thematizes the double bases of poetry in both emotional and literary experience, the effective fusion of which has led so many readers over time to interpret the poems autobiographically.

A further example of the Spaniard's relation to Petrarch can be found in Garcilaso's eleventh sonnet, the famous "Hermosas ninfas," in which the poet's tears, in sonnet 13 emblematically linked to poetry, also appear. According to Herrera, the opening line of the poem—"Hermosas ninfas, que en el rio metidas"—has its basis in Petrarch's sonnet 303, in which the nymphs are only one party in a general apostrophe to all of nature, which is invited to hear his woes. Garcilaso shifts the nymphs from Petrarch's woodlands ("o vaghi abitator de' verdi boschi, / o ninfe" [O wandering inhabitants of the green woods, o nymphs], *Rime sparse* 303.9–10) and places them instead in a liquid environment suggested by the following line, an allusion to the river Sorgue ("voi che 'l fresco erboso fondo / del liquido cristallo alberga et pasce" [you whom the grassy floor of the liquid crystal shelters and feeds], 10–11); the procedure again singles out an element and exploits its erotic potential. As an eclectic imitator he combines and develops reminiscences of Virgil, Sannazaro, Bernardo Tasso, and others, presenting the nymphs in a highly artificial underwater habitat, built of shining stones and glass columns. Throughout there is understandably an emphasis on their watery surroundings: they live in the river; the stones of their palace are shiny because wet; the crystal columns recall a foamy cascade; the nymphs are literally drunk ("embebecidas") with the medium that envelops them, one that acquires a special dimension when one recalls the multiple instances of water-related erotic myths in *canzone* 23. In this context the last two lines ("convertido en agua aquí llorando, / podréys allá d'espacio consolarme," 13–14) take on a particular significance. While the bulk of the sextet concentrates on the nymphs, Garcilaso's own potential transformation into a fountain in the last two lines again returns us to *canzone* 23 and the myth of Byblis; it thus functions as what Cruz calls an implied mythological metaphor, a device typical of Garcilaso (see "La mitología como retórica").

The commentators found nothing objectionable about this sonnet; Tamayo's explanation of the obvious, "El XI es a las lágrimas que el sentimiento de verse ausente le hacía derramar" (602), is the only hint that another interpretation might be possible. It is important to recognize that Garcilaso may have been employing erotic code-words in this poem, for "nymph" was an extremely common term used for prostitute (see Alonso Hernández, 555), while "weeping" was sometimes used for ejaculation (see Alzieu, 343), and riverbanks were places for sexual encounters (recall the *escudero's* attempts at seduction in *Lazarillo de Tormes*). Yet if there is some erotic ambiguity in the poem, it is only a small portion of the pleasure to be derived from it. There are no explicit descriptions of sexual acts in Garcilaso's poem, no suggestions of sexual plenitude; the riverine prostitutes, if that is what they are, are transformed into nymphs who pursue aristocratic pastimes, and even their bodies are not specifically invoked. The first-person point of view increases the lyric value by placing the reader in the poet's situation, just as the use of a subjective point of view in the earlier sonnet had placed the poet in Apollo's. The existence of alternative meanings gives this poem interest by creating tension between the traditional Petrarchan lament on which it is based and its transformation into a coy and aristocratic compliment initiating a sexual encounter. The poem thereby again serves as a critique of the very tradition from which it takes its point of departure.

Yet this ambiguity is but one element in the poem. The nymphs addressed in Petrarch's sonnet were purely rhetorical, existentially distinct from the weeping poet, whose transformation into a fountain, in the *canzone*, only underlined his isolation from the rest of the world. It is, however, not primarily the Petrarchan subtexts that give Garcilaso's poem its erotic dimension, but instead the description of the nymphs themselves, like court ladies sometimes weaving, sometimes gossiping about their lovers. By commanding them to leave off their occupations, "alçando / vuestras rubias cabeças a mirarme" (raising your blond heads to see me, 9–10), Garcilaso conveys that he and the nymphs belong to the same world, and that mythology is not merely a poetic adornment but a part of existence.[22] Their reality in turn makes plausible the poet's own potential transformation into the very water that courses around them. Once again the poem closes with a witticism implying that all is not lost, and that a union between himself and the nymphs through the medium of mythological metaphor is both possible and desirable. In this context the erotic potential of the two final words far exceeds what it attains if one bases the reading on the simple equivalence of nymphs and prostitutes; but the power of that eroticism is lost if, like Lapesa, one emphasizes the borrowing of details from Sannazaro rather than the basis in Petrarch.[23]

Tears again play a prominent if very different role in yet another poem, the sonnet "Estoy contino en lágrimas bañado."

> Estoy contino en lágrimas bañado,
> rompiendo el ayre con sospiros,
> y más me duele el no osar deziros
> que he llegado por vos a tal estado.
> (Rivers ed., 38.1–4)

I am continuously bathed in tears, breaking the air with my sighs, and it pains me most not to dare to tell you that I have reached this state because of you.

The date of this poem is completely uncertain, a problem compounded by its not being included in the first edition of Garcilaso's works and by its thematic similarity to, but stylistic differences from, sonnet 1 (see Lapesa, 197; Rivers ed., 162). As in many of Petrarch's poems, we find the poet here in an extreme state of desolation, with a familiar emphasis on his tears and sighs, while these are discounted as inconsequential in comparison to that silence which has been imposed on him and which keeps him from voicing his suffering directly to his beloved. Lapesa links this feature to the *cancionero* tradition, in which the poet's silence arises from a situation that forbids speech, and uses that association in turn to posit a series of poems characteristic of Garcilaso's early career:

> Las producciones que con mayor fundamento pueden considerarse anteriores a la estancia de Garcilaso en Nápoles abundan en rasgos no petrarquescos propios al de la lírica recopilada en los cancioneros. La sobriedad nerviosa va unida a una extraordinaria austeridad imaginativa: las canciones I y II, los sonetos I, IV y XXVI son desnuda exposición de afectos, vigorosa unas veces, tiernamente conmovedora otras, sin una imagen que se cruce en la escueta manifestación del íntimo sentir.
>
> (54)

> Those works which can most surely be considered prior to Garcilaso's stay in Naples abound in un-Petrarchan remnants more proper to the lyric gathered in the *cancioneros*. Nervous sobriety is united to an austere imagination: *canciones* 1 and 2, sonnets 1, 4, and 26 are a naked exposition of affects, sometimes vigorous, sometimes tenderly moving, but without a single image that might interfere with the direct manifestation of intimate feelings.

Yet in sonnet 38 the poet's silence is not something he boasts of because of his "greater gentility" (Lapesa, 53); rather, as in Petrarch, it is something imposed by the woman. The opening phrase both recalls and contrasts with *canzone* 23's "lagrima ancor non mi bagnava il petto" (nor tear yet bathed my breast, 27) as well as with the subsequent myth of Byblis, a punishment imposed on Petrarch for failing to keep silent. Thus Garcilaso opens his poem with a direct, pointed allusion to his model and to the issue of silencing, reinforced by the fourth line of the poem, imitated from *Rime sparse* 134.14 ("in questo stato son, Donna, per vui" [in this state am I, Lady, on account of you]; see Mele, 243). Silencing, for Petrarch, had caused him to resort to writing ("le vive voci m'erano interditte, / ond' io gridai con carta et con inconstro" [words spoken aloud were forbidden me; so I cried out with paper and ink], *Rime sparse* 23.98–99; see Nancy Vickers). Garcilaso alludes to the same impetus, while also invoking the Ovidian tradition of silent speech by boasting about his ability to transform his suffering into tears and sighs while not uttering the forbidden words. As the poem is addressed to the lady, he is, slyly, communicating the very thing that he pretends to keep hidden; as his suffering is sublimated into tears and sighs, so too his speech is sublimated into the writing of the poem, which will accomplish what is otherwise forbidden to him.

The rest of the poem continues to combine Petrarchan and *cancionero* reminiscences. Lines 5–6, "que viéndome do estoy y en lo que he andado / por el camino estrecho de seguiros," do indeed recall, as Rivers noted (ed., 162), the first lines of the first sonnet, "Quando me paro a contemplar mi 'stado / y a ver los passos por dó m'han traýdo." Yet even that (for Lapesa) exemplary instance of *cancionero* influence on Garcilaso had its roots, as Rivers notes (ed., 66), in Petrarch's sonnet, "Quand' io mi volgo indietro a mirar gli anni" (When I turn back to gaze at the years, *Rime sparse* 298.1). Yet undeniably there are *cancionero* elements in sonnet 38, particularly in the bleak landscape through which the poet wanders, reminiscent of Boscán's second *canción*, and which culminate in the almost surrealistic final image, praised by Herrera as an "hermosíssima alegoría" (388): "sobre todo, me falta ya la lumbre / de la esperança, con que andar solía / por la oscura región de vuestro olvido" (above all, I lack the light of hope, with which I once wandered through the dark regions of your forgetfulness, 12–14). Thus the poem has its basis in a textual deviation from Petrarch's *canzone* 23, is elaborated through reminiscences of both Petrarch and the *cancionero*, and closes with a witticism that is Garcilaso's own. The imitative technique here is no different from that of the other sonnets we have examined; just as in sonnet 11, eclectic sources, and their embedded erotic codes, are marshaled to meet the challenge posed by a Petrarchan *incipit*. Instead of constituting a distinct and inferior phase in Garcilaso's poetic trajectory, the *cancionero* influence is but one more of the many poetic resources on which he draws throughout his career.

One final example from Garcilaso's sonnets will allow us to assess his use of Petrarch:

> Un rato se levanta mi esperança,
> mas cansada d'averse levantado,
> torna a caer, que dexa, a mal mi grado,
> libre el lugar a la desconfiança.
> ¿Quién suffrirá tan áspera mudança
> del bien al mal? ¡O, coraçón cansado,
> esfuerça en la miseria de tu 'stado,
> que tras fortuna suele aver bonança!

> Yo mesmo emprenderé a fuerça de braços
> romper un monte que otro no rompiera,
> de mil inconvinientes muy espesso;
> muerte, prisión no pueden, ni embaraços,
> quitarme de yr a veros, como quiera,
> desnudo 'spirtu o hombre en carne y huesso.
>
> (sonnet 4)

My hope rises for a while. But tired from having risen it turns to fall, leaving, against my will, free space for despair. Who will suffer these harsh transformations from well-being to suffering? Oh tired heart! Make an effort, in your miserable state, for behind fortune there is often happiness.

I myself will undertake with the strength of my arms to break a mountain none other would break, dense with a thousand troubles. Neither death, nor prison, nor burdens can prevent me from seeing you, one way or another, a naked spirit or a man of flesh and bone.

Lapesa (83–85) sees this poem as the product of a middle period in Garcilaso's production, between Isabel Freire's wedding and her death, when he had not yet fully assimilated Petrarch's influence. Thus although the sonnet takes both its beginning and its conclusion from Petrarch's *canzone* 37, lines 5–6 closely parallel a source in Ausías March; above all, Garcilaso fails to imbue his poem with the melancholy of the Petrarchan original, transforming it instead into a supreme cry of independence, the grandiose boast of one who expects to govern himself even after death (85; see also Mariscal, 119). To these sources one might, with El Brocense, add Bernardo Tasso, Sannazaro, Theocritus, and Horace, and note an affinity to Garcilaso's own second eclogue; or, with Herrera, add sources in a hymn to Priapus and in Pliny, as well as a parallel in Garcilaso's second elegy. Yet whatever the sources, Lapesa is essentially correct; the bursting of the impeding mountain rewrites Petrarch's "me celan questi luoghi alpestri et fieri" (these mountainous and wild places hide them from me, *Rime sparse* 37.104), and Garcilaso's final lines are a far cry from Petrarch's, spoken to the *canzone* itself:

> non la toccar, ma reverente ai piedi
> le di' ch' io sarò là tosto ch' io possa,
> o spirto ignudo od uom di carne et d'ossa.
>
> (*Rime sparse* 37.118–20)

Do not touch it, but reverently at her feet tell her that I shall be there as soon as I can, either a disembodied spirit or a man of flesh and bone.

Garcilaso's poem is dynamic in conception; it begins with the familiar Petrarchan image of hope, which is so weary that being aroused it falls back again in exhaustion, leaving the way open for despair.[24] But Garcilaso urges the heart to rouse itself and offers with his own strength to break apart the mountain that is oppressing it, such that neither death, nor prison, nor burdens can prevent him, dead or alive, from attaining his goal. Thus although the poem begins with images of exhaustion and despair, it ends on notes of invincible strength. Yet while closely cleaving to his source text, he completely revises the implicit codes of Petrarchan love poetry. By emphasizing his ability to overcome suffering, he suggests his parallel ability to emulate and surpass Petrarch through a show of physical, emotional, and poetic strength. Once again, Garcilaso has used Petrarch as a launching pad for poems that are unmistakably the Spaniard's own.

The sonnets examined so far come from all of the phases in Garcilaso's poetic trajectory. In each instance he has taken a specific element from Petrarch—sometimes some lines, sometimes an image or a concept—and used it as the seed from which he then elaborates a poem through eclectic imitation of Sannazaro, Ausías March, the *cancionero*, and other influences. This imitative technique is one Garcilaso employed in the longer *canciones* as well. For example, the second *canción* begins with the very Petrarchan image of the poet "esparziendo / mis quexas d'una en una / al viento" (scattering my complaints one by one to the wind, 4–6), but the rest of the poem is developed with acute rhymes and wordplay more often associated with the *cancionero*; Lapesa at first classifies it with the early poems (55–56) but then concludes that it is Petrarchan in general tone if not in specific detail (75–76). Similar strategies of both composition and, later, interpretation exist for the third and fourth *canciones*. Often, too, the poems comment on a Petrarchan source, and so, like Boscán's collection, exist in tension with it. The knowledgeable reader of a sonnet like number 22 recognizes the source in *canzone* 23, understands how Garcilaso has altered its meaning, and sees what a suggestive line it was in the first place. Ultimately, the conflict with Petrarch is embodied in the very tension between formal, Italianate elements (genre, diction, the hendecasyllabic line) and the Castilian language itself.

Yet if in the sonnets Garcilaso plays with the conventions of Petrarchan poetry, he submits them to a thoroughgoing critique in two longer poems, the fifth *canción* (actually a Horatian ode in *liras*, a form borrowed from Bernardo Tasso), and the second eclogue, both from his later Neapolitan period. The transformation into a fountain of tears from sonnet 11 reappears in the *canción*, also known as the "Ode ad florem Gnidi." The poem is an appeal to Violante Sanseverino, a Neapolitan lady who has refused the attentions of a friend of Garcilaso's, and the friend's situation is thus that of a classic Petrarchan spurned lover. Lapesa, echoing Menéndez y Pelayo, calls the poem a precious toy (154), while Dunn has added much to our understanding by explicating some of its Neoplatonic dimensions. Yet this poem of Garcilaso's in particular demands to be read in terms of the "inelegant associations" Alzieu found typical of the erotic tradition (x).[25] Garcilaso's friend, Mario Galeota, is identified by means of a pun one-third of the way into the poem, "aquel cativo / . . . / que 'stá . . . / al remo condenado, / en la concha de Venus amarrado" (that captive condemned to row, bound in Venus's shell, verses 31–35). The image of the galley slave is meant to recall Galeota's name, and the Venus shell recalls the myth of Venus and Mars, which had occupied the first third of the poem. Yet the word "concha" had associations with female genitalia so indelicate that even Herrera could not overlook them:

> Fingen que Venus va en concha por el mar, dejando la causa principal, que no es tan honesta que la permita nuestra lengua; porque el mantenimiento de este género conmueve el incentivo de la lujuria.
>
> (411)

> They pretend that Venus traveled across the sea in a shell, leaving aside the principal reason, which is not so honest that our tongue would permit it; for maintaining this type of thing is an incentive to lust.

Tamayo in turn notes similar lascivious uses of the word by Plautus and Tibullus. As Dunn showed, this part of the poem is primarily an imitation and inversion of Horace, *Ode* I.8, where love for Lydia had made Sybaris effeminate. Here, however, it is precisely the Petrarchan situation of unreciprocated love that makes the friend a slave to a sexual object and keeps him from his manly duties; the blatantly obscene reference to the seashell signals a series of erotic code-words that allow interpretation of the succeeding stanzas:

> Por ti, como solía,
> del áspero cavallo no corrige
> la furia y gallardía,
> ni con freno la rige,
> ni con bivas espuelas ya l'aflige;
> por ti con diestra mano
> no rebuelve la espada presurosa,
> y en el dudoso llano
> huye la polvorosa
> palestra como sierpe ponçoñosa;
> por ti su blanda musa,
> en lugar de la cíthera sonante,
> tristes querellas usa
> que con llanto abundante
> hazen bañar el rostro del amante.
> (36–50)

Because of you he no longer, as he did, corrects the fury and boldness of the frenzied horse, nor controls it with his rein, nor with his living spurs afflicts it; because of you with skilled hand he does not wave the quick sword, and in the plain of doubt he flees the dusty field like a poisonous serpent; because of you his soft muse, in place of sounding the lyre, he makes sad complaints that with abundant tears bathe the lover's face.

Thus we have Galeota neither directing nor spurring his horse, no longer waving his sword in his hand, fleeing the battlefield as if it were a poisonous snake, and bathing his face in tears instead of playing the guitar. In the Alzieu anthology and the Alonso Hernández dictionary, we find that swords, horses, and snakes are all attested as phallic metaphors; weeping stands for ejaculation, guitars (like seashells) represent female sexual organs, and battlefields suggest beds (recall Garcilaso's own "y duro campo de batalla el lecho" [and a hard battlefield my bed], sonnet 17.8). The use of erotic codewords in this poem is all the more striking because of its placement in a new generic context, distinct from the *cancionero*, where tradition sanctioned it.

But how do these details add to our understanding of the ode? This question returns us to the beginning of the poem, for the most famous of all erotic battlefields was the "Justa de Marte y Venus." Like the story of Venus's birth, this myth had allegorical importance for the Neoplatonists, who saw it as the victory of love over war, the reconciliation of opposites, and the source of harmony; but in addition to these dimensions, it had tremendous potential as a story of sexual pleasure: in Ovid's version Mars, caught in the act, says the ridicule was well worth the time spent with Venus. Now this myth was introduced into Garcilaso's poem in a curious way, alluded to by means of a juxtaposition: using contrary-to-fact constructions, the poet tells Violante (already identified with Venus in that Nido, her neighborhood in Naples, is eponymous with the site of a temple to Aphrodite) that, were he able, he would not sing of Mars's fury but of her beauty and of the armor she wears. This armor, "el aspereza de que estás armada" (that harshness with which you are armed, 25), does double duty as an allusion to her treatment of Galeota and to Mars's armor, worn by the sexually victorious Venus.[26] Yet Garcilaso cannot sing of Violante's victory because it has not taken place. In Ovid there were two victors in the struggle: Venus triumphed, thereby proving the sexual superiority of women, but so did Mars, who did not have such a bad time of it. Garcilaso would rather sing of Venus than of Mars—that is, of love instead of war—but is faced with a martial woman and an emasculated man. He envisions a victory for Venus as one for the erotic principle whose image the woman Violante should be, yet by taking the opposite role, through her "aspereza," she robs Galeota of his just attributes. A joust between them in turn would allow Galeota to realize himself fully as a man, both sexually and militarily, by releasing his horse, waving the sword, going to battle, and so on. Indeed, just as Galeota has lost his masculinity because of his sexual frustration, so too Violante is threatened with an imminent loss of her female sexual identity as she turns into a statue, a permanently inaccessible image of Venus, cold and, through its hardness, more masculine than feminine. For her instruction, Garcilaso introduces at the conclusion of the ode the myth of Anaxarete, with an extended narration of her transformation into stone. As Rico suggests (337), this description recalls *canzone* 23, while the exchange of sexual roles invokes (ironically) the motif of the lover transformed into

the beloved; Cruz strengthens the connection to Petrarch by recall-
ing Laura's complex role as a Medusa figure, both petrifying the
poet's heart and being herself made stony by his idolatry (*Imita-
ción*, 67–69).

Far from being (as Lapesa put it, 155) a poem that does not capti-
vate the reader, who longs to lose himself in the poet's sweet, deep
soul, this occasional poem turns out to be one of Garcilaso's most
mature and personal creations, imbued not with the details of a
fictional autobiography, but with a meditation on the true functions
of love and passion. The poem thus represents an inversion not only
of Horace but of the entire courtly and Petrarchan code, with its
valuation of frustrated love. Furthermore, as Lázaro Carreter notes,
Garcilaso's purpose is to offer a demonstration of the strength of
love, interwoven with an appeal to a beauty on a friend's behalf,
showing us Galeota made a slave by Venus's shell, and thus materi-
alizing with malice what was usually sublimated ("La 'Ode,'" 125).
By infusing hendecasyllabic poetry with an erotic polysemy proper
to the Castilian tradition, Garcilaso seeks both to show and to criti-
cize the ultimate focus of Petrarchan fetishism. For Garcilaso, mov-
ing strongly toward the values embedded in the erotic code, sexual
consummation emerges as a necessity for men and women alike to
maintain both their proper social roles and their adult sexual identi-
ties. Tears like Apollo's are good for poetry but bad for life.

A situation similar to that of Mario Galeota occurs in the second
eclogue; there, the shepherd Salicio encounters Albanio beside a
fountain, and the latter describes how with the onset of adolescence
he fell prey to the attractions of his childhood companion, Camila.
One hot day, on returning from the hunt and cooling themselves by
the same deserted fountain, he admitted his love for her. The heat,
the isolation, and the presence of the fountain all seem to be point-
ing the narrative toward a prelapsarian consummation, but Camila
took offense and fled; later, when he encountered her yet again by
the fountain, he attempted to rape her. Since the late sixteenth cen-
tury critics have recognized the eighth *prosa* of Sannazaro's *Arcadia*
as the source for this episode; Azar's careful analysis shows how in
fact Garcilaso has assembled details from tales in the seventh,
eighth, and ninth *prose* (respectively, Sincero the courtly lover, Car-
ino the pastoral lover, and Clónico the mad lover). He thus carefully
reassembles the Petrarchan persona Sannazaro had taken apart and

reproduces that key situation, also present in Petrarch's *canzone* 23: it is the lover's confession of his sexuality that earns him the beloved's scorn, which in turn completely emasculates him. Yet by presenting the emotions in a quasi-dramatic form, not as his but as those of the shepherd Albanio, Garcilaso achieves a type of alienation effect (Ly, *distanciation* [280]; Cruz, *fragmentación* [*Imitación*, 94]) that allows him to present a critique of those emotions. As Cruz notes, Albanio personifies Petrarchism, and Garcilaso recognizes the fallacy of an always imitative Petrarchism that engraves the sentiment of absence on the figure of the lover, and the mimetic sterility that would eventually result from the continuous imitation of Sannazaro's pastoralism (ibid., 94). Albanio's suffering in no way ennobles him, for the rejected lover is presented as both mad and in the throes of a specifically adolescent passion, which, as in the ode, has robbed him of his proper social role, as indicated by the various references to his neglected sheep.

The myth of Narcissus is recalled twice in the narrative, when the characters look into the fountain to see their reflections: first Camila, who is told by Albanio that within it she will see the woman he loves; then Albanio himself, who goes mad thinking his body has been stolen. Upon seeing herself, Camila ran away, frightened by the sight of her adolescent self and of the new relationship to Albanio it implied.[27] It is important to interpret *fuente* not as gushing phallically, but as a still spring or a pool; only then does the secondary meaning of the word, as a female sexual metaphor, become clear (see Alonso Hernández, 371).[28] Then Albanio, seeing himself caught within it, goes mad and loses all power (he is unable to consummate his suicide, is knocked over by a mere gust of wind, and so on), because he is, like Galeota, the equivalent of a prisoner in Venus's shell. That the encounters in the first half of the poem all take place around the fountain further transform it into an *umbilicus mundi* that is the center of all the characters' lives. Significantly, Albanio's cure will be performed by Severo, who can control the course of rivers and who proclaims a prophecy given to him by the god of the Tormes. The duke of Alba, whose life is narrated in the second half of the poem, is noted for both his sexuality ("ardiendo y desseando estar ya echado" [burning and desiring to be laid], line 1416, a line Herrera found "bajísim[a] . . . obscenidad y torpeza" [the lowest obscenity and crudeness], 546) and his military prowess. The predominance of flowing over still waters in the second half of the poem further marks the shift to manhood and an active male sexuality.

For Garcilaso, as for Boscán, Petrarch is primarily a love poet; in the sonnets Garcilaso establishes a relationship with the Petrarchan love code through hyperbolic development or redirection and appropriation of motifs, but in the eclogue this code is finally revealed as an adolescent fantasy. As Cruz sees it, Garcilaso in the eclogues reinterprets Petrarchism in order to explore and exacerbate the problem of poetic imitation (*Imitación*, 91). Garcilaso's poetry depends on Petrarch's, but he struggles against an exclusively literary referent and tries to make it, if not mimetic, at least meaningful by reactivating those psychic elements latent in the Italian's poetry. In order to do so he employs erotic codes from the popular and *cancionero* traditions, yet these do not diminish the functional literariness of his poetry because they are as much literary codes as the Petrarchan one. Especially in the two longer poems analyzed here, they give the poems a semblance of realism that could be mistaken for mimesis; the poetry seems to be "about" something, and that "something" is closer to average human experience than is Petrarch's tortured Augustinian sensibility.

Our emphasis on intertextuality is thus not meant to diminish the poetry's capacity to convey meaning, but that meaning need not be limited to the emotions associated with the legend of Isabel Freire. The autobiographical interpretation of Garcilaso began in the Renaissance and has continued to the present day, in part because of the poems' rhetorical power, what Paul Julian Smith has called their sense of "presence." Smith goes on to note,

> The romantic, almost novelistic quality of the life of Garcilaso de la Vega (his love for Isabel Freire and his early death in battle) has lent force to the biographical approach of more traditional modern critics who tend to see the excellence of the poem in the extent to which it inspires a sense of intimacy between poet and reader, a sense of the poet as immediate presence or voice. Yet there is much evidence that, even in the case of Garcilaso, Golden Age readers had little interest in sentimental biography. Herrera's *Anotaciones* offer a minute analysis of Garcilaso's linguistic practice to the neglect of his amorous motivation.
>
> (*Writing*, 50)

Smith is not entirely right here: there existed Renaissance noveliza-
tions of the life of Petrarch based on his sonnets; the legend of Isabel
Freire dates to the seventeenth century, if not to Garcilaso's own day;
and even Herrera occasionally postulates a "real world" inspiration
for the poems. But Smith is correct in drawing our attention to Gar-
cilaso's more artificial compositions and using these rather than the
sentimental ones as paradigms; as we have seen, these artificial
compositions can be as communicative as the sentimental. Not all
emotions are amorous, however, even if presented in those terms,
and Garcilaso's poetry also lends itself to other interpretations. In
the following section we shall continue our analysis of Garcilaso by
examining two poems in terms of how the Castilian poet thematizes
and ultimately determines his place in literary history.

GARCILASO AND THE PRIMAL SCENE
OF INSTRUCTION

The first poem in which I find an allegorical account of Garcilaso's
relation to the Petrarchan tradition is his tenth sonnet, also one of
his most famous:

> ¡O dulces prendas por mi mal halladas,
> dulces y alegres quando Dios quería,
> juntas estáys en la memoria mía
> y con ella en mi muerte conjuradas!
> ¿Quién me dixera, quando las passadas
> oras que'n tanto bien por vos me vía,
> que me aviades de ser en algún día
> con tan grave dolor representadas?
> Pues en una ora junto me llevastes
> todo el bien que por términos me distes,
> lleváme junto el mal que me dexastes;
> si no, sospecharé que me pusistes
> en tantos bienes porque desseastes
> verme morir entre memorias tristes.

Oh sweet treasures, for my suffering encountered, sweet and joyful
when God so wanted, joined in my memory and sworn together with
it against my life! Who could have told me, in those past hours when
you caused me so much joy, that some day you would present your-
selves to me with so much pain?

For as in an hour you took away all that good which once you had
measured out, take away also the suffering you left me; if not, I will

suspect you put me amid such joys because you wished to see me die amid sad memories.

The most common interpretation of the poem was laid down by El Brocense. "Parece que habla con algunos cabellos de su dama" (he seems to speak to some locks of his lady's hair, 267), he declared, and went on to propose as the poem's point of departure a line from Virgil's *Aeneid:* "Dulces exuviae dum fata, Deusque sinebant" (Oh relics, sweet while fate and the gods allowed! 4.651). Herrera does not dispute this attribution but, analyzing the poem rhetorically as an extended example of prosopopoeia, he goes on to cite other instances of the trope in Ovid, Propertius, and Horace, as well as a contemporary example by Cristóbal Mosquera de Figueroa. He also finds a subtle echo of the second line in a poem by Diego Hurtado de Mendoza and sees a further source in Petrarch's *canzone* 50 ("Nella stagion . . ."); as he does not specify a particular line and there are no clear candidates, he may be referring to the general theme of the passage of time, which is the subject of that poem. This in turn suggests that Herrera subscribed to a more meditative interpretation of the sonnet—a notion echoed by Tamayo who, after praising the poem and again asserting its Virgilian source, explains that "su sujeto no es cosa señalada, sino cualquiera prenda de voluntad o imaginada o verdadera" (its subject is not indicated, but may be any token of her will, real or imagined, 602).

Yet in our own century critics have returned to the biographical gloss. As Elias Rivers notes in his commentary in the *Obras completas* (92), Heyward Keniston connects this poem with Nemoroso's address to his dead beloved's hair in the first eclogue and uses this link to determine that Garcilaso must have written the sonnet shortly after Isabel Freire's death. Tomás Navarro Tomás, William Entwistle, and Audrey Lumsden followed in Keniston's interpretative footsteps, the latter emphasizing the sonnet's greater abstraction. Lapesa, however, had some doubts, writing of this interpretation,

[N]ada obliga a ello; todas las frases del poema pueden explicarse por la presencia de cualquier objeto que, viva o muerta la amada, evocara en el poeta recuerdos de pretéritos días venturosos. Al no mencionarse las circunstancias concretas gana amplitud y profundidad la contraposición entre la felicidad perdida y el dolor presente.

(*Trayectoria*, 128)

Nothing requires it; all of the phrases in the poem can be explained by the presence of any object that, whether the beloved was dead or alive, evoked in the poet memories of past happy days. By not mentioning concrete circumstances, the juxtaposition of lost happiness and present sorrow gains in proportion and depth.

He notes the rhythmic bifurcation of the first line (". . . prendas | por . . ."), which emphasizes the two moments in time that are the theme of the poem; this pattern is repeated in lines 2 and 3 and ends only in the rhythmically tripartite fourth line, which both thematically and phonetically is subtly based on Petrarch's "o stelle congiurate a 'mpoverirme" (*Rime sparse* 329.2), but is strengthened through the substitution of the poet's death for his impoverishment. In one of his most nuanced analyses, Lapesa also notes the rhythmic irregularities of the second quatrain and the complex interplay of antitheses in the first tercet, which threaten to render the poem abstract and reminiscent of the *cancionero*, only to have the sense of emotional presence return in the closing lines. While the latter express the intensity of the poet's suffering, at the same time their poetic power underscores his strength.

Yet clearly for most twentieth-century critics the interpretative *contaminatio* with the first eclogue has led to a focus on the poem as an expression of mourning for a departed beloved. New readings of the sonnet were made possible by the contribution of Carroll Johnson. Taking as his point of departure Goodwyn's calling into question of the Isabel Freire legend, Johnson proposes reading Garcilaso's poem as being about the changing value of signifieds in a stable signifier. He notes that the Virgilian passage repeatedly cited as a source contains no references to hair, and that while El Brocense clearly had the first eclogue in mind when interpreting this sonnet, his only gloss to that passage in the eclogue is not to an event in Garcilaso's life but to its source in Sannazaro (290). He also recalls that by itself the word *prenda* means a bond or guarantee, or any other symbol of intent to comply with a promise. He summarizes: "A *prenda*, it seems, can be just about anything, material or otherwise. The essence of a *prenda* is not what it is materially, but that it stands for something else. It is a sign, whether of love, of willingness to repay a loan, of friendship or whatever" (291).[29] Because of the *prenda*'s status as a sign, Johnson sees an ampler meaning to the poem, as a meditation on the passage of time and on how "a signifier means whatever it means only within a particular signifying system or code, and that the same signifier in a different code means something different" (291–92). Yet if a *prenda* is a contract, or even a lock of hair given as a sign of love, its meaning does not change, only the poet's emotional relationship with it; in E. D. Hirsch, Jr.'s classic formulation, there has been a change not in meaning but in value (146).

Another possible meaning of *prenda* is booty or plunder; in light of Garcilaso's remarks in his preface to Boscán's *Cortegiano* translation and his struggle to appropriate Petrarch as outlined in the preceding section, the poetry of his Italian predecessor is a signifier likely to have affected the Castilian in this way. Garcilaso's words recall Bloom's description of the moment of poetic misprision, when a successor poet is seized by the desire to be a poet, engendered by the reading of his poetic father. That earlier voice cannot die, and indeed continues to live by dominating the poetic son it has engendered, who in turn seeks to tame a precursor "outrageously more alive than himself" (*Map*, 19). We have seen this contest in the poems in which Garcilaso repeatedly took an idea from Petrarch and wrestled it into his own poem. Garcilaso's tenth sonnet, in this interpretation, represents the reading of Petrarch, which to Garcilaso might once have seemed a happy experience, but which ultimately becomes a burden as the Italian's poetry continues to speak through his own; the texts that once brought him great pleasure now only bring sorrow. Able readers, like Herrera and particularly Lapesa, can detect even in the Virgilian "O dulces prendas" Petrarch's undeniable presence. As Lapesa pointed out, Garcilaso adapted Petrarch's sonnet by bringing into the poem the notion of his own death; thus the *prendas* are linked to the poet's inevitable demise in line 4, they bring him great pain in line 8, and in the final tercet he accuses them of having once seduced him with pleasure only in order to see him later die in pain. These details facilitate a Bloomean interpretation of the poem, for the death in question is that of Garcilaso as a pleasure-seeking but passive reader. Conversely, from this death there rises Garcilaso as a self-conscious Petrarchist poet. At the same time the object of his love changes from the poetry of others to his own; acknowledging Petrarch's poetic priority and glory leads him to desire the same thing. In effect, he too yearns for the crown made from Daphne's leaves.

This reading of the tenth sonnet opens up the possibility that other love poems can also be interpreted as metapoetic allegories. Such a reading would not exclude other referents, for the themes of frustration and desire that run throughout Garcilaso's corpus need not be limited by one particular motivation, be it unrequited love or the emperor's favor or Petrarch's priority. The poems only present anew the emotions themselves, reconstructed in and for the reader through the recourses of rhetoric; conversely, the expressions of emotion are overdetermined, and one can read back a host of motivations, both general and particular, as the biographical critics have done. Yet if it is difficult for readers to imagine Garcilaso as a slave in Apollo's shell, the reason lies in the way that Garcilaso writes himself into literary history, in his last and most complex poem: the third eclogue.

Almost all critics agree that this work was written during the poet's last military campaign against the French in Provence; the poem, which consists of forty-seven stanzas of eight hendecasyllables, is highly structured and easily divides and subdivides into parts (see Elias Rivers, "The Pastoral Paradox"; Fernández-Morera, 74). Three of the initial, prologic stanzas expand on the conflict between his active, military life and his desire to be a poet. Thus after declaring that fortune afflicts him and tears him away from home, he finds that the worst part is that "la carta / donde mi pluma en tu alabança mueva / ... / me quita" (that page on which I might move my pen to praise you . . . [fortune] takes away, 21–22, 24), preventing him from praising Doña María Osorio Pimentel (to whom the poem is dedicated) and, by extension, keeping him from being a poet. Yet he will succeed; Apollo and the Muses will find for him the necessary leisure, and

> Entre las armas del sangriento Marte,
> do apenas ay quien su furor contraste,
> hurté de tiempo aquesta breve suma,
> tomando ora la espada, ora la pluma.
> (37–41)

Amid the arms of bloody Mars where scarcely anyone can oppose his fury, I stole this brief quantity of time, wielding now the sword, now the pen.

These lines, imitated countless times in Spanish Renaissance litera-
ture, locate Garcilaso at the crux of the conflict between arms and
letters. The perfect balance of line 40, wherein each of these callings
is allocated an equal number of syllables and where they are in fact
linked by a comma-spanning synaloepha (to/man/do_o/ra/la_es/
pa/da_o/ra/la/plu/ma), shows Garcilaso not choosing between
one of these limiting options but successfully combining the two
offices. Although he uses the word *ocio*, Garcilaso is here clearly
recalling Castiglione's notion of *sprezzatura*, presenting this long,
polished, and highly artificial composition as the product of mo-
ments snatched here and there between battles. By doing so, he de-
stroys the traditional notion of *ocio* even more effectively than Bos-
cán had done in his translation of *Il Cortegiano* and in the preface
addressed to the duchess of Soma; *ocio* no longer means extensive
time for study, but brief instants of poetic activity, enough for the
composition of a line or two. At the same time, the practice of poetry
need no longer interfere with an active military life, which is ac-
corded equal value. Garcilaso thus succeeds in fashioning his image
in literary history: he will forever be known as the courtier poet who
healed the theoretical split between arms and letters and made the
pursuit of the latter a legitimate aristocratic activity. That these cru-
cial rhetorical and theoretical moves are nestled in the opening,
dedicatory stanzas of a pastoral poem further shows Garcilaso's
complete assimilation of the indirect, courtly manner of argumen-
tation.

The initial stanzas are also important because in them Garcilaso
establishes a complex relationship with his dedicatee, which both
draws on and subverts the Petrarchan tradition. The first seven stan-
zas constitute the dedication to the "illustre y hermosíssima María"
(illustrious and most beautiful María, 2), probably María Osorio Pi-
mentel, wife of Pedro de Toledo, Garcilaso's friend and viceroy of
Naples, to whom the first eclogue was dedicated. From the begin-
ning Garcilaso contrasts his desire to praise her with the constraints
imposed on him by his military activity. The first, imperfect verb
("Aquella voluntad . . . / / que'n mí de celebrar tu hermosura, /
. . . estar *solía*" [that desire to praise your beauty which *used to be* in
me], 1, 3–4) rhymes with *María* and seems to imply that the desire
to praise her is no longer there. But this reading is belied by the

second half of the octave, where he declares that in spite of the detour imposed on him by fortune, "está y estará tanto en mí clavada / quanto del cuerpo el alma acompañada" (it is now and always will be nailed into me, as long as my body is accompanied by my soul, 7–8). This theme is developed in the third to fifth stanzas, culminating in line 40. But the second stanza takes line 8 as its point of departure, as Garcilaso expresses his intention to continue praising Doña María after his death; his tongue, cold and dead in his mouth, will continue to sing in the voice he owes to her, while his soul singing alongside the Styx will, like Orpheus, arrest the waters of oblivion. Thus the first two stanzas set up a number of implied antitheses (past/present, life/death, remembering/forgetting) even as their efficacy is denied. On the one hand, Garcilaso declares that his poetry will prevent her being forgotten, but on the other hand he attributes his poetic voice to her ("la boz a ti devida" [that voice I owe to you], 12), employing a trope he had also used in sonnet 5 ("quanto yo escrivir de vos desseo: / vos sola lo escrivistes" [whatever I desire to write of you, you alone have written it], 2–3). In so doing, he implies an identification of poetry with love; he, like Apollo in the Daphne sonnet, will find in frustrated emotion the motivation for poetry. This connection is underscored by the word *clavada*, which vividly suggests that the specific moment in which he was made a poet occurred when the desire to praise her was nailed into him. At the same time, however, the connection is dissolved when the reader stops to consider that this is not a love poem but an eclogue, a highly artificial one at that, which exists as a companion piece to the earlier one. Garcilaso's desire to praise Doña María is not based on passionate love of a Petrarchan sort, but on her being the wife of his good and powerful friend. By making and then unmaking the connection between love and poetry, Garcilaso signals the purely rhetorical nature of his Petrarchism.[30]

In the sixth and seventh stanzas of the poem, Garcilaso asks Doña María to accept this offering even though it is a simple pastoral poem; his reason for adopting the low style is presumably his lack of time and the military encampments that have already taken him into the countryside.[31] By thus emphasizing the humility of the pastoral, he diverts attention away from the fact that except for the two opening stanzas the poem is not at all in praise of Doña María and in fact has nothing more to do with her. Instead, the rest of the work deals with four nymphs: stanzas 8–13 describe their emergence from the river into a *locus amoenus*, the central twenty-one stanzas (14–34) describe the tapestries the nymphs are weaving, and the closing thirteen stanzas present the song of two shepherds whom the nymphs overhear and the latter's return to the river.

The description of the nymphs' emergence from the water, their "coquettish gestures" (Fernández-Morera, 89), and their cleaving lasciviously through the river on their way to the shore, recalls the sonnet "Hermosas ninfas," while their riverside retreat, with ivy growing up the trunks of willows shielding it completely from the sun, the river nurturing the grass even as it gladdens the ear, birds flying overhead and bees buzzing, is a compendium of topics associated with the *locus amoenus*. These highly artificial and literary aspects contrast with Garcilaso's repeated insistence that the nymphs are emerging from the Tajo and that the retreat is located on its banks. The river's modern vernacular name, mentioned three times in as many stanzas, contrasts with the nymphs' neoclassical names, and the conflict between the two is but a continuation from the preface of a complex back-and-forth movement that places events sometimes in a vague mythological past, and sometimes in the real-world landscape of Garcilaso's own day. Such a contrast, inherited from Virgil, is typical of complex pastoral, meant to highlight the artificiality of the genre (see Bruno Snell, 291–92; Panofsky, 297–99). But the combination also has another effect; instead of working against the literariness of the pastoral, it asserts that sixteenth-century Spain is as worthy of pastoral literature, as capable of sustaining nymphs, as ancient Sicily or Arcadia. Garcilaso's nymphs, here as in "Hermosas ninfas," are as real as any others, and if they are evidently rhetorical constructions, they are also not merely the result of prosopopoeia, imitating and personifying their environment (see Elias Rivers, "Pastoral"; Cruz, *Imitación*, 108). By extension, Garcilaso thus presents himself as the fit heir to the classical tradition, going back beyond Petrarch, entitled to appropriate its figures (in both the mythological and the rhetorical sense) and use them to his own purposes.

The next eighteen stanzas, the heart of the poem, describe the tapestries that the nymphs are weaving. The first three tapestries are described in three stanzas each; Filódece weaves one which shows the Thracian river Estrimón and on its banks Eurydice, being

bitten by a snake. It also shows Orpheus descending to the under-
world and, after his impatience has robbed him of his wife, his
"quexa al monte solitario en vano" (vain complaint to the solitary
mountain, 144). The second tapestry, made by Dinámene, shows
Apollo absorbed in the hunt, about to be wounded by Cupid's
arrow; also Daphne, her hair flying in the wind, fleeing as the sun-
god pursues her, and her metamorphosis into a tree as he kisses
and embraces her. The third nymph, Climene, weaves a tapestry
showing a mountainside, and a boar mauling a youth who had ear-
lier wounded it; he is Adonis, as shown by Venus's lament over him,
her mouth placed on his in order to catch his last breath.

Details from all of these myths are incorporated into the fourth
tapestry, which takes nine stanzas to be described. Nise, its maker,

> no tomó a destajo
> de los passados casos la memoria,
> y en la lavor de su sotil trabajo
> no quiso entretexer antigua istoria.
> (193–96)

did not take as her task the memory of past episodes, and in the labor
of her subtle work did not wish to weave an ancient story.

She shows the Tajo circling a mountain topped by ancient buildings
(that is, the city of Toledo), and then watering the neighboring fields
"con artificio de las altas ruedas" (with the artifice of the water
wheels, 216). Nymphs can be seen coming out of the water, bearing
flowers to another nymph who lies on the bank, "entre las yervas
degollada" (with slit throat amid the grass, 230). Another nymph
identifies her:

> "Elissa soy, en cuyo nombre suena
> y se lamenta el monte cavernoso,
> testigo del dolor y grave pena
> en que por mí se aflige Nemoroso
> y llama 'Elissa'; 'Elissa' a boca llena
> responde el Tajo, y lleva pressuroso
> al mar de Lusitania el nombre mío."
> (241–47)

I am Elisa, with whose name the cavern-filled mountain sounds and
laments, witness to the pain and great sorrow with which Nemoroso

afflicts himself on my behalf, calling "Elisa," and full-mouthed, the Tajo responds "Elisa," hurriedly bearing off my name to the Lusitanian sea.

The tapestry also shows the story of their love, which Nise learned from Nemoroso himself.

Rhetorically, the descriptions of the tapestries are extended examples of ekphrasis (see Spitzer; Selig; Paterson; and Bergmann, 102–5). By describing the objects, the poet emphasizes their artificiality, which is further underlined by the importance he places on the materials of which they are made and the repeated use of terms related to painting. This process begins with an allusion to the Greek painters, whose works that of the nymphs could rival (111–20). Filódece "tenía figurada" (had drawn, 123) the banks of the Estrimón; "estava figurada . . . Eurídice" (Eurydice was drawn, 129–30); and Orpheus "figurado se vía" (drawn could be seen, 137). "Dinámene no menos artificio / mostrava en el lavor que avía texido" (Dinámene no less artifice showed in the work she had woven, 145–46); while in her tapestry, "Apollo en la pintura parecía" (Apollo in the painting appeared, 156). Climene, not to be outdone,

> llena de destreza y maña,
> el oro y las colores matizando,
> yva de hayas una gran montaña,
> de robles y de peñas variando;
> (169–72)

full of dexterity and skill, mixing gold with colors, gave variety to a mountain with beeches, oaks, and cliffs.

Nise, busy "en la lavor de su sotil trabajo" (in the labor of her subtle work, 195), "figuró" (drew, 199) the Tajo, which was "pintado" (painted, 201) on her tapestry, "la hermosa tela" (the handsome cloth, 217) and "esta tela artificiosa" (this artful cloth, 249). At the same time, each story takes place in an artificial natural setting— that is, nature within an artwork—and as such, each is a pastoral narrative in miniature. The plastic art employed by the nymphs to represent nature (and in turn re-presented to us by Garcilaso) is thus the functional equivalent of the verbal art used by the poet to create the *locus amoenus* within which the nymphs are working.

Artificiality is also stressed by two details of the last tapestry: the

buildings on top of a hill, representing Toledo, and the machines
that use the Tajo's water to irrigate the neighboring fields (see Elias
Rivers, "Pastoral"). These features serve to locate the events repre-
sented on the final tapestry in something like Garcilaso's own day,
while the description of the place where Elisa's body lies, sur-
rounded by nymphs, closely resembles that where the action is sup-
posedly taking place. Thus once again Garcilaso mixes the classical,
mythological past with the present. Nise is described as having cho-
sen a modern theme for her tapestry, and indeed she seems to be
depicting the very tale that would have formed the "basis" of Garci-
laso's own first eclogue, the companion piece to this one. To modern
biographical critics, Elisa represents Isabel Freire and Nemoroso,
Garcilaso himself; in the first eclogue, we get the immediate and
lyrical outpouring of his grief, while in Nise's tapestry, a more dis-
tanced narration. In this interpretation they get some support from
the Renaissance commentators, all of whom identify Elisa with
Freire, though not Nemoroso with Garcilaso. From an intertextual
perspective, however, the first eclogue is just one more subtext
which precedes this one, as do the texts of Ovid, Virgil, Theocritus,
and Petrarch from which Garcilaso takes the details that are illus-
trated in the first three tapestries.[32] These portray stories of unhappy
love from ancient literature, and by devoting the fourth tapestry to
Nemoroso's unhappiness, the poet is placing it on the same level as
the ancient examples—and, by implication, equating himself to his
predecessors.[33] Ekphrasis moreover is not the only link between
Nemoroso's story and the others'. Individual details of his story are
anticipated in them as well: the riverside setting is also present in
the Orpheus tapestry; the tree on which Elisa's epitaph is carved
is anticipated by the laurel that Apollo embraces; and the nymphs
lamenting over Elisa's body find their model in Venus's lament over
Adonis. Not only the details add up; there is also an incremental
growth in violence and sexuality, culminating in the final image of
Elisa with her throat cut.[34] The final tapestry is thus an object lesson
in imitation and amplification. By cannibalizing his own first ec-
logue as a source, Garcilaso represents himself as already a classic;
by making "his" tapestry the last in the series, he presents himself
as the heir and culmination of the tradition.

   This final point has an important repercussion, to which we shall
return; first, however, to the conclusion of the eclogue. The conclud-

ing portion of the poem consists of an amoebean competition between two shepherds singing of their loves; indeed, the nymphs are about to return to the river when they hear them approaching. In contrast to the tragic stories on the tapestries, these two are happy in love; the first shepherd, Tirreno, uses positive, sensual images to describe his beloved, while the second, Alcino, uses negative ones to contrast with her (see Fernández-Morera, 92–100). Although the song competition is modeled on Virgil's seventh eclogue, Garcilaso alters the motivation of the songs by eliminating the element of explicit competition, making the songs lyrical expressions of emotion. Tirreno's beloved seems all sweetness and light, while Alcino's seems harsher; but, again in contrast to the tapestries, both shepherds convey a happy sexuality, in the natural imagery and in their impatience "por ver ya el fin de un término tamaño, / deste día, para mí mayor que un año" (so as to see an end to the enormous term of this day, longer to me than a year, 319–20). Through the transition from the tapestries to the song Garcilaso puts Petrarchism behind him: it thus represents a shift from an obsession with the past (even Nise, as Paterson noted, had portrayed a historical event, however recent) to the present (see also Moreno Castillo). The tapestries represented violence and sexual frustration, focusing fetishistically on body parts: Eurydice's "blanco pie mordida / de la pequeña sierpe ponçoñosa" (white foot bitten by the small poisonous snake, 130–31); Daphne's hair, arms, and feet; Adonis's mouth. In contrast, the shepherds' songs express a fulfilled love in a pastoral setting. Above all there is a shift from the visually oriented ekphrasis of tapestries that are seen to songs that are heard, in which, as Ly suggests, the words in the intricate final stanzas seem chosen more for their sound than for particular sense (329). With this final transition Garcilaso reintroduces musicality into the aesthetics of hendecasyllabic poetry.

The location of the fourth tapestry and the length of its description (nine stanzas, equal to the other three put together) are no accident; I have already discussed how Garcilaso through this and other maneuvers represents himself as the fitting heir to the classical and Italian lyric traditions. There is yet another way to interpret this relationship, which, however, depends on a habit of reading somewhat alien to our own. To Renaissance readers, later texts could echo but earlier ones could also foretell. If the methods of typological interpretation are applied to the succession of tapestries, then Eurydice, Daphne, and Adonis are all figures of Elisa, and the poetry of Theocritus, Virgil, Ovid, Petrarch, and Sannazaro is not merely imitated but fulfilled in that of Garcilaso. Within the eclogue, as Barnard points out, this analogy is suggested by Garcilaso's self-presentation in the dedication as a successful Orpheus, in contrast to the failed Orpheus of the tapestry ("Garcilaso's Poetics"; see also Gallagher). Through the technique of self-figuration, which invites a typological reading, Garcilaso tropes his predecessors and achieves in his final poem what no other Spanish Renaissance poet would accomplish until Góngora: in a successful act of metalepsis, he reduces his sources to the status of predecessors.[35] No longer do they speak through him, perpetuated as a classically educated reader notes conscious and unconscious echoes of their works in Garcilaso's. Rather, it is Garcilaso himself who, in this poem at least, predominates and who seems dimly anticipated in the works of his poetic fathers, who are read through him. The result is a crucial one for the emergence of a national literature, as it makes possible the notion of Castilian-educated readers who turn to the classics only because of their interest in Garcilaso. But the impact of the metalepsis is not uniform, and the cost is a diminution in the appreciation of Garcilaso's rhetorical craft. For every Herrera annotating sources and techniques there would be a Prete Jacopín defending the poems as authentic and natural expressions of emotion; and the conflict continues to this day.

The powerlessness inherent in the Petrarchan sonnet as a genre can be read sentimentally, politically, or metapoetically, but it is also a feature of the genre. Because Petrarch (rather than Dante, Ariosto, or Aretino) is the canonic source for the genre, the formal elements take on the status of a sign, creating in the reader a horizon of expectations and indicating Garcilaso's entrance into a literary system. At the same time, his masterful use of Castilian shows his effective resistance to the Italian linguistic codes heretofore exclusively associated with the sonnet. Garcilaso's Petrarchism, with its graceful, seemingly artless blend of elements, fulfills Castiglionian requirements and is an appropriate trope for Charles V's international empire. The poetic glory Garcilaso ascribes to himself has an inherently political dimension, as the achievement of the half–century–old dream of a literary *translatio*.

As surely as Boscán, in the dedication to the duchess of Soma, wrote himself into literary history as the bridge between Petrarch and Garcilaso, so the latter in his third eclogue writes himself as the solution to the debate between arms and letters and as the fulfillment of Petrarch. The canonization of Garcilaso became one of the principal critical problems of the next fifty years, and it can be said to have been launched by the poet himself. The third eclogue is a subtle, and thus Castiglionian, exposition of Garcilaso's literary theory, a demonstration of and an argument for *sprezzatura*. With this poet, Spain attained the rarefied level of poetic glory. The victory, however, proved fleeting; Garcilaso's life was cut short, and there is an elegiac dimension to the posthumous publication of his works. Just as *Il Cortegiano* represented both nostalgia for Urbino and an attempt to negotiate a compromise with the realities of Castiglione's life, so too Boscán's evocations, in the preface, of the living Garcilaso's encouragements and the publication of his poetry point to an attempt to secure for his friend the immortality through fame that is only a simulacrum of living presence. Without the living Garcilaso, Spanish letters once more seem inferior to Italian, while the example of his achievements only adds a further layer of belatedness between Spanish poets and the Petrarchan source. Living up to the challenge of that belatedness became the preoccupation of the next generation.

4

Herrera and the Return to Style

In the years following the publication of Boscán's and Garcilaso's works, the latter's self-proclaimed status as the national heir to Virgil and Petrarch became widely recognized. As he was assimilated to these illustrious predecessors, he was also increasingly proclaimed a model for successors. Garcilaso's double role, as uniquely canonized poet and as stylistic model, is the underlying theme of the *Anotaciones*, Fernando de Herrera's massive commentary on his poetry. On the one hand, through glosses on Garcilaso's sources, Herrera (ca. 1534–1597) attempts to decenter him by locating him in a broad canon of models and imitators, including Herrera himself; on the other, he presents through his comments on Garcilaso's generic and rhetorical techniques a stylistically oriented theory of poetry. Garcilaso's example becomes the source of Herrera's own poetry, in which he uses intertextual allusion to locate himself as the latest heir and fruit of a poetic tradition that began with the ancients, was revived by Petrarch, and was naturalized by Garcilaso.

THE ACADEMIC CANONIZATION
OF GARCILASO

In the second half of the sixteenth century, the coalescing perception of modernity and the growth of national consciousness led to the formulation of national literary canons. Although some acknowledged the medieval poetic tradition, in all Garcilaso was granted a unique status as a rival to Petrarch, the only national poet worthy of imitation and the aristocratic hero who had succeeded in combining the practice of literature with military glory. In the preceding chapters, we saw the gradual canonization of Garcilaso, first as a distinguished courtier and linguistic role-model (Valdés), later as the culmination of efforts to reform Spanish lyric (Boscán) and as the Spanish Orpheus and the fulfillment of Virgil, Ovid, and Petrarch (Garcilaso himself). While there had been aristocratic authors before him, it was only the *exemplum* of Garcilaso's life, as Russell noted, that finally healed the breach between poetry and "a strong body of opinion which regarded it as both professionally risky and socially unbecoming for any member of the knightly class" (47; for documentation of Garcilaso's fame as both warrior and poet, see Gallego Morell, "Garcilaso de la Vega en los 'Cronistas'"). Even reactionary writers such as Cristóbal de Castillejo (ca. 1494–1550), who opposed the adoption of Italian forms, advanced the canonization by singling out Garcilaso and Boscán for blame (190–93). Writers of the next generation make even more explicit the parallels between Garcilaso and Petrarch, but also appropriate his example to diverse ends; we shall examine three quite different texts, each of which promotes the canonization of Garcilaso.

Like Castillejo, Gonzalo Argote de Molina (1549–ca. 1596) regretted the neglect of the old Spanish forms. His *Discurso sobre la poesía castellana* (1st ed. 1575), a treatise rather than an actual oration, divides into sections based on the verse forms being discussed; the first deals with "La copla castellana redondilla" or octosyllable.[1] Contesting Boscán's "A la duquesa de Soma," Argote characterizes this form as the most ancient and assigns it a genealogy including the Greeks in ancient times and, in modern days, the French (Ronsard is specifically named), the Italians, and the Basques, but the Spanish have made the most perfect use of it. It is the verse form used in the ballads in which the heroes of Castile are celebrated, and Argote defends its capacity for ornament, declaring it "compostura cierto graciosa, dulce, y de agradable facilidad, y capaz de todo el ornato que qualquier verso muy grave puede tener, si se les persuadiesse esto a los poetas deste tiempo que cada dia le van olvidando, por la gravedad y artificio de las rimas Ytalianas" (a composition that is certainly gracious, sweet, agreeably simple, and capable of all the ornaments a much graver verse could have, if one could convince the poets of our time, who neglect it more each day, in favor of the gravity and artifice of the Italian genres, 31). Argote also discusses "versos grandes," twelve to fourteen syllables long; some old Italian poems also use the form, but Argote believes it to be of Arabic origin and (confusing these two nations) quotes a Turkish poem to support this claim. Likewise he mentions "versos mayores," also neglected by contemporary poets in spite of their genuinely Spanish character.

Yet although Argote laments the neglect of these medieval Castilian forms, he acknowledges that only the hendecasyllable, or "verso Ytaliano," has brought greatness. Again countering Boscán, he asserts a Spanish origin for the form, quoting Mosén Jordi's version of Petrarch's "Pace non trovo . . . ," misdating it to 1250, and then claiming it was Petrarch's source.[2] More correctly, he disputes Boscán by pointing to Santillana's sonnets, nearly forgotten in the sixteenth century. Leaving aside the question of priority, the Spanish have in any case surpassed the Italians; the hendecasyllable,

> al cabo de algunos siglos que andava desterrado de su naturaleza ha buelto a España, donde a sido bien rescebido y tractado como natural; y aun se puede dezir que en nuestra lengua, por la elegancia y dulçura della, es mas liso y sonoro que alguna vez paresce en la Ytaliana.
>
> (43)

> after all the centuries of exile, has returned to Spain, where it has been well received and treated as a native; and it can even be said that in our language, because of its elegance and sweetness, it is smoother and more sonorous than it ever seemed in Italian.

This achievement, however, is due to Garcilaso, "que en la dulçura y lindeza de conceptos, y en el arte y elegancia no deve nada al Petrarcha, ni a los de mas excelentes poetas de Ytalia" (who in the sweetness and beauty of concepts, and in skill and elegance owes nothing to Petrarch or to the other great poets of Italy, 44). Thus Argote attempts to relieve Spanish poets of any debt to Petrarch and the Italians, though at the cost of setting up Garcilaso as a national counter-model. As far as the characteristics of the hendecasyllable are concerned, Argote, echoing Boscán, finds it learned, grave, and receptive to all sorts of ornaments and figures; among all kinds of poetry, it is the most worthy of the term "heroic." Thus while he agrees with Castillejo that the chief virtue of the traditional forms is their hispanicity, this decreases in value if the hendecasyllable too can claim to be legitimately Spanish.

With its genre-by-genre arrangement, Argote's treatise looks back to Encina and anticipates the return to systematic poetics in the subsequent decades; he also demonstrates an unusual acquaintance with French poetry. His judgments are balanced: he feels a certain nostalgia for the traditional genres but gives the Italian forms their due; and while he asserts the historical precedence of Santillana's efforts, he concedes that Boscán and Garcilaso had to reintroduce the sonnet and that Garcilaso surpassed not only Santillana, but his Italian models as well—an important concession from one intent on not setting up an exclusive canon. Boscán and Garcilaso are recognized for effecting a radical transformation of Spanish poetry, the former as an important historical link, and the latter as the preeminent poet whose achievements eclipsed all predecessors, both Italian and Spanish, thus sealing the success of the new genres and becoming both model and measuring rod for his contemporaries and successors. The "heroism" of the hendecasyllable is particularly striking because Argote's examples come from lyric rather than epic sources, suggesting that to him the sonnet is the modern equivalent of the epic in the hierarchy of genres, and that Garcilaso's use of it provides the evidence for resolving, in Spain's favor, the cultural rivalry with Italy.

Argote presents Garcilaso as the only Spaniard who could compete with the Italians; in him alone was the *translatio* achieved. El Brocense (Francisco Sánchez de las Brozas, 1523–1601) further elevates Garcilaso to canonical status through his 1574 edition of the poet's works. Indeed, by designating him a writer deserving of textual revision and commentary, El Brocense classicizes him by the very act of exercising the humanist hermeneutic upon his works. In his preface, El Brocense counters those who complain about his documentation of Garcilaso's borrowings by declaring,

> [N]o tengo por buen poeta al que no imita los excelentes antiguos. Y si me preguntan, porqué entre tantos millares de Poetas, como nuestra España tiene, tan pocos se pueden contar dignos deste nombre, digo, que no ay otra razon, sino porque les faltan las ciencias, lenguas, y dotrina para saber imitar. Ningun Poeta Latino ay, que en su genero no aya imitado a otros.
>
> (*Opera omnia*, 4.36)

> I do not esteem as a good poet one who has not imitated the best of the ancient authors. And if I am asked why, among the thousands of poets we have in Spain, so few are worthy of the name, I would say that there is no other reason, but that they lack the science, languages, and learning to know how to imitate. There are no Latin poets who did not, in their genres, imitate others.

As El Brocense thus differentiates between Garcilaso and the mass of others, he redefines him as a learned rather than courtly poet. He also clarifies his understanding of imitation as a process within generic categories, but across boundaries of time and language; citing (as had Federico Fregoso in the *Cortegiano*) the hoary example of Virgil and Homer, his language betrays the concern with military conquest that is at the root of the *translatio:*

> Ansi como es muestra de grandes fuerzas sacar de las manos de Hercules la maza, y quedarse con ella; ansi tomar a Homero sus versos y hacerlos propios, es erudicion, que a pocos se comunica. Lo mismo se puede decir de nuestro Poeta, que aplica y traslada los versos y sentencias de otros Poetas tan a su proposito, y con tanta destreza, que ya no se llaman agenos, sino suyos; y mas gloria merece por esto, que no si de su cabeza los compusiera.
>
> (ibid.)

> Just as it is a sign of great strength to take his club from the hands of Hercules and keep it, so to take from Homer his verses and make them one's own is erudition, which is given to few. The same can be said of our poet, who applies and transfers the verses and thoughts of other poets for his own ends, with such skill that they are no longer alien, but his; and this deserves even greater glory than if he had composed them in his own head.

El Brocense also defends his treatment of Garcilaso by pointing to the example of the Italian commentaries on Ariosto and Sannazaro; just as they had succeeded in canonizing those authors, so he proposes to do the same for Garcilaso (4.37). Indeed, he achieves his aim in the commentary proper, as he reinforces Garcilaso's stature by situating him, through a restricted genealogy of sources, among Virgil, Horace, Ovid, Petrarch, Sannazaro, Ariosto, Bembo, and Bernardo Tasso (see Javitch, "Shaping"). That this view subjected El Brocense to the censure of others such as Jerónimo de Lomas Cantoral (who declared, "solo hieren al que à dado / el mundo justo Lauro y digno assiento" [they only injure him who gave to the world a just laurel and a worthy location], quoted in Coster, 56) points to the split between those who continued to subscribe to the aesthetics of *sprezzatura* and those who seek to improve the language by neo-Ciceronian means.[3]

Clearly El Brocense was influenced by Ciceronian theories of imitation and attempted to prove that Garcilaso was a relatively Ciceronian imitator. The ultimate step in the canonization process can be found in the brief treatise "Discurso sobre la lengua castellana," by Ambrosio de Morales (1513–1591).[4] As a literary oration, Morales's work is Ciceronian in genre and style as well as ideology. His purpose is to encourage the cultivation of Spanish letters, and his first step is to argue for the legitimacy of literary studies by citing the familiar example of the Greeks and the Romans, who did not scorn the development of their native linguistic skills. Thus Plutarch continued to write in Greek after many years' residence in Rome, and Cicero through his power of speech became preeminent in the political arena, while translating the best of the Greek philosophers into Latin. Morales also draws parallels between the ancients and the modern-day Italians, "exercitándose todos con gran cuydado en su lenguaje; y aunque saben los que entre ellos son doctos, el Latín por excelencia, escriven muy poco en esta lengua y muy mucho en la suya" (exercising themselves with such care for their language, that although the learned among them have excellent Latin, they write little in this language and much more in their own, 181). As further instances of this dedication to the mother tongue, he points to the discussion in the *Cortegiano* over whether Petrarch or Boccaccio should be the correct model, and to Bembo, who wrote a book dedicated specifically to the codification and improvement of the Italian language. There are no learned men in Italy who do not dedicate themselves to the illustration of their language, learning Greek and Latin only "para tener llaves con que puedan abrir los thesoros de entrambos, y enriquescer su vulgar con tales despojos" (to have keys with which they can open both treasures, and enrich their vernacular with these spoils, 181).

One may question Morales's actual familiarity with the Italian situation: there were indeed many Italians who wrote not in the vernacular but in Latin, and the adoption of the vernacular was the subject of, if anything, greater controversy in Italy than in Spain. Moreover, his representation of the linguistic discussion in the *Cortegiano* is, as Terracini points out (*Lingua come problema*, 170), a singularly Bembist one. Despite these errors, Morales represents the Italians, along with the Romans and the Greeks, as models of a people who cultivated their own language; he brings them into the "Discurso" only to contrast with the Spanish. Most of Morales's examples are taken from Cicero, Quintilian, and Bembo, and they provide an ideologically appropriate introduction for the exposition of his theory of an educated language.

This topic takes up the next section of the "Discurso"; here, Morales argues for a middle path between vulgarity and affectation. In the 1546 version of the "Discurso," the latter seemed the greater threat, and Morales concedes that some writers sin by using foreign words and new ways of speaking that few understand, only because they desire to be different from others, and not from a wish to speak the same language with greater prudence and care (183). Such people give linguistic cultivation a bad name, for true eloquence such as Cicero's comes not from the use of unusual words but from craft in the selection and arrangement of everyday vocabulary to attain grace, variety, melody and sweetness in the sounds, and the like. True elegance could not be further from affectation:

> ¿Y este pulir desta manera la habla quán ageno, quán differente, y quán contrario es de la affectación? El cielo y la tierra, lo blanco y lo negro, lo claro y lo escuro, no están más lexos de ser una cosa, que éstas dos de juntarse, o parescerse. Pero tanto no condenemos en nuestro lenguaje el cuydado del bien hablar, sino dolámonos de ver que estamos tan fuera de quererlo y saberlo hazer, que tenemos por mal hecho aun sólo intentarlo, y lo que sería gran virtud y excelencia, culpamos con o vicio y fealdad.
>
> (184)

> This polishing of speech: how alien, how different, how contrary is it to affectation? Sky and earth, black and white, clear and murky are not farther from being the same thing than are these two from joining or resembling each other. Therefore let us not condemn the dedication to good speech in our language, but instead lament that we are so far from desiring and knowing how to do it, that we hold it wrong even to attempt it, and that that which should be a great virtue and excellence, we blame as a vice or a blemish.

Subject matter, too, has contributed to the lack of literary development; echoing Nebrija and Garcilaso, Morales grants that books written in Spanish have attained great popularity, but declares them to be of no interest to the learned. Indeed, their despair has not been without cause, for nothing is written in Castilian save love stories and fables (186). As a result, Spanish literature has earned the same contempt that Diogenes Laertius had for perfumes when he cursed "los hombres desonestos y afeminados, que por usar mal de cosa tan preciosa, han hecho que los hombres virtuosos no puedan honestamente gozar della" (unchaste and effeminate men, who by misusing something so precious, have made it such that virtuous men cannot honestly take pleasure in it, 186).

Morales's emphasis on the dangers of affectation shows the influence of Castiglionian aesthetics even as he adopts a more strictly Bembist/Ciceronian position on questions of style. The Castiglionian rejection of affectation is balanced by Morales's choice of a monologic genre and the Ciceronian style in which it is written. Genre and style are as much signs of Morales's ideology as his actual arguments; in place of the give-and-take of interlocutors, opposing views are reduced to silence, the ultimate Ciceronian hell, and survive only by implication. Similarly, Valdés's reliance on his own colloquial speech, "sin afetación ninguna escrivo como hablo" (without any affectation I write as I speak, 154), gives way to a style in which the ersatz orality of oratory apes writing. Moreover, it is difficult to tell what affectations Morales rejects, for while he pleads for an everyday, common vocabulary, he had earlier praised the Italians for incorporating into their language "despojos," booty taken from Latin and Greek, thus indicating an openness to neologisms and loanwords.

Indeed, whatever it was that prompted this section of the "Discurso," in the later, revised version the condemnation of affectation is preceded by an expanded discussion of the dangers of untutored speech. While affectation is a consequence of ambition, carelessness (*descuydo*) is the result of the lack of pride in their language shown by the Spaniards, who treat it instead with scorn and vituperation (181–82). Believing that as nature teaches language, she is the mistress of its perfection, Spaniards hold anything that departs from common usage to be a vile affectation, and they reserve care and dedication for the study of Greek and Latin, overlooking the distinctions among the speech of rustics, of city dwellers, and of courtiers. The Romans took care that children learn language from a woman because women are more conservative in their usage; would such care be necessary if eloquence came naturally? Nature needs the help of art:

> [A]yudada naturaleza con el mejor uso, saca más ventaja y perfeción.
> ¿Pues qué los otros que todo lo tienen en Castellano por affectado?
> Éstos quieren condenar nuestra lengua a un estraño abatimiento, y

como enterrarla biva, donde miserablemente se corrompa y pierda
todo su lustre, su lindeza y hermosura. . . . Yo no digo que afeytes
nuestra lengua Castellana, sino que le laves la cara. No le pintes en
el rostro, mas quítale la suziedad. No la vistas de bordados ni re-
camos, mas no le mengües un buen atavío de vestido, que aderece
con gravedad.

(182)

When nature is helped with good practice, it gains profit and perfec-
tion. So what of the others who hold everything in Castilian affected?
They want to condemn our language to a strange decline, and to bury
it alive, where it will miserably decompose and lose all its luster, its
beauty, its handsomeness. . . . I do not say you should powder our
language, but wash its face. Do not paint its countenance, but take
away the dirt. Do not dress it with brocades and embroidery, but do
not begrudge it good clothing so that it may dress with gravity.

In this series of highly repetitive, conventional, and sometimes con-
tradictory metaphors, one can see Morales groping for an appro-
priate way to express the balance between nature and art. Most of
them are subtractive: good speech is pure, like mother's milk, clean,
free of cosmetics, and polished. But to deprive language of embel-
lishment is also to take away its beauty and to bury it alive. Through
the comparison to perfume, something naturally pleasing in itself
but abhorrent when used by effeminate men, Morales tries to give
language an element of masculinity, perhaps to counterbalance the
earlier remarks about the mother tongue. Morales also appeals to
masculinity and in particular to the aristocracy through his use of
examples drawn from the lives of noble Romans to support his ar-
gument, and through the military word *despojo*.

In addition to the general suspicion with which Spaniards regard
any attempts to ornament the language, Morales sees one other
cause for this lamentable state of affairs: the lack of examples to
imitate. In the closing section of the "Discurso" he attempts to extri-
cate the language from this situation by pointing to those few Span-
ish writers who could indeed serve as models. His principal interest
is in prose, and the models range from the fifteenth-century Fer-
nando del Pulgar to Boscán's translation of the *Cortegiano*. Morales
then addresses lyric poetry, praising Boscán for having introduced
to Spanish a variety of genres, such that it is in no way inferior to
Italian. These borrowings would be of little value, however, if it were
not for Garcilaso:

Luz muy esclarescida de nuestra nación, que ya no se contentan sus obras con ganar la victoria y el despojo de la Toscana, sino con lo mejor de lo Latino traen la competencia, y no menos que con lo muy precioso de Virgilio y Horacio se enrriquescen.

(187)

The most splendid light of our nation, whose works no longer content themselves with victories and spoils from the Tuscans, but now compete with the best of the Latin, and enrich themselves with nothing less than the most precious of Virgil and Horace.

On their face, these words, first published in the 1546 edition and then retained forty years later, imply an end to the cultural struggle with Italy and the relationship of inferiority it engendered; the Spanish have now matched the modern Italians and compete directly with the classics. Yet the praise of Garcilaso is belied by the spirit of competition with Italy that permeates the entire "Discurso," and which was its point of departure. The paucity of acceptable models reinforces the sense of inferiority and recalls the terms of Garcilaso's preface to the *Cortegiano* translation. Paradoxically, Morales's work thus betrays an enormous contempt for Spanish letters, and even as it condemns this contempt in others, it reaffirms it. He has nothing to say about the repeated attempts of writers from the time of Nebrija on to ennoble Spanish; no poets before Boscán are mentioned, and none after Garcilaso.[5] This neglect is particularly striking when one remembers that this is no simple list of good writers, rather, a list of authors to be imitated in an exclusive way. Moreover, the position of Spanish relative to Italian and the classics is only potentially one of equality; Boscán did his best by importing the genres, but in terms of actual achievements other than Garcilaso's, it lags behind.

Yet despite his criticism Morales does not, as did Nebrija, Valdés, and especially Boscán, offer any radical alternatives. On the contrary, as a Ciceronian his position is hyperconservative: his call for greater erudition and care does not involve a rejection of courtly ideals, as shown by his repeated praise for Castiglione's book; and the inclusion of Garcilaso, in a canon limited largely to historians and other prose writers, affirms his unique status among humanists and courtiers alike. Most important of all, Garcilaso's role as the singular model shows, as early as 1546, the potential fossilization of the Spanish Petrarchist tradition. What had begun as a movement to open poetry to new forms and new diction threatens to become a restricted, official code for lyric poetry.

By the final quarter of the sixteenth century Garcilaso had emerged as the prince of Spanish poets and the national rival to Petrarch. Yet attempts such as Morales's to legitimize Spanish literature only reveal a deep pessimism, according to which Garcilaso's accomplishments were unique, while the rest of Spanish literature remained backward. When he expressed a national feeling of inferiority to Italy, Morales was not only echoing the trope of Spanish belatedness but also using it to raise Garcilaso to the status of a Cicero or a Petrarch, someone whose attainments would only with difficulty be equaled. To Amado Alonso, Morales's emphasis on amelioration of the language and on the use of literary models makes him an early champion of artistic hegemony over the language (88–93). Yet it is not at all clear that Morales has an aesthetic rather than a utilitarian purpose in championing good usage, and his biographical situation shows how Garcilaso could be appropriated by groups other than Boscán's courtly circle of readers.[6] In the 1546 edition of the "Discurso," published only three years after Garcilaso's works and at the beginning of his time at Alcalá, Morales emphasizes the dangers of affectation; but by 1586, at the end of his academic and bureaucratic career, the lack of cultivation seems the greater danger. In such a context Garcilaso was valuable as a model who could demonstrate the need for erudition and especially for the kind of education that the universities dispensed and Morales himself possessed. El Brocense too had ties to both the nobility and the university: in his childhood he was a page to the Portuguese king, John III, and later a courtier to Philip II's first wife, Maria; and although he gave up the court for the university, he continued to have friends in high places who effectively protected him from the Inquisition until 1600 (see Bell, 27–58, esp. 30–31). Through their representations of Garcilaso, both Morales and El Brocense seek to appropriate his example to legitimize a university education as a source of linguistic excellence; Garcilaso's canonization, expressed in Castiglionian and Ciceronian terms, rested on the analogous pillars of the aristocracy, the bureaucracy, and the academy.

At a time in which, as Lynch put it (2.15), the king was his own chief civil servant, Morales's interest in prose may be due to the need for better writers in the royal bureaucracy; Donisotti, in his introduction to Bembo, speculated on a similar motivation for the Italian's Ciceronianism (35–37). Moreover, that a discussion of Boscán's translation as a model for prose leads Morales into the topic of poetry shows the association in his mind between the *Cortegiano* and the Spanish Petrarchist school, as well as the latter's status as the preferred form of lyric poetry. Morales's cultural formalism parallels the political formalism of Philip II, in whose reign the forms but not the substance of Charles V's imperial system were perpetuated: where the peripatetic Charles had tried to be, in his person or through viceregal appointments often drawn from his own family, the ruler of each of his separate realms, Philip increasingly subordinated his realms to a bureaucracy based in Castile.[7] With the reduction of the status of Italy to one resembling a colony, the usefulness of Italian culture as an indication of the monarchy's internationalism naturally declined, while the perceived cultural superiority of the Italians rankled all the more.

Yet the hurdle posed by the canonization of Garcilaso was not only social. The initial canon, with its basis in limited ideological, linguistic, and literary criteria, easily posed a challenge to later writers. By emphasizing the importance of canonic imitation and citing Garcilaso as the only model for poets, El Brocense and Morales succeed in turning him into a strong, blocking poet and burden Spanish poets with an added degree of poetic belatedness, as they must struggle not only against Petrarch and the Italians but against one of their own compatriots, now dead for fifty years. For a revisionist, paradoxical response to that challenge, we must turn away from the academy and to another poet, Fernando de Herrera, and his *Anotaciones.*

HERRERA'S *ANOTACIONES* I:
DECENTERING GARCILASO

Garcilaso's canonization, grounded in both aesthetic and sociolinguistic criteria, only increased the burden on a socially marginal successor such as Fernando de Herrera. In his *Anotaciones,* or notes to Garcilaso's work (1580), Herrera tried to make room for himself in this highly restricted canon by redefining it, so that Garcilaso was no longer at its center. Doing so meant using the commentary in a subversive way, for commentaries were most often employed, as by

El Brocense, as paratexts that promoted canonization. Herrera, however, took advantage of the opportunities offered by the commentary as a genre to put forward a version of literary history that is a carefully crafted fiction used for polemical purposes. His notes attempt to widen the reader's intertextual location of Garcilaso's poetry, while the profusion of source citations undermines the poet's image as a courtier whose poems were acts of *sprezzatura;* instead Herrera appropriates him as a predecessor for the learned kind of poetry that he himself writes. At the same time the nature of Herrera's proposed sources challenged the narrow kind of imitation and canonization championed by El Brocense. Herrera seized the opportunity to quote sources and analogues, inserting himself into the intertext through the inclusion of translations of classical poetry and quotations of his own poems, as well as through the very quantity of annotations, which dwarfs the original texts. Moreover, the overly learned citations have a countereffect, as the mass of contradictory information subverts the very notion of authority and thus of canonicity. This interpretation of the *Anotaciones* finds support in the responses of contemporary readers.

As Herrera found, a move to displace Garcilaso was viewed as an attack on the forces controlling the canon. These were principally the Castilian nobility, who could claim Garcilaso as one of their own, a warrior who, by fighting against the Turks, was a modern crusader and thus linked national identity (war against Muslims), literary achievement (ascendancy over Italy), and the new empire. It also included the authorities at the Universities of Salamanca and Alcalá, who since Nebrija had been asserting their control over the Castilian dialect, which was itself achieving linguistic hegemony throughout Spain.[8] Herrera, as an Andalusian autodidact of unknown origins, was thoroughly excluded from both groups.[9] The controversy surrounding the reception of the commentary thus demonstrates both Herrera's poetic struggle against an overwhelming predecessor and the social dimensions of the conflict over control of the literary language. Garcilaso's canonization, joined to the continuing sense of Spanish belatedness, resulted in both a crisis for vernacular humanism and a multiple threat to Herrera. While Garcilaso's fame as a courtier and a military hero may have made poetry respectable for the nobility, it also threatened to make it their prerogative; it is no accident that from the time of Valdés, Garcilaso—a nobleman and a Castilian—had been invoked as a linguistic authority. Thus Herrera's attack is not so much directed against Garcilaso, whose ameliorating effect on the language Herrera must admire, but against the notion of a canon, the ideologies that govern its formation, and the institutions that control it. In order to reduce Garcilaso's presence, Herrera attempts to alter the reader's conception of Garcilaso as a perfect soldier-poet, turning him instead into a scholar more like Herrera himself, and less the original and unique figure presented in Morales's *Discurso*. That this was Herrera's intent was recognized and resisted by his earliest readers; the passion of the defenses of Garcilaso by "Prete Jacopín" (pseudonym for Juan Fernández de Velasco, d. 1613) and Tomás Tamayo de Vargas (1588–1641), among others, underlines the poet's special position in the canon and attests to the radical nature of Herrera's views.[10]

Herrera himself is quite forthright about his intention to replace the ideal of the courtier-poet. The preface to the *Anotaciones* presents the humanist aim of educating the young, "para que no se pierda la poesía española en la oscuridad de la ignorancia" (so that Spanish poetry not be lost in the darkness of ignorance, 307), as had writers from Nebrija to Morales.[11] But shortly thereafter, in the very first note, Herrera connects this very darkness to the profession of arms:

> [L]os españoles, ocupados en las armas con perpetua solicitud hasta acabar de restituir su reino a la religión cristiana, no pudiendo entre aquel tumulto y rigor de hierro acudir a la quietud y sosiego de estos estudios, quedaron por la mayor parte ajenos de su noticia; y a pena pueden difícilmente ilustrar las tinieblas de la oscuridad, en que se hallaron por tan largo espacio de años.
>
> (313)

> The Spanish, occupied exclusively by arms until they had finished restoring their kingdom to the Christian religion, unable amid that struggle and the clash of iron to heed the quiet and solace of these studies, remained for the most part far from [poetry's] regard. Barely and only with difficulty can they light up the darkness in which they found themselves for so many years.

In a manner typical of the commentary, this important statement is buried halfway into the first note; here, Herrera tries to combine the conventional rhetoric of the preface with the assertion that it is impossible to be both a warrior (as were Garcilaso and, of course, the *condestable* Fernández de Velasco) and a true man of letters. It is with this subversive idea that Herrera begins his revisionary account of Garcilaso's place in the canon.

Equally subversive are Herrera's techniques, for to accomplish his displacement of Garcilaso he takes advantage of several features of the commentary as a genre. As Javitch shows (*Proclaiming*, 3–10, 48–70; idem, "The Shaping"), commentaries on Ariosto's *Orlando Furioso* were written specifically to promote canonization through the careful citation of select sources, an effect copied by El Brocense and also achieved by E. K.'s glosses on Spenser. Because of these precedents and the associations of a commentary with classical scholarship and the study of canon law, Herrera's work would seem to be underlining Garcilaso's canonical stature. By its very nature, however, a commentary creates what Berman called a coming-and-going (90), a centrifugal effect disrupting the reading of the original by drawing attention away from the source text commented upon, and directing it instead to the annotations as an alternate text. Thus capitalizing on the genre's agonistic possibilities, Herrera attempts through these notes to replace the restricted canon El Brocense had earlier created. The new, open canon in turn poses a challenge to the very notions of literary authority and canonicity.

Herrera utilizes these features of the commentary in several ways. His primary technique is to redefine the readers' notion of Garcilaso's intertextuality, not only by emphasizing the degree to which he imitated earlier poets, but by also expanding the canon of sources. For example, with little or no introduction (e.g., "la imitación es de" [it is an imitation of]), he glosses three lines from Garcilaso's sonnet 7 with two quotes from Propertius, one from Tibullus, and another one from Bembo (*Anotaciones*, 334–35). For other lines in the poem he gives references to Virgil, Ovid, Horace, Bernardo Tasso, and Diego Hurtado de Mendoza (328–34); El Brocense had cited only Horace and Tasso (267), and Tamayo later limited himself to an emendation of the text (600). Similarly, he provides for sonnet 11 references to Petrarch, Gerolamo Muzio, Virgil, Claudian, and Tasso (342–44), while El Brocense made references only to Virgil and Sannazaro (268), and Tamayo again only edited the text (602).

El Brocense, by his restricted canon, sought to identify Garcilaso as a practitioner of Ciceronian/Petrarchan imitation; while Herrera's citations are recognizably from the same tradition of source criticism, their effect is different from that of the other commentaries, and they must be put in the context of a correct understanding of Renaissance imitation theory and poetic practice. It is a commonplace of Renaissance scholarship that the use of sources is not in itself derogatory; yet as we saw, El Brocense himself was criticized for emphasizing Garcilaso's use of imitation. Although Herrera does not directly enter the debate over the proper way to imitate, by stressing the diverse sources for Garcilaso's poetry he points in the direction of a more eclectic approach to imitation, espoused earlier by Erasmus, as well as by Castiglione through his use of the bee metaphor. This is the kind of imitation Herrera himself practiced, and he seeks to legitimize it by appropriating for himself Garcilaso's example. But by stressing the use of imitation he also indirectly opens a line of attack on Garcilaso, for imitation was not a universally recognized virtue. Such "modern" concepts such as originality, self-expression, and plagiarism were not unknown during the Renaissance, and many literary theorists, following Horace and Quintilian, identified imitation more with the apprenticeship of young poets than with the mature achievements of those who themselves are to be models.[12] Herrera himself was accused of copying from Julius Caesar Scaliger by Prete Jacopín (see Coster, 54–57, 166–68), and Quevedo maligned him as "ladrón y no poeta" (thief and no poet; Komanecky, 126) for supposedly stealing from Francisco de la Torre. Furthermore, it was on the very question of Garcilaso's originality and sincerity that Tamayo chose to declare his distance from Herrera:

> Si Herrera se persuadió que Garcilaso no usó color retórico en sus versos, de que antes no hubiese consultado o su memoria, o sus libros, engañóse sin duda, porque los afectos naturales en hombres de ingenio, y más en materias amorosas, no requieren estudio particular o para su expresión, o para su perfección. La naturaleza sola . . . los pule, los dilata, los perfecciona.
>
> (597)

> If Herrera persuaded himself that Garcilaso did not employ the colors of rhetoric in his poems without first consulting his memory or his books, doubtless he deceived himself, for natural affections in men of genius, particularly in matters of love, require no particular study for their expression or perfection. Nature alone . . . polishes them, enlarges them, perfects them.

Moreover, in addition to implying Garcilaso's debt to minor po-
ets, Herrera's many source citations make it difficult for a reader to
know the context in which these poems should be read, for while
the multiplicity of sources is impressive, it is not entirely to the
point. Garcilaso was probably not specifically imitating Propertius
and Tibullus in sonnet 7, the example given earlier; he may have
been imitating Bembo, whose poem is the closest in time and the
most similar, but more likely he was employing a commonplace that
the other poets also employed. An even more important question,
however, is why Herrera wishes his readers to believe that Garcilaso
is familiar with these poets. The identification of multiple sources
for Garcilaso's poems forces Garcilaso to compete within a broader
canon, thus undoing the narrowing efforts of Morales and El Bro-
cense. It also allows Herrera to trumpet his own learning, the depth
of which was questioned by subsequent writers.[13] In addition, he
not only shows off his knowledge but implies an equal or even
greater degree of learning on Garcilaso's part—Garcilaso must have
been quite a scholar himself to have known all of these often obscure
classical and Italian poets. This may be true, but it undermines Gar-
cilaso's reputation as an ideal soldier-poet. Herrera would have us
see Garcilaso's poems not as acts of *sprezzatura* but instead as the
results of much labor and scholarship, a point Tamayo both recog-
nized and objected to:

> ¿Quién creerá que tuvo necesidad de guía el ingenio felicísimo de
> nuestro Poeta, ni tiempo su corta vida tan bien ocupada para imitar
> con tanta particularidad cosas que sin dificultad a cualquiera se ofre-
> cieran . . . ? Fuera de que muchas veces son sólo lugares comunes.
>
> (597; see Almeida, 57)

> Who will believe that the happy genius of our poet had the need of
> such a guide, or that in his short, well-spent life he had the time to
> imitate with so much care things that without any difficulty are avail-
> able to anyone . . . ? Not to mention that often they are only common-
> places.

Tamayo's comments are important for they reveal Garcilaso's reputa-
tion as a poet of such genius that he had no need for learning; it is
Herrera's intention to subvert this image, not only in order to attack
Garcilaso's unique canonical status but also to locate him on the
poets' side of the soldier/poet division and to appropriate him as a

predecessor for learned poetry. His source citations are suspect, for he attempts through them to alter the reader's perception of the nature of the poetry, from spontaneous to learned, and to change accordingly the reader's assessment of Garcilaso's achievement.

If Herrera seeks to expand the canon of possible sources, he also tries to turn Garcilaso into just one more member of a poetic movement by also quoting other sixteenth-century Spanish poets who imitated the same lines. Thus, for sonnet 17, line 8, after giving Petrarch as a source, he also quotes, without any introduction, similar lines from Boscán and Diego Hurtado de Mendoza (362). At times, these excerpts from sources and parallel examples become quite lengthy. For sonnet 6, for example, he gives four sources, and parallels by Bernadim Ribeiro and Diego Hurtado de Mendoza (326–27). For sonnet 4, he gives, at various points, sources in Theocritus, a hymn to Priapus, Pliny, and Petrarch; while as parallels he cites Camoens, Juan Saez Zumeta, Fernando de Cangas (two examples), Diego Hurtado de Mendoza, and an entire sonnet by Gutierre de Cetina (323–24). The use of complete sonnets is particularly important, for Herrera includes this second poem in spite of its having very little in common with Garcilaso's at all. The only detail the two sonnets share is the notion of vain hope, and had Herrera merely wanted another instance of the same motif, he could have quoted just the last two lines of Cetina's poem. By incorporating the entire poem, he diverts the reader's attention from the tenuous thematic connection and toward Cetina's poem as an alternate text, a different but equal way of handling the same motif. The inclusion of parallels such as these has the cumulative effect of decentering Garcilaso as the key poet of the sixteenth century, implying that the other poets, too, achieved the equivalent of what Garcilaso achieved.

Herrera is also not adverse to presenting even his own poems as parallels to Garcilaso's. The phrase "dejad un rato" in sonnet 11 reminds Herrera of "haber hecho un soneto, que para que tenga vida y no se pierda en silencio y oscuridad, . . . me atrevo entrejerillos [i.e., los versos] en estos excelentísimos de Garcilaso" (having written a sonnet which, in order that it have life and not be lost in silence and obscurity, . . . I dare to introduce them [i.e., the verses] among these excellent ones of Garcilaso's, 343). The text of Herrera's sonnet follows; similar quotations of his own poems also accompany sonnets 8 and 12 (two poems). Moreover, this is not the only method

Herrera employs to introduce his own works into the commentary, for he often provides a Spanish translation of texts in Italian and Latin. His versions depart considerably from the originals and thus themselves are parallel imitations of Garcilaso's models. For example, Herrera translates the texts from Propertius and Tibullus mentioned above, producing translations that are themselves more like imitations of the source texts. The translations tend to begin literally but undergo amplification as he goes along, and he translates these three elegiac couplets into three different verse forms. The result is thus relatively "free" translations, not unlike the Garcilaso poems that Herrera is glossing.[14]

Together with the other Spanish imitations, Herrera's translations create a context for Garcilaso's poems which in turn, when read along with their sources, are themselves perceived as imitations. The accumulation of unlikely sources, translations from the classics, and alternative imitations results in a further diminution of Garcilaso's text as a unique literary event and the sole focus of interest; it becomes one of many possible texts. At the same time, the other imitations gain stature by being offered as parallels to Garcilaso's poetry, which serves to increase the reputation not only of Mendoza, Cetina, Boscán, and the other Spaniards, but also of Herrera himself, both directly as a poet and indirectly as a translator, an effect recognized and criticized by Prete Jacopín in his response:

> I vos que dixistes que no pretendíades más que la fidelidad de las traductiones, ¿no pudiérades traduzir más fielmente? ... [S]in respeto ni consideración ponéis vuestros versos con los del Petrarca, Ariosto, don Diego de Mendoça i otros grandes poetas, queriendo correr parejas con ellos.
>
> (118)

> And you who said you had pretended to nothing more than fidelity with your translations, couldn't you translate more faithfully? ... [W]ith neither respect nor consideration, you place your verses among those of Petrarch, Ariosto, Don Diego Hurtado de Mendoza, and other great poets, wishing to equal them.

As Asensio has shown, this indeed became the most controversial feature of Herrera's work: El Brocense himself complained about the intrusion of Herrera's own poetry into the commentary, and in 1639 the Portuguese commentator Faría y Sousa was still complaining:

"singularmente me instiga el ver traídos tantos lugares sin propó-
sito, i Poesías propias i de amigos" (it still particularly galls me to
see him bringing in so many quotations to no end, particularly his
own and those of his friends; quoted in Asensio, "El Brocense," 24).[15]

Yet it is not only through those annotations containing sources
and parallel imitations that Herrera attempts to decenter Garcilaso;
the extended notes on a word or a literary technique also tend to
deflect interest away from the poems, by their very length emphasiz-
ing the commentary as an alternate discourse and challenging the
concept of literary authority. His commentary to these lines from
sonnet 16 offers an example:

> ni aquel fiero rüydo contrahecho
> d'aquel que para Júppiter fue hecho
> por manos de Vulcano artificiosas.
> (6–8)

> nor that fierce noise which mimicked
> that other one which for Jupiter
> was made by Vulcan's skillful hands.

Herrera glosses *Vulcano* by giving extensive mythological informa-
tion. Citing Cicero, Homer, Hesiod, Lucian, and Diodorus Siculus,
he identifies five such deities in the ancient world, while also quot-
ing Marcus Varro's etymological explanation for the name (358).
Herrera then goes on to explain Vulcan's various attributes, includ-
ing the reasons for his association with lightning, his fall from
heaven, and his lameness. His other sources include Eusebius, Val-
erius Flaccus, Apollodorus, Pausanias, Lucan, Lorenzo of Anania,
Dionysus of Alexandria, Galen, St. Isidore, and more. Herrera's use
of so many authorities broadens the canon of knowledge a poet
might have and redefines it in a European rather than a Spanish
context, yet the net result of this piling on of information is that the
sources cancel one another out. The original poem could have been
understood by anyone with an idea of Vulcan's connection with
thunder; the annotations only confuse the reader, draw attention
away from the poetic text, and by raising too many possibilities
make interpretation of the poem impossible. Moreover, this is not
an isolated case of overglossing; in fact, it is a device that Herrera
employs quite often. Among the other items that receive such ency-
clopedic treatment are mythological figures such as Diana, Tityrus,

and Orpheus, allegorical ones such as sleep (*sueño*) and *nemesis*, concepts such as *idea*, and even geographical references such as the Danube River.

These encyclopedic glosses further identify poetry with scholarship, and so promote literature as an activity incompatible with the knightly profession of arms.[16] But the overly learned citations also have a countereffect: the mass of contradictory information brings into question whether any single one of these authorities can be correct, and by so doing undermines the notions of authority and canonicity, for it challenges the common-sense interpretability of the texts. By multiplying and thus diluting authority, the obscure citations further weaken the notion of a limited canon and thus further diminish Garcilaso's position as an authoritative model.

Herrera achieves the same decentering effect in his comments on the literary genres and techniques employed by Garcilaso; once again, attention is focused away from the poem and instead on a particular genre or trope as a thing in itself.[17] Significantly, these comments amount to small treatises embedded in the *Anotaciones* and are the sections most often quoted, independently of the Garcilaso poem to which they are appended. In them, one can most clearly see Herrera's conception of literary history and the subtle ways he redefines Garcilaso's place within it. To Herrera, a genre exists independently of the poems that compose it. In his very first note, he characterizes the sonnet as "la más hermosa composición, y de mayor artificio y gracia de cuantas tiene la poesía italiana y española" (the most beautiful composition, with more artifice and grace than any other poetry, Italian or Spanish, 308) and discusses the various literary techniques he considers most appropriate for sonnets. Historically, the greatest writer of sonnets was Petrarch, who was also the first great imitator, for he not only imitated the Provençal poets who directly preceded him but went back to the Romans as well. After Petrarch there was a gap in poetry writing, ended in the early sixteenth century by Sannazaro and especially Bembo. Herrera credits Santillana with being the first to bring poetic eloquence from Italy to Spain, approvingly quoting an entire sonnet; and he lists Boscán, Mendoza, Cetina, and finally Garcilaso coming after him. Through this list Herrera attempts a subtle displacement: by introducing six intermediaries between Petrarch and Garcilaso and slightly altering the actual chronology of sonnet writers in

Spain (Garcilaso should precede Cetina and Mendoza), Herrera locates him farther from the source. Thus he emphasizes Garcilaso's position as the latest (but not necessarily the last) link in a European tradition, rather than as the beginning and end of a Spanish one.

Herrera's comments on the elegy are similar. In the course of his history of the genre, he reiterates the myth of the dark age that descended on Italy and Spain after the invasion of the Goths. Although the Italians were the first to restore poetry, the Spanish language "es sin alguna comparación más grave y de mayor espíritu y magnificencia que todas las que más se estiman de las vulgares" (is without comparison graver and of greater spirit and magnificence than all those which are most esteemed among the vernaculars, 417–18). Yet in words that echo Nebrija's and Encina's, Herrera expresses his sense that Spanish remains in danger, "porque aunque ahora lo vemos en la más levantada cumbre que jamás se ha visto . . . antes amenaza declinación que crecimiento" (for although we now see it at the highest peak on which it has ever been seen . . . decline seems more imminent than growth, 419).

Coster took these comments of Herrera's at face value and asserted that Herrera was ignorant of the Spanish lyric before Boscán, save for the works of Santillana, which Herrera would have known through his acquaintance with Argote de Molina, who possessed a manuscript of his works (89, 311–12).[18] In fact, Herrera has enough references to Ausías March, Juan de Mena, and others to demonstrate at least some familiarity with earlier lyrics. Rather, Herrera has again fashioned his version of Spanish literary history for primarily polemical ends. What is remarkable about this passage is not his apparent ignorance of medieval Spanish lyric but his overt expression, at the end of the sixteenth century, of the fear that had been implicit in Spanish considerations of literary history since the end of the preceding century: that Spanish letters are at their peak and about to decline. He writes his annotations to combat the threat of oblivion that was first expressed by Nebrija and later echoed by Encina, Boscán, and Morales, in a discourse that had paralleled that of national and then imperial expansion.[19] Herrera does not think that the creativity of Spanish poets has been fully dissipated, only that the desire to outdo the achievements of the canonized past must be recultivated—and here it is clear that the past must refer not just to Rome or even to Rome and Italy but also to the immediate Spanish past, and in particular to Garcilaso. It is the job of the poet to express common sentiments in new and elevated ways, "y cuanto es más común, siendo tratado con novedad, tanto es de mayor espíritu, y, si se puede decir, más divino. Esto es lo que pretendió Petrarca, y por qué resplandecen más sus obras" (for what is most common, if treated in a new way, is thus of greater spirit and, one might say, is more divine. This is what Petrarch attempted, and why his works are so brilliant, 420).[20]

Petrarch should thus once again become the model, as he was for Garcilaso, but as a scholar-poet and for his use of both imitation and invention. This idea is developed in several of the later entries, in which Herrera returns to the situation of Spanish in comparison to other languages. The need for more achievements comes out, finally, in a long diatribe near the end of the *Anotaciones*, appended as a note to eclogue 2. Herrera glosses the phrase *el osado español* (the daring Spaniard, line 1539) with a complaint about Italians who deride the Spanish. To counter them, he catalogs the achievements of the Iberian nation from the time of Hannibal to the present. These achievements are primarily military:

> Porque los despojos ganados de Italia y Francia, la reducción de toda España a la religión de Cristo, y las victorias de Africa, son hazañas maravillosas, pero semejantes a otras de los grandes príncipes; mas comenzar a levantar la cabeza contra la grandeza de Francia, y quebrantar su soberbia, teniendo tantos contrarios y quejosos en España, y crecer en tanta reputación y en tanto imperio con perpetuo curso de dichosos sucesos, y penetrar sus banderas lo encubierto de la tierra por mares no conocidos, es hecho mayor que todos los que se saben de algún rey cristiano.
>
> (554)

> For the spoils won from Italy and France, the reduction of all of Spain to the Christian religion, and the African victories, are marvelous exploits but similar to others of great princes. But to begin to lift one's head against the greatness of France and to break her pride, considering the many critics and whiners in Spain, and to grow in reputation and empire with an endless string of happy successes, penetrating with her flag the hidden parts of the earth over unknown seas, is a deed greater than any others known of a Christian king.

Herrera's tone is different here from what it was at the beginning of the *Anotaciones;* the Spaniards' martial daring is indeed a virtue, but its efficacy in securing fame has been limited because it remains unpublicized.[21] The contempt cannot be blamed entirely on the Italians; the Spanish too are at fault for failing to appreciate the special importance of the man of letters:

> Mas ¿para qué me alargo con tanta demasía en estos ejemplos? Pues sabemos que no faltaron a España en algún tiempo varones heroicos; faltaron escritores cuerdos y sabios que los dedicasen con inmortal estilo a la eternidad de la memoria.
>
> (555)

> But why do I go on with this excess of examples? For we know that Spain has never lacked heroes; she has only lacked sound and wise writers who with an immortal style can commit them to everlasting memory.

Here Herrera returns to the theme first sounded at the very beginning of the *Anotaciones:* the critical importance of poetry, the complemental nature of arms and letters, and thus the need for professional poets. Invoking the trope of the poet as the source of fame, he implies that courtiers such as Garcilaso who compose poetry as amateurs, while capable of great achievements, are not able to bring Spain the international reputation it deserves. Moreover, the canonization of Garcilaso is partly responsible for this impasse for, far from bringing Spain literary glory that surpasses Italy's, it has led to stagnation in the development of Spanish letters by perpetuating the myth of the courtier-poet. What Spain needs are men dedicated entirely to letters; the scholar-poet is not inferior to the man of arms, but instead his fitting successor, the only one capable of completing the ascendancy of Spain. Indeed, only he will be able to complete the task that was merely begun by the great warriors of the past.

At issue in Herrera's commentary is the evaluation of Garcilaso's stature in comparison to that of his predecessors and successors. Certainly Herrera greatly values both Garcilaso's poetry and that tradition which he sees stretching from the ancient world, through the Provençal and Italian poets, to Garcilaso and his Spanish contemporaries.[22] To Herrera, however, it is necessary that Garcilaso be viewed simply as part of that broad tradition, rather than as its culmination, for if the latter is the case, then there is little room for successors. Herrera reading Garcilaso becomes a bit like Petrarch touring Rome and imagining the ruins beneath the ground (see

Greene, 88–93): in effect Herrera subreads Garcilaso, dismembering with his annotations the unity of the text in a search for other texts hidden therein. He thus claims an access to the text's origins that eludes his contemporaries, and may have eluded Garcilaso himself.

Yet as Waller noted apropos of Petrarch, "the 'father' in Freud could be considered not only a biological entity, but also the representative within the family structure of the whole sociological and political matrix in terms of which the child will have to re-define him- or herself in order to move from the position of a child to the position of an adult" (36). In a broad perspective the *Anotaciones* represent a reaction to canon formation, analogous to the controversy over Ariosto in Italy, or to Du Bellay's demolition of Sebillet's French national canon in the *Deffence et illustration de la langue francoyse* (1549), wherein as Saulnier has shown there were also elements of class conflict. Herrera's concern with poetry as a calling in its own right is evident in the appearance of his own poetry two years later, the first major poetry collection prepared for publication by its author since Boscán's, forty years earlier (see "Love and Allusion," below). Yet Herrera's target was not so much Garcilaso's poetry as its position in the canon, and to the degree that Herrera felt it necessary to break with the literary establishment, he certainly succeeded (see Bianchini, "Herrera and Prete Jacopín"). In this context, Herrera's designation of Petrarch as the true model is not only an attempt to find a predecessor who combined the practice of scholarship with the composition of poetry, but to substitute a remote, less threatening, and Italian poetic father for a proximate, intimidating, and Castilian one. His use of a commentary as his vehicle is not as paradoxical as it might seem, for if it classicizes Garcilaso, by subjecting him to the humanist hermeneutic it also proclaims his remoteness and highlights the discontinuities in the poetic tradition.

Once again Bloom's theory of poetic agon provides a vocabulary with which to restate a Renaissance controversy: the question is whether Garcilaso successfully performed an act of metalepsis (as he himself implied, in the third eclogue), transforming earlier poets into predecessors, or whether he is just one more poet who contributed his own clinamen or swerve to the tradition. Our own conception of Garcilaso as a very strong poet must not blind us to Herrera's different point of view, that of a poet who directly struggled with Garcilaso's legacy. The *Anotaciones* can be read independently of the propriety of their remarks about Garcilaso, as the fiction of Herrera's contest with an overwhelming predecessor. The publication of the *Anotaciones* in 1580 may be taken as a demonstration of Herrera's successful appropriation of prior literature, and of his readiness to overcome his reticence and publish his own poems. The first readers recognized that his commentary was not a neutral literary history, but ironically Herrera's own subsequent inclusion in the canon, as much for the *Anotaciones* as for his poetry, eliminated this reading, because he owes that canonization to a paratext dependent on Garcilaso and because such intracanonic struggles seemed unbecoming. By rereading Herrera through the eyes of his critics we gain the insight to reconstruct the family romance of that conflict; an active misreading on our part restores the fiction that originally animated Herrera's work.

HERRERA'S *ANOTACIONES* II:
THE POET'S EYE

In the preceding section we examined Herrera's *Anotaciones* in terms of their overall decentering technique applied to Garcilaso's poems as canonical texts, focusing on the source citations and thematic glosses. Herrera's explicit comments on literary theory also deserve examination; while many are derived from classical and Italian sources, his expression of these ideas in Spanish places them in the context of tendencies we have been examining since Nebrija. In this section we will focus on Herrera's emphasis on sensual, and particularly visual, imagery as it relates to his theory of metaphor; on his theory of translation and its importance for the illustration of the language and for literary history; and on his genre theory and its relation to the *translatio*.

One of Herrera's first glosses deals with metaphor. Garcilaso's sonnet 2 reads, "Mis lágrimas han sido derramadas / donde la sequedad y el aspereza / dieron mal fruto dellas, y mi suerte" (My tears have been spilt where drought and harshness yielded a bad harvest from them and my fortune, 9–11). Herrera draws the reader's attention to what he calls this "traslación de la agricultura" (318) and explains that "traslación," or metaphor, is the most common of figures. He begins with a linguistic and philosophical exposition of the need for metaphor: things have names, and while words or names are but signs for things, words can also be made to refer to something else; the Greeks called this "tropos de la mudanza del entendimiento, y Aristóteles del verbo *metaphérou* que es trasfiero, metáforas, y los latinos traslaciones" (tropes of changed meaning, and Aristotle, from the verb *metaphérou*, which means transfer, metaphors, and the Romans called them *traslaciones*, 318). Figures of this type are almost always pleasing because they result in brevity instead of "revueltas y torcimientos de vanas palabras" (twisting and turning of worthless words, 319) and because the resulting expressions are more unusual and interesting. The use of metaphor can thus be preferable to the use of the name itself, as long as the virtue of clarity is observed and the connection is immediately apparent; clarity results in an intellectual fusion between the writer and the audience such that "el que oye va llevado con la cogitación y pensamiento a otra parte" (he who hears is transported by this thinking to another place, 319).

Yet although metaphor is consequently an intellectual process, it is also a sensual one; and although Herrera conceives of metaphors springing from any of the senses, he gives the place of honor to visual figures:

> Porque el olor de la cortesanía, la blandura y terneza de la humanidad, el murmurio del mar, y la dulzura de la oración, son deducidas de los demás sentidos. Pero las [translaciones] de los ojos son mucho más agudas y de mayor eficacia y vehemencia, porque ponen casi en la presencia del ánimo las cosas que no pudimos mirar ni ver.
>
> (319)

> For the odor of courtiership, the softness and tenderness of humanity, the murmur of the sea, and the sweetness of speech are derived from the other senses. But those [metaphors] derived from eyesight are much more acute and of greater efficacy and vehemence because they almost place before the soul things we cannot see.

Metaphors were first employed out of necessity, to discuss things that had no name, but because they embellished an oration, they came to be employed for their own sake. The trope has enormous potential, as almost any word can be transferred to a new "place," while the only inherent danger, easily avoided, is taking words from places that are not in themselves noble. Moreover, because the purpose of a metaphor is to clarify, the words should be taken from a neighboring field: "[C]onviene que la traslación sea vengonzosa, que significa de cosa cercana y fácil, porque se hace áspera cuando se deduce de lugar muy apartado; o cuando es tan oscura, que tiene necesidad de exposición" (It is desirable that the comparison be becoming, which means from something proximate and simple, for it becomes harsh when derived from a distant place, or when it is so obscure that it needs to be explained, 320). Naturally, a certain moderation should be exercised in the quantity of metaphors in a single composition, but there is no absolute limit. Herrera concludes by drawing distinctions between metaphor and simile and between metaphor and catachresis, while explaining the relation between metaphor and allegory.

Herrera's account of the origin of metaphor extends the privileged position this figure held in Spanish Petrarchist theory and practice.[23] For Herrera, metaphor is not merely an ornament like the other figures, but one with a special heuristic value, for it allows us to talk about things that have no names and to establish relations not previously perceived. Herrera's views thus constitute a secular variant of the metaphor theory of Fray Luis de León and St. John of the Cross.[24] As a consequence, clarity is essential, for the very purpose of metaphor is to enlighten. Herrera amplifies the importance of clarity in his note on Garcilaso's sonnet "Hermosas ninfas." After praising the splendor of the poem (342), he goes on to assert that its clarity results from the placement of words in an order that lends itself to comprehension. Herrera proceeds:

> Es importantísima la claridad en el verso; y si falta en él, se pierde toda la gracia, y la hermosura de la poesía . . . porque las palabras son imágenes de los pensamientos. Debe ser la claridad que nace de ellas luciente, suelta, libre, blanda y entera; no oscura, no intrincada, no forzada, no áspera y despedazada.
>
> (ibid.)

> Clarity is extremely important in poetry; if it is lacking, all the grace and all the beauty in the poem are lost . . . for as words are images of thoughts, the clarity that comes from them should be resplendent, loose, free, soft, and complete, not dark, not intricate, not forced, not harsh, not dissociated.

Yet the term is itself a visual metaphor, and by emphasizing it Herrera further reveals the priority of sight in his system of literary aesthetics. As important as its meaning is, it is only one of many visual ingredients in Herrera's aesthetic vocabulary, and by associating it with metaphor he again highlights the visual and conceptual elements of the latter.[25]

This concern with the visual may in part be due to Neoplatonic theory, for Herrera stresses its importance in glossing terms such as love (328), spirits (336), and beauty (*hermosura*, 367), all of which are explained in terms of sight perception. Similarly, the efficacy of metaphor was explained in terms of placing the previously unseen before the reader's eye. The concern with eyesight leads Herrera to an equivalence between the poet and the painter, as in his gloss on Garcilaso's representation, in the first elegy, of the Tormes as a river-god surrounded by nymphs. Blurring the distinction between ekphrastic description of artistic works and actual painting, Herrera alludes to representations of river-gods with the heads and horns of a bull. He begins by using the verb *fingir* ("los *fingían* los antiguos con cabezas de bueyes o toros con cuernos" [the ancients pretended they had heads of oxen or bulls, along with horns]); he then uses *pintar* in an ambiguous manner that may refer either to painting or to poetry ("y por otra razón lo *pintan* con cuernos" [and for other reasons they paint it with horns]); and finally he uses *pintar* in a totally metaphoric way with reference to a poetic text ("Claudiano ... *pinta* diferentemente de esta tristeza al Po" [Claudian ... paints the Po differently without this sadness], 432–33). Not surprisingly, Herrera's diction here echoes that of Garcilaso's description of the nymphs' tapestries in the third eclogue. Herrera's slip into the same figural language betrays his Horatian concept of the poet as a painter of scenes for a reader's visual imagination, but it again underscores the primacy of the visual as the foundation of poetry.[26]

This emphasis on the visual does not mean that Herrera was unconcerned with matters of sound; indeed, several entries in the commentary are devoted exclusively to the sound of certain lines.[27] For example, he glosses Garcilaso's line "y si no le fabrico y le renuevo" (elegy 2, line 163), commenting that vowels sound more sweetly than consonants, for there is no one who does not understand that the frequent and dense gathering of vowels can lead to a long phrase, but also one that is overstuffed and degenerate; the joining or collision of vowels is called synaloepha. Elsewhere he discusses the appropriateness of enjambment to the hendecasyllable. But just as he rejects hyperbaton, one of the very licenses fifteenth-century theorists such as Encina had particularly endorsed, so too he rejects the aural aesthetics of octosyllabic poetry, in terms that recall Boscán's "A la duquesa de Soma":

> Verdad es, que el número mueve y deleita, y causa la admiración; pero nace el número de la frasis. . . . ¿Qué cosa hay más sin arte y sin juicio, y que con más importuna molestia canse las orejas, que oyen, que trabar sílabas y palabras siempre con un sonido y tenor?
>
> (420)

> It is true that meter moves and delights, and causes admiration; but meter should result from the phrasing. . . . What is less artful and discriminating, and with more aggravation wearies ears that hear, than always to bind syllables and words with the same sound and tenor?

Elsewhere we see Herrera, even when describing the effects of sound, resorting to the vocabulary of sight, as when he refers to "aquella viva claridad y elegancia de luz con que resplandecen en las orejas" (that lively clarity and elegance of light with which they shine in the ears, 511). The effect here is not only synesthesia but also an inadvertent revelation of the position of sight and sound in his aesthetic hierarchy.

Herrera's distinctions among visual, aural, and logical techniques is reflected in his theory of literary translation. Herrera turns to this topic in the context of the situation of Spanish in comparison to other languages, an issue that arises in several of the later entries. Commenting on Garcilaso's description of a hunt in the second eclogue, Herrera points out that the passage is a near translation of the eighth *prosa* of Sannazaro's *Arcadia*. Instead of criticizing Garcilaso's plagiarism, as Prete Jacopín implies (131), Herrera deems the translation so well done that it demonstrates the capacity of Spanish to express any topic that has previously been expressed in another language. Nonetheless, each language has its own qualities, which are difficult to translate:

> [M]as hay algunas cosas dichas con tanta viveza y propriedad y significación en cada particular y nativo lenguaje . . . que aunque las hagan vecinas y moradoras de otra habla, nunca retienen la gracia de su primera naturaleza. Porque tienen algunas propriedades y virtudes la hermosura de la lengua toscana, la gracia de la francesa, la

agudeza y magnificencia de la española, que trocadas con las extrañas, aunque tengan el sentido, pierden aquella flexión y medida de palabras o números. . . . Y así quieren los que saben, que el que imita no proponga tanto decir lo que los otros dijeron, como lo que no dijeron.

(ibid.)

But some things are said with such vividness and propriety and meaning in each particular and native language, that even if made residents of a neighboring speech, they never retain the grace of their first nature. For the handsomeness of Italian, the grace of French, and the wit and magnificence of Spanish have their own properties and virtues, but if exchanged with other languages, that flexibility and measure of the words or numbers is lost. . . . And thus the wise wish that the imitator not attempt to say what others said, but what they did not say.

Herrera here joins the perennial Renaissance debate over the efficacy of translation; it is somewhat surprising, in view of the many translations that he himself offers, to see him come down against the possibility of translations accurately reflecting the originals, even though this was the position of most Renaissance theorists who concerned themselves with literary translation in the abstract. Yet this seemingly contradictory appraisal of Garcilaso can be resolved if one reviews the criteria for success. Spanish is as good as any other language, and there is nothing expressible in another language that cannot be said also in Spanish. Concepts have an existence that is independent of the expression in any one language, and they are consequently translatable in spite of each language's having its own unique virtues. Herrera's description of these virtues—the beauty of Italian, the grace of French, the wit of Spanish—has a Castiglionian air about it, not least in its lack of specificity. Thus, along with most Renaissance theorists, Herrera sees the possibility for translating the *res* but not the *verba;* he differs from many others in not restricting *res* to philosophical and scientific writings, but positing a literary *res* that can be translated.[28] This is precisely what Garcilaso does with the passage from Sannazaro, restating it and imitating it in Spanish. But he does not attempt to reproduce it exactly in Spanish, for the special qualities of the original, which cannot be matched even in neighboring languages, are associated not with matter but with the character of the language.

Herrera also comes close to defining imitation as a form of trans-

lation, as when he says of Garcilaso's first elegy, "esta elegía es tra-
ducida, aunque acrecentada mucho, y variada hermosamente" (this
elegy is translated, though much augmented and freely altered;
450). Here Herrera restates the value of innovativeness to the good
imitator and transfers it to the translator; typically, he also illustrates
the principle through the structure of the note itself. As usual, he
begins by giving the text of the model, but then comments,

> Bien sé que son molestas a los que saben las traducciones desnudas
> de artificio, y sin algún ornato . . . pero no atiendo en esta parte satis-
> facer sus gustos, sino los de los hombres que carecen de la noticia de
> estas cosas; y por esta causa vuelvo en español los versos peregrinos
> de nuestra lengua.
>
> (452)

> I know well that these translations, naked of artifice and without any
> ornament, are a bother to those who know [the original languages]
> . . . but I do not attempt in this part to satisfy their taste, rather that
> of those who have no knowledge of these things; and for this reason
> I turn into Spanish those poems which are foreign to our language.

Whatever pedants may think, translations will always have a role to
play as long as Spaniards remain ignorant of foreign literature; He-
rrera thus sets up his own translation, which follows, as an alternate
to Garcilaso's, its presence justified on the same grounds of the
translator's license. While Herrera's focus on intervernacular transla-
tion between related languages recalls Boscán and Garcilaso, his
precision about translation theory stands in contrast to their pre-
faces to the *Cortegiano* translation (see the first section of chapter 2).
Boscán's emphasis had been on the reception of the subject matter
and on the desirability of thereby illuminating Spanish literature;
Garcilaso's, on Boscán's skill in remaining faithful to the original
while maintaining a pure Castilian style. Although Herrera praises
Garcilaso's transformation of Sannazaro, it is not for its fidelity to
the original, and much less for enriching the Spanish language with
a rendition of a bird hunt; rather, his focus is on the technical and
philosophical issues of literary translation.

A bit farther on Herrera takes up the problem of translating scien-
tific *res* with no Spanish equivalents. Although Castiglione, through
Canossa, had defended the use of neologisms in an ever-mutable
language, Boscán and Garcilaso had come out against them as signs

of affectation. Herrera, by contrast, is positive about their use, for "lícito es a los escritores de una lengua valerse de las voces de otra" (it is legitimate for writers in one language to use words from another, 471). Thus unlike Boscán, who had sacrificed specificity in seeking to use only Spanish words to render Castiglione's Italian, Herrera recommends the borrowing of words from the source language: "Divídese en dos especies la formación de los vocablos nuevos: por necesidad para exprimir pensamientos de Teología y Filosofía y las cosas nuevas que se hallan ahora, y por ornamento" (The formation of new words can be divided into two kinds: for the expression of philosophical and theological ideas and of the new things that are now being found, and for ornament, 527). Naturally, he is more interested in the latter of these processes, in which words are borrowed for poetic effect. In language similar to Castiglione's, Herrera recommends the enrichment of Spanish by borrowing words from ancient and foreign languages, and justifies this effort by pointing to the example of the Romans and the way in which they enriched Latin by borrowing even from the barbarians.[29] Languages mature slowly, and none suddenly attain perfection; it is legitimate to engender new tropes, for thus was Latin enriched. Herrera would allow the use of neologisms in Spanish because it is a living language, in contrast to Latin, whose vocabulary survives only through those relics of ancient writers which still exist. Garcilaso himself incorporated Latinisms and Italianisms into his poetry, and others should not fear to do likewise: "Apártese este rústico miedo de nuestro ánimo; sigamos el ejemplo de aquellos antiguos varones que enriquecieron el sermón romano con las voces griegas y peregrinas y con las bárbaras mismas" (Let this rustic fear flee from our souls; let us follow the example of those ancient noblemen who enriched Latin discourse with words that were Greek and foreign and even barbarian, 525). By polarizing linguistic attitudes into those of "rústicos" and those of "varones," Herrera makes the same distinction as Morales, though replacing "booty," *despojos*, with "words," *voces*. The concept of linguistic booty resurfaces, moreover, in the next page of the commentary, where Herrera argues that there is no language that cannot stand to be enriched "con los más estimados despojos de Italia y Grecia, y de los otros reinos peregrinos, puede[se] vestir y aderezar su patria y amplialla con hermosura" (with the most esteemed spoils of Italy and Greece and other foreign realms, can his country dress, adorn, and amplify itself with beauty, 526), as long as one has art and judgment. Similarly, he argues that one author's not using a word does not mean that others cannot, and thus, in effect, that there are no canonical linguistic models.

This claim, ironically, allows Herrera to defend Garcilaso's use of *orejas* instead of the more elevated *oídos*, complaining about the tyranny "que nos obliga a conservar estos advertimientos, nacidos no de razón o causa alguna, sino de sola presunción y arrogancia" (that forces us to heed these strictures, born not from reason or cause, but from presumption and arrogance, 522). Yet by arguing that these strictures should no longer be applicable, now that Spaniards "osamos navegar el anchísimo Océano y descubrir los tesoros de que estuvieron ajenos nuestros padres" (dare to navigate the wide ocean and to discover the treasures that were unknown to our fathers, 522–23), Herrera reverts to the idea of a cultural backwardness that lags behind imperial accomplishments; implicit in these remarks is an admission that Spanish is not as rich as he had earlier made it out to be, and that it still needs to strive for greater richness. Thus the principle of linguistic freedom concords with the thrust of the entire commentary, which is precisely that, great as Garcilaso's achievement—and by extension the linguistic tools of his day—may have been, Spanish should not stagnate but aspire to still greater achievements on both the literary and the linguistic levels. And those who have the duty to effect just this improvement are the poets, who

> hablan en otra lengua y no son las mismas cosas que trata el poeta que las que el orador, ni unas mismas leyes y observaciones. . . . [E]s la poesía abundantísima y exuberante y rica en todo, libre y de su derecho y jurisdicción sola sin sujeción alguna y maravillosamente idónea en el ministerio de la lengua y copia de palabras por sí.
>
> (527)

> speak in another language, for the poet does not speak of the same things as the orator, nor does he follow the same laws and observances. . . . Poetry is most abundant and exuberant and rich in everything, free and by its right and jurisdiction separate, without any subordination, in itself marvelously independent in administering the language and the wealth of words.

Thus just as Herrera's theory about the possibility of literary translation is tied to his interest in visual and sensual imagery, his interest in its effect is connected to the question of enriching the language through neologisms, as the state is enriched by foreign wealth. Just as a political aristocracy rules the country, so too a poetic aristocracy must exercise hegemony over the language, if the *translatio* is to be realized. Once again, the key issues are the extent of Garcilaso's accomplishments, and the need for their continuation and extension.[30]

The *translatio* in turn serves as a foundation for Herrera's genre theories. Herrera has notes on all of the major genres employed by Garcilaso: the sonnet, the *canción*, the elegy, the eclogue, and the "estanzas o rimas octavas" of the third eclogue.[31] In all cases, one of his principal concerns is to relate these modern genres, as much as possible, to classical equivalents and to account for their use by Garcilaso in modern Spain. Thus at the head of the first note he presents the sonnet as the modern heir of the epigram, the ode, and the elegy, fully capable of treating all subjects and of being ornamented. Indeed, it is harder than the epigram because its length is limited and because, in addition to meter, the poet has to concern himself with rhyme, formal considerations that can place constraints on the use of ornamentation. This definition by analogy and contrast is not historicized until much later, when Herrera recounts the form's modern origins: Petrarch was "el primero que los labró bien y levantó en la más alta cumbre de la acabada hermosura y fuerza perfecta de la poesía" (the first who forged them well, and raised them to the highest peak of finished beauty and perfect force of poetry, 309–10), followed, after a gap of some centuries, by Sannazaro and Bembo who, though judged harsh and affected in his diction and style, was the first true expert on the flowers that adorn Latin and Italian poetry (311).[32] In his gloss on the *canción*, Herrera identifies it with classical lyric, giving a long history that traces it from the Greek odes of Anacreon, Pindar, and Sappho through Horace, but without mentioning the more immediate Italian or Provençal antecedents or the fifteenth-century Spanish genre. The elegy too is traced back to its classical roots, with particular praise for Tibullus and, as noted, an account of the dark age that set in after the fall of Rome to the barbarians, while the eclogue is likewise characterized by references to ancient poets such as Daphnis, Moscus, Bion, Theocritus, and of course Virgil. Herrera sees Petrarch and Boccaccio as the first to have written eclogues since antiquity, although their eclogues, as well as those of Pontano, are not worth remembering (475). Instead, Sannazaro is singled out as the greatest modern Italian writer of eclogues, while Boccaccio is credited with inventing the *rima octava*, in which he was succeeded by Poliziano and Ariosto. This accumulation of classical and Italian poets is not meant, however, to heighten his Spanish readers' awareness of Italian literature, for on the contrary Herrera feels that the Spanish writers of his day have given themselves over too greatly to admiration of the Tuscans:

> Pero no sé cómo sufrirán los nuestros, que con tanta admiración celebran [más] la lengua, el modo del decir, la gracia y los pensamientos de los escritores toscanos, que ose yo afirmar, que la lengua común de España. . . . Porque me parece, que más fácilmente condescenderán con mi opinión los italianos, que tienen algún conocimiento de la nuestra, que los españoles, que ponen más cuidado en la inteligencia de la lengua extranjera, que de la suya.
>
> (312)

> I do not know how ours can bear it, for with so much more admiration they praise the language, mode of speaking, grace, and thoughts of the Tuscan writers than, I dare say, the common language of Spain. . . . For it seems to me that those Italians who have knowledge of our language would more easily coincide with my opinion than would Spaniards, who place more care in the knowledge of a foreign language than of their own.

Here, in language similar to Morales's, Herrera castigates his fellow poets for neglecting their native vernacular. Yet that this neglect does not take the form of poetic composition in the classical languages, but, instead, of excessive imitation of Italian, underlines the canonical and classical status that the Italians have received. Underlying this passage is Herrera's variation on the basic trope of the Spanish Renaissance: the lists of antecedents in each genre exist precisely because they are Garcilaso's antecedents, and thus he emerges as the great mediator who imported and legitimized these foreign forms, the originator rather than the culmination of the *translatio*.

Herrera's comments on these genres extend beyond their history to their intrinsic features; while using them as a way to differentiate himself from the aristocratic, Castiglione-based aesthetics of Garcilaso and Boscán, he also takes advantage of the succession of genres to present a full-scale prescription for lyric poetry as practiced in

Renaissance Spain. For the sonnet he provides one of the earliest formal descriptions in Spanish, noting that it is composed of fourteen hendecasyllabic lines divided into two quatrains and two tercets, with one set of rhymes in the quatrains and another in the tercets. These requirements make it difficult for the inexperienced poet: because of the poem's concentrated nature any mistake stands out, and Herrera recommends that its theme should be a single "sentencia ingeniosa y aguda" (thought both ingenious and sharp, 308), avoiding obscurity but not descending into facility. Indeed, in language that specifically counters the recommendations of Valdés, Boscán, and Garcilaso, Herrera condemns the identification of writing with speech:

> [E]n este pecado caen muchos, que piensan acabar una grande hazaña cuando escriben de la manera que hablan; como si no fuese diferente el descuido y llaneza, que demanda el sermón común, de la observación, que pide el artificio y cuidado de quien escribe. No reprehendo la facilidad, sino la afectación della.
>
> (308; see Almeida 103)

> Many fall into this sin, thinking they have accomplished a great deed when they write as they speak, as if there were no difference between the carelessness and plainness called for in common speech, and the degree of observation called for by the skill and care of someone who writes. I do not reprove true facility, but only its affectation.

Not surprisingly, clarity is recommended, without contortions to accommodate the rhyme, but equally reprehensible are the lack of vigor, the use of low language, and having the rhyme dictate the matter rather than the other way around. Latin poets enjoyed greater freedom because modern poetry, in addition to meter, requires rhyme, while the rhythm of the hendecasyllable is not as malleable as it might seem, for any eleven syllables do not necessarily constitute a line of verse.

Herrera's comments on the sonnet introduce both the formal and the thematic requirements of lyric poetry. This course is continued in his remarks on the *canción*, which, as already noted, Herrera identifies with the very roots of lyricism itself. To Herrera, this is above all the genre of love; and, citing Anacreon as one of the first great lyric poets, he invests it with the Greek poet's sensuality:

[E]s su poesía toda amatoria, que como dice Pausanias en la *Ática*, fue el primero, después de Safo, que gastó gran parte de sus versos en declarar sus amores. Porque nació sólo para juegos y cantos y danzas y besos y convites, todo entregado en deleites sensuales y de gula. Mas aunque tiene viles y abatidas consideraciones y deseos, no se puede dejar de conceder que dice con mucho donaire, y que en aquella poesía mélica no esté todo lleno de miel y dulzura y gracia entre todos los griegos y latinos y vulgares.

(392)

His poetry is all about love, for as Pausanias said in the *Attica*, he was the first, after Sappho, who spent the greater part of his poems in declaring his love. For he was born only for games and songs and dances and kisses and banquets, completely given over to the pleasures of the senses and of the palate. But although he has low and vile considerations and desires, one cannot but concede that he speaks with elegance, and that Melic poetry is not all full of sweetness and honey and grace, among all the other Greeks, Romans, and vernacular [writers].

In contrast, Pindar is given relatively short shrift, while Sappho is praised as a woman of great spirit, admirable in the declaration of her passions and secret love (393). In contrast to Greek, Latin literature was relatively weak in lyric poets save for Horace, who alone is worthy of being read; yet Herrera's comments about him are restrained, with more space devoted to an ambivalent condemnation of Catullus's love poetry. The note concludes with the observation that a *canción* can be subdivided into stanzas, whose length, verses, and rhyme are consistent but free for the poet to determine, and that it is usually concluded with a shorter epilogue.

Herrera returns to the topic of love poetry in the note on the elegy; after analyzing the origin of its name and discussing its history in ancient Rome, Herrera concludes that it is a very flexible genre, capable of absorbing a great variety of attitudes:

Y porque los escritores de versos amorosos o esperan, o desesperan, o deshacen sus pensamientos, y inducen otros nuevos, y los mudan y pervierten, o ruegan, o se quejan, o alegran, o alaban la hermosura de su dama, o explican su propria vida, y cuentan sus fortunas con los demás sentimientos del ánimo, que ellos declaran en varias ocasiones, conviniendo que este género de poesía sea mixto . . . y por esto no se deben juzgar todos por un ejemplo, ni ser comprendidos en el rigor de una misma censura.

(417)

For the writers of these love poems either hope or despair, or undo their thoughts and introduce new ones, and change and pervert them, or beg, or complain, or rejoice, or praise the beauty of their beloved, or justify their own lives, and tell of their fortunes along with the other sentiments of the soul, which they declare on various occasions, for poetry of this type should be varied . . . and for this reason all should not be judged by a single example, nor included in the severity of a single censure.

Although this is a fair description of Roman elegy and not incorrect in pointing out the classical genre's variety, the comment could also serve as a definition of Petrarchist lyric. This coincidence of course is not accidental: the Roman elegists were among the principal sources of influence on Petrarch himself, and the connection is strengthened when Herrera identifies *terza rima* as the modern metrical equivalent of the elegiac couplet, and Dante and Petrarch as its chief practitioners. Yet coming after the notes on the sonnet and the *canción*, these remarks further Herrera's exposition of the historical link between the modern lyric and the Petrarchist model. Thus while the poet's principal themes should be his hope and his despair, the undoing of reason, praise of the beloved's beauty, and the like, infinite variety is also possible in love poetry, and no single model should be canonical. In the context of Herrera's own time, this is not a warning against the unique imitation of Tibullus, Propertius, or Ovid (none of them hypercanonical), nor even of Petrarch, but of Garcilaso, as singled out by El Brocense and Morales.

Just as Herrera's remarks on the *canción* and the elegy focus on subject matter as much as on form, so too do his comments on the eclogue. These have fountains with the sweetest water, and are full of trees with the largest fruit and plants and vines of incredible abundance (473). Thus Herrera identifies richness and fertility, metaphors of *copia*, as the genre's distinguishing characteristics, rather than the pleasantness of the Arcadian place. Again, too, love is the principal subject of the poems:

La materia de esta poesía es las cosas y obras de los pastores, mayormente sus amores; pero simples y sin daño, no funestos con rabia de celos, no manchados con adulterios; competencias de rivales, pero sin muerte y sangre. Los dones que dan a sus amadas, tienen más estimación por la voluntad, que por el precio.

(474)

The subject of these poems is the possessions and works of shepherds, particularly their loves; but these should be simple and without harm, not doleful with furious jealousy, nor stained with adultery; with competitions among rivals, but with neither death nor blood. The gifts they give to their beloveds should be more valued for their intention than for their worth.

In eclogues, diction should always be elegant; words should taste of the earth and the fields, but not without gracefulness, nor should they be ignorant or archaic. Rather, rusticity should always be tempered with a vocabulary appropriate to tender sentiments. Thus, Virgil and Sannazaro are praised, while Mantuan and Encina are censured; here, above all, Garcilaso has matched the achievements of his predecessors.

Nearly absent from Herrera's poetic theory is any discussion of the epic. Because of the commentary's paratextual status, the genres that Herrera defines are necessarily those that Garcilaso employed, and the near identification of lyric with love poetry is a result of what he and his significant predecessors made of it. However much Herrera may want to decenter Garcilaso, he stands between the Sevillian and the earlier poets, a lens that focuses as much as a barrier that impedes. Thus Herrera's neglect of the epic in the *Anotaciones* is not just the result of a rejection of Aristotelian theory, but a nearly inevitable consequence of the fact that Garcilaso himself did not practice it.[33] Moreover, because Garcilaso and Petrarch largely neglected the epic, at least in the vernacular, in favor of lyric, for Herrera the lyric takes the place of epic in the hierarchy of genres, as can be seen in his notes on these lines from the dedication of Garcilaso's first eclogue to Pedro de Toledo, viceroy of Naples:

> el árbol de vitoria
> que ciñe estrechamente
> tu glorïosa frente
> dé lugar a la yedra que se planta.
> (35–38)

Let the tree of victory that tightly girds your glorious forehead give way to the planted ivy.

Glossing the words *el arbol*, Herrera declares that the garland on the viceroy's brow must have been the laurel, which in ancient times had crowned military heroes and epic poets. Thus he opens the note with a quote from Petrarch, "Arbor vittoriosa triunfale, / onor d'imperadori et di poeti" (Victorious triumphal tree, the honor of emperors and of poets, *Rime sparse* 263.1–2). Yet standing at the head of the note, these lines, from the foremost modern lyric poet and devotee of the laurel, mark the historical transition from epic to lyric. Imitating Garcilaso's instructions to the viceroy (doff the laurel, put on the ivy), Herrera's note proceeds through an account of the poetic attributes of the laurel, the myrtle (used in ancient times by love poets), and finally the ivy, "de los líricos" (of the lyric poets, 477). This plant is also the most appropriate for learned poets, for "es de fuera verde y dentro amarilla; y por eso coronan de ella a los poetas, amarillos del estudio, mas su gloria, y la que celebran, florida y verde mucho tiempo" (it is green on the outside and yellow within; and for this reason it crowned those poets who were pallid from their studies, while their glory, and that of whom they praise, is always green and in bloom, ibid.). Herrera goes on to explain the sacred associations of the ivy: Jupiter wore it after defeating the Titans, and when mixed with wine it leads not to a vile drunkenness but to a near frenzy; the plant is named after a dancer who died in the course of performing for Bacchus, and who was subsequently transformed into a vine. By shifting the topic of a note ostensibly glossing the laurel, from military heroism and the epic to lyric poetry and art, Herrera echoes Garcilaso's advice (shed one garland in favor of another) but also traces, allegorically, what he sees as the course of literary history. In fact, Herrera had ample opportunities to digress on the nature of epic, such as the notes on the second half of the second eclogue, on the *rima octava,* and on the other poems in which Garcilaso declares a preference for love poetry over epic poetry (such as the fifth *canción* and the third eclogue). Herrera's avoidance of the topic must therefore be taken as both deliberate and significant.[34] His most "epic" note is that on "el osado español," discussed in the preceding section; in the context of Herrera's poetic theory as a whole, it becomes clear that the glory that poets will bring to Spain is not just parallel to, but distinct from, that of her military victories. Spaniards must take on Italians not on that military battlefield where they have already been victorious, but on the literary battlefield of the lyric poem.

To Elias Rivers, Herrera represents a retreat from the Garcilasan ideal of indirect poetics, back to the systematic, Nebrijan mold (see "Some Ideas" and "L'humanisme linguistique"). Undeniably, Herrera's annotations do revel in a demonstration of encyclopedic erudition antithetical to the school of Castiglione, and he rejects the prosaic model of poetry approximating the speech of courtiers. He emphasizes instead what is proper for the heightened language of poetry through his attention to genres, figures, and even phonetic techniques. Yet there is little that is systematic about Herrera's exposition, either in content or in arrangement. Historically, the *Anotaciones* are a transitional text; and while his descriptions of the formal requirements of the various genres, particularly the sonnet, are unusual for his time, it would be impossible to write a poem merely following his precepts. He presupposes familiarity with the forms, and for more prescriptive definitions one must look in Sánchez de Lima's *El arte poética en romance castellano* (also 1580) or wait for Díaz Rengifo's *Arte poética española*, ten years later. Similarly, his aesthetic ideas are more methodically presented in Robles's *Culto sevillano*, which Herrera influenced. His paratextual dependence on Garcilaso shows Herrera's continued resistance to theory, which places the *Anotaciones* at the cusp of the transition to the Baroque preceptive and analytical treatises of the following century.

Although the arrangement of Herrera's notes seems chaotic, overall they are governed by a limited set of principles: on the one hand, the need to displace Garcilaso from his position at the center of Spanish poetry; on the other, the nature of that poetry as determined by Garcilaso's example. Above all, he emphasizes the importance of sensual (particularly visual) and intellectual elements in poetic ornamentation, and the continuing delay in the completion of the *translatio*. Underlying these ideas is the conviction that lyric poetry is the proper successor to the epic, and thus is the ground on which national literary achievements must be judged. The context, both historical and stylistic, in which Herrera places Garcilaso is "Italia y Grecia," the Greco-Roman-Italian tradition whose foremost modern representative is Petrarch. Writing the *Anotaciones* reenacts the hermeneutic circle: such are the expectations with which Herrera reads Garcilaso, and such is what he subreads in Garcilaso's poems. The same circular process lies behind the creation of Herrera's own poetry, and it is with this method that his poems should be read.

LOVE AND ALLUSION: PETRARCH
AND GARCILASO IN THE POETRY
OF HERRERA

The remainder of this chapter examines Herrera's poetry in terms of the related issues of arrangement, intertextuality, and interpretation. These aspects of his poetry have been neglected, in part because critics have been diverted by the textual issues surrounding his work and by attempts to apply narrowly the stylistic categories of the *Anotaciones*. Moreover, Herrera's poetry is clothed in a nearly seamless garment of conventional Neoplatonism and Petrarchism, which stands in the way of a true intertextual reading. Often Herrera seems either to imitate slavishly, or else to adopt a style, instead of struggling to appropriate and revise particular poems. Yet our emphasis on subreading Herrera's texts and on treating some of them as metapoems is not a generic approach to Petrarchist poetry, but one motivated by Herrera's own allusive technique; the resulting interpretations are meant not to supplant the conventional understanding but to show how intertextual tension competes with the surface unity of the poems. Herrera's adoption of neglected genres and techniques, in an attempt to go beyond Garcilaso, results in hyper-Petrarchan texts that successfully emulate their models.

Herrera's poetry has not received as much critical or interpretative attention as that of other Spanish Renaissance poets, perhaps because of the textual controversies that cannot be definitively resolved. There are three principal sources for his poetry. The first is the *Cisne del Betis*, manuscript 10.159 of the Biblioteca Nacional in Madrid, dated 1578 and containing the works of several poets from Seville; the Herrera portion, containing early versions and otherwise unknown poems, was published by Blecua as Herrera's *Rimas inéditas* in 1948. The second and most authentic source is the 1582 edition *Algunas obras de Fernando de Herrera*, prepared by the poet himself, dedicated to the marqués de Tarifa, and containing one hundred poems. For the remaining seventeen years of his life, however, the poet published no more poetry, and the next edition of his works, the 1619 *Versos de Fernando de Herrera emendados y divididos por él en tres libros*, has been controversial from the start. It was prepared (according to Enrique Duarte's prologue) by the painter Francisco Pacheco on the basis of "cuadernos i borradores" (quartos and drafts) that survived the "naufragio" (shipwreck) after the poet's death, in which was lost a manuscript of his poems, "que él tenía corregidas de última mano, i encuadernadas para darlas a la imprenta" (which he had definitively corrected in his own hand, and bound for printing). Dedicated by Pacheco to Gaspar de Guzmán, count of Olivares (and future *privado* to Philip IV), it contains 365 poems, including almost the entire contents of the 1582 edition but in new versions and in a new arrangement; the degree to which the emendations and the ordering of the poems reflect Herrera's intentions is much disputed. Thus many poems exist in two or even three versions.[35]

That Herrera published his own poetry is significant; he was the first major author since Boscán to attempt to bring to print a significant body of work in his own lifetime (and Boscán, of course, died just before seeing the fruits of this effort).[36] Like Boscán, Herrera takes advantage of print to imitate Petrarch by organizing his poems; in both printed editions, as in the *Rime sparse* and in Boscán's second book—but in contrast to the Garcilaso editions—poetic genres are intermixed rather than separated. Moreover, although some of his poems celebrate historical events or are addressed to contemporaries, most are about his love for "Luz" (usually identified with Leonor, wife of his patron, the count of Gelves), who thus plays a role analogous to Laura's as both signified (a forbidden love) and signifier (the focal point of the collection). This analogy serves as a sign in its own right, linking the two collections; in view of Laura's identification with the dawn and Luz's with sunlight, it creates overlapping semantic fields which in turn increase the possibilities for intertextual reference. As Hernández Esteban put it,

> Creemos que mejor que ningún otro poeta del Renacimiento español, es en la poesía de Herrera donde hay una más profunda comprensión de la fusión Dafne-Laura que lleva a cabo Petrarcha, y su recuperación le permite a Herrera no sólo imitar en una vía de continuidad poética, sino a la vez separarse, diferenciarse del modelo.
>
> (405)

> We believe that, more than in any other poet of the Spanish Renaissance, in Herrera's poetry there is a profound comprehension of that fusion of Daphne and Laura which Petrarch realizes, and its recovery permits Herrera not only to imitate in a path of poetic continuity, but also to separate and distance himself from the model.

Like Boscán, Herrera expects readers to be familiar with his prede-
cessors' work and takes advantage of the expectations that will
thereby have been formed. The process is circular: on a macrotextual
level, the very act of arranging the texts serves an allusive function
which, in turn, reinforces the allusions that, on the microtextual
level of individual poems, create the illusion of a series of "snap-
shots" constituting a narrative.

The poems in the 1582 edition are undoubtedly authentic and, as
the title indicates, it was meant to be a selection of Herrera's works
and a demonstration of his poetic ability to an audience of fellow
literati. The very act of publishing them, and the fact that the count-
ess of Gelves had died the previous year, mitigate their reading as
love poems in a strictly communicative sense. Within the anthology
there is an attempt to present them in a sequence, as can be seen in
certain groups of poems or "nodes" about a particular theme; yet
an autobiographical or even narratological interpretation is difficult.
Unlike Boscán, who suggests a fictional autobiography, Herrera
uses the opening poems not to describe an *enamoramiento* but to
set the tone for the anthology, and the arrangement of the poems
highlights Herrera's use of Petrarch and Garcilaso as models. In the
first lines of the opening sonnet,

> Osè, i temi; mas pudo la osadia
> tanto, que despreciè el temor cobarde.
> subi a do el fuego mas m'enciende i arde,
> cuanto mas la esperança se desvia.
> Gastè en error la edad florida mia.
>
> (*AO* 1.1–5)

> I dared and I feared, but my daring proved so great that I despised
> fearful cowardice; I rose to where fire most ignites me, the more that
> hope is left behind. I spent in error my florid age.

the verbs are in the preterit, implying actions that are past and
completed, upon which the poet looks back from a state of greater
wisdom. In this choice of tense, and in the reference to his wasted
youth, the verses suggest a connection to the prefatory sonnets of
Petrarch and Boscán, an *imitatio vitae* culminating in conversion and
a palinode. Yet in the subsequent lines the poet switches to a present
tense, indicative of continuing and cyclical actions. Here the refer-
ences seem to be more to Garcilaso, particularly sonnet 4, in the

poet's attempts to rise, his subsequent fall, and his determination to persevere.

Considering the poem's apparent prefatory function, one would expect the subsequent sonnets to illuminate or take off from this starting point, but instead they continue in the same vein. Thus the prefatory nature of *AO* 1 results from the horizon of expectations, conditioned by Petrarch, Bembo (see Cruz, *Imitación*, 26–33), and Boscán, that the reader brings to it. It is not truly liminal, but an integral part of what is to follow, as is borne out by its displacement, in *V*, from a prefatory position to the middle of book 3. Yet its function in relation to the rest of *AO* is as much in the intertextual connections that it signals as in the message it explicitly conveys. With this sonnet Herrera takes advantage of those horizons he knows the reader will bring to the poem and reinforces them; by thus exacerbating them, he lends ambiguity to the poem's reference: his daring, his fear, and his *furor* may be taken poetically as well as erotically. By invoking his predecessors Herrera attempts, as in the *Anotaciones*, to locate his own poems as the latest entry in the Petrarchan tradition.

A similar exploitation of the reader's horizons takes place at the conclusion of *AO*; Macrí (591) has seen in this final poem a palinode, although in *V* this poem too is displaced to the middle of book 3. Yet the preterit in the first quatrain ("en un incendio no acabado / ardí" [in an unfinished fire I burned], 1–2) is no more indicative of perfected action than it was in the first sonnet, as the present indicative of the second quatrain "I aora (ô vano error) en este estado, . . . pierdo en ti lo mejor de mi cuidado" (and now [oh vain error] in this state . . . I lose in you the greatest of my cares, 5, 8) makes clear. Similarly, the final lines, spoken to love as indirect commands to the beloved, do not suggest repentance: "Abra la luz la niebla a tus engaños, / antes qu'el lazo rompa el tiempo, i muerto / sea el fuego del tardo ielo mio" (Let light pierce the fog of your deceits, before time breaks the bonds and the fire by my final ice is killed, *AO* 78.12–14). These subjunctives do not indicate immediate action; instead, they convey the poet's wishes, as yet unfulfilled. Macrí notes in these lines the use of the fundamental ice–fire antithesis, citing numerous precedents in Petrarch, such as sonnet 220, "che mi cuocono il cor in ghiaccio e 'n foco" (that burn my heart in ice and fire, 14). Yet in Petrarch ice and fire are paradoxically, and oxymoronically, united, while in Herrera the final stanza sets up a complicated set of oppositions. In the first line of the tercet, *luz*, with her light and heat, must break through the cold, dark shadows of love itself; while *muerto*, the final word of the second line, though syntactically independent, suggests that death would be the result of time's broken bonds and that the fire that gives him light will be extinguished by the iciness of fatality. Thus on first reading, it is the poet himself whose death is in question. Yet in Herrera's poetic vocabulary, *lazo*, bond or knot, is often a metaphor for hair (see Macrí, 223; Kossoff, 180), and as such is a synecdoche for the beloved. She too is consequently in danger of dissolution by time, as her beauty fades and icy indifference comes to replace the fiery passion he once felt. Finally, the loosened bonds are also those of love itself, which will die with him, as will the fire of life and of poetic creation, which creates the light he loves: when he dies, *Luz*, who exists only as his poetic creation, will die also. Thus Herrera simultaneously fragments his Petrarchan source into an allegory of external opposites (love and the beloved, life and death, fire and ice) operating on him as a unified subject, threatens the beloved with a *carpe diem*, and internalizes the opposites into a self-centered love song to his own poetic creation.

The opening and closing poems in *AO* allude to Petrarch and Garcilaso in a general way; as interesting, in terms of specific intertextual competition, is the node that precedes the conclusion (*AO* 73–75), which recapitulates Garcilaso's theme of love as a journey. The series is introduced by sonnet *AO* 73, where the poet compares his burden to that of Atlas and Hercules, in that he too has sustained the heavens "do el Amor se cria; / i donde reina eterna la belleza" (where Love is raised and where eternal beauty reigns, 11–12); as in sonnet 1, this burden can be construed poetically as much as erotically. The following sonnet, "Dond'el dolor me lleva, buelvo el passo" (Where pain leads me, I turn my steps, *AO* 74.1) has the poet retracing footsteps in a repeating cycle of hope and despair which was also Garcilaso's; the word *passo* recalls the Toledan's "y a ver los passos por dó m'han traýdo" (to see where my steps have brought me, 1.2), while other details suggest connections with Garcilaso's sonnets 6 and 4, and thence to Garcilaso's own sources in Petrarch, Ausías March, and the *cancionero* tradition. The most specific connections, however, occur in Herrera's next poem:

Sigo por un desierto no tratado,
sin luz, sin guia, en confusion perdido,
el vano error, que solo m'à traido
a la miseria del mas triste estado.
Cuanto m'alàrgo mas, voi mas errado,
i a mayores peligros ofrecido.
dexar atras el mal m'es defendido;
qu'el passo del remedio està cerrado.

(*AO* 75.1–8)

Through an unexplored desert, without light or guide, in confusion lost, I follow vain error, which only has brought me to the misery of the most woeful state. The further I travel, the more I am in error, and to greater perils offered. To leave affliction behind is forbidden, for the path of remedy is closed.

Here, as in the preceding sonnet, a number of details recall various places in Garcilaso, but above all Herrera rewrites the conclusion of Garcilaso's "Estoy contino en lágrimas bañado":

Y si quiero subir a la alta cumbre,
a cada paso espántanme en la vía
ejemplos tristes de los que han caýdo;
sobre todo, me falta ya la lumbre
de la esperança, con que andar solía
por la oscura región de vuestro olvido.

(Rivers ed., 38.9–14)

And if I wish to climb to the high summit, at each step I am frightened by the sad examples of those who have fallen; above all, I lack the light of hope, with which I once wandered through the dark regions of your forgetfulness.

Herrera both preserves and intensifies Garcilaso's desert landscape, particularly in rendering more external and objective that which, in his predecessor, is clearly an internal state. This process is clearest in the transformation of the light/hope metaphor; in Garcilaso they are directly identified, but in Herrera the link is left ambivalent. Thus, through Garcilaso, *luz* (line 2) refers narrowly to hope, but in the context of the collection as a whole all other associations are also brought into play. Similarly, the eleventh line of Garcilaso's poem, about the failure of his predecessors, creates a context for ambiguity in Herrera. In line 3, *solo* may mean either that his error has only brought him misery or that it has brought him alone misery; if the latter, then Herrera is pretending to have no predecessors even as the reader recognizes that, if anything, an excess of predecessors and models is more truly the case. The more Herrera perseveres in this path, the more *errado*, the more Petrarchan, he becomes, and the more subject to the dangers of imitation; surpassing the limitations, in both the erotic and the literary senses, of Petrarchan love is forbidden to him, while for him as for Garcilaso ("si me quiero tornar para hüyros / desmayo, viendo atrás lo que he dexado" [if I wish to turn to flee you, I faint, seeing at my back what I have left behind], 38.7–8) retreat is impossible. There are no alternatives to Petrarchan imitation open to a poet who wishes to challenge and outdo his predecessors; the field of battle has been chosen for him.[37]

The opening and closing poems of *AO* are not truly liminal texts, though they are read as such by those who bring to bear on the anthology a horizon of expectations shaped by Petrarch and Boscán. Herrera exploits that horizon, both to obtain such a reading and to underline the allusive links between his anthology and the poetry of his predecessors, particularly Petrarch and Garcilaso, whom he proposes to transcend. In the node immediately preceding the final sonnet, he makes repeated allusions to Garcilaso's journey poems, portraying himself as both surpassing but also limited to the path his predecessors trod. In contrast to *AO*, *V* presents a completely different approach to organization, and however much edited by Pacheco, its title asserts that it contains the corpus of Herrera's poetry presented in canonical order. The 365 poems in *V* are grouped into three books, each of which begins with a truly liminal sonnet about the challenge posed, respectively, by the modern love poets (book 1), the Roman elegists (book 2), and the epic poets (book 3).

The liminal status of *V* 1.1 can be seen in its opening lines. The first quatrain recapitulates several themes from Petrarch's first sonnet, particularly the notions of vain error, hopelessness, and the tyranny the senses exercised over him; these details are greatly accentuated from the earlier version of the poem in *CdB* and show the adaptation of a preexistent sonnet to fit the requirements of a liminal poem. The second quatrain then describes the poetic process itself:

Mueve la voz Amor de mi gemido,
i esfuerça'l triste coraçon cansado,
porque, siendo en mis cartas celebrado,
d'el s'aprovéche nunca el ciego Olvido.
(*V* 1.1.5–8)

Love moves the voice of my cries and gives strength to my tired, sad heart, so that by being celebrated in my writing, blind Oblivion may never overcome him.

Here again the manuscript version of the poem has been revised, replacing *canto* with *gemido,* a more extreme word but one which through metonymy retains the same referent, and introducing *cartas,* an insinuation of writing, thus incorporating both the oral and scriptive components of poetry. Just as Garcilaso in the third eclogue spoke with a voice that belonged to another, so Herrera presents Love as an autonomous force compelling the poet to speak his cries and forcing him to praise Love through his writing, so that its power may never be forgotten. Then in the tercets Herrera invites the reader, who in his rhymes "sabe i vê'l rigor de su tormento" (knows and sees the severity of his torment, *V* 1.1.9), to rejoice in recognizing their affinity, while those who are ignorant of it should flee, for "para libres almas no es el canto / de quien sus daños cuenta por vitoria" (the song of him who counts his wounds a victory is not for free souls, *V* 1.1.13–14). In the original version there was no division into two classes of readers, and thus the second major allusion in the poem, to Ausías March's "Qui no és trist de mos dictats no cur" (see Cuevas edition, 501), is—like the Petrarchan references— accentuated in the process of revision. Through these references Herrera locates both his love and his poetic process in the tradition of the modern love lyric. Unlike Petrarch and Boscán, however, who at least pretended to welcome an untutored audience that would stand to profit from the lessons of love, Herrera seeks only sympathetic and thus cultured readers. While Boscán forced the knowledgeable reader to fictionalize himself as both a poetic and an erotic naïf, ignorant of both Petrarchan love and Petrarchist poetry, Herrera only wants an audience that can share his manipulation of the Petrarchist love themes; and while this poem, like *AO* 1, sets the emotional tone for what is to follow, in thus standing apart from the poetry and commenting on its origins, and in constituting its audience, it is more truly liminal than "Osè i temi."

In the preceding section we saw how for Herrera the lyric genres come to take the place of the epic as the guarantors of national glory. A similar sentiment is expressed in the liminal sonnet to book 3 of *V*:

> Las armas fieras cánte
>
> . . .
>
> quien en l'Aonia selva ornò su frente,
>
> . . .
>
> Que yo solo (si Amor tal bien consiente)
> mi pura Estrella, cánto vuestra lumbre;
> que m'afina en las llamas de su gloria.
> (*V* 3.1.1, 9, 12–14)

Let him who on Ionia crowned his brow, sing of fierce arms; I, if love consents, my pure star, will sing only of your light, which refines me in its glory.

Here Herrera connects the transition from epic to lyric to the *translatio* from Greece to Spain, and from the ancients to the moderns: epic was good enough for Homer but only praise of his beloved will do for Herrera. Yet as many critics have commented, in the process of supplanting the epic, the lyric genres take on many of its characteristics, in diction as well as theme.[38] As McInnis noted, Herrera directly refers to his choice of genres in *AO* 49:

> Que bien sè qu'es mayor la insine gloria
> de quien Melas bañò i el Mincio frio,
> de quien llorò en Tebro sus enojos.
> Mas que hare, si toda mi memoria
> ocupa Amor, tirano señor mio?
> (*AO* 49.9–13)

For I well know that the greatest glory belongs to him whom Melas bathed, and the cold Mincio, to him who into the Tiber wept his passion. But what can I do if my entire memory is occupied by Love, my tyrant lord?

Here Herrera employs the names of rivers antonomastically to refer to the poets of antiquity: the Anatolian Melas stands for Homer, the singer of Troy, while Mantua, Virgil's birthplace, is on the banks of the Mincio; the Tiber is thought to refer to Tibullus (see Cuevas's notes, 419, but also the discussion below). The speaker, in contrast, has been deprived of memory, an essential property of the epic poet, while enslaved by love and his beloved's eyes. Yet the full impact of the poem can only be judged in terms of its "node" and the specific allusions to a similar node also near the center of the *Rime sparse*. The poem's context, largely preserved in *V*, is important: it is immediately preceded by the sonnet "Rompio la prora en dura roca abierta" (My open prow was broken by a hard rock) in which, with epic diction that recalls Homer and Virgil, the poet describes his shipwreck and his arrival in an unknown land. Yet the conclusion of that poem reveals that the shipwreck is but an allegory for love, for "en el golfo de Cupido / ninguno navegò, qu'al fin deshecho, / no se perdiesse falto de ventura" (in Cupid's gulf no one navigates who is not at the end unmade, lost for lack of fortune, *AO* 48.12–14).[39] It is followed by a sonnet in which the poet addresses the certain ignominy that awaits him:

> Pierdo, tu culpa Amor, pierdo engañado,
> siguiendo tu esperança prometida,
> el mas florido tiempo de mi vida,
> sin nombre, en ciego olvido sepultado.
>
> (*AO* 50.1–4)

I lost through your fault, Love, and, deceived while following your promised hope, I spent the most florid period of my life namelessly buried in blind oblivion.

The poet then goes on to assert that he will no longer squander his time in this way, for while he has seen how a captive can twist his hands and free himself from chains binding his feet, he himself could never erase from his heart that which even death cannot remove. All three poems, then, deal with the decision to write lyric poetry instead of epic, a decision Herrera presents in terms of a necessity because of his love; in *V*, the node is appropriately placed in book 3, dedicated to the contrast between epic and lyric.

Herrera's choice of the lyric over the epic is overdetermined, however; in addition to the demands of love, the choice imitates Garcilaso's, who himself wrote lyrics instead of epics. The conflict between epic and lyric is also the topic of a number of poems by Petrarch, who worried that the attention he devoted to the vernacular lyric was diverting him from completion of his Latin epic, *Africa*.

Petrarch's sonnets 186–88 thus provide an important context for these poems of Herrera's. In sonnet 186, Petrarch declares Laura to be worthy of epic treatment: Virgil and Homer themselves, had they known her, would have scorned Aeneas, Achilles, and Odysseus, and devoted themselves to praising her instead. He also compares her to Scipio, the subject of the *Africa*. In 187 he retells the anecdote of Alexander the Great approaching Achilles' tomb and yearning for a poet who might secure for him a comparable immortality; Laura, too, deserves a greater poet:

> Ché d'Omero disgnissima e d'Orfeo
> o del pastor ch' ancor Mantova onora,
> ch' andassen sempre lei sola cantando,
> stella difforme et fato sol qui reo
> commise a tal che 'l suo bel nome adora
> ma forse scema sue lode parlando.
> *(Rime sparse* 187.9–14)

For she is worthy of Homer and Orpheus and of the shepherd whom Mantua still honors, worthy to have them always singing only of her, but a deformed star and her fate, cruel only in this, have entrusted her to one who adores her lovely name but perhaps mars her praise when he speaks.

Thus Petrarch establishes an ideological precedent for the treatment of the beloved as an epic theme; what he declares himself to have failed to accomplish, "l'un stil coll'altro misto" (one style with the other combined, *Rime sparse* 186.4), Herrera carries out through his epic diction in lyric poems and his use of lyric genres for epic themes (as in the *canción* dedicated to the Battle of Lepanto). Moreover, where Petrarch predicts that Laura, because of his inadequate poetry, is destined to be forgotten, Herrera asserts that Luz's fame will survive, for his own memory is fully occupied by Love and not distracted by an ongoing epic project.

In reality, of course, quite the opposite is true, as even Herrera would have recognized. Laura was immortalized by Petrarch's lyrics much more effectively than Luz, and Herrera's memory is as full of distractions as any epic poet's. The very process of alluding to predecessors in terms of riverine antonomasias is itself suggested by Petrarch, who in sonnet 247 refers to Demosthenes, Cicero, Homer, and Virgil by the names of their birthplaces. Yet in his imitation, Herrera outdoes Petrarch by mentioning not the well-known cities but the rather less-known rivers; to solve the allusive puzzle of the poem, the reader is forced to resort to compendia of information like the *Anotaciones*. This poem further cries out for such a commentary, because the allusions tend toward the obscure: Mincio flows past Mantua, and thus clearly refers to Virgil, but Melas, while probably referring to Homer, opens a host of geographical possibilities in Asia Minor. The Tiber in turn is obscure in just the opposite way, for while everyone knows it flows past Rome, no single poet is specified; in that the sonnet refers to epic poets, Ovid or even Ennius (mentioned in *Rime sparse* 186) is as likely the object as Tibullus.

Herrera thus establishes a link between this node of three sonnets and a similar node in the *Rime sparse;* the connection is made even stronger by the opening lines of Petrarch's sonnet 189, "Passa la nave mia colma d'oblio / per aspro mare a mezza notte il verno / enfra Scilla et Caribdi" (My ship laden with forgetfulness passes through a harsh sea, at midnight, in winter, between Scylla and Charybdis, *Rime sparse* 189.1–3), which have a clear affinity with the closing of Herrera's "Rompio la prora," particularly in its revised version (*V* 3.48). There are further allusions in this set of poems to subtexts by Petrarch, Boscán, and Garcilaso: the "florido tiempo" of *AO* 50.3 recalls Petrarch's frequent use of *età fiorita*, although Petrarch uses it in reference more to Laura's youth than to his own, and the shipwreck theme in "Rompio la prora" likewise invokes one of the key themes in the *Rime sparse*, which, as we saw in chapter 3, was significantly reworked by Boscán. Behind the conversion implicit in "Pierdo, tu culpa Amor" there lies an allusion to the Pauline figure of the child and the adult, also crucial to Boscán, while the opening line of *AO* 49, "Esperè un tiempo, i fue esperança vana" (I hoped for a time, but hope was in vain), recalls Garcilaso's "Un rato se levanta mi esperança" (My hope rises for a while, 4.1). Most of all, the prison imagery of *AO* 50 suggests an imitation and development of Garcilaso's several incarceration poems, including sonnet 2, sonnet 4, and especially the third *canción*. The allusions to Boscán and Garcilaso, and particularly the link between this node and the similar one in Petrarch's *Rime sparse*, break down Herrera's preference for lyric over epic as a free choice, showing it instead as the price for entry into the modern lyrical tradition.

In the liminal poems and in related nodes, we examined how

Herrera defines his relationship with Petrarch. Just as these poems have a specific set of poems in the *Rime sparse* as their principal source, Garcilaso's poetry provides the stimulus for other texts, which moreover allow us to explore the development of conventional Petrarchan metaphor. The opening image of *V* 1.31,

> Yo vi, a mi dulce Lumbre qu'esparzia
> sus crespas ondas d'oro al manso viento,
> i con tierno i suave movimiento,
> mi duro coraçon enternecia
>
> (*V* 1.31.1–4)

I saw my sweet Light who spread her golden curls to the tame wind and, with a soft and tender movement, mollified my hard heart

recalls a similar image from one of Garcilaso's most famous sonnets:

> Y en tanto que'l cabello, que'n la vena
> del oro s'escogió, con buelo presto
> por el hermoso cuello blanco, enhiesto,
> el viento mueve, esparze y desordena.
>
> (23.5–8)

And insofar as the wind moves, spreads, and disorders your hair, chosen from a vein of gold, with a quick flight along your handsome white neck.

Common to both poems is the identification of the beloved's hair with gold, the wind's movement, and the key verb *esparcir*; note, however, that in Herrera's version the woman actively scatters her hair to the wind, while in Garcilaso her hair is a passive object that the wind scatters. The similarities with Garcilaso have actually been strengthened in the revision of the poem. The *CdB* version's "Sirena dividía" has been replaced by "Lumbre qu'esparzia," and this change in turn influenced line 3, where "i, con tierno" took the place of "y en voz tierna," with its allusion to the Siren's singing; she survives only in the oceanic "crespas ondas" of line 2.[40] The Siren has much stronger associations with Petrarch than with Garcilaso, and the process of revision, in addition to moving the poem closer to Garcilaso, substitutes Herrera's personal myth (*lumbre*, a synonym for *luz*) for the more public allusion borrowed from Petrarch.

Yet the poem, even in its 1619 version, still has strong Petrarchan resonances. The traditional source for Garcilaso's poem, cited by El Brocense (269), is a sonnet by Bernardo Tasso that opens "Mentre che l'aureo crin v'ondeggia intorno / a l'ampia fronte con leggiadro errore" (while golden curls with light disorder wave about your wide forehead); although that may be true for the poem as a whole, both Garcilaso's and Herrera's descriptions of the wind-tussled hair are more reminiscent of several places in Petrarch, such as sonnet 90,

> Erano i capei d'oro a l'aura sparsi
> che 'n mille dolci nodi gli avolgea,
> e 'l vago lume oltra misura ardea
> di quei begli occhi, ch' or ne son sì scarsi
> *(Rime sparse* 90.1–4)

Her golden hair was loosed to the breeze, which turned it in a thousand sweet knots, and the lovely light burned without measure in her eyes, which are now so stingy of it

and in Herrera's case even sonnet 156, "I' vidi in terra angelici costumi" (I saw on earth angelic qualities, *Rime sparse* 156.1). Petrarch's sonnet 90 is in turn closely modeled on the description of Venus in the first book of the *Aeneid*. Thus through his imitation Herrera subreads in Garcilaso not only the well-known source in Bernardo Tasso but an entire poetic tradition, and brings it to the fore. The subreading of Garcilaso's sources thus encapsulates literary history, including the shift from epic to lyric as Petrarch takes the image from Virgil, the *translatio* from Rome/Italy as Garcilaso imitates the Italians, and culminates with Herrera's own place at the end of the tradition, in a position to draw upon its riches for his own *copia*.

In this poem we saw Herrera heightening the affinity with Garcilaso. Yet another poem based on Garcilaso's twenty-third sonnet shows a different kind of transformation process:

> A ora, que cubrio de blanco ielo
> el oro la hermosa Aurora mia;
> blanco es el puro Sol, i blanco el dia,
> i blanco el color lúcido d'el cielo.
> Blancas todas tus viras; que recelo,
> es blanco el arco i rayos d'alegria,
> Amor; con que me hieres aporfia,
> blanco tu ardiente fuego i frio ielo.
> Mas que puedo esperar d'esta blancura;

pues tiene'n blanca nieve'l pecho tierno
contra mi fiera llama defendido?
O beldad sin amor! ô mi Ventura!
qu'abrasado en vigor de fuego eterno,
muero en un blanco ielo convertido.

(*V* 1.75)

Now that the gold of my handsome dawn is covered with white ice, the pure sun is white, the day is white, and white is the lucent color of the sky. White are your darts that I distrust, white is the bow and the rays of joy with which, Love, you wound me repeatedly, white your burning fire and your cold ice. But what can I hope for from this whiteness, for it has her tender breast defended with white snow from my fierce flame? Oh loveless beauty, oh my fortune, that while blazing in an eternal fire, I die into white ice converted.

The transformations from the *CdB* to the 1619 version have been masterfully analyzed by Pepe Sarno: as she notes, the word *blanco* and its variants, occurring ten times in the course of the sonnet, assume the role of key words in the semantic system of the sonnet ("Bianco il ghiaccio," 461). Opposing its semantic supremacy, however, are words containing the phonemes /r/ and /o/; this pattern, established by the initial word of the sonnet, is associated with the key concept of *oro*, symbol of light as well as the color of the beloved's hair. This feature is common to both versions of the poem; however, Pepe Sarno also stresses how in the revision the final word of the first line is changed from *velo* to *ielo*, thus creating an identical rhyme with line 8, and how Herrera reinforces the repetition by changing "nieve fría" to "blanco ielo" in line 14.[41] As she notes,

Se fonicamente la variante *velo/ielo* si rivela in P fattore unificante delle rime, semanticamente la sua presenza è molto più incisiva. *Velo* e *ielo* definiscono ambiti semantici diversissimi: il primo, il velo di B, rientra nel campo dell'abbigliamento femminile e mobilita valori connotativi di impalpabile morbidezza, leggerezza, delicatezza ecc.; il secondo, il *ielo* di P, rimane completamente estraneo a questa sfera semantica ed acquista una connotazione di rigida freddezza.

(ibid., 463)

If phonetically the variants *velo/ielo* are revealed in *P* [i.e., *V*] as a unifying factor in the rhyme, semantically their presence is much more incisive. *Velo* and *ielo* define very different semantic fields: the first, the veil in *B* [*CdB*], directs us to the field of women's dress and allows connotations of impalpable morbidity, lightness, delicacy, etc.;

the second, the ice in *P,* remains completely extraneous to this seman-
tic sphere and acquires a connotation of rigid cold.

Similarly, "el color del claro cielo" becomes "el color lúcido del
cielo": *lúcido,* in addition to its semantic connection to *Luz,* is more
proper to ice than to the veil, with its connotations of brilliant trans-
parency (ibid., 464). Other transformations in the quatrains include
the change from "blancas tus flechas son" to "blancas todas tus
viras," resulting in the diminution of soft ells and greater concentra-
tion in syntax. The same effect is achieved in the tercet through
strengthening the enjambment and hyperbaton in lines 10–11, and
by the substitution of "contra mi fiera llama" for "tiene contra mi
alma" (line 11) because of the former's opposition, in terms of tem-
perature and color, to the "blanco ielo" and the threat it poses to
the "pecho tierno" of the preceding line. The tercets also contain
a shift of focus from the beloved (to whom the first "blanco ielo"
refers) to the poet (himself converted to ice in the final line).

The shifts thus intensify the poem's central conceit, the transfor-
mation of the beloved from warm gold to cold ice. The imitation
that underlies the poem is of the notion of the beloved's hair cov-
ered with snow, as expressed by Garcilaso, "antes que'l tiempo
ayrado / cubra de nieve la hermosa cumbre" (before angry time
covers with snow the beautiful summit, 23.10–11); just as the phonic
pattern shines from beneath the semantic one, so too Garcilaso's
poem hovers just beneath the surface. Yet instead of drawing out
the lesson of that poem, that youth should be enjoyed before it
fades, Herrera turns it on its head: if the beloved's gold is turned
white, then it follows that everything associated with her must turn
white as well. In the revision of the poem, Herrera intensifies his
own association with fire, here representative of passion; the ice–fire
antithesis thus becomes the motivation for the tercets, in the last
line of which he too must surrender to ice and death. In this way he
turns the moral of Garcilaso's poem, "todo lo mudará la edad
ligera / por no hazer mudança en su costumbre" (fickle age will
change everything so as not to change its custom, 23.13–14), inward
against himself: by being changed into ice, he becomes what the
beloved already is, and the sonnet thus embodies what Rico consid-
ers the fundamental trope of Spanish Petrarchism, "el amante en
amada transformado" (lover into beloved transformed). In contrast

to *V* 1.31 where, in the course of revising the poem, Herrera brought out the affinities to Garcilaso, here he disguises them, thus eliminating the veil that would fall lightly upon the beloved's golden hair (which has strong Petrarchan connotations as well), as well as the snow in the closing line. Instead, he closes the revised poem with an image of hard ice, water made mineral, akin to Petrarch's "l'indurato ghiaccio" (the hardened ice, *Rime sparse* 66.29). This semantic emphasis on concentration and hardening is mirrored stylistically in the revisions to the poem, through such details as the increased complexity of the hyperbaton and the use of the more erudite *vira* instead of *flecha*.

Herrera's allusions to Petrarch are not only structural and semantic but generic as well. As noted at the beginning of this section, Herrera uses the very act of organizing his collection as a sign through which he asserts a relationship with his predecessors. He also does so through his choice of genres: while most of his poems are sonnets, *canciones*, elegies, epistles, eclogues, and octaves—the genres made canonical in Spanish by Garcilaso—Herrera tries to outdo his predecessor by naturalizing one of the most distinctive of Petrarchan genres, the sestina. Herrera's sestinas, by their form, call attention to themselves as self-consciously Petrarchan productions, and not surprisingly Herrera often uses them to thematize his relation to the poetic tradition. One such poem is the first sestina of book 1, "Vn verde Lauro, en mi dichoso tiempo." [42] Cuevas, in his notes (520), connects the poem to Petrarch's "Giovene donna sotto un verde lauro" (*Rime sparse* 30), while Hernández Esteban (405) links it through the coincidence of some rhyme words to "A la dolce ombra de le belle frondi" (*Rime sparse* 142). Herrera's poem shares with both of these others a sense of nostalgia for time past but, as will be shown, its link to "A la dolce ombra" goes beyond identity of rhyme words.

Herrera's poem is unusual in that here the poet virtually forsakes his usual repertoire of visual images associated with light (gold, fire, stars, the sun) and instead adopts an equally visual and equally Petrarchan set of images associated with trees, rivers, and forests. As Hernández Esteban noted, the word *Lauro* recurs in each stanza, always in the middle of a line, and thus it forms a vertical axis linking the stanzas that competes with the self-contained cycle of the rhyme words, all of which are directly or indirectly related to it. The first stanzas describe the poet's fall from grace:

> Vn verde Lauro, en mi dichoso tiempo,
> solia darme sombra, i con sus hojas
> mi frente coronava junto a Betis:
> entonces yo en su gloria alçava el canto,
> i resonava como el blanco Cisne;
> la Soledad testigo fue, i el bosque.
> Despues que al bien me dio principio el bosque,
> i en la sombra gozè d'el dulce tiempo,
> i cantè como cuando muere'l Cisne,
> el Lauro me negò sus verdes hojas.
> i en triste se trocó el alegre canto,
> i se admiró de mi lamento Betis.
>
> (*V*, sest. 1.1.1–12)

A green Laurel, in my happy time, used to give me shade, and with its leaves crown my forehead by the Betis: then I raised my song to its glory, and it resounded like the white Swan; Solitude and the forest were witnesses. But after the forest gave me my start in virtue, and in the shade I enjoyed the sweet time and sang as when the Swan dies, the Laurel denied me its green leaves, and my happy song became sad, and the Betis was astonished at my lament.

In the first stanza, all of the disparate elements are in unity: the laurel shaded him and crowned his brow, so that he sang in the forest like a swan.[43] The result was a truly blessed time, captured by the phrase "dichoso tiempo" which also echoes the first line of Petrarch's *canzone* 23, "Nel dolce tempo de la prima etade." As in *canzone* 23 and in the *sestine*, the primal state comes to a quick end, and the rest of the poem is taken up with the consequences of his exclusion. The succeeding stanzas repeat the narrative of his alienation: the forest has closed in and barred him from the laurel, which consequently no longer crowns him; he seeks it but is reduced to crying his lament like a swan along the river's bank, which alone hears his song.

At first reading it seems as if this poem restates one more time the Herreran theme of hope followed by despair, with the complete and successful appropriation of Petrarch's imagery resulting in an identification of Luz with Laura on the levels of both the signifieds (the beloveds that the poems are about) and the signifiers (the superstructure of associations based on their names).⁴⁴ A second look at the poem, however, reveals the presence of a word sharing sememes with Herrera's usual repertory: *sombra*, used twice in the opening stanzas to describe the nature of his prelapsarian state. Ordinarily Herrera uses the word in tandem with terms like *olvido* (see Macrí, 317; also Kossoff, 308) to indicate the state of being isolated from the beloved; the poet's intimacy with the green laurel, then, effectively protected him but also cut him off from the sun. At that time he was also covered with the laurel leaves; we know from the *Anotaciones* that these are associated with poetry, and Petrarch himself used the word *fronde* to mean both leaf and page. Thus when Herrera states that in his solitude he sang its praises, he is referring not just to a tree, or to a woman, but to a state of being in communion with poetry itself. In the second stanza, however, as the tree denies him its shade, his song becomes like that of a dying swan, and the Betis—symbolic of Seville and by extension of all Spain—admires his cry. His exclusion from the laurel is consequently compensated by the development of his own poetry, of a proper voice which is that of the lament.

The succeeding stanzas emphasize the interposition of the forest between him and the laurel: "Yo busco el Lauro . . . / i està cerrado en el espesso bosque" (I seek the Laurel . . . and it is closed off in the dense forest, 13–14); "el Lauro, i verdes hojas, / que m'impiden tratar el duro bosque" (the Laurel and the green leaves that the forest impedes me from treating, 21–22); and "aquel bosque / que del Lauro defiendeme las hojas" (that forest that bars me from the Laurel's green leaves, 29–30). In the closing stanzas, however, the power relationship is reversed:

> Pues ya no me corono de las hojas
> enmudesca de oi mas el tierno canto;
> assi vea desnudo al triste bosque,
> i llore mi dolor el blanco Cisne,
> que tiende'l lecho en el sobervio Betis;
> pues el Lauro me falta, i dexa el tiempo.
>   Entristeceme'l tiempo, el Lauro, i hojas,
> el canto no me agrada, el blanco Cisne
> lamente'n Betis, i arda en fuego el bosque.
>   (31–39)

For as I no longer crown myself with the leaves, from now on may the tender song be silenced; let me see the sad forest denuded, and let the white Swan weep my pain, that makes his bed in the proud Betis; for the Laurel is denied to me, and time allows it. Time, the Laurel, and the leaves sadden me, and the song no longer pleases me; let the white Swan lament on the Betis, and let fire consume the forest.

Here Herrera rejects the tone of nostalgia that governed the rest of the poem and asserts an independence from his prior mode. If the crown of laurel is to be no longer his, then he will renounce the tender mode and allow the trees to lose their leaves; this image is intensified in the final line of the poem, when he predicts the trees' conflagration. *Fuego* is yet again from Herrera's own repertoire of images; as an antonomasia for Luz, its consuming of the forest indicates not an association with Laura but an antagonism to, and an ultimate destruction of, the original.

The residual presence of these items from Herrera's standard vocabulary, then, works against the identification of Laura and Luz and sets them up as opposites. In this context, Herrera's model is worth reviewing. Petrarch too set up an opposition between the tree and the light:

> A la dolce ombra de le belle frondi
> corsi fuggendo un dispietato lume
> che 'n fin qua giù m'ardea dal terzo cielo;
> et disgombrava già di neve i poggi
> l'aura amorosa che rinova il tempo,
> et fiorian per le piagge l'erbe e i rami.
> Non vide il mondo sì leggiadri rami
> né mosse il vento mai sì verdi frondi
> come a me si mostrar quel primo tempo,
> tal che temendo de l'ardente lume
> non volsi al mio refugio ombra di poggi,
> ma da la pianta più gradita in cielo.
> (*Rime sparse* 142.1–12)

To the sweet shade of those beautiful leaves I ran, fleeing a pitiless light that was burning down upon me from the third heaven; and already the snow was disappearing from the hills thanks to the loving breeze that renews the season, and through the meadows the grass bloomed and the branches. The world never saw such graceful branches nor did the wind ever move such green leaves as showed themselves to me in that first season; so that, fearing the burning light, I chose for my refuge no shade of hills but that of the tree most favored in Heaven.

On a narrative level, for Petrarch the laurel tree functions as a source
of protection from a burning sun that beats down on the poet, and
whose shade creates a veritable *locus amoenus* with a fresh breeze,
melting snow, and flowers. At the same time, the light that torments
Petrarch comes from the third heaven, that of Venus, and so on an
allegorical level the shade that the tree offers is in some sense a
respite from the pangs of lust. Borrowing the motif of the lost laurel
from "Giovene donna," Herrera combines the two poems to offer a
vision of a lost paradise in which there was plenitude and fulfill-
ment, both erotic and poetic. Yet notably absent from Herrera's
poem is any sense of divine salvation, which comes into play at the
conclusion to "A la dolce ombra," when Petrarch declares he must
substitute another tree if he is to obtain permanent rest: "Altr'amor,
altre frondi, et altro lume, / altro salir al ciel per altri poggi / cerco
(che n'è ben tempo), et altri rami" (Another love, other leaves, and
another light, another climbing to Heaven by other hills I seek [for
it is indeed time], and other branches, *Rime sparse* 142.37–39). Unlike
Petrarch, Herrera does not offer himself a transcendent escape from
his obsessions.

Through his use of the form and of thematic material from Pe-
trarch, Herrera turns the sestina into the site of a struggle for su-
premacy signaled by his transferring the laurel to the banks of the
Betis. His initial enjoyment of the shady bower was also a time of
nurturing and apprenticeship, when he freely took from the tree's
leaves, but his song went unheard; his satisfaction with the source
precluded any frustration that could be displaced to poetry of his
own. This situation lasted until he began to sing like a dying swan,
which is to say in a sacred and immortal way; then, as a response
to his song, the laurel forsook him, but the Betis was astonished at
his song. Whatever the source for the image of the swan, it is a
proclamation of the poet's own strength, his transformation from
the youthful status of reader into a rival poet. Yet if the laurel repre-
sents the source of poetry, and as such Petrarch, the trees that closed
in, cutting him off from his onetime source, are the intervening gen-
erations of poets, the realization of his lack of priority even as an
imitator. Instead of intimidating him, however, they only led him to
sing even more, and to declare war on the forest. Ultimately, Herrera
takes comfort in a vision of surpassing his model, his ardor threat-
ening to destroy it. This vision, however, remains on the level of a

fantasy, as the subjunctive verbs of lines 31–39 indicate. Moreover, the central axis of the *Lauro* is stronger than the rotating cycle of the rhyme words. Herrera's appropriation of the genre thus proves to be but a dream of priority, in which the poetic fathers are killed and the orphan reigns in their place. As a fantasy, it reinforces its opposite fiction, which thus assumes the mantle of "reality": necessarily cut off from Petrarch by time and the intervening achievements of rival poets, Herrera is truly an orphan, yet one attempting to renew the fecundity of the line.

The poem stands thus in marked contrast to Garcilaso's confident assertion of his own metalepsis in the third eclogue, for through his generic, stylistic, and thematic choices Herrera reveals a dependency on his predecessors, particularly Garcilaso and Petrarch. Dependency is not the same thing as identity, however, and in the best of his poems Herrera displays a seriousness and a mad intensity that, on its own terms (for instance, the metaphorization of the beloved's body, the emanation of sememes from the beloved's name), nearly raises him above even these predecessors. Moreover, if Herrera's poetry was insufficiently strong to overcome Garcilaso's, as a poet-critic he certainly overcame his predecessors, and in spite of the rejection by his contemporaries he has come to be regarded as the father of literary criticism in Spain. Throughout both his poetry and his criticism he shows himself a powerful reader, embellishing his material with wide erudition and stylistic imagination. Himself a literary connoisseur, he appeals to the same, and his achievements would shine brighter were it not for Góngora, whose work he seems not to have known.

5

Góngora, Quevedo, and the End of Petrarchism in Spain

At first glance, the transition from the sixteenth century to the seventeenth in Spain can seem like the beginning of a decline; the national enthusiasm that Herrera could feel after the 1571 victory at Lepanto gives way to the so-called *desengaño* or disappointment of the new century, heralded by unsuccessful wars with England and France, rebellions in the Netherlands and Aragon, the 1588 defeat of the Armada, the 1596 bankruptcy, and the plague of 1600. Yet contemporaries need not have perceived the decline so clearly: Philip III (1598–1621) may have abdicated responsibility to a favorite or *privado*, but his reign was one of relative peace, as internal turmoil kept France distracted and a truce was achieved in the Netherlands, and it saw the emergence of Baroque culture, Spain's true "Golden Age," the time of Lope de Vega, Cervantes, and Calderón.[1] In addition to the stylistic transformations common throughout Europe, the characteristics of Spanish Baroque lyric include the revival of Castilian genres such as the *romance* (ballad) and *letrilla* (short song lyric), often employing formal techniques such as octosyllabic and acute verse and assonant rhyme, and the emergence of social satire as a theme; while in the realm of theory, systematic treatments of poetics become the norm. Thus in contrast to Boscán, Garcilaso, and Herrera, whose forays into these genres were clearly secondary works, writers such as Luis de Góngora y Argote (1561–1627) and Francisco de Quevedo (1580–1645) left behind a far more heterogeneous body of work. There are nonetheless significant areas of continuity, and in examining the seventeenth century this study will focus on what is most distinctively "Renaissance" about Góngora's and Quevedo's work, in particular secular love poems in hendecasyllabic verse that are in competition both with the classical and Italian lyric traditions (the latter now expanded to include poets such as Torquato Tasso and Giambattista Marino), and with earlier Spanish poets who had already achieved canonical status. As in the sixteenth century these poems, and their related paratexts, reveal a continuing worry about the legitimacy of Spanish culture and about the cultural primacy of a long-subjugated Italy.

GÓNGORA AND THE POETICS
OF FULFILLMENT

The eclecticism of Góngora, and his more than successful metalepsis of his predecessors, might exempt him from the main trajectory of this study. While clearly nurtured by Petrarchist poetry, even at an early age he was not dependent on Petrarch alone but on a tradition that included Ovid, Horace, Virgil, and less canonized classical authors; other Italian poets, notably Bernardo and Torquato Tasso; as well as Spanish predecessors. Yet he must be taken into account, for his redirection of the Petrarchist tradition subverted its canons to the point that they were nearly redefined, necessitating a direct return to Petrarch by his younger contemporary, Quevedo. Góngora's most obviously Petrarchist works are his love sonnets, numbering forty-five in Ciplijauskaité's critical edition.[2] Chronologically, this category can be further subdivided into twenty-six poems dating from 1582 to 1585; thirteen poems from 1594 to 1609; and five poems from 1620 to 1623. They thus span all stages of the poet's career, from a novitiate in his twenties to his maturity (Góngora completed his most famous poems, the *Soledades* and the *Fábula de Polifemo y Galatea*, in 1612) to his old age, and allow us to examine his shifting orientation vis-à-vis the Petrarchist tradition. Moreover, as Jammes noted, the twenty-six early sonnets, while not a collection, do constitute a corpus that can be examined independently of the other poems. To Jammes, Góngora in these poems follows models so closely that they contain little that had not been used many times earlier and very little that did not figure in Garcilaso; the latter's pervasive influence is evident both in thematic details such as the conventional idealization of the beloved, the pastoral landscape and classical names, and so on; as well as in the diction and the smooth flow of the hendecasyllabic lines (362–63).

Yet imitation does not preclude difference, and Góngora's poetry contains significant departures from Garcilaso as well. Two famous *carpe diem* poems, "Mientras por competir con tu cabello" (*Sonetos* 151) and "Illvstre i hermossissima Maria" (*Sonetos* 152, its *incipit* a line from Garcilaso's third eclogue), are particularly good examples. Though termed love sonnets in the Vicuña and Hozes editions, they were reclassified under the rubric "morales, sacros, varios" (moral, sacred, and various) in the Chacón manuscript; Terracini (*I codici,* 101–21) correctly situates "Mientras por competir" between the "strict" *carpe diem* tradition, represented by poems such as Garcilaso's sonnet 23 and Bernardo Tasso's "Mentre che l'aureo crin," and the more "moral" *memento mori* tradition, evident in Herrera's "Oh soberbia y cruel en tu belleza" (*Anotaciones,* 374). Yet more than the emphasis on the beloved's decay and ultimate death differentiates Góngora's sonnets from Garcilaso's. In "Mientras por competir," the linear succession of hair, forehead, lips, and neck becomes through repetition a cycle and then a vertical axis in the poem, as the features are gradually transformed, first into metaphorical equivalents (gold, lilies, carnations, crystal) and ultimately into earth, smoke, dust, shadow, and nothing. This metamorphosis creates competing linear and vertical axes that draw attention to the poem's own verbal artistry and away from the natural processes of enjoyment and transformation that it describes. Moreover, by joining the *carpe diem* and *memento mori* motifs, Góngora violates Christian norms of decorum but recalls an earlier pagan tradition. Thus even when most imitative of Garcilaso, Góngora pushes at the boundaries of canonical categories and heightens the autoreferentiality of the poems.[3]

Similarly, on a moral level, the *alba* poem "Ia besando vnas manos crystalinas" (*Sonetos* 62) challenges the bounds of even Garcilaso's lax standards of decorum (the perception of which had become considerably stricter, in the course of his canonization by the commentators), while the conventional metaphors used to describe the woman (for instance, "ia quebrando en aquellas perlas finas/ palabras dulces" [now breaking sweet words against those fine pearls], 5–6) work against the reader's perception of her as an erotic whole rather than a collection of attributes transformed into textures and colors (see Calcraft, 31–34). This is even more true of "De pvra honestidad templo sagrado" (*Sonetos* 55), where the representation of the beloved as a temple and an idol (see Bergmann, 293–95) is morally offensive, while the emphasis on metaphorical construction (in a double sense: the building of the temple, the building of the poem) privileges aesthetic ingenuity over eroticism. These last two poems are significant because alone among Góngora's love sonnets they were criticized by the Jesuit Juan Pineda in a report to the Inquisition after the Vicuña edition of Góngora's works.[4] Pineda criticizes as indecent the moral content of "Ia besando" along with the style of "De pvra honestidad," characterized as "loca exageración de profanos poetas, que en boca de un sacerdote . . . se haze más intolerable" (the mad exaggeration of a profane poet, which in the mouth of a priest. . . becomes even more intolerable, xxxii). Thus Pineda seizes on the twin issues of stylistic and moral unsuitability, suggesting a complete rejection of the Petrarchist style as Góngora practiced it.

A further look at two early sonnets will enable us to explore Góngora's combination and manipulation of sources. Garcilaso's sonnet 23 lies visibly behind Góngora's *carpe diem* poems; it can also be perceived in "Al tramontar del sol," written, according to the Chacón manuscript, in 1582:

> Al tramontar del Sol la Nimpha mia,
> de flores despojando el verde llano,
> quantas troncaba la hermosa mano,
> tantas el blanco pie crecer hacia.
> Ondéàbale el viento que corria
> el oro fino con error galano,
> qual verde hoja de alamo loçano
> se mueue al roxo despuntar de'l dia.
> Mas luego que ciñò sus sienes bellas
> de los varios despojos de su falda,
> (termino puesto al oro, i a la nieue)
> iurarè, que luciò mas su guirnalda,
> con ser de flores, la otra ser de estrellas,
> que la que illustra el cielo en luces nueue.
>
> (*Sonetos* 57)

At the setting of the sun my nymph, divesting the green plain of flowers, as many as her lovely hand exchanged, so many her white foot would cause to grow. The wind made waves around her which caused the fine gold to run with gallant error, as the green leaf of a luxuriant poplar moves when the red sun starts out the day. But after she girt her beautiful temples with the various spoils of her skirt (forming a boundary between the gold and the snow), I would have sworn that her garland shone more, though made of flowers, than that made of stars, with which the other one illuminates the sky with nine lights.

The first-person verb in line 12, *iurarè*, introduces an element of subjectivity into what is otherwise a nearly ekphrastic description, asserting that the poem reports something that the poet actually saw (thus García de Salcedo Coronel, in his 1644 commentary, subtitles it "con ocasion de aver salido su dama una tarde al campo, descrive D. Luis en este Soneto su hermosura" [on the occasion of his lady having gone to the countryside one afternoon, Don Luis describes her beauty in this sonnet], 2.367). The poem, however, is highly artificial; again, the linear narration is countered by a vertical accumulation of four separate *agudezas* (witticisms), one for each section of the poem. In the first quatrain the woman's passing creates as many flowers as she picks, in the second there is an ingenious description of her wind-blown hair, in the third there is another of the garland she places around her head, and in the fourth that garland is declared superior to Ariadne's crown of stars. Salcedo Coronel identifies as the principal sources for the poem Claudian's epyllion *De raptu Proserpinae* and Torquato Tasso's sonnet "Colei che sovra ogni altra amo ed onoro"; while the former provides the idea of plundering the ground of its flowers (*pratorum spoliatur* versus Tasso's *coglier*), the latter is the source for her restoration of the blossoms ("ma non tanti la man cogliea di loro / quanti fra l'erbe il bianco piè n'apriva" [but her hand did not pick so many of them as her foot caused to open amid the grass]). Similarly, Salcedo Coronel names Claudian as the source for the flower garland binding her hair, while Hyginius, Ovid, and Prudentius are all cited for mentioning Ariadne's crown. Unlike the *agudeza* in the first quatrain, the final three, on a linguistic level at least, are more properly Góngora's own: Claudian does not describe the garland as a boundary between gold and snow (obvious metaphors for hair and forehead; see Brockhaus, 22), while none of the mythographers uses language particularly like Góngora's to describe Ariadne's crown.

Most interesting for us is the second quatrain. Salcedo Coronel correctly divides it into two parts: the description of the wind blowing her hair and the comparison to leaves in a breeze at sunset. For the first, he gives as a source Torquato Tasso's sonnet, "ondeggiavano sparsi i bei crin d'oro / ond'Amor mille e mille lacci ordiva" (her beautiful golden locks were scattered in waves, where Love ordered a thousand knots). In addition, he cites the same lines by Bernardo Tasso given by El Brocense and Herrera as the source for Garcilaso's sonnet 23, "mentre che l'aureo crin v'ondeggia intorno / a l'ampia frente con legiadro errore" (while golden curls wave with light disorder around your wide forehead), and suggests places in Horace and Ovid's *Metamorphoses* as possible sources for both Tassos' poems. For the swaying leaves, he also cites descriptions from Ovid's *Ars amandi* and from Flavius Corippus. As in Herrera's commentary, this accumulation of source citations is not entirely to the point. The emphasis on sources for each section of the poem obscures the second quatrain's function as a unifying factor: the sunset and the green leaves recall the first quatrain, as does the play of colors, which in turn anticipates the first tercet (where the contrast between white and gold replaces that between green and red); the sunset also anticipates the nighttime of Ariadne's crown of stars.[5] Salcedo Coronel's particular set of sources for the wind-blown hair also obscures a more obvious and appropriate chain, going through Garcilaso's poem (a model, as we have seen, for other early poems of Góngora's) to Petrarch and Virgil. Thus while Salcedo Coronel correctly underlines the artificiality of Góngora's sonnet, he ironically diminishes the poem's true originality, which lies not in the descriptive depiction of a real-life event but in the way that Góngora manipulates the very artifice he derives from the tradition.

Moreover, while the commentator gives no sources from Petrarch, the key elements of the poem—a vision of the beloved surrounded by flowers and with the wind blowing her hair, even the detail of her restoring the flowers with her footsteps—are clearly Petrarchan.[6] This connection gives added significance to the metaphor of leaves waving in a red sunset—on the one hand they are a vehicle for the tenor, her hair waving in the wind, but on the other they suggest the leaves of the laurel tree waving, after Daphne's transformation, in the glare of a red sun burning with frustrated passion. Petrarch's descriptions of Laura walking on the flowers generally have an iconic dimension—she is caught in the act of moving—but a voyeuristic one as well, for the sight of her is all that Petrarch will ever enjoy. Through its mythological and textual allusions, however, Góngora's poem summons up more active lovers: Pluto, Apollo, and Bacchus. Like Garcilaso, Góngora revitalizes the latent sexuality in Petrarchism, but transforms the lover into a predatory figure, possibly a rapist.[7] Thus although on a textual level the poem is prompted by a convergence of details in Claudian and Torquato Tasso, its field of allusion is even broader than Salcedo Coronel suggests, while the poet subverts the very rules of decorum that give structure and coherence to the love-poetry tradition.

The gold and snow in line 11 of this poem are metaphors for hair and skin; by this time, the identification was so strong that its status as metaphor is almost lost and the words are functionally synonymous. Góngora exploits the strongly conventional character of Petrarchan metaphor in a sonnet from 1585, "Avnque a rocas de fee ligada vea / con laços de oro la hermosa naue" (Though bound to rocks of faith I see with golden knots the handsome ship; *Sonetos* 80). The poem is based on a familiar metaphor of the lover as a ship in a storm, here extended into an allegory about the inconstancy of good fortune in love, as Salcedo Coronel explains in his commentary:

> Escriue Don Luis a algun amigo suyo este Soneto, y en metafora de vna naue descriue el incierto estado de qualquier amante, aun estando fauorecido, y el riesgo que en la mayor tranquilidad se puede prometer de la inconstancia de vn mar tan mal seguro, como el del Amor. Confirma esto con exemplo de las agenas calamidades, a cuya causa dize: que no le fiará dèl, sino le assegura del peligro, que reconoce aduertido, con razon, y discurso eficaz.
>
> (2.463)

> Don Luis writes this sonnet to some friend of his, and through the metaphor of a ship describes the uncertain state of any lover, even when favored, and the risk that even in the greatest serenity can be foretold from such an uncertain sea as that of love. He confirms this with examples from others' calamities, which lead him to say that he will have no trust unless he is reassured about the danger, which he concedes he has been warned about, by reason and an effective discourse.

Interpretation of the poem, however, is more difficult than the commentator suggests; he is helped by reading it in terms of a sonnet by Torquato Tasso, which he declares Góngora "expressly imitated." In Tasso's poem the poet, speaking in the first person, indeed presents himself as a ship close to the shore, leery of the temporarily favorable wind. Góngora however objectively describes a handsome ship linked by golden knots to the rocks of faith, raising a host of questions. Salcedo Coronel dutifully explicates the golden knots as "los dorados cabellos de la dama" (the lady's golden hair, 2.464), which they conventionally represent; but in this context the metaphor is unenlightening. Is the beloved the ship, apparently linked to fidelity but always in danger of slipping away? Or is the lover himself the ship, which would be better off sailing away from this false sense of security? Similarly, a few lines later he glosses "en el aspecto celestial se lea" (may in the celestial aspect be read) with "el hermoso rostro del objeto amado" (the lovely visage of the beloved object), conflating omens in the sky with the light reflected off the beloved's eyes. As a result, what seemed to be a straightforward allegory is refracted by Salcedo Coronel's commentary into a number of different interpretations, some of which privilege certain metaphors, some others.

The problem becomes even more acute in the closing tercets:

> he visto blanquéàndo las arenas
> de tantos nunca sepultados huessos,
> que el mar de amor tubieron por seguro;
>   que del no fio; si sus fluxos gruessos
> con el timon, o con la voz no enfrenas
> ô dulce Arion, ô sabio Palynuro.
>   (*Sonetos* 80.9–14)

> I have seen the sands whitened by never-buried bones of those who held the sea of love to be safe; thus I will not trust it, unless its great waves with rudder, or with voice, you restrain, oh sweet Arion, oh wise Palinurus.

The first two lines closely imitate Tasso's poem, but Góngora subreads in it its own Virgilian source, as the final lines indicate: in the *Aeneid*, the image of the bone-covered beach occurs in a description of the Sirens' home and immediately precedes the account of Palinurus falling asleep at the helm. Salcedo Coronel turns verbal somersaults attempting to explain these lines, first clarifying that "fluxos gruessos" means tempestuous waves and then interpreting these to mean that "no fiará del Amor, viendo escarmientos tales, sino le asegura su discurso, y su sabia providencia" (he will not trust Love, seeing such injuries, unless reassured by his speech and his wise foresight). Yet the cynical lover who mistrusts the beloved's constancy and advises for himself a retreat may himself be fooled, for a reader knows more than to rely on Arion's candor or Pali- nurus's judgment: the connection to the *Aeneid* ironizes the final lines, for Palinurus did not prove to be an effective pilot, while Ar- ion saved his own life through cunning as much as through sweet- ness. Thus the elegant chiasmus (rudder : Palinurus :: voice : Arion) disguises a reassuring but false set of analogies, which serve as ob- ject models of the dangers of trusting artful appearance instead of underlying reality.

According to Ciplijauskaité, the bones washed up on the shore reminded Gates of the soaked trophies in Garcilaso's sonnet 7, yet they also bear some kinship to the dead predecessors of his sonnet 38, "ejemplos tristes de los que han caýdo" (sad examples of the fallen). Through these allusions Góngora asserts a link to the Petrar- chist tradition, even as the suggestive but untelling metaphors and mythological allusions subvert the capacity of the tradition to gener- ate new poetry on any level other than the stylistic. Here, as in the sonnet "No destroçada naue," he directs the warning as much to a prospective poet as to a recalcitrant lover: "A Dios Nympha crûel, quedaos con ella / dura roca, red de oro, alegre prado" (Good-bye cruel nymph, you may keep her, hard rock, golden net, joyful meadow, *Sonetos* 73.13–14). As Jammes put it, tears in the long run give way to rebellion (361); significantly, "Avnque a rocas de fee" is the last love sonnet in the Chacón manuscript before a nine-year hiatus.

Góngora's inversion of Petrarchist codes is not limited to his love sonnets; perhaps the most effective upending of Petrarchism in the Spanish Golden Age occurs in the *Fábula de Polifemo y Galatea,* which recounts the myth, from Ovid's *Metamorphoses,* of the Cyclops Poly- phemus and his unrequited love for the nymph Galatea, who in turn loves only the handsome shepherd Acis. In Góngora's version Polyphemus is constantly making noise, whether whistling to his animals, playing monstrous musical instruments of his own cre- ation, or singing to Galatea, celebrating her beauty, boasting of his wealth, and imploring her to overlook his physical ugliness.[8] It is precisely from him that Galatea flees when she finds a secluded pool and stops to take a nap. There she is discovered by Acis as he is having a drink; instead of waking her, he leaves her some gifts and pretends to fall asleep on the other side. Stirred nonetheless by

his noise, Galatea fears it is Polyphemus, but finding the gifts she
realizes it must be someone else. She then sees Acis across the pond:

> El bulto vio, y, haciéndolo dormido,
> librada en un pie toda sobre él pende
> (urbana al sueño, bárbara al mentido
> retórico silencio que no entiende).
> (lines 257–60;
> *Góngora y el "Polifemo,"* 3.179)

She saw the form and, believing it asleep, balanced on one foot over
him she hangs (urbane to sleep, barbaric to the mendacious rhetorical
silence that she does not understand).

These lines have been controversial since Góngora's own day, with
critical attention focused on Galatea's exact posture in line 258.
Other details, however, are also worth examining. Vilanova (*Las
fuentes,* 2.212–14) quotes the commentators Salcedo Coronel and
José Pellicer on the word *bulto:* both agree that it means something
perceived indistinctly and that it is therefore a subjective description
of Galatea's point of view.[9] But Covarrubias's dictionary offers addi-
tional possibilities, defining the word as something hidden by a
cloth, also as a supine statue or effigy. It was employed several times
in pastoral romances to describe sleeping shepherdesses, and in
Montemayor's *Diana* it refers specifically to the shape of the breasts
beneath her clothing. Vilanova concludes that Góngora thus plays
on the resemblance between Acis, extended over the grass, pre-
tending to be asleep, and a statue or effigy. These meanings are
suggestive: they emphasize Galatea's view of Acis as an inert body
to be evaluated aesthetically and sexually for its vigor; just as Mon-
temayor used *bulto* to refer to breasts, so too it can suggest that part
of the male anatomy normally kept under clothing.

In this context, the last two lines of the quatrain also demand
some attention. Vilanova argues that Góngora bases himself on the
classic notion of *bárbaro* as "alien" (*Las fuentes,* 2.220), and from this
developed the clever antithesis, in which Galatea is urbane to sleep
because she is familiar with and kind to it, wishing to reciprocate
the courtesy shown by the youth who did not wake her. Vilanova
agrees with the commentators that she is a barbarian to "el mentido
retórico silencio" because she has had no experience of Acis's silent
eloquence, and he connects this passage with the established trope

of mute speech employed by Ovid, Petrarch, and Garcilaso. He does not, however, note the widely divergent emotional values such a trope elicited in these three writers, all of which Góngora recapitulates; nor does he comment on the accumulation of adjectives: Acis is not merely silent but also both deceitful and rhetorical. In this way his "technique" contrasts with Polyphemus's, which was neither mendacious nor silent. By means of his feigned sleep, Acis employs the only method that could in fact succeed with Galatea, because it does not frighten her off by making evident from the beginning his sexual desire. Yet his is a rhetorical silence, meant to persuade and to conceal the fact that he has as much desire as Polyphemus. As Dámaso Alonso notes, citing the commentator Andrés de la Cuesta, rhetoricians teach us not only how and when to speak, but when and where to keep silent (*Góngora y el "Polifemo,"* 3.183). By practicing silence and pretending to be asleep, Acis also turns the tables on Galatea, who awakens and sees him sleeping just as he had spied her asleep; just as he peered at her and found her desirable, so she too examines him and discovers the incarnation of her fantasies. This seduction by the fountain thus invokes and, at the same time, inverts the Actaeon myth that had closed Petrarch's *canzone* 23 and the frustrated love scene in Garcilaso's second eclogue. By his pretended silence Acis seduces the girl denied to the more Petrarchist lover, Polyphemus.

Mute speech is meant to convey love through the eyes when silence for whatever reason had been imposed. Here, however, the "sleeping" Acis, with his closed eyes, transforms Galatea into a voyeuse, hovering over him like a hawk over a chick. Her actions are in line with Góngora's frequent representation of a predatory sexuality, further inverted by being ascribed to a woman. Jammes notes that traditionally Acis was the least interesting member of the sexual triangle, and that Góngora had succeeded, by presenting him as a hunter, in remasculinizing the somewhat effeminate presentation in Ovid (538). Yet Góngora actually goes further; as Paul Julian Smith puts it, "in the *Polifemo* we find an unregulated circulation of signs and, indeed, of sexes" (*The Body,* 66). On the plot level Galatea, represented earlier in the poem as a traditional *ninfa esquiva* ever in flight from her suitors, is masculinized when placed in the male role of penetrating Acis's bower and viewing the sleeping sex object; on the textual level, as Smith notes, Acis is feminized when his body is described in terms of surfaces and details, using metaphorical techniques normally reserved for descriptions of women.[10] Jammes is correct in noting how, by maintaining both Acis's and Galatea's silence, Góngora deprives this episode of dramatic power and turns it into a type of mime (543–45); but I would disagree with his determination that by inventing a 160-line scene absent from Ovid, Góngora shows how for him love is a strikingly profound and varied emotion (538) and that the scene proves the degree to which Góngora was seduced by the theme (543). Rather, I would agree with Smith that here Góngora accomplishes just the opposite, reducing love to "figures or commonplaces of love, not icons of authentic or instinctive sentiment" (*The Body*, 62), and furthermore inverting the ways in which these love and sex roles had previously been inscribed by the tradition. By opening a space for an inquisitive, active sexuality on Galatea's part, Góngora also makes possible all kinds of sexual behavior proscribed in the Petrarchist tradition and by extension in Renaissance Spanish society as a whole.

Late in his life Góngora returned to the love sonnet, and although these poems demonstrate his most mature style, they also preserve formal and thematic tendencies, such as indeterminate metaphor and a predatory sexuality, that we have observed in his earliest works. One example of his late love sonnets is "Prision de'l nacar" (*Sonetos* 97), written in 1620, describing a woman who pricks her finger while removing a diamond ring. Considering the poet's age at the time this poem was written, Jammes judged the poem a courtly exercise and asserted that Góngora could not have witnessed such a small incident without any interest, nor be in the habit at that age of playing the gallant lover (317); Blecua, by contrast, defended it precisely as a literary exercise that may have provided the author a poetic distraction from his travails. The opening quatrain consists of a violent hyperbaton that explains how a diamond, in its hardness a shining imitator of the poet's steadfastness, and like him imprisoned in gold, in turn was a prison for the beloved's "nacar articulado" (articulated mother-of-pearl)—that is, her finger. As Blecua and Brockhaus (30) both note, the quatrain has a circular structure like that of the ring itself, beginning and ending with a variant of the word *prision*, which suggests three prisons: of the finger in the ring, of the diamond in its setting, and of the poet himself caught in the net of hair. Salcedo Coronel explains the appropriateness of the metaphor "nacar articulado" in terms of references by Ovid and Juvenal to fingers as *articulis,* to mother-of-pearl as the site where jewels (*gemma*) are created, and to *articulos* as the Latin word for the nodes on the vine from which flowers bloom, blossoms that are also called *gemma* and which resemble great gems on a finger. The poem thus describes a woman's knuckles adorned with a monstrously large diamond, but, as Blecua pointed out, the signified is nearly lost in the elaboration of the signifier, through the use of hyperbaton, of erudite vocabulary, and of allusions to precious materials. The rest of the poem continues these practices, adding enjambments and diereses (which Salcedo Coronel found excessive); the words *ai* and *laton* in the first tercet clash with this texture but do not really subvert it. Indeed, the final tercet redoubles the emphasis on beauty, as the effect of blood on her hand is compared to the red veins on Indian marble and to jealous Aurora dropping carnation petals on snow.

As Salcedo Coronel noted, the two final images, in this very combination, can be found in book 12 of the *Aeneid* in a description of Lavinia's face. By and large, however, he provides not so much sources for this poem as glosses explaining the images, often in terms of other poems by Góngora. Thus, for the first tercet, "Mas ai, que insidíòso laton breue / en los crystales de su bella mano / sacrilego diuina sangre beue" (But ouch! that insidious small piece of brass from the crystal of her beautiful hand sacrilegiously drinks divine blood, *Sonetos* 97.9–11), he zeroes in on the metal drinking in blood from her crystalline hands, and refers the reader to his comments on an earlier sonnet, "En el crystal de tu Diuina mano / de Amor bebi el dulcissimo veneno" (From the crystal of your divine hand I drank the sweetest poison [1609], *Sonetos* 93.1–2). There in turn he had declared that "en metafora de los vasos de cristal en que se suele beber, descrive D. Luis la blancura y belleza de la mano de su dama, que pudo enamorarle" (through the metaphor of the crystal glass from which he used to drink, Don Luis describes the whiteness and beauty of his lady's hand, which made him fall in love) and referred the reader to parallels not only in Virgil, Propertius, Terence, and other Latin poets, but also in Góngora's own *Polifemo,* specifically Galatea drinking in Acis's beauty. Thus the principal characteristics of the sonnet, to a Renaissance reader like Salcedo Coronel, are its somewhat overly artistic metrical structure and erudite vocabulary; the imitation of a Virgilian trope describing the effect of red blood on white skin; and an allusion to Góngora's own earlier poems in which he describes drinking in the beloved's beauty as from a crystal glass. Salcedo Coronel's gloss is disconcerting because it focuses on a sanguivorous detail of the poem and suggests either a bizarre love by the inanimate of the animate (the ring had indeed been ripped off by its petrarchanly disdainful owner), or else that the poet's love increases as he takes aesthetic pleasure in the scene of her injury.[11]

"Prision d'el nacar" thus continues the tradition of predatory sexuality, excessive metaphorization, and self-referentiality which can be traced back to Góngora's earliest love sonnets; the poet's style evolves, but the aesthetic principles remain remarkably constant throughout his career. Moreover, like early sonnets that lent themselves to a metapoetic interpretation (such as "De pura honestidad": construction of a temple/construction of the poem; "No destroçada naue": farewell to the nymph/farewell to Petrarchism), so too do these late ones. The ring drinking the blood of the lady's beauty, with its extensive field of intertextual references, suggests a gruesome revision of the digestive metaphor for imitation, used since Seneca. Similarly, the poem in which a bee, mistaking a sleeping nymph's lips for a flower, stings her but thereby rescues her from a prowling satyr recalls the apian metaphor and suggests a self-representation of the poet-as-bee as rescuer of beauty from a satyr who could well represent the notoriously ugly Quevedo. Góngora's imagery in these poems may seem decadent and, in Jammes' words, lacking in authenticity (317), but his self-representation, late in life, as the imbiber of the Italo-classical tradition competes in its implied metalepsis with Garcilaso's third eclogue.

In both practice and theory Góngora transformed Spanish lyric. Although precedents for his stylistic techniques existed in other poets, particularly Herrera and Camoens, Góngora developed them in an idiosyncratic manner that lent itself to analysis, imitation, and parody. His poetry also unleashed a torrent of critical commentary that, while drawing on late sixteenth-century critics such as Herrera, ultimately resulted in the highly sophisticated systems of Spanish Baroque poetics.[12] Above all, Góngora transformed the subsequent perception of the canon. As Schulz-Buschhaus points out, Góngora from the very beginning of his career imitated well-known poets who had been designated in the sixteenth century as representative of Italian literature; the result of these obvious imitations of canonical sources is an announcement of both his entry into a preexisting discourse and of his intention to compete with well-known predecessors, with the ultimate goal of autocanonization. Salcedo Coronel saw Góngora, in "Prision de'l nacar," primarily troping himself; by imitating himself Góngora, like Garcilaso in the third eclogue, raises his own poetry to the level of his classical and Italian predecessors. Yet while Garcilaso's self-referential poem opens a route of escape in the shepherds' concluding song, Góngora turns the Petrarchan tradition back on itself, and by placing both Petrarch and Garcilaso on the same level as Ovid, Tasso, and even Claudian, Góngora begins to end the privileged position of the Petrarchist model in Spanish lyric poetry. The result is what Sánchez Robayna calls a hypernorm in decadence. He goes on to say,

> El canon técnico-formal e 'ideológico' del petrarquismo, su estética de la exasperación, el recuerdo y la *irrealidad*, pasa a una suerte de automatismo que es el estadio inicial de la caída de su funcionamiento como tradición literaria.
>
> (38)

> The technico-formal and "ideological" canon of Petrarchism, its aesthetic of exasperation, memory, and irreality, pass on to a sort of automatism that is the beginning of its failure to function as a literary tradition.

Góngora breaks the metonymy between poetic and erotic frustration, transforming the old pose of masculine suffering and female indifference into a free zone for poetic play; from the beginning of his career, the discourse of denial rings false, for it coexists with a poetics of fulfillment. Yet as Sánchez Robayna further notes, Góngora would nonetheless preserve the Petrarchist system; "no existe en ningún caso un efecto *destructivo* de la tradición petrarquista . . . la parodia no está llevada por una intención absolutamente *negativa*" (there are no cases of a destructive effect on the Petrarchist tradition . . . the parody is not led by a purely negative intent, 43).[13] By positing himself as the fulfillment of the preexisting poetic traditions, however, Góngora leaves little room for serious successors; only a radical return to Petrarch as a model can open new ground, though at the risk of destroying the now weakened state of Petrarchist lyric. For just such a final assault on Petrarchist poetry, we must turn to Quevedo.

PARODIC PETRARCHISM IN
CANTA SOLA A LISI

In his sonnet collection *Canta sola a Lisi y a la amorosa pasión de su amante*, Francisco de Quevedo once more attempts to redirect the course of Spanish lyric poetry so as to recover Petrarch's moral seriousness and correct Spain's continuing cultural inferiority. To do so, Quevedo appropriates Boscán's autobiographical pose, along with his pretense of instructing the reader about love and poetry; the Lisi poems, taken cumulatively and in order, teach the reader that beautiful poetry results not from noble sentiments but from efficacious rhetoric. By embedding echoes, imitations, and quotations from his major Spanish and Italian predecessors within his own discourse, Quevedo reveals the construction of the Petrarchan subject but also defamiliarizes it, making possible a new reading and a new rewriting of the Petrarchist tradition. The Lisi cycle begins with tightly organized sonnets built around a central idea or *concepto*, but soon decays into poems with elaborate metaphors and an erudite vocabulary that recall Góngora. The central poem, "Cerrar podrá," makes crucial allusion to the Orpheus myth in Garcilaso and Petrarch; from then on, the second part of the collection consists mostly of poems about death and decay that, in style and imagery, echo Boscán and the *cancionero*. Like Góngora, Quevedo imitates canonical sources, but unlike him, he does not naturalize them within his own discourse, instead embedding quotations and allusions so that they stand out and remain foreign. Although its moral content connects the Lisi cycle to Quevedo's metaphysical poems, the crucial lesson of the cycle is the absence of an authentic poetic voice and the breakdown of Petrarchan rhetoric, features that connect these poems to Quevedo's satirical and burlesque verse.

Revisionist criticism has tended to play down the distinction between Góngora and Quevedo, concluding, as does Warnke, that both poets "are rooted in the same habit of mind and the same conception of art" (59). Yet the opposition between these poets is not a misguided invention. Behind Quevedo's accusations against Góngora of heresy or covert Judaism, his major objections, as Collard recognized, were that Góngora practiced obscurity for its own sake (69) and that he attempted to undo the bond between poetry and moral instruction which had been the former's traditional defense, overthrowing the old notion of the poet-prophet and substituting for it that of the poet-artificer who has made himself by dint of his talent and erudition (102). To Quevedo it seemed that Góngora cloaked trivial subject matter in overly elaborate rhetorical dress and violated the principles of clarity, as expounded in Herrera's *Anotaciones:* difficulty of thought along with simplicity of style is an ideal, and the sonnet, as the modern equivalent to the epigram, should have as its basis a single thought or *concepto.* The example of Góngora's poetry was particularly threatening to the continued practice of Petrarchism, which had been subverted not only by the Córdoban's sonnets but also by his most notorious poems, the *Soledades* and the *Polifemo,* hendecasyllabic compositions steeped in Petrarchism on both the stylistic and the narrative levels. If these poems were truly the culmination of Spanish Petrarchism, they could forever mark the incapacity of Spanish poetry to equal the moral seriousness of the Italian original. His opponents' task, then, was to develop a love poetry that recuperated the element of moral instruction present in Petrarch, and that through single-mindedness and austerity could embody traditional Castilian stylistic virtues. Quevedo composed love poetry throughout his life, but the major vehicle for his reformulation of Petrarchism is his love-poem collection, *Canta sola a Lisi.*

The Lisi cycle is remarkable for a number of reasons, not the least of which is its very macrotextuality. While sonnet collections had become quite the norm in other European countries during the sixteenth century, in Spain, as we have seen, they remained the exception—perhaps, as Walters supposes (*Poems,* xiv–xv), because Spanish poets continued to shy away from publishing their own poetry and thus were unable to guarantee that their poems would appear in a particular order. Among Quevedo's predecessors, only Boscán and Herrera had composed and published such collections. Yet these are significant predecessors, for both poets are extremely important in Spanish literary history as self-conscious theorizers about lyric poetry and about the imitation of Petrarch. Boscán lamented the state of Spanish poetry and proposed the adoption of Italian verse forms in imitation of Petrarch as a way for Spain to attain a poetic greatness to match its political and military achievements; Herrera, forty years later, still deplored the inferiority of Spanish poetry and blamed it on the lack of professional poets who, in imitation of Petrarch, would devote themselves to the study of letters and thus recover poetry from courtiers and other amateurs. Thus Quevedo, by also writing a collection, inserts himself into a rather short genealogy of self-conscious reformers, both of whom looked to Petrarch as their poetic father. Boscán and Herrera were not, however, the principal poets of the Spanish Renaissance; the best known were Garcilaso de la Vega and Góngora himself. As the "Prince of Castilian poets," Garcilaso in particular was responsible for the subsequent popularity of Petrarchist imitation among almost all of the poets from the Iberian peninsula, a line that could be construed as leading directly to Góngora. Thus by writing Petrarchan love sonnets, Quevedo also inserts himself in yet another, far larger genealogy of Spanish poets, asserting that the house of Petrarch has not come to an end and that there is yet room enough for another successor.

As noted above, few Spanish poets of the Renaissance published their own work, and Quevedo was not an exception in this regard. The Lisi collection poses a particular problem for critics because there is very little verifiable information regarding its composition and the arrangement of the poems. The bulk of them first appeared in the posthumous compilation of Quevedo's poems entitled *El Parnasso español*, published in 1648 by the poet's friend and literary executor, José González de Salas.[14] In his preface to the Lisi collection, González de Salas notes the uniqueness of Petrarch's love for Laura and that this love, as recorded in the *Rime sparse*, was partly responsible for his fame:

> Famosa es mucho la memoria, desde el segundo o tercero siglo antecedente, del ilustre y elegante poeta, entre los toscanos, Francisco Petrarca; y no menos aún también entre los latinos. Pero no creo que el esplendor que contruyo a su fama, de la celebración de su Laura tanto repetida, querrá ceder al que más le adorne entre sus muchos méritos. . . . [L]a vira que de Laura flecharon los ojos, ansí dentro introdujo su veneno, que veinte y un años permaneció constante, sin que su pasión se remitiese; que esos fueron los que desde el principio de su amor ella tuvo de vida, y diez ansimismo que él después sobrevivió igualmente su amante.
>
> (1.117)[15]

For the past two or three centuries, the memory of the illustrious and elegant poet Francis Petrarch has been greatly celebrated among the Tuscans and no less among the Latins. But I do not believe that he would wish the splendor that induced his reputation, of praising his Laura repeatedly, to give way to any of the other merits that most distinguish him. . . . The dart from Laura that wounded his eyes introduced its poison within him, so that for twenty-one years he remained constant, without his passion diminishing; and those were the years after the beginning of his love that she had life, for he then survived her by ten years, as her lover just the same.

Thus González de Salas construes Petrarch's collection as having its basis in biographical facts, a single love to which the poet remained faithful throughout his life. González de Salas also ascribes to Quevedo a similar affection and takes partial credit for the final ordering of the poems in the 1648 edition, though following Quevedo's specific intention of imitating Petrarch in the "autobiographical" arrangement:

Confieso, pues, ahora, que advirtiendo el discurso enamorado que se colige del contexto de esta sección, que yo reduje a la forma que hoy tiene, vine a persuadirme que mucho quiso nuestro poeta este su amor semejase al que habemos insinuado del Petrarca. El ocioso que con particularidad fuese confiriendo los sonetos aquí contenidos con los que en las rimas se leen del poeta toscano, grande paridad hallaría sin duda, que quiso Don Francisco imitar en esta expresión de sus afectos.

(ibid.)

I confess then that taking note of the love discourse that can be gathered from the content of this section, which I reduced to the form it now has, I came to persuade myself that our poet very much wanted his love to resemble that of Petrarch's we have already discussed. The person of leisure who were carefully to compare these sonnets with those which can be read among the Tuscan poet's works will doubtless find great similarities, for Don Francisco wished to imitate him in this expression of his affections.

Thus to Quevedo Petrarch was a double model, both for his twenty-two-year love for Lisi and for his determination to chronicle it in verse; equivocating between history and fiction, emotion and rhetoric, González de Salas concludes that "mucho parentesco, en fin, habemos de dar en estas dos tan parecidas afecciones, como en la significación que tienen los conceptos con que ambos las manifestaron en sus poesías" (in the end we must admit that there is a great family relationship between these two very similar loves, just as in the meaning of those concepts with which they both manifest their love in their poems, 1.117).[16]

While the order of the Lisi poems in *El Parnasso* has not always seemed correct to every critic, with no other textual evidence to go on one is forced, if the collection is to be considered at all, to accept what Blanco Aguinaga called González de Salas's "orden magistral" (magisterial order, 317) as at least a tentative possibility.[17] Just as complicated as the ordering of the poems is the question of their dating. Very few of the poems appear in any datable manuscripts; early versions of three (poems 3, 36, and 45) are in a manuscript compiled in 1627–28, while early, autograph versions of four more (poems 30, 42, 43, from *El Parnasso* and 3 from *Las tres Musas*) are bound together with a poem datable to 1634. Thus there is no obvious correlation between the date of the poems and their order in the sequence, much less any reason to believe that they are actually autobiographical.[18] But the general range (1620s–1630s) makes these poems relatively late ones and coincides with the period in Quevedo's life in which he edited the poems of Fray Luis de León and Francisco de la Torre, as antidotes to what was considered by opponents and supporters alike the excess of the Gongoristic school.[19]

In view of the fact that at this time Quevedo was thus engaged in an attempt to redefine Spanish literary history for the preceding hundred years, it is not surprising that when one views the poems as a collection, one sees Quevedo not just telling a story of an unrequited love but recapitulating the course of Spanish Petrarchist poetry, and then proposing a correction of his own that approximates the love poems to Quevedo's so-called metaphysical or moral style. The Lisi collection opens with poems that suggest an attempt at a reformed Petrarchism. The very first sonnet, a type of *enamoramiento* poem, is built around the idea that his falling in love was not an act of free will; it is based on an antithesis between freedom, represented in the first quatrain by words such as *libre* and *albedrío*, and slavery, represented by *prisión* and *conquistada:*

¿Qué importa blasonar del albedrío,
alma, de eterna y libre tan preciada,
si va en prisión de un ceño, y, conquistada,
padece en un cabello señorío?
(L1/B442.1–4)

What is the use of boasting of free will, and of the freedom and eter-
nity of the valued soul, if it can be imprisoned by a frown and, con-
quered, suffers the mastery of a lock of hair?

This antithesis is carried into the succeeding stanzas, where the poet
associates his earlier, preamatory state with good government and
his present condition with political tyranny; throughout, he alludes
to Petrarchan details such as Lisi's face, hair, eyes, and mouth, as
well as her absolute indifference to his poetic efforts, conventionally
represented as *gemidos* (cries). Self-contained, like Herrera's Luz, she
neither prides herself on her victory nor feels any pity for his suffer-
ing. The ideas of the poem are straightforward—at least to a reader
familiar with Petrarchan conventions—and so too is their presenta-
tion.[20] Most lines contain a complete thought, and enjambments,
where they occur, only separate a verb from its subject or its object.
The poet does employ hyperbatons, but generally they take the
form of placing the subject at the end of a clause, and therefore
closer to a second verb of which it is also the subject. The only ex-
ception is the first tercet, "Una risa, unos ojos, unas manos / todo
mi corazón y mis sentidos / saquearon, hermosos y tiranos" (A
smile, some eyes, some hands, lovely but tyrannical, pillaged all my
heart and senses, 9–11), in which the epithets "hermosos y tiranos"
are displaced to line 11, separated from the nouns they describe,
"risa-ojos-manos," by the intervening "corazón y sentidos." Perhaps
the slightly contorted syntax is meant to represent the moment of
his enslavement; in any case the epithets thus form a bridge to line
13, where "risa-ojos-manos" remain the subject rather than the more
proximate "gemidos."

Similarly, the third poem of the collection is also built around a
single antithetical idea:

Los que ciego me ven de haber llorado
y las lágrimas saben que he vertido,
admiran de que, en fuentes dividido
o en lluvias, ya no corra derramado.

Pero mi corazón arde admirado
(porque en tus llamas, Lisi, está encendido)
de no verme en centellas repartido,
y en humo negro y llamas desatado.
En mí no vencen largos y altos ríos
a incendios, que animosos me maltratan,
ni el llanto se defiende de sus bríos.
La agua y el fuego en mí de paces tratan;
y amigos son, por ser contrarios míos;
y los dos, por matarme, no se matan.

(L3/B444)

Those who see me blind from weeping and know the tears I have poured out are surprised that, divided into fountains or deluges, I do not yet flow away spilled. But my heart burns in wonder (for by your flames, Lisi, it is ignited), at not seeing me scattered in sparks, and into black smoke and flames unfastened. Great high rivers do not in me defeat the fires that as enemies mistreat me, nor does weeping guard itself from their brightness. Water and fire have made a truce in me and become friends, in being my adversaries; the two, to kill me, do not kill each other.

Here Quevedo plays with the reader: the first quatrain is devoted to water and the second to fire, but the tercets resolve the apparently divergent topics by taking as their theme the reconciliation of these opposites, for rivers cannot vanquish his fire, and his tears are impervious to flames; fire and water have struck a truce, together they wage war against him. The playful ingenuity of the poem is reinforced by the structure. Both quatrains are worded in terms of the surprise of viewers at his resistance to dissolution. In the first one, unfamiliar spectators remark that he fails to divide into twin fountains or rainstorms, and the verbal juxtaposition of opposites in the first line ("ciego me ven") suggests the ambiguity of association: he is blinded by his weeping, but they are blind in their incomprehension. The second quatrain repeats the basic structure but shifts the locus of the gaze from outside to within; now it is his burning heart that is surprised at the poet's not scattering into sparks, or disintegrating into black smoke and flames.[21] Through his use of two opposing themes in the quatrains, Quevedo at first prompts the reader's censure, only to resolve this disapproval at the recognition, in the tercets, of the single antithesis. The reversal makes the reader aware of the reading process and turns the poem in on itself, an effect also achieved by the artful, parallel structure of the quatrains.

Self-consciousness about the reading of an artistic text is also achieved by the poem's conventionality: González de Salas points to its source in Sannazaro's *Miraris liquidum*, quoted by Herrera in the *Anotaciones* as a gloss on the word "contrarios" in the final line of Garcilaso's second elegy ("y assí, diverso entre contrarios muero" ([and thus divided amid opposites I die]). As Herrera shows, by Garcilaso's time the mutual canceling out of the lover's tearful eyes and his fiery heart had become a commonplace. Consiglio, however, notes a further debt to a *ballata* of Petrarch's:

> Qual foco non avrian già spento et morto
> l'onde che gli occhi tristi versan sempre?
> Amor, avegna mi sia tardi accorto,
> vol che tra duo contrari mi distempre,
>   et tende lacci in sì diverse tempre
> che quand' ò più speranza che 'l cor n'esca,
> allor più nel bel viso mi rinvesca.
>   (*Rime sparse* 55.11–17)

> What fire would not have been put out by the floods that my sad eyes are always pouring forth? Love, though I have been tardy in seeing it, wishes me to be untuned between two contraries; and he puts out snares of such different temper that, when I most hope that my heart can get free of them, then he most enlimes me again with that lovely face.

This is the source for the closing conceit of Quevedo's poem: these two opposites not only cancel each other out but are so arranged by love as to prolong the lover's life and thus his suffering. This life-and-death issue will become a key theme throughout the Lisi cycle. Through his imitation of Petrarch and Sannazaro, Quevedo locates his poem in the Italian love-lyric tradition, and like Boscán a century earlier uses this context to create tension between the reader's expectations and the actual poem. In contrast to Petrarch's drawing out of the consequences of the fire/water antithesis, Quevedo's conclusion, that the two instead of killing each other will kill him, seems abrupt; Quevedo depends on the reader's complicity in understanding that the concise reference to death is to be taken as a metonymy for the sufferings of love, yet frustrates the reader's desire for and expectations of a more poetic exposition, such as those in Petrarch and Sannazaro. Moreover, the word *matar*, used twice in the final line of Quevedo's sonnet ("y los dos, por matarme, no se matan"), is from a relatively lower stylistic register than the rest of the poem, and thus anchors it to a Castilian alternative, the *cancionero* tradition.[22]

The combination of Petrarchist and *cancionero* features suggests other Spanish predecessors, notably Garcilaso, whose "Hermosas ninfas" is echoed in Quevedo's fountain of tears. But Quevedo's "blind" viewers in the first line, who do not understand why the poet does not melt, particularly recall Boscán's semiotically unqualified interpreters, ignorant about the nature of true love. As in Boscán's collection, the deficient interpreters stand for unqualified readers, who need instruction in the nature of love poetry; and as in Boscán the intent is ironic, though in a different way. Boscán pretended to address readers ignorant of Petrarchism even while imitating Petrarch in ways that well-versed readers would recognize. Quevedo forces readers to constitute themselves in the same way, even while depending on their recognition of Petrarchist subtexts to help them understand the poem. By imitating Boscán, Quevedo suggests, a century later, that the Spanish have never learned their lessons and need to be reinstructed. In its thematic concern with fire and water, its self-consciously artful construction, and its clear designation of subtexts in terms of which the poem must be read, this sonnet is typical of the Lisi cycle and, as much as the opening poem, it sets the tone for what is to follow.

The reader in need of instruction about love is directly addressed in the very next poem:

> Tú, que la paz del mar, ¡oh navegante!,
> molestas, codicioso y diligente,
> por sangrarle las venas al Oriente
> del más rubio metal, rico y flamante,
>   detente aquí; no pases adelante;
> hártate de tesoros, brevemente,
> en donde Lisi peina de su frente
> hebra sutil en ondas fulminante.
>   (L4/B445.1–8)

You who molest the peace of the sea, oh navigator both greedy and diligent, so as to bleed the veins of the Orient of the blondest metal, rich and flaming, stay here; go no farther; sate yourself with treasures,

quickly, where Lisi combs from her forehead delicate fibers into ful-
minating waves.

Here the reader is fictionalized as a member of the Spanish ruling
class, engaged in the recovery of riches from the New World. The
animating trope in these lines is the conventional comparison of
Lisi's hair to gold; the third line recalls, in a distant way, Garcilaso's
"cabello, que'n la vena / del oro s'escogió" (hair culled from a vein
of gold, 23.5–6) as well as Petrarch's "Onde tolse Amor l'oro et di
qual vena / per far due treccie bionde?" (Where and from what
mine did Love take the gold to make two blond tresses? *Rime sparse*
220.1–2). But the paronomasia (veins of gold, veins of blood) reads
a monstrous dimension back into the Petrarchan tradition and into
the imperial enterprise, ripping and bleeding gold from the earth
of Spain's overseas possessions. The use of navigation images in this
context also undermines one of the key Petrarchan tropes, that of
the lover as sailor, while giving the poem a Horatian dimension
(see Walters, *Franciso de Quevedo*, 91–94; and more generally Lerner,
"Quevedo"). Yet the physicality of this description, far greater than
Garcilaso's much-criticized "entre las yervas degollada" (eclogue
3.230), breaks the decorum of the collection even more strongly than
the "por matarme, no me matan" of the preceding poem. Prosodic
decorum is also broken by the repeated caesuras and irregular
rhythms of the first six lines, which disturb the flow of the verse;
not until lines 7–8, with their timeworn comparison and Latinate
vocabulary, do the hendecasyllables flow smoothly.

The rest of the poem dissipates the tight focus of the quatrains,
asserting that not only gold but pearls, dyes, flowers, and even stars
can be had, respectively, from Lisi's laughter, lips, cheeks, and eyes.
The idea behind the poem thus shifts away from the hair/gold con-
ceit to a series of metaphorical celebrations of Lisi's body; as a cata-
log, it recalls poems such as Góngora's "De pvra honestidad templo
sagrado" (*Sonetos* 55). A specific reference to Columbus underlines
the contrast between love and empire, which, considering the highly
formalistic nature of the poem, can itself be taken as the opposition
between letters (the production of metaphorical riches through the
celebration of Lisi) and arms (actual conquest, exploration, and ex-
ploitation overseas). The degeneration into Gongorine tropes, as
well as the exaltation of literature, and thus of *verba* over *res*, suggest

that the true intended reading is an ironic one; what is striking about the poem is not the second half, with its smooth progression of Gongorine metaphors, but the violent verses of the beginning. The true lesson of the poem is not that love is preferable to empire and that poetic riches are better than material ones, but the opposite. As both an example of the Gongorine approach to Petrarchist poetry and a critique thereof, the sonnet forms a bridge to the elaborate poems typical of the first half of the Lisi cycle.

An example is the seventh sonnet of the collection, "Si mis párpados, Lisi, labios fueran" (B448). The key conceit here is a comparison between the poet's eyelids and his lips; were this only true, it would allow him to be constantly kissing Lisi by means of the invisible rays through which lovers communicate; denuded, they could be secretly united in public. To Paul Julian Smith (*Quevedo*, 165–68), the poem is grounded in the simplest kind of metaphor, that based on resemblance, thus fulfilling contemporary criteria of brevity, clarity, and novelty (although the latter is somewhat strained, in view of the parallels in Ovid and Marino). It also plays on a Neoplatonic notion that formed the basis of a Garcilaso sonnet, "De aquella vista pura y excellente" (8). Yet much of the vocabulary is alien to Garcilaso, either because of excessive physicality (*labios, besos*), or of excessive erudition (*hidrópicos*), features that suggest an affinity with Góngora; line 5 ("tus bellezas, hidrópicos, bebieran") specifically recalls Góngora's "en el crystal de tu Diuina mano / de Amor bebi el dulcissimo veneno" (in the crystal of your divine hand I drank the sweetest poison of love; *Sonetos* 93.1–2). The Ovidian tone of the poem is also alien to the unusually serious Neoplatonism of the Garcilaso sonnet. Quevedo instead takes the trope of lovers' silent speech and returns to it the comicality of Ovid in the *Amores* signaling to his mistress in her husband's very presence: "De invisible comercio mantenidos, / y desnudos de cuerpo los favores, / gozaran mis potencias y sentidos" (Maintained by invisible commerce and denuded of body, my powers and senses will enjoy your favors, L7/B448.9–11). "Desnudos de cuerpo" refers to the spirits that have shed their bodies, but the phrase cannot help suggesting naked bodies invisibly cavorting as they enjoy paradoxically secret but public sexual relations, an element exacerbated by the words *gozar, potencia,* and *sentidos* in the final line (see Elias Rivers, "Language and Reality," 28–29). Similarly, Quevedo exploits all the implications of *co-*

mercio: though ostensibly a description of the lovers trading glances, it suggests sexual intercourse and even the exchange of money for sexual favors. Indeed, the prostitute too enjoys a status both furtive (because illegal) and public (because she is available to all). These insinuations of irregular sexuality, as much as the stylistic echoes, suggest the approximation to Góngora.[23]

The immediately following poem works in a similar fashion:

> En crespa tempestad de el oro undoso,
> nada golfos de luz ardiente y pura
> mi corazón, sediento de hermosura,
> si el cabello deslazas generoso.
>   Leandro, en mar de fuego proceloso,
> su amor ostenta, su vivir apura;
> Icaro, en senda de oro mal segura,
> arde sus alas por morir glorioso.
>   Con pretensión de fénix, encendidas
> sus esperanzas, que difuntas lloro,
> intenta que su muerte engendre vidas.
>   Avaro y rico y pobre, en el tesoro,
> el castigo y la hambre imita a Midas,
> Tántalo en fugitiva fuente de oro.
>
> (L8/B449)

In a curly tempest of wavy gold my heart, thirsting for beauty, swims gulfs of pure burning light, if you unfasten your abundant hair. Leander in the sea of tempestuous fire, it [the heart] displays its love and expedites its life; Icarus on an unsure golden path, it burns its wings, more gloriously to die. With pretense of a phoenix, its hopes (whose death I weep) aflame, it intends its death to engender lives. Avaricious and rich and poor, in its treasure, its punishment, and its hunger it imitates Midas, and Tantalus in a fleeting fountain of gold.

This sonnet is based on the conceits that the beloved's blond hair is like gold in color and like waves in form.[24] By combining these two images, Quevedo sets his heart swimming through a curly tempest of wavy gold and through gulfs of pure burning light; in so doing his heart is like Leander risking his life in a sea of fire and like Icarus burning his wings on the golden path. Together, these images and allusions recapitulate Spanish Petrarchan poetry. Garcilaso, as we have seen, compared the beloved's hair to gold, and Góngora used the image in the first line of his imitation of Garcilaso, "Mientras por competir con tu cabello." The radiance of golden hair made it a key concept for Herrera, who organized his sonnet collection around the allegorical value of Luz, the beloved's name, and Lope de Vega had made a sea of the beloved's hair and a boat of her comb. Similarly, the mythological allusions recall other poetry. The Hero and Leander myth formed the basis of an epyllion by Boscán, and Garcilaso has a sonnet on the same theme; Icarus too was the subject of a poem by Garcilaso and was invoked by Herrera in the opening lines of the first sonnet in his collection. The myth of the phoenix was also employed by Herrera, but most famously by Góngora in the first *Soledad;* in addition, it anticipates the very next sonnet in the Lisi collection. In this regard it is like the myth of Midas, as both refer externally to subtexts and internally to the Lisi cycle itself, where they serve as key, recurrent mythological allusions.[25] Above all, Quevedo's poem alludes, though indirectly, back to Petrarch, who often used *onda* as a metonymy for the sea or for his tears, but never as a metaphor for Laura's hair, and who frequently employed the stormy sea as a metaphor for his emotion:

> Non d'atra et tempestosa onda marina
> fuggio in porto giamai stanco nocchiero,
> com' io dal fosco et torbido pensero
> fuggo ove 'l gran desio mi sprona e 'nchina.
> *(Rime sparse* 151.1–4)

> Never did weary pilot flee to port from the black tempestuous wave
> of the sea, as I flee from my dark and turbid care to where my great
> desire spurs and inclines me.

Quevedo reads these lines of Petrarch's through the lens of the subsequent metaphorization of *onda* by the Spanish Petrarchist tradition; the navigator tossing on the black waves of despair is rewritten as the poet's boat on Lisi's golden curls. Petrarch's presence also establishes a link to Quevedo's own navigation poems, the preceding "Tú, que la paz del mar" and the subsequent Petrarchist tempest poem, "Molesta el ponto Bóreas" (L13/B454).

Moreover, it is not only through intertextual references that the sonnet points to earlier poetry; its very style is reminiscent of Góngora's excesses, generally so despised by Quevedo. The entire poem is based on rather trivial, time-worn comparisons, hyperbolically expanded and compounded by mythological allusions. The hyperbatons of the first quatrain disguise the subject—*corazón*—which, as González de Salas himself pointed out, is through appositions the unspoken subject of all of the succeeding sentences as well, while the metaphorical referent of the first line (hair) is not identified until the fourth. Grammatically, lines 5–6 and 7–8 are parallel, while line 6 breaks down into a *bimembre*, Góngora's trademark device. Line 10 confuses the reader by having the poet himself as the subject of the verb, *lloro*, while line 12 contains a polysyndeton, another *culteranista* feature. The closing allusion to Tantalus recalls the word *sediento* ("thirsty") in line 3 and thus invokes a sensation that plays an important part both in Góngora's poetry and throughout the Lisi collection.

The technique of embedding quotations, imitations, and allusions within his poems is one Quevedo employs throughout the Lisi cycle, and it frequently serves, as in the preceding poems, to recapitulate the course of Petrarchist poetry. Sonnet 10, "¿Cómo es tan largo en mí dolor tan fuerte" (How can such a strong pain last so long in me, B451), begins with a direct quote from Boscán and proceeds through a series of rhetorical questions to the subject of mute speech. As Close puts it, "by introducing his sonnet with a quotation from Boscán Quevedo makes each of the rhetorical questions in the first six lines an echo of Boscán's question. What I believe that Quevedo has done is to adapt Guarini ('Amante poco,' # 54) in such a way as to recall the plainness, paradoxical point, and latent despair of Boscán's lines" (846). To her, Quevedo forms a pastiche of Boscán's plain style but sharpens it, then meditates on silence in a Petrarchan manner, and concludes with a series of Gongorine *agudezas:* "Suspiros, del dolor mudos despojos, / también la boca a razonar aprende, / como con llanto y sin hablar los ojos" (Sighs, those silent spoils of pain, the mouth also learns to recite, as do the eyes with tears but no speech, L10/B451.12–14). Similarly the twenty-fourth sonnet, "En breve cárcel traigo aprisionado" (B465, discussed by Blanco-Morel and by Olivares, 67–74), also recalls the Petrarchan tradition. The poem describes a portrait of Lisi that the poet carries in a ring; as a poem about a memento, it belongs to the same genre as Garcilaso's "Dulces prendas." But whereas that poem concentrated on the poet's evolving emotional reaction to this enduring reminder, Quevedo's is devoted to the paradox of the entire universe, in other words, what Lisi is to him, being contained in such a small space. The ring specifically recalls Góngora's sonnet

"Prision de nacar" (*Sonetos* 97), while the description of the heavens in the fourth and fifth lines contains a blatant echo of the opening of Góngora's *Soledades;* the pearls, diamonds, and rubies contained in the ring (and ingeniously in a single line: "perlas que, en un diamante, por rubíes" [pearls that, in a diamond, through rubies], 10) are metaphors for Lisi's teeth, disdain (see the note by González de Salas), and lips, recalling the earlier allusions to imperial wealth and the catalogs of Lisi's body in sonnets 2 and 4. The sonnet's most famous line, "relámpagos de risa carmesíes" (carmine lightning-bolts of laughter, 13), imitates Petrarch's "e 'l lampeggiar de l'angelico riso" (and the lightning of the angelic smile, *Rime sparse* 292.6).[26] Yet again, sonnet 29 (B470), which opens with an elaborate hyperbaton, is dedicated, as González de Salas pointed out, to a comparison between Lisi and a magnet; in both style and content it recalls the description of Galatea as a magnet in Góngora's *Polifemo* (stanza 25), in which she attracts (and arouses) Acis, "venablo de Cúpido" (Cupid's javelin), itself a subversion of Petrarch's "e 'l colpo è di saetta et non di spiedo" (and the blow is from an arrow, not a spear, *Rime sparse* 174.11).

The result of these imitations is, on the one hand, self-canonization into the Petrarchan tradition, coupled with, on the other hand, a dismemberment of Quevedo's own texts. Canonizing commentary, such as that performed by El Brocense on Garcilaso or by Salcedo Coronel on Góngora, is unnecessary, for the sources are neither obscure nor concealed, but both canonical and obvious; the poet will not allow any mistakes concerning the tradition to which he belongs. The predecessors' texts appear undigested, and the bee metaphor for imitation would be inapplicable here, for what Quevedo presents within the poems of his own collection is more like a bouquet or anthology of the Petrarchist tradition. Quevedo's use of this preexisting material is not merely a case of his employing Petrarchan commonplaces, or of the *rifacimento* of poems by obscure Italian or Spanish predecessors (although Quevedo also does both of these things). The borrowings stand out, undigested. If to a degree the poems succeed in creating the impression of a strong poetic voice actively recounting deeply felt emotion, they also underline the conventionality of such an emotion, which can only be expressed secondhand, using time-worn tropes borrowed from other poets. The excesses of the rhetoric make them difficult to read, drawing further attention to their status as products of a rhetorical tradition. Their ludic value is emphasized, and Quevedo is able to show himself a master of the very styles he most disdained.

The process of recapitulation culminates in the most famous of all Quevedo's poems, "Amor constante más allá de la muerte" (Love loyal even beyond death):

> Cerrar podrá mis ojos la postrera
> sombra que me llevare el blanco día,
> y podrá desatar esta alma mía
> hora a su afán ansioso lisonjera;
>   mas no, de esotra parte, en la ribera,
> dejará la memoria, en donde ardía:
> nadar sabe mi llama la agua fría,
> y perder el respeto a ley severa.
>   Alma a quien todo un diós prisión ha sido,
> venas que humor a tanto fuego han dado,
> medulas que han gloriosamente ardido,
>   su cuerpo dejarán, no su cuidado;
> serán ceniza, mas tendrá sentido;
> polvo serán, mas polvo enamorado.
>
> (L31/B472)

That final shadow which will take white day from me may close my eyes, and it may unfasten this soul of mine, flattering at that hour my anxious desire; but it will not, at that other shore, leave the memory in which it burned, for my flame knows how to swim the cold water, and how to lose its respect for harsh laws. A soul which has imprisoned an entire god/which has been entirely imprisoned by a god, veins that have brought humors to so much fire, marrow that has gloriously burned, will leave behind their body but not their care; they will be ash, but it will have feeling; they will be dust, but dust in love.

The poem has been praised as the most beautiful sonnet in Spanish; the vibrant first and last lines, in particular, most exemplify Quevedo's mastery of the rhetoric of presence. Much of its force derives from Quevedo's deployment of stylistic resources, achieving a careful balance of parallels and antitheses which mimics argumentation while moving, rather than persuading, the reader.[27] Yet as Close put it, "The *form* of the logical argument is strong—indeed, it is sustained by the repeated use of verbs in the defiant future indicative . . . the argument, however, is fallacious" (854). Throughout the poem hyperbatons and enjambments separate nouns from adjectives and verbs from their subjects and their objects, so that, as Lázaro Carreter noted, the poem is not so much about triumph over death as about decay. This theme is mirrored in the decomposing grammar of the sonnet's sentences, which contrasts with the highly Latinate syntax of the early poems which, while sometimes difficult, could always be straightened out. The poem begins with a verb in the infinitive, so there is necessarily a hyperbaton. Although the phrase "mis ojos podrán cerrar" (my eyes might close) would make grammatical sense, *ojos*, being plural, can only be the object of the verb *cerrar*, because *podrá* is in the singular. *Sombra*, shadow, seems to be the next best candidate for a subject, but it opens another ambiguity: what then is the subject of the verb in line 2? Is the final shadow taking away the white day, or the other way around? The main verb in line 3 is again *podrá*, so the shadow might again be the subject here, or it might be *hora*, while line 4 might describe *sombra*, *día*, or *alma*. *Sombra* or *alma* might be the subject in line 6 (although Lázaro Carreter believes it to be *hora*, from line 4), leaving memory behind in a place made somewhat obscure by the use of three prepositional phrases (*de* esotra parte, *en* la ribera, *en* donde ardía) in two lines. Line 9 again presents a problem: has the soul imprisoned a god, or vice-versa, or both? The first tercet contains, as Lázaro Carreter characterized it, three subjects in search of a predicate: the principal nouns of lines 9–11 (*alma*, *venas*, and *medulas*) together seem to be the subjects of the verb in line 12, *dejarán*, which is appropriately plural, save that while one may talk of the soul leaving behind the body, veins and marrow are parts of it and certainly do not leave after death.[28] The latter two seem to be the appropriate subjects for the final two *seráns*, but what is one to make of the apparently freestanding "mas tendrá sentido?" It may be a description of the soul, or of the body, or of *ceniza*, or, like "perder el respeto" in line 8, a colloquialism, here meaning simply "it will make sense."

There is a contradiction, then, between the poem's tight rhetorical structure of parallels and oppositions, which suggest an almost dialectical presentation of meaning, and a syntactic structure that challenges any facile interpretation.[29] Yet its position in the collection facilitates its interpretation: many of the tropes come not only from the Petrarchan tradition in general, but from the Lisi cycle itself, where "Cerrar podrá" follows immediately after the sonnet marking the tenth anniversary of his meeting with Lisi, and thus the halfway point in the affair. As we have already seen, the key antithesis of fire and water was the topic of one of the first sonnets in the collection, while the references to flames and ashes prompted Naumann to assert that this poem, like "En crespa tempestad," invokes the myth of the phoenix. Other poems too anticipated themes in "Cerrar podrá" (see Walters, *Francisco de Quevedo*, 124–27). In sonnet 19, the poet wishes that love truly engendered death; then his cold ashes would continue to burn, while his soul would keep the flame and carry it across Lethe, achieving a kind of immortality:

> De esotra parte de la muerte dura,
> vivirán en mi sombra mis cuidados,
> y más allá del Lethe mi memoria.
> Triunfará del olvido tu hermosura;
> mi pura fe y ardiente, de los hados.
> (L19/B460.9–13)[30]

On the far side of harsh death, my cares will live in my shade, and memory will survive beyond the Lethe. Your beauty will triumph over oblivion, my pure and burning faith, over the fates.

The immediately following poem, which marks the sixth anniversary of his falling in love with Lisi, employs much of the crucial vocabulary of "Cerrar podrá" (such as *postrer, desatar*), as the poet combines an anticipation of his poetic immortality with a Boscán-like warning to those reading the poem in hope of instruction about love. Even the poem immediately preceding "Cerrar podrá" anticipates it. There the poet writes of the sweet fire that courses through his veins, proclaiming that this love will grant him immortality: "Llama que a la inmortal vida trasciende, / ni teme con el cuerpo sepultura, / ni el tiempo la marchita ni la ofende" (That flame which transcends to immortal life neither fears interment with the body nor that time will diminish or harm it, L30/B471.12–14). The word *marchita* is important, for it figures prominently in the closing tercet of Garcilaso's *carpe diem* sonnet, "En tanto que de rosa" (23). The connection is a crucial one, for the trope of constancy in love is precisely the antithesis of the notion of endless mutability inherent in the *carpe diem*; as Garcilaso put it, "todo lo mudará la edad ligera / por no hazer mudança en su costumbre" (the light age must change everything so as not to change its habit, 13–14). Indeed, as

Blanco Aguinaga observed (316), "Cerrar podrá," launched in defiance against the "severe law," is also equally directed against the most common expression of that law in the seventeenth century, Góngora's verse, "En tierra, en humo, en poluo, en sombra, en nada" (Into earth, into smoke, into dust, into shade, into nothing, *Sonetos* 151.14), which Quevedo himself echoes in his closing line. The power of this poem, then, resides in part in the gathering of tropes that had been scattered throughout the first half of the Lisi cycle, but also in its upending of the earlier facile correlation of love and death. As Paul Julian Smith concludes, "if Quevedo has become a 'famous lover,' if his monument has achieved immortality, it is not because of the authenticity or originality of his sentiment, but because of the consummate skill of his expression. Others may have loved more sincerely, few have loved so eloquently" (*Quevedo*, 175).

Debts to other poets have also been recognized: while according to Borges the final *agudeza* is taken from Propertius (61), María Rosa Lida de Malkiel has shown very close affinities between Quevedo's sonnet and poems by Herrera and Camoens ("Para las fuentes," 373–75). Yet there is also an important allusion to Garcilaso's third eclogue:

> Y aun no se me figura que me toca
> aqueste officio solamente'n vida,
> mas con la lengua muerta y fria en la boca
> pienso mover la boz a ti devida;
> libre mi alma de su estrecha roca,
> por el Estygio lago conduzida,
> celebrandot'irá, y aquel sonido
> hará parar las aguas del olvido.
>
> (9–16)

Nor does it seem to me that this is my duty only in life; for with my tongue dead and cold in my mouth I plan to move the voice I owe to you. When my soul is freed of its narrow rock, and along the Stygian lake is led, it will go praising you, and that sound will force a halt to the waters of oblivion.

Quevedo uses these lines as the kernel of his own poem: he too will continue, after death, to remember his love for Lisi; the flame crossing the cold water is not just a repetition of the icy fire motif but an assertion of a memory that survives the passage of Lethe. Yet, as Naumann noted, Quevedo also changes the emphasis from the power of the beloved to inspire emotion that endures after death to the lover himself, and from the power of poetry to immortalize to the power of love to endure. Yet that lover will die; whatever the ameliorating effect of the final conceit, his body will decay into ashes and dust. As these semantic fields elsewhere in Quevedo's poetry are associated with death, the *memento mori* is directed not at a resistant love object but at the poet himself.

Garcilaso's lines mediate between Quevedo's poem and its true mythological roots; in them Garcilaso pretends that even after death he will, like Orpheus, continue to celebrate, in the underworld, the beauties of María de Toledo, the vicereine of Naples to whom he dedicates his poem. Although Garcilaso here reduces the myth to a decorative device that allows him to play at being Orpheus to María's Eurydice, the allusion gains depth from Garcilaso's other Orpheus poems; the language in them includes imitations of numerous classical and Italian sources, including Virgil, Ovid, Poliziano, and Sannazaro, which is not surprising in view of Garcilaso's eclectic approach to imitation. But the presentation of Orpheus as ancestral *ur*-poet and *ur*-lover echoes Petrarch, for whom Orpheus is the "ultimate prototype" (Sturm-Maddox, 93) because his dedication to Laura outlived her death. Petrarch often alludes to the myth, and he directly invoked it in *sestina* 332, a poem that—like Quevedo's— deals with the failure of poetry and specifically with the incapacity of love poetry to transcend death:

> Ove è condutto il mio amoroso stile?
> a parlar d'ira, a ragionar di morte.
> U' sono i versi, u' son giunte le rime
> che gentil cor udia pensoso et lieto?
> Ov' è 'l favoleggiar d'amor le notti?
> Or non parl' io né penso altro che pianto.
> (*Rime sparse* 332.13–18)

Where has it been led, my amorous style? to speak of sorrow, to talk about death. Where are the verses, where are the rhymes that a noble heart used to hear thoughtful and glad? Where is that talking of love all the night? Now I speak and think of nothing but weeping.

The word *giunte* in line 15 is important because it shows how, in retrospect, Petrarch sees his poetry once joined together where now it is scattered (*rime sparse*—the title of the collection). Although Petrarch laments that his poetry is unlike Orpheus's in being unable to bring back the beloved, in fact the Greek poet too failed; by looking back at Eurydice he lost her, and his own subsequent death was due to the dismemberment and scattering of his body.

Yet still to be explained is the notable absence from Quevedo's sonnet of the Orpheus myth. Quevedo tropes Petrarch's lines by alluding to them through Garcilaso's bridge text but eliminating any reference to the power of poetry somehow to immortalize and free both the poet and the object of the poetry from the inevitable decay that is the other side of the *carpe diem*. If the poet is to turn to ashes and dust, so too certainly will Lisi, and so too will the pages on which the poem is written. The here-and-now eroticism of the early poems proves to be only an illusion, no defense at all against the fact of the poet's own mortality. It is thus appropriate that Quevedo's crypto-Orphic poem should be entitled "Love faithful even after death" and should begin with references to eyesight (the cause of Orpheus's failure) and an unfastened body (Orpheus torn limb from limb). Yet the death invoked in Quevedo's poem is not Lisi's but his own. Thus this poem marks the beginning of that part of the sonnet cycle which might be called *in morte*, save that Lisi is almost forgotten and the poems are concerned almost exclusively with the poet's own impending death.

As Blanco Aguinaga noted, the majority of the poems that are "approximations" of "Cerrar podrá" come before it, while in those which follow the fire dissolves into ashes (317 n. 33). The next poem ("Éstas son y serán" [These are and will be], L32/B473), for example, repeats some of the key images and words from "Cerrar podrá": the word *postrera* itself, the beach, the notion of love surviving death. But the nature of love, and thus of the poem, has changed. Death is no longer something to be defied, but something to be anticipated as it brings a purification; it is for that reason that these are the final tears he will waste ("perderé," line 3) on Lisi. Instead, he will soar in spirit and burn above the sun, while back on earth his lifeless visage will serve as its own epitaph, proclaiming wordlessly to all travelers, "Ya fue gloria de Amor hacerme guerra" (It was Love's glory to have made war on me, 14). The poem is something of a failed palinode: on the one hand it leads the reader to expect a new attitude to love, but on the other hand its Neoplatonism seems forced and the heroic closing line a poor and derivative

cousin to the final line of "Cerrar podrá." Moreover, the closing has
no organic relationship with the rest of the poem, which lacks a
central image, a single clear thought to animate it, in contrast to the
highly focused poems at the beginning of the collection. Several
phrases recall Garcilaso: for example, there are the otherwise unex-
plained foreign beaches, "playas extranjeras" (5) which suggest the
"tierra ajena" (foreign land) of Garcilaso's third *canción* (16), and
above all the phrase "espíritu desnudo" (naked spirit, 9), used by
Garcilaso in the final line of sonnet 4 and copied, in turn, from Pe-
trarch's *canzone* 37. For Garcilaso, too, the phrase indicated a deter-
mination to love even after death, but it did not suggest a spiritual-
ization of his emotion or a devaluation of physical desire. In its tone
of heroic defiance, Garcilaso's sonnet was closer to "Cerrar podrá";
Quevedo, by contrast, uses the phrase to launch the second half of
the Lisi cycle, which focuses on the consequences of bodily deterio-
ration, anticipated in the closing line of "Cerrar podrá." By doing
so Quevedo corrects both Garcilaso and his own earlier, erotically
suggestive phrase "desnudos de cuerpo" (L7/B448.10). In contrast
to those earlier poems, however, this one seems weak and uncon-
vincing, and it soon gives way to a direct contemplation of decay.
Where the body and its appetites had earlier been positively valo-
rized through eroticism or a "thirst" for Lisi's beauty, these same
words are now turned against the poet, as the forces arrayed against
him eat and suck away his vitality. At the same time, the later poems
lack the tight organization and unifying vision that characterized
the earlier ones, underlining the poet's dissolution and failure.

In the second section of the Lisi cycle Quevedo also continues to
employ the imitative technique that characterized the first part, but
with a change in diction and rhetoric, and with a shift of subtexts
away from Góngora, toward Boscán and the *cancionero*.[31] In the fol-
lowing poem ("¿Qué buscas, porfiado pensamiento" [What do you
seek, obstinate thought?], L33/B474), as Close has shown, Quevedo
addresses thoughts that are absent because they have gone in search
of Lisi; the theme is derived from the *cancionero*, and was employed
by Boscán, Garcilaso, and Herrera. The line "Yo muero, Lisi, preso
y desterrado" (I die, Lisi, imprisoned and in exile, 9) again recalls
Garcilaso's third *canción*, and once more the poem strings together
motifs without a central idea. Similarly, the next poem personifies
death and represents life as a journey:

¡Qué perezosos pies, qué entretenidos
pasos lleva la muerte por mis daños!
El camino me alargan los engaños
y en mí se escandalizan los perdidos.
(L34/B475.1–4)

What indolent feet, what inattentive steps death takes, for my misfortune! Deceits lengthen my journey and the damned are scandalized by me.

These too are *cancionero* themes previously employed by Boscán and Garcilaso, and in this poem Quevedo twice directly quotes Boscán (see Close, 851). What is ingenious about the sonnet, however, is not the worn-out prosopopoeia with which it opens, but the way Quevedo draws out its implications: if death is like a person, then it has feet, it can be lazy or diligent, and its delays are as much the result of whimsy as an intentional prolongation of the poet's suffering. This poem also contains the following lines: "Y por descaminar mis desengaños, / me disimulan la verdad los años" (And in order to dis-walk my disillusion, the years dissemble the truth to me, L34/ B475.6–7). Underlying these words are again the conventional ideas of life as a journey and of life prolonged through hopes that verge on fantasy. To combine them, Quevedo seizes on the word *desengaño* (a key concept in the Spanish Renaissance), borrows the prefix, and then attaches it to *caminar*, creating a neologism that implies living life backward, undoing the process of enlightenment and falling back into deception. As an image it recalls details such as Garcilaso's sonnet 38 ("si me quiero tornar para hüyros, / desmayo, viendo atrás lo que he dexado" [if I wish to turn to flee you, I faint, seeing at my back what I have left behind], 7–8) and sonnet 6 ("si a mudarme a dar un passo pruevo, / allí por los cabellos soy tornado" [if I try to turn to take a step, there by my hair am I pulled back around], 3–4); while the play on the sound *des-* is a technique that again recalls the *cancionero*, it also contributes to the semantic field of decay, destruction, falling apart. It reappears a few poems later in yet another journey sonnet with affinities to Boscán and Garcilaso, "Cargado voy de mí" (I am weighed down with myself, L37/B478; as Fucilla, 200–201 and Close, 851 point out, the opening line is a direct quote from Boscán), in words such as *desdichada, desordenado*, and in the phrase "por no desandar lo caminado." Both "Qué perezosos pies" and "Cargado voy de mí" demonstrate a concern with educating the reader about love, and in this regard they recall earlier poems in the Lisi cycle such as "Tú, que la paz del mar"; however, they are meant to serve as warnings against love, and thus Quevedo copies Boscán's pose: "don't love as I do" translates into "write as I do."

Many of these tendencies come together in the forty-fourth sonnet of the collection:

> En los claustros de l'alma la herida
> yace callada; mas consume, hambrienta,
> la vida, que en mis venas alimenta
> llama por las medulas extendida.
> Bebe el ardor, hidrópica, mi vida,
> que ya, ceniza amante y macilenta,
> cadáver del incendio hermoso, ostenta
> su luz en humo y noche fallecida.
> (L44/B485.1–8)

In the cloisters of my soul the wound lies quiet; but hungrily it consumes the life that in my veins feeds a flame that extends through my marrow. My dropsied life drinks the fire as now, emaciated and loving ash, the remains of the lovely fire, it displays its extinguished light in smoke and darkness.

Close sees the basis for the quatrains in the motif, often employed by Petrarch, of the heart consumed by fire (for instance, *Rime sparse* 202 and 207); one could also note here echoes of "Cerrar podrá," including the word *venas* and the phrases "llama por las medulas extendida" and "ceniza amante." The tone of this poem, however, is completely different, with no sense of triumph over death. The flame is directly opposed to life, which is consumed by a spiritual injury, in its silence inimical to poetry. Here, for the first time since "Cerrar podrá," there is a sense of struggle against overwhelming odds, yet now it ends in defeat: his life, after feeding the flames of love, is reduced to a cadaver and ashes at once sickly and loving, vainly attempting to shine through the smoke and gloom. Most striking of all is the opening line: the cloister of the soul implies a central space but also a void, a wall pierced by arches, emptiness, nothing. Without recourse to verbal echo the poem, as much as "Cerrar podrá," suggests Góngora's "En tierra, en humo, en polvo, en sombra, en nada," stripped of *carpe diem* eroticism and turned in against the poet himself (the very move Sor Juana Inez de la Cruz would make). Caesuras, enjambment, and irregular rhythm stand in the way of smoothly flowing hendecasyllables, and the poet's power seems exhausted as his verse decays into prose. After these quatrains, the tercets seem a disappointment:

> La gente esquivo y me es horror el día;
> dilato en largas voces negro llanto,
> que a sordo mar mi ardiente pena envía.
> A los suspiros di la voz del canto;
> la confusión inunda l'alma mía;
> mi corazón es reino del espanto.
> (L44/B485.9–14)

I flee people and am horrified by the day; I extend in long cries my black weeping, which to a silent sea my burning pain sends. To cries I gave the voice of song; confusion floods my soul; my heart is a realm of terror.

This conclusion contains several of the most formulaic and trite of Petrarchist figures. Yet paradoxically this weakness is also the poem's strength; by ending the poem in this manner, Quevedo achieves several important goals. First, he demonstrates the exhaustion that was only described in the opening of the poem; the effort necessary for the production of the strikingly original opening line, the metaphorical illness sapping his poetic vitality, leaves him unable to continue, so he must resort to an almost schoolboy Petrarchism in order to bring the poem to a conclusion. Second, these lines give us a lesson about how to read Petrarch. The countless imitations of the preceding hundred years, and particularly the mock horrors of Góngora, from the jealous Cyclops to the bee's sting, have inured readers to the true horror of Petrarch's emotion, the confusion in his soul and the anguish in his heart that are complementary to his poetry, the sighs not yet sublimated into song. By placing this Petrarchan imitation at the conclusion of the sonnet, Quevedo tries to get us to read it anew, to defamiliarize it and thus make possible a new reading, and a new rewriting, of Petrarch.[32] The poet is not merely suffering because of sexual frustration, or even because of unrequited love; rather, he suffers because it is in the nature of passion to induce suffering, regardless of reciprocation or consummation. The love he feels for Lisi is a cancer eating him from within, and unlike Boscán's poem collection, this one will not end with a declaration that love is in itself good. By taking this position, Quevedo undermines the amoral presuppositions of Spanish Petrarchist poetry, which had never questioned the lover's right to love. What torments the poet is not Lisi, but a love he himself should have rejected.

In this poem Quevedo also gives the reader a lesson in understanding poetry. Quevedo's use of quotations is worth comparing to Garcilaso's; both use them intertextually, but in different ways. When Garcilaso quoted Petrarch, as in the last line of sonnet 22, "non esservi passato oltra la gonna" (not having penetrated the gown), he initiated a dialogue with the Italian writer, highlighting the foreignness of the quotation by keeping it in Italian. This foreignness, most obviously a matter of language, was also a matter of ideology, and the quotation continued to focus in on its original context, serving as a reminder of Petrarch's virginity. But when Garcilaso worked the quotation syntactically into his own poem, he also appropriated it into his own discourse and ideology. The result was a joke, what Castiglione in his second book called "pronta acutezza," and as the butt of the joke was Petrarch, it is also something of a light-hearted polemic or parody; in Bakhtin's words, it "introduces into that discourse a semantic intention that is directly opposed to the original one" (Problems, 193; see also Todorov, 70).

Quevedo incorporates quotations into his poems much more polyphonically; they appear here and there, disguised in the warp and woof of his own discourse, unmarked but not unrecognizable. The results range from stylization to parody to what Bakhtin (ibid., 197) called "hidden polemic," in which others' words influence the author's speech, forcing it to alter itself. In Quevedo the original voices continue to speak through his text, even to determine what he can say and how he says it. He also speaks, however, through the alien voices: the authentic voice of the Lisi cycle is impossible to distinguish from the incorporated voice of the predecessors, because it largely consists of the amalgamation of those voices. The relation of the tercets (in "En los claustros") to the entire poem is like that of the ekphrastic descriptions of tapestries to Garcilaso's entire third eclogue: they stand out like quotations, seemingly not a part of the poet's own voice, his authentic discourse. In reality, however, both poems are rhetorical constructions, the description of the Tajo circling Toledo no less so than the ekphrases, the quatrains no less than the tercets (see Johnson). To think one encounters the poet any more in the one than in the other is to allow oneself to be deceived, to fall into the trap of looking for (and thinking one has found) poetic presence. Poetry, Quevedo teaches us, is really about absence, about the poet hiding rather than revealing himself through rhetoric.[33]

A few poems later death brings the collection to an end; the only surprising thing about this event is that it is Lisi rather than the poet himself who dies. Her death, coming immediately after the sonnet marking the twenty-second anniversary of the poet's love, is the only biographical "fact" about her in the entire collection, and in the last few sonnets the reader nearly forgets her independent existence as the poems dwell more and more on the poet's state of mind. The same can even be said of the sonnet marking her death, which mostly dwells on the poet's own suffering, closing with an ingenious paradox about his continuing inability to see her: "Celosa debo de tener la suerte, / pues viendo, ¡oh Lisi!, que por verte muero, / con la vida me estorba el poder verte" (I must have a jealous fate, for seeing, oh Lisi, that to see you I die, with life it keeps me from seeing you, L51/B492.12–14). Lisi's death, like everything else in the collection, was determined by the model; as González de Salas himself observed, Quevedo loved her a year longer than Petrarch loved Laura, yet wrote no poems after her death, and the absence of such poems suggests a failure to fulfill the very vows he made in "Cerrar podrá." Where the reader most expects, as in Petrarch and Boscán, a spiritualization of love, the poet provides instead a cheeky epitaph in the form of a madrigal on a sculpted portrait of Lisi. There Quevedo compares the sculpture to nature's own portrait; while both have made Lisi white and cold, the sculptor did a better job, for "vuelta te advierte en piedra ingrata, / de lo que tú te hiciste te retrata" (he proclaims you turned into ungrateful stone, of what you made of yourself, he portrays you, B507.13–14; see Moore). With its levity and its focus on an ingenious comparison of Lisi's character to that of a statue, this poem harks back to the first half of the collection, as well as nodding in the direction of Garcilaso's fifth *canción*. But there is more to it than at first meets the eye: by declaring the sculptural representation superior to nature's, "que no sabe / del jazmín distinguirte y de la rosa" (which knows not how to distinguish you from jasmine or rose, B507.11–12), Quevedo undoes the colorist metaphorization prevalent not only in Garcilaso, Herrera, and Góngora but in the first poems of the Lisi cycle itself. In stressing the appropriateness to Lisi of the statue's cold, white hardness, Quevedo alludes to the discourse about the relative superiority of painting and sculpture which had its Spanish *locus classicus* in Boscán's translation of Castiglione, and which has important ramifications for poetry, identified with painting by Garcilaso, Herrera, and Góngora. Quevedo rejects their easy pictorialism, and as he himself is the true sculptor who made the appropriately harsh portrait of Lisi, he lays claim to the rhetorical virtue of conceptual hardness, a line that stretches (in the vernaculars) from Dante, through Petrarch, to the *cancionero*.

The *Canta sola a Lisi* can be read, then, as an effort once more to rewrite Spanish literary history and to correct its relation to Italy's. To do so, however, Quevedo first has to undo the journey Spanish poetry has taken for nearly 150 years; after Góngora, Quevedo understands that it is not enough merely to present an alternative. The Lisi cycle, containing undigested quotations of earlier poetry within its own highly rhetorical texture, transforms the quotations into synecdoches of their sources and raises readers' awareness that those too were rhetorical. Just as a strong metaphor can alter the perception of reality, so that one never sees the tenor without thinking of the vehicle, so Quevedo would have readers' perceptions of literature changed so that one cannot read the originals without thinking of their dismemberment and incorporation into the Lisi cycle. By doing so Quevedo runs two risks. The first is that of being too representational; in terms of the final madrigal, of reproducing too well the flowers of amatory rhetoric and thus having his *imitatio* mistaken for mimesis. The second danger, however, is of being too hard, with the result that Petrarchism will lose its capacity to generate new amatory texts and that the entire edifice of Spanish Renaissance poetry will be destroyed. Yet this second peril may well have been his goal; as Claudio Guillén put it (amplifying Rafael Alberti), "Sí, Quevedo agota el idioma, se alabanza sobre el lenguaje y construye mundos verbales, pero no para que los hombres mejoren, sino por cuanto la realidad . . . no admite mejoría, cambio, transformación ni alivio" (Yes, Quevedo wears out speech, prides himself on being above language and constructs verbal worlds, not to better humanity, but because reality . . . admits no improvement, change, transformation, or relief, 505).

Thus the destruction of amatory rhetoric is an integral part of Quevedo's larger project, that of representing a human reality that is in its essence both abhorrent and unalterable. In the final section we will examine the relationship of Petrarchism, the Lisi cycle, and Quevedo's so-called metaphysical and burlesque poetry, and assess his success at redirecting, one last time, the perception of literary history.

CONCLUSION: THE END OF PETRARCHISM IN SPAIN

Within the Quevedo canon, the *Canta sola a Lisi* occupies a special place, seemingly distanced from the pessimism of many of his other works. Yet its emphasis on death and decay makes it thematically similar to his metaphysical poetry, while his reliance on the rhetoric of absence results in its having much in common with his burlesque works. In the latter one can see, in a harsher light, the same insistence on the meaninglessness of amatory rhetoric, as well as his attempt to explode its privileged position in the imperial literary system by introducing into the sonnet the un-Petrarchan, but otherwise prevalent discourses of anti-Semitism, misogyny, and homophobia (see Mariscal, 38).

Many critics have observed the community of style between the poems in the second half of the Lisi cycle and Quevedo's so-called metaphysical poetry, including his earlier macrotextual collection, *Heráclito cristiano* (1613).[34] The similarities include the emphasis on thirst, death, and decay, along with the technique of ending or beginning a poem with a striking *agudeza*. Moreover, these coincidences do not exist only because Quevedo consistently wrote similar poetry over the course of twenty years; there are enough specific verbal echoes of the *Heráclito* in the Lisi cycle to show that the poet was imitating and cannibalizing his own earlier poetry as much as he was that of Petrarch, Boscán, Garcilaso, Góngora, and others. The coincidences also exist because the *Heráclito* was Quevedo's first attempt at a reformed Petrarchist poetry collection: that is to say, in the *Heráclito*, as in the final poems of the Lisi cycle, he attempted to use motifs drawn from the Petrarchan tradition toward moral rather than erotic ends. Perhaps the most striking instance is the opening of Psalm 9, "Cuando me vuelvo atrás a ver los años / que han nevado la edad florida mía (when I turn back to see the years that have snowed upon my florid time, B21.1–2). In the context of the *Rime sparse* alone, the topics of life as a journey and youth as the floral season of one's life are merely recognizable; in the context of subsequent Spanish Petrarchist poetry, they are paramount, canonized as such by Garcilaso and Herrera.[35] Yet he also introduces his own variation, the notion of the years falling like snow on the flowers of his youth. On the textual level, the image combines reminiscences of flower petals gently falling on Laura in "Chiare fresche et dolci acque" (*Rime sparse* 126) with Laura "più bianca et più fredda che neve" (whiter and colder than snow) from "Giovene donna" (*Rime sparse* 30.2). The image shifts the focus away from spring and youth to winter and old age, but it also suggests the snow of Quevedo's own cold style blanketing over the poetry of his florid Spanish predecessors so that there will be no trace of it, thus allowing him to return to the original Petrarchan image-hoard. Through techniques such as these, Quevedo attempts to locate his *Heráclito* in the Petrarch/Garcilaso tradition, but the discontinuities are too great, and as an effort to reform that tradition the collection failed. Moreover, such obvious allusions to Petrarch and Garcilaso are relatively rare in the *Heráclito*, composed before the widespread circulation of Góngora's great poems and before the publication of Herrera's *Versos*, at a time when Quevedo perhaps felt less keenly the challenge of reclaiming literary history.

Less often noted than the resemblance of the Lisi cycle to the moral poetry is its approximation to the satirical verse.[36] Many of these poems are constructed using the very techniques of metaphorization associated with Góngora and *culteranismo*. For example, the famous poem about a nose, "Érase un hombre a una nariz pegado" (There once was a man stuck to a nose, B513), consists of a series of metaphorical elaborations of a large nose: it is a sword, a sundial, an elephant lying on its back, a pyramid, and so forth. Only the metonymic eleventh line, "los doces tribus de narices era" (twelve tribes of noses was it), reveals that his true intention was not only to impress the reader with his wit but to impugn someone's (Góngora's?) purity of blood.[37] Similarly, the poem about a woman

in a large dress, "Si eres campana, ¿dónde está el badajo?" (if you
are a bell, where is the clapper, B516), likewise consists of a series
of metaphorical vehicles based on a single tenor: she is a bell, a
pyramid (again), a sugar loaf, a capital, a surgeon's case, and so on
(see Lerner, *Metáfora*). Other poems deal with metaphor in a more
oblique and deconstructive manner:

> Si no duerme su cara con Filena,
> ni con sus dientes come, y su vestido
> las tres partes le hurta a su marido,
> y la cuarta el afeite le cercena;
> 　si entera con él come, y con él cena,
> mas debajo del lecho mal cumplido
> todo su bulto esconde, reducido
> a chapinzanco y moño por almena,
> 　¿por qué te espantas, Fabio, que, abrazado
> a su mujer, la busque y la pregone,
> si, desnuda, se halla descasado?
> 　Si cuentas por mujer lo que compone
> a la mujer, no acuestes a tu lado
> la mujer, sino el fardo que se pone.
>
> 　　　　　　　　　　　　　(B522)

If Filena does not sleep with her face, nor with her teeth eat, and if
her clothing robs three-fourths of her from her husband while the rest
her makeup shears away, and if she eats whole with him and with
him dines, but beneath the unconsummated bed all her bulk is hid-
den, reduced to a shoe heel with a wig for a roof, why does it frighten
you, Fabio, that embracing his wife, he looks and calls for her if, when
she is naked, he finds himself unmarried? If you count as woman
what woman is made of, don't lay a woman next to you, but instead
the bundles that she wears.

One could read this sonnet as the intersection of two common
themes in Quevedo's satirical poetry: on the one hand, derision of
women who wear too much makeup, which, when removed, reveals
ugliness (see Mas, 34–41); and on the other, a critique of marriage
wherein husbands are generally victims of their wives' deceptions
(Mas, 85–124). Filena's disappearance, however, also turns this into
a poem about absence, and features such as the Latinate names, the
hyperbatons, and the genre itself suggest that it be read in terms of
the Petrarchan tradition. What causes her husband to seek and call
out to her is that when her ornaments—her clothes and her cosmet-

ics—are removed, he finds neither a naked beauty, as he expects, nor an ugly woman, as the reader of Quevedo's other poems on the same theme would expect, but instead nothing at all. The very terms used here to describe Filena's behavior, painting her face and over-dressing, resonate in the critical debate over lyric poetry, for they were also used, metaphorically, by the opponents of a style they found excessive, ornate, even effeminate. When Filena removes her adornments, she is revealed as the ultimate figure of absence, leaving her husband unmarried and frustrated, reduced to the status of a Petrarchan lover. Like Góngora's poetry she is all signifier and no signified, all *verba* and no *res*. By satirizing these practices, Quevedo seeks to rescue lyric poetry from the feminized realm of decorative poets to the sinewy world of masculine action and empire.

The need to redeem poetry from mere verbal beauty is a constant in much of Quevedo's lyric, and his violent anti-Petrarchism often takes the form of de-idealization of language, of love, and of the body. In the Lisi cycle, it was expressed, as we have seen, through a parodic subversion that forced the reader to question the very nature of love poetry. In other poems, the attack is much more direct as Quevedo violates the stylistic and thematic registers associated with the sonnet. Petrarchism's *ur*-myth is upended when Apollo, chasing Daphne, is reminded that Danae raised her skirt for a shower of gold, and advised that "si la quieres gozar, paga y no alumbres" (if you want to enjoy her, pay up instead of shining, B536.4).[38] All women become whores, good for nothing but sex in return for pay ("¡Oh barata y alegre putería!" [Oh cheap and delightful whoredom!]; see Mas, 30–31, 134–36); poems about prostitution and ugliness lead to poems in which the body, tenor of the most famous Petrarchan metaphors, is revealed in all its corporality (see Read). There are sonnets about eating food and sonnets about worms eating dead bodies; sonnets about farts and assholes, sonnets about sodomy. Every time Quevedo uses words like *ojo de culo* and *pedo, puto* and *coño*, he transgresses the rules of *sprezzatura* and decorum and soils the genre of Castiglione, Boscán, and Garcilaso. This technique is especially clear in a poem such as "Este cíclope, no sicilïano" (This Cyclops, not Sicilian, B832), which begins with ten lines of Gongorine stylistic devices and mediates through "esta cima del vicio y del insulto" (this mountaintop of vice and insult, 11) to a conclusion, "éste, en quien hoy los pedos son sirenas, / éste es el culo, en Góngora y en culto, / que un bujarrón le conociera apenas" (this one, in whom today farts are sirens, this is the asshole, in Góngora and in cultish, which even a Sodomite would scarcely recognize, 12–14). What is shocking here is the quick transition from *cultismos* to obscenities. Yet the theme of homosexuality (an Italian vice; see Mas, 185) in the final line resonates back through the entire poem, in the various allusions to Italy and in the metaphorical disguising of the anus, suggesting that Góngora too obscures the same vice. This attribution of concealed homosexuality has implications on both the biographical level, as an insult, and the rhetorical, as a denigration of Góngora's style (recall Morales's complaints about effeminate men). The violation of the decorum is only more obvious here because of the context of the *cultismos*, but it is present whenever obscene language was used in a sonnet, the privileged genre of Petrarchism and of imperial culture.[39] Moreover these violations are not merely lexical; they are ideological as well, for however prevalent the social attitudes they represent may have been, they had no place in the Petrarchist tradition.

Although both Góngora and Quevedo satirized the court in verse, they were also ambitious courtiers who used their fame as poets to advance their careers (the former rising to the post of honorary royal chaplain to Philip III, the latter enjoying a diplomatic career until the fall of his patron, the duke of Osuna, in 1621). They also experienced a similar reversal of fortune, their ultimate *desengaño* motivated in part by personal poverty and disappointment. As Bloom expressed it (*Breaking*, 13), the struggle to rewrite one's predecessors is parallel to the quest for wealth, for professional advancement, and for sexual fulfillment; all four, directly or indirectly, are the objects of Góngora's and Quevedo's poetic desire. Petrarchism, however, privileges the relationship of eros with poetry, expressing other desires through metonymy. Thus we return to the quotation from Kerrigan and Braden at the end of the introduction, equating sex and poetry: "Artistic and sexual ambitions are interchangeable; they can be substituted for each other in the course of reaching countless bargains. A solitude stocked with images may be preferable to having an amorous partner. The value of postponement, hedonistic as well as moral, is considerable" (188). By throwing out the Petrarchan sexual myth, Quevedo throws out with it the particular historical form of the Renaissance search for priority.

From Boscán's profeminist writing to Herrera's love for the countess of Gelves, the legitimacy of lyric love, on its own terms, went unquestioned because it was part and parcel of a system of legitimization that included classical and Italian literature, Spanish culture, and even the state. If implicit in the Petrarchan pose there was a plea for fulfillment, autonomy, and priority, it was also quite clear that these desires could only be attained within the privileged grounds of the poems themselves. Góngora tested the system as far as it would go, but his intention was not to destroy it. Quevedo does take that step, calling into question all forms of legitimacy, sexual, literary, cultural, and political (see on this point McCallum and Zahareas); and by merging Petrarchism and the burlesque he tosses out one of the few vehicles for establishing one's legitimacy as a lover and as a poet. By making the Petrarchan erotic dream seem illegitimate, he dismisses other fantasies as well. The sonnet about verbal and mineral wealth, "Tú, que la paz del mar" (L4/B445), is particularly instructive in this regard: read with the proper irony, it teaches that words do not create wealth, only the blood and labor of the mines do, and Spain's gold now comes from abroad, not from the sands of the Tajo. Quevedo is not opposed to the Spanish empire per se, but he wants it seen for what it is. Finally, by undermining the Petrarchan sonnet, Quevedo also calls off the cultural competition with Italy, which in the age of Philip IV he deems irrelevant. Read symbolically, the split between Quevedo's amorous sonnets and his satirical ones is neither as great nor as inexplicable as it might seem: his women are garrulous because of the logorrhea with which the muse infected Góngora (and, truth be told, Quevedo himself); they are wanton because the muse has given herself to every male poet for 150 years: to Encina, to Boscán, to Garcilaso, to Herrera, even to celibate churchmen like Fray Luis de León and to rhetorical pederasts like Góngora. But Lisi is cold and hard because the muse is to him always diamondlike and stony, because language always resists, and because poetry is always a struggle.

Quevedo's moral reading of Petrarch is not necessarily superior to previous ones, and if it seems superior, that is only because its very belatedness allows it to subsume the linguistic, thematic, generic, and stylistic readings of his predecessors. At the same time Quevedo uses his moral deconstruction of Petrarch to invalidate all of those previous readings. In contrast to Góngora, whose styliza-tion was inclusive, Quevedo's parody highlights difference and breaks down the tradition into its components. He thus challenges the validity of a stylizing metalepsis; in contrast to Garcilaso and Góngora, he is come not to fulfill the Petrarchan tradition but to destroy it. His own aim is to effect a retrospective clinamen stronger than Góngora's metalepsis, which would allow the pretense of a di-rect return to the source. In his more mundane moments, this desire takes the form of an attempt to reclaim Petrarch and Garcilaso as his own, rather than as Góngora's, predecessors, by rewriting literary history through activities such as editing the poetry of Fray Luis de León. On a more fantastic level, the intention is to replace Boscán, Garcilaso, Herrera, and Góngora and to set himself up at the head of the Spanish Petrarchist tradition (hence perhaps the unseemly obsession in the Lisi cycle with the second-rate Boscán). The fantasy can be seen in a satire, written after purchasing the house where Góngora lived, in order to evict him:

> Y págalo Quevedo
> porque compró la casa en que vivías,
> molde de hacer arpías;
> y me ha certificado el pobre cojo
> que de tu habitación quedó de modo
> la casa y barrio todo,
> hediendo a Polifemos estantíos,
> coturnos tenebrosos y sombríos,
> y con tufo tan vil de *Soledades,*
> que para perfumarla
> y desengongorarla
> de vapores tan crasos,
> quemó como pastillas Garcilasos:
> pues era con tu vaho el aposento
> *sombra del sol y tósigo del viento.*
> (B841.121–35)

Quevedo pays for it because he bought the house in which you lived, that mold for making harpies; the poor lame man has certified to me that your bedroom, like the house and the entire neighborhood, reeked of stagnant Polifemos, dark and shadowy buskins, and with such vile fumes of the *Soledades,* that to perfume it and degongorize it of such crass vapors he burned pills of Garcilasos: for the room was, with your breath, *a shadow of the sun and a poison for the wind.*

Burning Garcilaso like incense may produce a better perfume than Góngora's feet and breath, but it also sacrifices and destroys him, leaving a direct conduit from the great Italian father to this the last of his orphans. This is how Quevedo would have written himself into literary history; whether he achieved it is a different question, to which one can only give a historically conditioned answer. Different ages have held different evaluations of Góngora's, Quevedo's, and even Garcilaso's relative stature. Any judgment rendered on Bloom's strategies is ultimately dependent on the historical process of canon formation; for indeed, the Bloomean paradigms are in the end only models for trying to describe and understand the hermeneutically circular process of canonization. Aesthetic and historical evaluation are ultimately the same; canonized poets are read as strong, because strong poets constitute the canon. To an amazing degree, Spanish Renaissance poets succeeded in writing themselves into the canon as they saw fit, such that what we think of them today is what they wanted us to think; this determination is the sign of their strength. This very strength, however, can interfere with their being read as anything but our own poetic fathers. Only with conscious effort can we displace ourselves to see them again, like Herrera, as orphans excluded from the shade of the laurel tree. Only then can we appreciate the enormous hermeneutic freedom derived from their status as orphans, to sidestep proximate models and to use the cultural belatedness of the Renaissance humanists as a defense against poetic belatedness vis à vis their most immediate predecessors.

1. Notes

1. Thus Bembo's literary theory is at odds with his reputation as a Neo-platonist, which is based on the love theory of his 1505 dialogue *Gli Asolani*, and on the speech "he" gives in book 4 of Castiglione's *Cortegiano*.

2. On the role of Bembo's letter to Pico in the evolution of imitation theory, see Santangelo; Greene, 171–77; and Cruz, *Imitación*, 24–26. Bembo's rejection of a metaphysical, inspirational theory of poetry approximates twentieth-century hermeneutic and phenomenological approaches that emphasize reading and writing; see Kennedy, 1–2, 16–18, particularly his references to Gadamer and Ingarden.

3. Bembo's arguments here are an echo of the trope of the *translatio studii*, which was to become crucial for the Renaissance outside Italy; see the section below on "Spanish Alterity and the Language of Empire."

4. Thus to Ferguson the idea of a "renaissance," in contrast to other period concepts such as both "antiquity" and "middle ages," is rooted in the cultural self-consciousness that existed at the time. By deriving our characterization of the "Renaissance" from the self-concept of the humanists, the term can be historicized, freed on the one hand from nineteenth-century Burckhardtian associations, and distinguished, on the other, from our own set of period concepts; see Waller, 5–8; also Kerrigan and Braden, 7: "The movement that counts, what we now call humanism, takes decisive form under Petrarch's inspiration and influence in the fourteenth century and is accompanied from the first with propaganda about its historic momentousness."

5. To Curtius, the creation of new tropes such as these can signal a major historical transition, for tropes "reflect the sequence of psychological periods. But in all poetical topoi the style of expression is historically determined. Now there are also topoi which are wanting throughout Antiquity down to the Augustan Age. . . . They have a twofold interest. First, as regards literary biology, we can observe in them the *genesis of new topoi*. Thus our knowledge of the genetics of the formal elements of literature is widened. Secondly, these topoi are indications of a changed psychological state; indications which are comprehensible in no other way" (82). Thus just as ancient tropes have a history that can be traced, so too do modern tropes such as the tripartite model of history, the idea of a Renaissance, the pairing of Petrarch and Boccaccio (as models of learning or of ignorance), and many

other expressions used by the humanists; and the development of these new tropes is indicative of the psychological changes that characterize period boundaries.

6. For a typology of Renaissance tropes that describe "following," transformative imitation, and emulation, along with their classical sources, see Pigman.

7. For the sake of consistency all quotations from Petrarch's *Familiares* (English: *Letters on Familiar Matters*) are taken from the translation by Aldo Bernardo.

8. For a nuanced Bloomean approach to Petrarch's poetry that takes as its point of departure his theory of history, see Waller.

9. Curtius's chief concern here is to reject Burkhardtian and essentialist notions of the renaissance as a "real" event in history (5–6), rather than as a change in perception expressed through certain tropes. To Curtius, the true revival of Latin literature occurred in twelfth-century France (53–54, 255), and Spain had hardly any share in this movement (385–87); as a consequence, its development of a vernacular literature lagged considerably behind the French. On the other hand, Spain's continuing medievalism contributed to the strength of those features of the Baroque which entailed a revival of medieval culture (on this point see Díaz y Díaz). Curtius calls this phenomenon the cultural "belatedness" of Spain (541–43).

10. Curtius locates the origin of this notion in Ecclesiasticus 10:8, "sovereignty passes from nation to nation on account of injustice and insolence and wealth." In the West, this passage was first used to explain the *translatio imperii*, the rise and fall of empires and the shifts in political domination; later, it became a justification for the legitimacy of the Carolingian empire (29). Yet the movement that granted legitimacy to the Carolingians would not do very much for sixteenth-century Frenchmen or Spaniards claiming to be the true heirs of Rome; thus, like the Italian humanists shifting the date of the "renaissance," they constantly postpone the date of the transfer and argue that the events of their own day constitute the true movement of culture away from Italy.

11. These statements in praise of Santillana are clearly a form of panegyric; while Curtius warns us against taking such tropes as literal statements of fact or true sentiment, they do reflect a predisposition to believe that culture is in need of revival, that warriors are insufficiently dedicated to letters, etc.

12. Born Antonio Martínez de Calar y Jarava into a middle-class family in the village of Lebrija (the ancient Nebrissa Veneria), forty-five miles south of Seville, Nebrija studied at Salamanca and then at the Spanish college in Bologna, where he spent a decade. Upon his return to Spain he occupied a number of academic posts and also served powerful members of the church hierarchy and the nobility. In 1481 he published a Latin textbook, the *Introductiones latinae* and, at the request of the queen, prepared a Spanish translation (published about 1486); during the late 1480s and 1490s he wrote and published his Latin–Spanish dictionaries, his Spanish grammar, and other

works. In later years he participated in the preparation of the polyglot Bible and in 1514 was awarded a special chair of rhetoric at the new University of Alcalá. Along with his philological accomplishments, Nebrija was instrumental in bringing the printing press to Salamanca: the second book published in the city was his *Introductiones,* and he may also have directed the press, a situation necessarily covert because its mercantile associations would have been incompatible with a university position. Both his son and his grandson became printers, however, and most of the incunables published in Salamanca were either by Nebrija or by authors connected to his circle; he was also the first author to claim a copyright in Spain. On his connections to the press see Haebler; Cuesta Gutiérrez. Information on Nebrija's life, drawn primarily from autobiographical assertions in the prologues to his works, can be found in the Quilis edition of the *Gramática,* 9–18, from which I also quote.

13. On the implicit positing of a *medium aevum* during this fourteen-hundred-year gap, and its connection to the historical theories of the Italian humanists, see Guerrero Ramos.

14. Generally, however, Nebrija relies not so much on literary usage as on aristocratic norms, giving the grammar, in spite of the prescriptive bias of the prologue, a decidedly descriptive slant (see Zamora).

15. Encina was born in or near Salamanca in 1468, and was probably of *converso* origin. His father was a shoemaker, but the poet received a university education. He may have studied with Nebrija; the latter alludes in the grammar to a friend writing an art of poetry (see Quilis), while Encina himself refers admiringly to Nebrija, and the 1496 volume is one of several books by members of Nebrija's circle published in Salamanca during those years (and by the same press as had printed Nebrija's grammar). From 1486 Encina sang with the cathedral choir and served as a page to Gutierre Alvarez de Toledo, chancellor of the university and brother of Fadrique, the second duke of Alba, and in 1492 Encina passed into the latter's service as master of ceremonies, a sort of poet, composer, and dramatist in residence. Yet this post seems to have proved frustrating, for while it allowed him to associate with the highest levels of the aristocracy, he had become in essence a glorified servant (see Andrews and, most recently, Yarbro-Bejarano and ter Horst, "The Duke and Duchess"). In 1498 he failed to obtain the post of choirmaster at Salamanca, and shortly thereafter left Spain for Rome, where Alexander VI, Julius II, and Leo X successively were his patrons. Up to 1523 Encina divided his time between Rome and Malaga, where he was officially archdeacon until 1519. In that year, he was appointed prior of the cathedral chapter at León and was ordained a priest. He took up residence at León in 1523, and died there in 1529 or 1530.

16. A modern edition of the "Arte" can be found in volume 1 of the *Obras completas,* from which I cite; Rambaldo's introduction contains biographical information about the poet and a useful summary of earlier scholarship. Among the studies of the treatise, that of Andrews remains remarkable for its assessment of the work in terms of Encina's psychological and

244 Notes to Pages 26–35

social preoccupations; in many ways Andrews's book launched modern Encina scholarship. See also Shepard, 19–22; López Estrada; and the two studies by Clarke, which emphasize the prosodic aspects of the work.

17. Andrews comments extensively on this passage, noting how the false modesty of "mi flaco saber" results in a strong dissociation of word from intent (77–80).

18. The attempt to appropriate ancient authors such as Seneca and Quintilian to the national tradition as Spaniards was common in the fifteenth century; see Di Camillo, 124 and Weiss, 12, 233.

19. Andrews sees the notion of posthumous fame as something of an obsession for Encina, and differentiates it from Nebrija's messianic remarks (172 n. 9). Yet surely the concern with personal fame is related both to the worry about the nation's cultural future and to Encina's desire for fame in his own lifetime.

20. Etymologically *copla* means "couplet"; the rule of four is an echo of the earlier couplets of two sixteen-syllable lines, which were subsequently divided into their component hemistichs.

21. López Estrada connects Encina's concern with "galas" with the medieval, sound-oriented poetic tradition (156–57 and 161–62); to Martí (37, 87), this emphasis tied Encina to the medieval poetic tradition and disqualified the "Arte" from being a true Renaissance *Ars*.

22. On the theoretical significance of the concept of "secondary" writers, see *Il «minore»*, particularly the essays by Macrí and Stella.

23. Various points of view on Bloom's relevance to the study of Renaissance imitation may be found in Javitch, "Imitations of Imitations," 216–17; Colombí-Monguió, 138–39; and most recently Mariscal, 107.

24. These categories are not dissimilar to Pigman's notions of "following" and "dissimulative" imitation, and (as Bakhtin himself concedes) while the theoretical distinctions are clear, differentiating between parody, stylization, and imitation in the concrete historical examples of particular texts is far more difficult and partly a matter of judgment on the reader's part. On parody see, in addition to Bakhtin and Hutcheon, Todorov, 68–74; O. M. Freidenberg, "The Origin of Parody," in *Semiotics and Structuralism* [1976], 269–83; Bromwich; and, in a Spanish context, Cruz, *Imitación*, 46–48; and Sánchez Robayna.

25. As Bloom himself expressed it, his "chief purpose is necessarily to present one reader's critical vision, in the context both of the criticism and poetry of his own generation. . . . A theory of poetry that presents itself as a severe poem, reliant upon aphorism, apothegm, and a quite personal (though thoroughly traditional) mythic pattern, still may be judged, and may ask to be judged, as an argument" (*Anxiety*, 12–13). He also notes the crucial relationship between revisionary misreadings and the construction of the canon (*Map*, 35–37). See also Lentricchia: "No theorist writing in the United States today has succeeded, as Bloom has, in returning poetry to history" (342).

26. See Alonso, *Poesía española*, 19–42; and Paul Julian Smith, *Quevedo*, 5–11.

27. The history of Spanish Petrarchism is treated by Manero Sorolla in a useful but brief chapter consisting mostly of a listing of poets, major and minor, belonging to the various generations, with pertinent bibliography (83–102).

28. Even-Zohar's model also accommodates Raymond Williams's categories of dominant, emergent, and residual elements in a culture (121–27), profitably used by Mariscal in his discussion of Petrarchism (37, 110).

2. POETIC THEORY IN THE REIGN OF CHARLES V: CASTIGLIONE AND THE SPANISH RENAISSANCE

1. An exception to this rule is Javitch, who connects the courtly aesthetization of the self promoted in Castiglione's book with an openness to lyric poetry among the Tudor aristocracy. "The poet's manipulations of language or of perspective are but part of a larger characteristic of poetry that would be preeminently attractive to courtly society: its playfulness. The milieu as well as the ideal individual depicted in the *Cortegiano* are constantly inclined to play" (*Poetry*, 88). While his thesis is also applicable to Spain in a general way, here we are concerned with how *Il libro del Cortegiano*, read in a Spanish context, promoted the specific change in poetic genres that occurred at this time, under the very leadership of its Spanish translators, and how it otherwise influenced the course of Spanish poetry and poetic theory. See also Darst, *Juan Boscán*, 25–26.

2. Boscán's translation is the object of Morreale's careful analysis. Hers is, however, as she admits (13), a study of the words used by Boscán to express other words in Castiglione's text, of the ways in which Boscán represented the minutiae of Italian court life, of the proportion of Latinisms in each version, etc. My own discussion, while drawing on Morreale's contributions, is not so much concerned with words per se as with the reception of Castiglione's ideas. Most quotations are taken from Boscán's translation because that is the version that Renaissance Spaniards would most likely have read, and because it documents Boscán's and Garcilaso's interpretation of Castiglione; where necessary, the Italian text is also quoted and cited by book and chapter. Needless to say, Boscán and Garcilaso themselves read the Italian original, and they would not have been alone in doing so.

3. On Castiglione's cyclical theory of language see Wayne Rebhorn, "The Enduring Word," in Hanning and Rosand, 69–90.

4. On the Italian *questione della lingua* see Hall, Mazzacurati; and on its relevance to Spain, see Terracini, *Lingua come problema*.

5. See also Gemmingen who, though recognizing that the linguistic discussion proper refers to the Italian *questione*, sees the standards as applicable elsewhere, particularly in the fostering of decorum; Kinney, who asserts that the book teaches "not the facts that constitute knowledge, but the opinions and gestures that compose *performance*" (91); and Javitch, *Poetry*.

6. Such synesthesia, albeit more limited in scope, is already implicit in Castiglione's principal subtexts; see Eduardo Saccone, *"Grazia, Sprezzatura, Affetazione* in the *Courtier"* (in Hanning and Rosand, 45–67), who notes that for Cicero and Quintilian, not showing effort is a desirable quality in both oratory and painting, if not in all areas of life.

7. See Morreale, 187; and on the ethical ambivalence *otium* acquired in the Renaissance, see Vickers, "Leisure."

8. This further step is taken by Juan de Valdés in the *Diálogo de la lengua,* when he comments that "la gentileza del metro castellano consiste en que de tal manera sea metro que parezca prosa, y que lo que se scrive se dize como se diría en prosa" (the excellence of Spanish verse consists in its being verse that resembles prose, so that what is written is said as if it were prose, 164). Valdés was strongly influenced by Castiglione (see Terracini, *Lingua come problema,* 145–48 and 210–11 n. 107); his dialogue, written ca. 1535, is extremely important for gauging Spanish linguistic and literary attitudes at the height of Charles's reign. Bibliography on Valdés relevant to the present study includes Amado Alonso; Asensio, "La lengua"; and above all Lore Terracini's essays gathered in *Lingua come problema,* particularly "Tradizione illustre," originally published in 1964. More recently Ana Vian Herrero uses a formalist approach to elucidate the ideological and linguistic ramifications of the shifting alliances among the speakers.

9. As Guidi has shown ("Reformulations"), Castiglione's praise of the Spanish became more accentuated as it became clear that Charles rather than Francis I would be elected emperor, and in the final redaction of the *Cortegiano,* done in Spain after Castiglione's arrival as papal nuncio.

10. Such a synthesis is not unlike the one Du Bellay makes when appropriating Sperone Speroni's *Dialogo delle lingue;* see Navarrete, "Strategies of Appropriation."

11. As Morreale noted (170–71), when abstract concepts threaten to monopolize his attention for too long, Castiglione stops, as if to take leave of a topic that is not appropriate for the work. Courtiership, grace, and *sprezzatura* all exclude an exposition that is uniform and doctrinal, whence the variety of phraseology and syntax in the *Cortegiano.* The *Cortegiano* thus was the stimulus that caused Boscán to give us one of the richest and most stylistically varied works of the sixteenth century; a new breadth of perspectives and a richness of expression never before equaled are made available here for personal description and moral praise.

12. *Traducir,* the modern word for translation, was then a relative neologism in Spanish; the more traditional term had indeed been *romancear,* while Nebrija had preferred another Latinism, *trasladar.*

13. See Margaret Ferguson, who analyzes the image of theft in Du Bellay's *Deffence,* concluding that it betrays an ambivalent attitude about imitation as a violation (46–50).

14. Boscán limits his critique of contemporary literature to a general rejection of most translations; more important for him is the feminist question. All possible criticism of the book's subject matter is phrased in terms

of a misogynistic critique of its appropriateness for women, and then deflated by appealing to the example of Doña Gerónima herself. With a different set of characters, these rhetorical strategies—the assertions that Garcilaso sent him the book and that Doña Gerónima encouraged him to persevere, and the attempt to ingratiate himself with the dedicatee through praise of women's intellectual capabilities—were to reappear nine years later in the preface to Boscán's poetry.

15. Diego Hurtado de Mendoza, in his own right a noted poet in both traditional and Italian verse forms and a descendant of Santillana, was a son of the count of Tendilla, governor of Granada, and served Charles V as ambassador to Rome and Venice.

16. Valdés himself recommended Garcilaso as an authority on courtiership and thus on language, commenting, "más quisiera satisfazer a Garcilasso de la Vega, con otros dos cavalleros de la corte del emperador que yo conozco" (I would rather satisfy Garcilaso de la Vega, along with two other gentlemen from the emperor's court whom I know, 94); see Elias Rivers, "L'humanisme linguistique."

17. A Castiglionian precedent for this type of imputation exists in the papal ambassador's polemic against Juan de Valdés's brother Alfonso, which included references to his Jewish descent; see Terracini, *Lingua come problema*, 211.

18. The identification of the new verse forms with the emperor was to have long-term implications that outlived Boscán and Garcilaso, as Petrarchist poetry became the semiofficial lyric poetry of the Spanish monarchy; see chapters 4 and 5, below. Yet the metonymic association between poetry and empire in Spain differs from its position in England, where the situation of courtiers vying for favor from a "virgin queen" led to a metaphorical association between Elizabeth and Laura, and gave a different political edge to the function of Petrarchist lyric (see Parker, 61–66; Dasenbrock, 70–81).

19. As Celt has argued, that Boscán had fully mastered these nuances is itself open to question; this however would only have made the hendecasyllable seem to him all the more prosaic.

20. See, for example, Marasso Rocca; although, as Fucilla noted, even if Boscán had not in 1526 had his memorable conversation with Navagero in Granada, within a few years the Italian school would have triumphed in Spain (1). See also Celt (83) for a discussion of other ways Boscán has been represented in literary histories.

21. There is in fact a brief verse dedication, "¿A quién daré mis amorosos versos?" at the beginning of book 1 (though written in hendecasyllables), of no theoretical interest. Perhaps the convention of some kind of dedicatory preface at the beginning was too much for Boscán to overcome.

22. As Armisén commented, a brief mention of Boscán's letter has come to be an unavoidable commonplace and has given rise to conclusions that are worth reconsidering (359); he proceeds to perform a step-by-step rhetorical analysis of the preface and to consider its possible relationship to San-

tillana's letter (359–78). In addition to the studies already cited, see also Rivers's brief "Nota sobre Bernardo Tasso" and Manero Sorolla, 73–77.

3. BOSCÁN, GARCILASO, AND THE CODES
OF EROTIC POETRY

1. The question of Boscán's knowledge of his predecessors' work has not been settled. Most recently, Armisén has argued that Boscán may have been familiar with the fifteenth-century marqués de Santillana's prose prologue, if not with his translations and imitations of Petrarch (359–62, 366). In any case, in both the letter and the poetry Boscán presents himself as the first Spanish Petrarchist.

2. Thus it is not surprising that Menéndez y Pelayo and Lapesa, both of whom cite the Knapp edition, had nothing to say about the collection as a whole, while Crawford's attempts to date specific sonnets in the collection, and to correlate them on a biographical basis with *coplas* from the first book, are antithetical to the notion of a macrotext and disregard the poet's own statement that he ceased writing *coplas* when he began writing hendecasyllabic poetry. Only Parducci, though apparently unfamiliar with the early editions, recognized that certain *canciones* belong with certain sonnets (35), and analyzed them as two parallel collections.

3. Even this edition confuses the issue by sequentially numbering the poems beginning with the first poem of book 1; thus, the first poem of book 2 is numbered "XXIX" (the 1543 edition had no numbering). To facilitate discussion of book 2 and also reference to the Riquer edition, from which I generally quote, I will first refer to poems by their order in book 2 and then by their number in the 1957 edition; thus, "sonnet 1 (XXIX)," etc.

4. Since 1957 there have been several studies of Boscán's poetry, all of which in some way take into account its macrotextual status. See especially Darst, *Juan Boscán*, who at first declares the collection a unified whole, but then separately discusses the sonnets and the *canciones*; Armisén, whose analysis, using Lotman's *Structure of the Artistic Text* as a theoretical base, is thorough; and Cruz, *Imitación*, who concentrates on the *canciones* and on intertextual connections to Petrarch and Bembo.

5. As Menéndez y Pelayo aptly put it, Boscán's sonnets are, if ingenious, metaphysical and abstract (281). Darst agrees that an "exemplificative impetus" lies behind the decision to avoid the "personal and idiosyncratic" (*Juan Boscán*, 54); this feature connects Boscán to that fifteenth-century Petrarchism discussed by both Farinelli and Rico, in which love remained an abstraction and specific Petrarchan details were incorporated, as *topoi*, in poems written in traditional Spanish genres. But Boscán's use of hendecasyllabic sonnets and *canciones* and their combination into a collection gives his poetry an amplitude that differentiates him from those predecessors.

6. In other poems, of course, Petrarch presents himself writing his poetry, while Boscán also employs words such as *oíd* which suggest an oral status.

7. Although poets could have expressed Petrarchist love in the tradi-

tional lyric genres, those working in the older formal system were often bound by its thematic constraints as well. See for example Jones's discussions of Encina's love poetry (in *The Golden Age* and "Juan del Encina"); to him, the love in the traditional Spanish lyric differed from Petrarchan love in several crucial ways, and he credits this difference with Encina's imperviousness to formal Italian influences on his love lyrics, even as his dramatic and pastoral works reflect marked Italian tendencies. In passing, he remarks that Spanish literature had to wait until Boscán and Garcilaso for poets who were receptive to the Petrarchan conception of love, and this in turn facilitated their receptivity to the formal and aesthetic aspects of the Italian love lyric.

8. On similar problems in the writer–audience relationship in Petrarch, see Kennedy, 22–41.

9. Armisén comes to a similar conclusion, arguing that there are three implied "moments" in each poem—the time of the love experience, that of the poem's composition, and that of its reading (12)—but he fails to note a disjunction between the implied poet-lover and the actual poet, who has more in common with the reader. This irony, as Genot notes (40), while much more typical of narrative than of lyric poetry, is also quintessentially Petrarchan; Petrarch himself wrote of "mio primo giovenile errore, / quand' era in parte altr' uom da quel ch' i' sono" (my first youthful error, when I was in part another man from what I am now, *Rime sparse*, 1.3–4). On the connection between narrativity and macrotextuality see Navarrete, "Boiardo's *Pastorali*," 37–38.

10. See Genot: 'L'*ego* lirico si esprime con e nel presente, e magari con e in una successione di presenti" (The lyric *I* expresses itself with and in the present, and at best with and in a succession of presents, 44).

11. To Morreale, these lines are an example of Boscán's inadequate command of poetic language (275), while Armisén connects this and all his difficulties with narration to the inexpressibility *topos* (9–19), and Egido to a poetics of silence (97–98). Cruz also discusses the poem in terms of the preceding sonnets and of the Petrarchan paradigm, noting that the extended form of the *canción* allows him to amplify and invert the game in Petrarch (*Imitación*, 54).

12. In spite of the opening lines, the opening stanza conjures up a desolate landscape to which the poet is exiled, repeatedly emphasizing his loneliness. This preoccupation with abstract suffering in place of concrete physical description has led critics such as Menéndez y Pelayo (286–87) and Morreale (256–60) to see in the poem a persistence of *cancionero* aesthetics, and indeed the subsequent stanzas reprise some of the stylistic features of *cancionero* poetry, including the repetition of words such as "apartarme / de quien jamás osé pensar partirme" (to separate myself from her from whom I never dared to think of separating myself; 15–16) and "conviene consolarme" (it is convenient to console myself; 18). These, however, are the types of wordplay praised by Castiglione and Valdés, and they never threaten the stylistic plainness and prosaic quality of the verse.

13. The first of these examples is a variation on the trope of the lover transformed into the beloved, one of the most canonical in fifteenth-century Petrarchism; see Rico.

14. Darst (*Juan Boscán*, 66–67, 77–80) notes several of the biblical allusions in the final poems. For a close and sensitive reading of the concluding sonnets see also Armisén, 400–404.

15. Boscán's views here parallel Edmund Spenser's later Reformation-inspired notion of marriage as the truest form of chastity; see Dasenbrock, 32–84. Together with the biblical imagery, this link suggests a stronger Erasmist influence on Boscán than has hitherto been recognized.

16. The historical and aesthetic issues that preoccupy Boscán in the preface are recast, in the poetry, as a critique of the insufficiency of both the *cancionero* and the Petrarchan erotic codes. Though clearly a close reader of Petrarch, Boscán seems uninterested in other dimensions of the Italian's poetry (the political, the Augustinian, etc.).

17. Even here Boscán's strategy is profoundly Petrarchistic; as Kennedy noted, "manipulating the rhetorical means of the Petrarchan poem is a poet in control of his craft, capable of making and handling allusions to the Classical and Christian traditions and of transforming all that he approaches into a creative moral synthesis that is at once definitive and artistic" (40).

18. These commentaries, along with that by José Nicolás de Azara (1765), are gathered by Gallego Morell in *Garcilaso de la Vega y sus comentaristas*, from which I cite.

19. The biographical interpretation of Garcilaso is not entirely anachronistic, however, for it has its roots in the Renaissance practice of reading Petrarch, Bembo, and other poets; see Cruz, *Imitación*, 26–33. For Lapesa's response to the "new biography" see his essay "Poesía y realidad."

20. *Rime sparse* 70 also contains individual phrases that Garcilaso may have been imitating. To Ana María Snell, one of the few critics to take Garcilaso's poem seriously, the final verse is completely in agreement with the epigrammatic and anecdotal nature of the piece, which is no more than an ingenious development of the single thought it contains; the final verse, both seed and culmination, makes the poem a literary exercise in Barthes's sense of the term. See also Levisi, who emphasizes the importance of sight in this poem and elsewhere in Garcilaso's poetry, and Gargano, 27–54.

21. For a rhetorical analysis of the *agudeza* see Barnard, *The Myth*, 128–30.

22. In this regard they anticipate the nymphs in the third eclogue, who emerge not from an ancient mythological river but from the Tajo, right outside modern Toledo. See also Mariscal, who comments that in this poem there is no isolation of the poetic from nature (118).

23. Moreover, to the degree that the nymphs and the river represent the poetic tradition, and that tears are emblematic of poetry, the poem can be read as an allegory of the dissolution of the poet's self in the face of Petrarch's text. Bembo in fact cited *Rime sparse* 303 as one of Petrarch's most beautiful compositions, emphasizing the sound structure and the alterna-

tion of "feminine" vowels with "masculine" consonants, an erotic encounter thus thematicized by Garcilaso.

24. Foley sees in the *levanta/cae* pair a drawing-out of an antithesis, while the tercets serve as an extended gloss on the Petrarchan concept of *volere* (198–99, 204–5).

25. See Lázaro Carreter, "La 'Ode,'" who comments that there is a latent slyness in the poem that has never been appreciated (121).

26. Lázaro Carreter considers the contrary-to-fact clause to be an imitation of Propertius 2.1.17–26, and suggests this poem as the source for Garcilaso's allusive mythological strategy as well. He also proposes an erotic interpretation of the poem's title, with "flor" referring to Sanseverino's virginity.

27. The full implications of her anti-Narcissan flight can be glossed with a poem from the erotic tradition, sonnet 32 in the Alzieu anthology. There a woman, wishing to behold her private parts, stands at the water's edge, lifts up her skirt, and thanks the reflection for the wealth it has brought her, only to fall in the water when she tries to kiss it. The woman in this sonnet, while slightly silly and even narcissistic, is proud of her sexuality and pleased with the social benefits her situation confers on her, while Camila flees from her sexually adult body and the new social role it implies.

28. Zimic comes close to this interpretation: he believes that Camila's extreme reaction is motivated by her realization of her own attraction to Albanio, and recalls how for St. John of the Cross the fountain was a symbol of love (51).

29. Indeed, the word is used in the sense of a token in Garcilaso's third *canción*, "mientras de mí otra prenda no tuviere" (while having no other token from me, 32), a poem that also echoes sonnet 10 in its emphasis on changed fortunes, "pues á sido en un ora / todo aquello deshecho / en que toda mi vida fue gastada" (while in an hour all has been undone, on which I had spent my entire life, 43–45). Here again the biographical critics differ: Navarro saw in these lines a reference to Garcilaso's loss of favor with the emperor, but Keniston again perceived a connection to Isabel Freire's death; see the Rivers edition, 186.

30. See Paul Julian Smith, who notes that "the María addressed (whoever she may have been) is certainly not the Isabel whose death inspires the poem as a whole and who has always been taken to be the source of the poet's inspiration" (*Writing*, 53). He also sees a further contradiction in the emphasis on poetic voice in the opening stanzas, belied by the recourse to writing (*pluma*) in the subsequent ones; to him it is actually the pen, not the voice, that grants immortality. Yet even Garcilaso was not so far from the oral tradition, which effectively bequeathed immortality on Achilles and Hector in Homeric times, and on the host of heroes remembered in the *romancero*.

31. As Gallego Morell noted ("Estudio crítico," 23), Garcilaso's pastoralism is conventionally seen as an escape from his military undertakings; but it would be more correct to underline the paradox of this escape to nature

not from military encampments—which are in nature—but from the environment of the court and the literary academies, from the social occasions in which Italian ladies showed off their equally artificial clothes, coiffures, and wit, and from the conversations about literary themes among the writers he befriended. The bee's flight above the flower-strewn ground is farther from humanist circles than from the line of march.

32. Petrarch himself, in his *canzone 70,* ended the first four stanzas with a quote from a preceding Provençal or Italian poet, but then concluded the final stanza with the first line from his own *canzone 23*; the use of tapestries may in itself also allude to Ariosto's *Orlando furioso,* known as "la gran tela." On Garcilaso's relation to his models, Barnard comments, "Garcilaso's subversion of his models points to their insufficiency and achieves a secret victory over them. The result is not only a unique poetic vision but one that rivals the models in accuracy of presentation. And yet in the correction lies a poetic strategy" ("Garcilaso's Poetics," 319–20).

33. See Paterson; also Bayo, 143. More recently, Johnson has restated the effect in Freudian terms: "The notions of competition and replacement liken Garcilaso to the Oedipal son who wants to replace his father with his mother, except that Garcilaso (any poem is after all a fantasy) is successful. Furthermore, having usurped the father's role, Garcilaso now also continues in the normal function of the son: to identify with the father by imitating him and in that sense to keep him alive" (302–3).

34. There is a long tradition, summarized by Zimic, that attempts to emend "degollada" to "ygualada," i.e., stretched out, or interpreting the original word to mean exsanguinated and thus to reconcile it with Isabel Freire's death in childbirth. Zimic makes a case for a metaphorical understanding of "degollada"; stronger still is the argument that Garcilaso meant what he wrote in what is after all a fiction. See also Martínez-López; Lapesa, "Poesía y realidad."

35. See also Cruz, *Imitación,* 120. The notion that Garcilaso has achieved what Bloom calls a metalepsis of his predecessors is thus not a subjective aesthetic-historical assessment, but an interpretation of the poem, a restatement in Bloomean terms of how Garcilaso has written himself into literary history.

4. HERRERA AND THE RETURN TO STYLE

1. The *Discurso* was first published as an addendum to Argote's edition of *El conde Lucanor;* for a discussion, see Martí, 193–95.

2. As Tiscornia points out in his notes (Argote, 103–8), Argote's misinformation is taken from Beuter's *Primera parte de la cronica de toda España* (1546).

3. On imitation theory in El Brocense's commentary, see Vilanova, *Las fuentes,* 1.15–17, who emphasizes the eclecticism implicit in imitation of "los excelentes antiguos," at the expense of the relatively restricted canon within which El Brocense situates Garcilaso; on the defenses of Garcilaso by Jeró-

nimo de los Cobos and Jerónimo de Lomas Cantoral, see Coster, 54–57; Gallego Morell, *Garcilaso*, 24–25.

4. Ambrosio de Morales's "Discurso," as Terracini indicated, serves as a bridge between the early and the late sixteenth century, in terms of both ideology and its peculiar publishing history: first printed in 1546 as a prologue to F. Pérez de Oliva's "Diálogo de la dignidad del hombre," in the anthology *Obras que F. Cervantes de Salazar ha hecho, glosado y traducido* (Alcalá, 1546), it was extensively rewritten before its second appearance as the preface to the *Obras del Maestro F. Pérez de Oliva con algunas de Ambrosio de Morales* (Córdoba, 1586). Modern editions tend to combine the two versions; references here are to the critical edition by Valeria Scorpioni, which distinguishes the alterations made in 1586. See her introduction for a full account of the textual problems, and Terracini, *Lingua come problema*, 167–82.

5. In doing so, as Terracini notes (ibid., 125–27), he employs the trope of praise for the language and blame for its practitioners, dominant in many sixteenth-century discussions.

6. The son of a professor at Alcalá, Morales followed his uncle Pérez de Oliva to Salamanca, then returned to Alcalá as a student, professor, and ultimately rector of the royal college of San Felipe y Santiago. Among his students were John of Austria, Charles V's illegitimate son, and Bernardo de Rojas y Sandoval, future inquisitor-general and archbishop of Toledo, and he was rewarded with the post of royal chronicler in 1563. His career was thus intimately linked to the university as training ground for the upper nobility, and to the king as dispenser of patronage. See Redel, 88–97, 113, 121–26.

7. See Lynch, 1.54, 192–95. In part this development was inevitable, in that Spain alone, with its American empire, could finance Philip's wars; see Rodríguez-Salgado, 223–52. Although the process of centralization and conciliar administration had already begun under Charles, under Philip the constitutional independence of the Italian realms was reduced to a fiction, albeit a crucial one whose forms had to be observed.

8. See Amado Alonso, 51–100. The crux here is the question of the Spanish national language, an issue that differs from the Italian *questione della lingua* in important details: in Italy Tuscan was opposed to a cosmopolitan courtly language, while in Spain the courtly language is associated with Castilian. Boscán and Garcilaso themselves almost always used the term *castellano* rather than *español* to refer to their language; so too did Argote de Molina and Morales, both Andalusians but with ties to the nobility. But Herrera, as Alonso points out, consistently used the term *español* and gave it ideological value as indicative of a language belonging to all Spaniards, not just Castilians. More recent but brief treatment of the issue can be found in Lapesa, *Historia*, 291–315.

9. But see Mariscal, who emphasizes Herrera's dependence on aristocratic patronage (122). Born into a modest family, Herrera studied with the humanist Pedro Fernández de Castilleja but is not known to have taken any university degree. From 1559 his patron was the count of Gelves, whose

wife, Leonor, is thought to have been the "Luz" to whom Herrera dedicated his poetry; in 1566 he took minor orders and received a small benefice, on which he lived for the rest of his life, refusing ecclesiastic advancement. Herrera published little before the Garcilaso notes in 1580; his patrons both died in 1581, and a year later Herrera published a small collection of poetic works. The poet himself died in 1597; a much-expanded posthumous edition of his poetry appeared in 1619 (see the section on "Love and Allusion," below).

10. Prete Jacopín's *Observaciones* . . . *en defensa del Príncipe de los Poetas Castellanos Garci-lasso de la Vega* . . . *contra las Anotaciones de Fernando de Herrera poeta sevillano* were probably written in 1581, and Herrera wrote a reply, probably in the mid-1580s; see Montero, 27–37. Fernández de Velasco, count of Haro and duke of Frías, became hereditary *condestable* (chief military officer) of Castile in 1585 and governor of Milan in 1592. He studied at Salamanca with El Brocense, with whom he later corresponded, and, as a fellow member of the extended Mendoza family, he was a distant relative of Garcilaso. His work, together with Herrera's response, can be found in Montero, whose introduction and notes contain valuable information. In 1622 Tamayo, drawing on Fernández de Velasco, published his own notes to Garcilaso's works in competition with Herrera's. On other replies to Herrera see Montero's introduction, 17–63 and 83–87; also Almeida, 37–78; on the relationship between Fernández de Velasco and Tamayo, see Alatorre; and on El Brocense's own reply to Herrera, see Asensio, "El Brocense."

11. Major studies of the *Anotaciones* include Coster; Macrí; Bianchini, "The *Anotaciones*," which perhaps overemphasizes its Neoplatonic aspects but is otherwise an excellent guide to the work; and Almeida, which argues for the similarity between Herrera's literary views and those of the twentieth-century Anglo-American New Critics. See also Vilanova, "Fernando de Herrera"; Brancaforte; Amado Alonso, 80–99 Darst, *Imitatio*, 58–63; and Bianchini, "Fernando de Herrera's *Anotaciones*."

12. On Erasmus's resistance to Ciceronianism see Greene, 181–86; Cave, 138–46. The connection is suggestive, for although Prete Jacopín admitted (108) that there was nothing in the *Anotaciones* contrary to Christian doctrine, the comment suggests a nagging thought that something was wrong. The commentary is indeed heterodox in the challenge it poses to the notion of literary authority. Further discussions of Spanish imitation theory can be found in Vilanova, *Las fuentes*, 1.15–43; Darst, *Imitatio*, 51–83; and Paul Julian Smith, *Writing*, 30–42. On Renaissance concepts of originality see Greene, 171–75.

13. The question of Herrera's direct knowledge of classical literature has been debated since early in this century. Scholars have pointed out that Greek poets are always quoted in translation, and that even quotations from Latin poets are often limited to well-known incipits or to quotations to be found in secondary sources with which Herrera was familiar. Beach led the charge against Herrera in 1908; he was refuted by Lida de Malkiel in "La

tradición clásica." More recently, Almeida has addressed the same question. See also di Benedetto, Pring-Mill, and Brancaforte.

14. In general, Renaissance translation theory and practice need to be further investigated; for ideas about "literal" translation, see Norton, whose book demonstrates the necessity of reconsidering accepted generalizations about the subject. Bianchini ("The *Anotaciones*") sees Herrera's translations as the result of his stated intention to write for an unlearned audience, a reason at odds with his deeper conviction that poetry is an elite activity; this conviction surfaces in the omission of translations for incipits and other selections that Herrera meant the educated to recognize. As Elias Rivers points out ("L'humanisme"), El Brocense himself was equally guilty of introducing translations into a commentary with the aim of canonizing an author—Fray Luis de León, his colleague at Salamanca. Herrera's translation practice is considered by Navarro Durán, who compares his version of Horace's "Diffugere nives" with an earlier translation by Francisco de Medrano. She quotes Dámaso Alonso and Stephen Reckert's assessment, that Medrano imitates the movement of the model—a long line followed by a short one—but finds that in Herrera's version the linked tercets contribute to the amplification and separate the translation from the original (504). See also Macrí, 68–76.

15. Herrera himself responded to Prete Jacopín, in terms that reveal his aspiration to a literary aristocracy: "Quien puede quitar a F.d.H., que méscle sus versos con los de F. Petrarca i d. Diego de Mendoça . . . ? Porque bien puede un Soldado, por despreciado i cobarde que sea, arremeter a la bateria, con los mas valientes, sin que por esta osadia alcánce tanta gloria, como los que la merecen por su valor, i por los cargos que tienen. Agradecedme esta semejança, traida de la milicia; que por daros contento, vino a este proposito. Porque sin duda, segun se colige de vuestra Apologia, deveis ser mas soldado que ombre de letras" (Who can deny F.d.H. the right to mix his verses with those of Petrarch and Diego Hurtado de Mendoza . . . ? A soldier, no matter how despised and cowardly, can attack a battery along with the most valiant, without thereby attaining as much glory as those that deserve it by their valor and responsibilities. Thank me for this analogy, taken from the world of the military, and purposely used in order to please you, for without doubt, judging from your apology, you are more a soldier than a man of letters; Montero, 223). The use of a military comparison, while poking fun at Fernández de Velasco's literary pretensions, suggests the equality between the poet and the warrior and undoes the courtly ideal of wielding both the pen and the sword.

16. Coster recognized the importance of erudition for Herrera, and his views were echoed by Bianchini, for whom these learned glosses "illuminate the breadth of Herrera's curiosity and erudition, and portray the nature of Renaissance encyclopedic learning as it was exemplified by a Spanish man of letters. They also indicate the type and range of erudition that Herrera wanted to associate with a poetic vocation" ("The *Anotaciones*," 206;

see also 211). Randel sees a connection between Herrera's method in the *Anotaciones* and his historical research, while Collard points out that *culto* and *docto* were terms used approvingly by Herrera when referring to others' poems (8–10).

17. This tactic too was a focus of objections from El Brocense and Faría y Sousa; as Asensio showed (in "El Brocense") the former, in a preface to Luis Gómez de Tapia's translation and notes to Camoens's *Lusiads,* praises it in terms that clearly allude to Herrera: "No ha querido embutir aquí fábulas, ni orígenes de vocablos, ni definiciones de amor, de ira, de gula, de fortaleza, ni vanagloria, ni a propósito de la muerte o de la vida traer Sonetos suyos, ni agenos, ni quiso tratar las figuras y tropos que se ofrecían en esta obra" (He has not wanted to stuff it with myths, nor with etymologies, nor with definitions of love, anger, gluttony, and fortitude, nor with vainglory, nor to bring in his own sonnets and those of others on the topics of life and death, nor did he want to comment on the figures and tropes used in this work; quoted in Asensio, "El Brocense," 20).

18. On Herrera's relationship with Argote de Molina, see also C. C. Smith, "Fernando de Herrera," who attributes Herrera's predilection for archaisms to Argote's antiquarian influence.

19. Harald Weinrich argues that Herrera, like Nebrija, conceives of Spanish literature as young and immature. Yet his arguments are not entirely persuasive, for they overlook the anxiety expressed by Herrera over the failure of Spanish to develop adequately; Weinrich's views may be affected by the cognizance, unavailable to Herrera, that the true Golden Age of Spanish literature lay in the next generation. Once again the active trope here is the *translatio studii.* For other discussions of Herrera's antecedents on this point, see also Bianchini, "The *Anotaciones"*; Terracini, *Lingua come problema,* 125–27. Interestingly, as Carron points out, after Francis I was denied the imperial crown, the French lost interest in the connection between the *translatio imperii* and the *translatio studii.*

20. To Almeida, Herrera's emphasis on innovation approximates him to T. S. Eliot's notion that "bad poets deface what they take, and good poets make it into something better, [or] at least different" (Almeida, 85). Yet here Herrera goes beyond the tropes of emulation to a position similar to Shklovsky's theory of defamiliarization, in which the poet avoids the limits set by the model text. Such an attitude may in turn account for the formal and thematic freedom Herrera exercises and recommends in translations (see the second section on the *Anotaciones,* below).

21. At this point in the poem Garcilaso had set up an opposition between the Spaniard and the "cautious" Italian (line 1545); Herrera moves from an explanation and amplification of Garcilaso to handing the Italians a reason for their sense of superiority: the inferiority of Spanish letters. The note itself is an example of Herrera's decentering technique, as he himself recognizes in its first words, "quiero discurrir" (I want to digress; 552). On this passage see also Randel, 105–8.

22. Both Bianchini ("The *Anotaciones"*) and Almeida comment on the

importance of tradition to Herrera. Bianchini sees him inserting himself in the tradition by writing his commentary on Garcilaso just as Bembo wrote one on Petrarch; Almeida compares Herrera's interest in tradition to the concept as it came to be understood by T. S. Eliot, Cleanth Brooks, etc. (85).

23. Bianchini sees Herrera placing "his authority in support of metaphor as the undisputed domain of the poets, where they may exercise creativity without limitation ("Fernando," 166); she also notes that much of the discussion of metaphor is taken not from Aristotle, whom Herrera repeatedly cites, but from Cicero. For a discussion of metaphor's Aristotelian roots, see Ricoeur; on the importance of this Aristotelian tradition to Italian Renaissance theorists, see Breitenbürger; and on its significance to twentieth-century critical thought, see Miller. Herrera's theory of metaphor in some ways parallels that of early New Critics such as T. E. Hulme, who emphasizes the importance of the visual ("the poet is constantly in presence of a vividly felt physical visual scene") and of innovation and *enargeia* ("it is only when you get these fresh metaphors and epithets employed that you get this vivid conviction which constitutes the purely aesthetic emotions . . . metaphors soon run their course and die"; quoted in Miller, 17, 18). On metaphor and *enargeia* in Renaissance theory, see also Montgomery, 66, 178, 210.

24. Both Fray Luis and St. John developed theological theories of metaphor. The former analyzes the function of culturally specific metaphors in the Song of Songs and the need to understand them as equivalent to Petrarchan images; for St. John, metaphors are the only means of expressing the richness of the mystical experience. On Fray Luis, see Thompson, 7–12, 27–35; on St. John, see López Barralt, Wilhelmsen.

25. The concept of *claridad* is a classical stylistic virtue: Castillejo, for example, praised the clarity and brevity of the traditional lyric (194), and Robles (perhaps following Herrera) associated it with metaphor; Paul Julian Smith sees it as a feature of *enargeia* and as one of Quevedo's principal preoccupations (*Quevedo*, 140–54). See also McInnis, 156; Darst, "Las palabras," 92–95.

26. For a discussion of the centrality of the visual as the root of poetic imagery, see Welsh, who considers critics such as Ezra Pound, William Carlos Williams, and Northrop Frye. Herrera's rigorous analysis of the thought process behind Garcilaso's metaphors recalls Lotman and Uspenskii's insistence on the Baroque age as the period of transition from the absolute clarity of mythological identification to the scientific symbolism of modern metaphor (see the essay "Myth—Name—Culture," *Semiotics and Structuralism*, 3–32). As noted in chapter 3, Garcilaso's nymphs are more than just metaphors or other rhetorical constructs; but to Herrera the vividness of Garcilaso's evocations, through their clarity of syntax and pictorial description, is more important than the questionable presence of mythological beings in Spanish rivers. On how metaphors can "lie," see Montgomery, 178–84.

27. For views that emphasize Herrera's phonic theories, see William Fer-

guson who sees them as derived primarily from Bembo; and Alcina Rovira, who stresses the connection to Pontano.

28. Bianchini, "Fernando," sees Herrera combining the notion of literary *res* and literary *verba*, believing that to him the *verba* is the *res* of literature. But Herrera is quite specific about maintaining the distinction and explaining that, while the aural qualities of each language are inevitably lost in translation, there is more to poetry than just sound. The somewhat enigmatic advice to the imitator, "no proponga tanto decir lo que los otros dijeron, como lo que no dijeron" (do not attempt to say what others said, but what they did not say, 511), may need to be interpreted literally, with the emphasis on the oral/aural implications of "said" (*dijeron*), and thus the particular graces unique to the source language. Herrera's ideas about literary translatability are remarkably close to those of Pound, who linked the translatability of a text to the relative importance of phanopoeia (visual imagery, which is very translatable) and melopoeia (phonic patterns, which are generally untranslatable); see *How to Read*. For relevant discussions of Renaissance translation theory, see Norton; also Navarrete, "The Renaissance Preface" and "Strategies of Appropriation."

29. Coster correctly notes the effort toward naturalization implicit in this idea, and points out that Herrera would encourage borrowings from all sources, not just Latin (390).

30. Indeed, to sustain the *translatio* as a workable model, Herrera employs throughout the *Anotaciones* the phrase "Italia y Grecia," which combines ancient Rome with modern Italy and then couples it to Greece, yielding Spain's two immediate predecessors (Greece and Rome/Italy) in cultural and imperial primacy.

31. Among studies of Herrera's generic definitions, see Coster, who devotes a chapter to each of the genres Herrera defines, quoting at length from the *Anotaciones* and comparing Herrera's definitions to examples from his own poetic output; and Bianchini, "The *Anotaciones*" and "Fernando." In the latter, she notes the general paucity of prescriptive definitions in Herrera's generic discussions.

32. In presenting a gap between Petrarch and Sannazaro, Herrera here, as elsewhere, reflects his assimilation of Bembo's appropriation of humanist belatedness and his tripartite history of vernacular poetry.

33. In contrast to near contemporaries such as Ercilla, Lope de Vega, and even Góngora, Herrera never composed an epic, mostly limiting himself in his poetry to the genres Garcilaso employed. To Bianchini, "Fernando," the *Anotaciones* are free both from the Aristotelian emphasis on tragedy and epic and from the Horatian insistence on utility; McInnis also comments on Herrera's neglect of the epic.

34. Herrera's comments on the *rimas octavas* are limited to an uncharacteristically brief history, a description of the rhyme, and a digression on the differences between rhyme and rhythm. Thus he does not connect it, as the modern epic meter, to the classical dactylic hexameter. See, however, Gallego Morell (*Estudios*, 54–60) and Vilanova ("Fernando"), both of whom

perceive in Herrera a frustrated desire to write an epic, expressed in the early *canción* on the Battle of Lepanto and in the quasi-epic diction of his love sonnets. Yet the use of the *canción* in that instance marks precisely the modern role of lyric as the successor to the ancient epic, as does the assumption of such diction into the sonnet. I will return to this issue in the next section.

35. Herrera was addicted to revising his own poetry, and little is actually known about the circumstances surrounding the compilation of each of these editions. Even his own 1582 edition may represent not a definitive version of his poetry, honed to his satisfaction, but a selection printed in an effort to ingratiate himself with a potential patron in the wake of the deaths of the count and countess of Gelves the preceding year; certainly, the title of the book suggests that it is far from a complete edition. Nor do we know anything about the drafts from which Pacheco worked (Blecua considers them pre-1578, Battaglia and Macrí, post-1582) or the extent to which these revisions and—equally important—this arrangement of the poems reflect the lost manuscript that Duarte mentioned. The textual dispute is not likely to be settled; for résumés see Pepe Sarno, "Se non Herrera, chi?" and "La 'luz,'" 409–11 (she favors the later edition as reflecting Herrera's intentions) and Cuevas's introduction in *Poesía castellana*, 87–99 (he does not). My own position is that, regardless of the degree of Pacheco's intervention, the 1619 edition is an important document in the history of Spanish Petrarchism, containing poems that are generally denser in imagery and arranged in ways that create specific interpretative contexts. The Cuevas edition reconstructs the sequence in which the poems originally appeared in both 1582 and 1619, but as I sometimes emphasize the evolution of a poem from edition to edition, I therefore quote the original editions. To indicate the provenance of a particular text, I employ, in place of the usual *sigla B* (for Blecua), *H* (for Herrera), and *P* (for Pacheco), which undermine the latter's authority, the abbreviations *CdB* for the *Cisne del Betis* manuscript, *AO* for the 1582 edition, and *V* for the 1619.

36. The only poet between Boscán and Herrera to have published his own poetry was Pedro de Padilla, who published a volume in 1580 and another in 1582; see Rodríguez Moñino, 7–12.

37. At the same time, as García Berrio has argued, there are no alternatives for the poet who wishes to proclaim an otherwise illicit love—only Petrarchism, which insists on the illegitimacy of love, provides an outlet and a way of legitimizing such emotions.

38. See, e.g., Gallego Morell, *Estudios*, 54–60; Macrí, 68–73. To Woods, the mixing of genres calls attention to the "relation between different genres and the problems of writing poetry" (128).

39. This ending becomes more Homeric in *V* 3.48, "que ninguno de Cupido / seguro navegò el profundo estrecho; / que no perdiesse al cabo la ventura" (for no one certain of Cupid sailed the deep strait who did not in the end lose his fortune, 12–14).

40. As *onda* is a metaphor for wavy hair, there is a certain redundancy

in calling it *crespa*, but one of which Herrera himself approves: "no hay alguno tan ignorante, que no conozca que la *nieve* es *blanca*, el *sol dorado*, la *luna argentada*, y que éstos son demasiados epítetos, pero tienen en la poesía no mediana gracia" (no one is so ignorant who will not know that snow is white, the sun golden, the moon silver, and that these epithets are redundant, yet they have in poetry no small grace, *Anotaciones*, 344). *Onda* is only one of many metaphors for hair, such as *anillo, cadena, lazo, nudo*, etc., that Herrera employs; while the metaphorization of the beloved's body has its roots in Petrarch (e.g., "né posso dal bel nodo omai dar crollo / . . . / dico le chiome bionde e 'l crespo laccio" [nor can I shake loose that lovely knot . . . I mean the blond locks and the curling snare, *Rime sparse* 197.7, 9]), Herrera, who as we have seen privileges metaphor in the *Anotaciones*, carries it much farther. As a stylistic device metaphorization will come to be identified with Góngora and then be parodied by Quevedo; see chapter 5, below.

41. Cf. Micó, who traces the history and use of identical rhyme, culminating in Herrera, but who concludes that in this poem the substitution of *ielo* for *velo* was an editor's or printer's error.

42. Though first published in *V*, it is in fact an early poem, as its appearance in *CdB* indicates.

43. To Hernández Esteban, the swan exists in the poem as a private symbol of Herrera's, and thus as a rival to the borrowed symbol of the laurel tree (409); after considering various possibilities, she decides that its presence is principally an echo of *canzone* 23. Yet Herrera's assertions in the *Anotaciones* (519), which she cites (413), that the swan is sacred to Apollo and that it sings at its death because its soul rejoices at the approach of immortality, are also relevant, as I will show.

44. For a semiotic analysis of Renaissance literary onomastics, but with primarily French examples, see Rigolot.

5. GÓNGORA, QUEVEDO, AND THE END OF
PETRARCHISM IN SPAIN

NOTE: Arthur Terry's *Seventeenth-century Spanish Poetry: The Power of Artiface* (Cambridge: Cambridge University Press, 1993) was published too late to be taken into account during the writing of this chapter.

1. For political and economic histories of Baroque Spain see Kamen and the second volume of Lynch; for cultural analysis see above all Maravall, who emphasizes points such as a consciousness of crisis and *desengaño* as defining topics, a theatricality that points toward a mass culture with elements of kitsch, representations of life as a burden (*cuidado*) and as labyrinth, and a poetry that satirizes the world it once praised.

2. In addition, one might add up to five other sonnets classified as love poems in Vicuña or Chacón; see Calcraft, 13–15. References here are to the principal textual sources for Góngora's poetry: the edition published by Juan López de Vicuña (1627, but based on an early manuscript); the edition compiled by Gonzalo Hoces y Córdoba (published 1633); the Chacón

manuscript, compiled by Antonio Chacón Ponce de León with the author's collaboration in the last years of his life; and Biruté Ciplijauskaité's modern critical edition of the sonnets, which takes Chacón as its basis. All of these sources classify the sonnets by topic (love, praise, etc.); within each category Chacón and Ciplijauskaité further order the sonnets by date.

3. On this sonnet see also di Pinto; Foster and Foster; Phillips; and Jammes, 366–67, who asserts that compared to Garcilaso, Góngora is more precious, richer, and brighter, but that the image of beauty that imposes itself on us in the course of this poem is like a gold or ivory statue, somewhat deceptive, and lacking that human pulse which one feels in Garcilaso (366).

4. On Pineda see Alonso's introduction to the facsimile of the Vicuña edition, xxix–xli; as Alonso points out, Pineda's animosity results from his being the butt of a satirical sonnet by Góngora in 1610 (xxxix). Ultimately the Vicuña edition was banned not because of its contents but because the author's name did not appear on the title page and because the book bore an unauthorized dedication from Vicuña to the grand inquisitor.

5. On the plasticity of Góngora's use of colors, in contrast to Herrera's more usual emphasis on translucence, see Orozco Díaz.

6. See for example *canzone* 126: "erba et fior che la gonna / leggiadra ricoverse / co l'angelico seno, / aere sacro sereno / ove Amor co' begli occhi il cor m'aperse" (grass and flowers that her rich garment covered along with her angelic breast, sacred bright air where Love opened my heart with her lovely eyes, 7–11); *canzone* 127: "le bionde treccie sopra 'l collo sciolte / ov' ogni latte perderia sua prova, / e le guancie ch' adorna un dolce foco. / Ma pur che l'ora un poco / fior bianchi et gialli per le piaggie mova, / torna a la mente il loco / e 'l primo dì ch' i' vidi a l'aura sparsi / i capei d'oro ond' io sì subito arsi" (the blond tresses loosened on her neck, where every milk loses by comparison, and the cheeks adorned with a sweet fire. If the breeze but a little moves the white and yellow flowers in the meadows, the place comes back to mind and the first day when I saw freed to the air the golden hair from which I so quickly caught fire, 77–84); and, for the restoration of flowers, sonnet 165: "Come 'l candido pie' per l'erba fresca / i dolci passi onestamente move, / vertù che 'ntorno i fiori apra et rinove / de le tenere piante sue par ch' esca" (As her white foot through the green grass virtuously moves its sweet steps, a power that all around her opens and renews the flowers seems to issue from her tender soles, 1–4).

7. This is a theme to which the poet in fact returns in his late sonnet "Al tronco Filis de vn laurel sagrado" (*Sonetos* 98, 1621), in which a satyr stalks a sleeping nymph who is saved, in turn, by a providential bee stinging the lips it has mistaken for a flower.

8. These thematic elements of Polyphemus's song are also present in Salicio's lament from Garcilaso's first eclogue, also addressed to a nymph named "Galatea."

9. Pellicer underlines this point by noting the use of the subjective verb *ver* rather than the more objective *mirar* (Vilanova, *Las fuentes*, 2.212).

10. Vilanova notes that Torquato Tasso employed a similar situation when Armida fell in love with the sleeping Rinaldo's "muta eloquenza" (*Gerusalemme liberata* 14.66; Vilanova, *Las fuentes*, 2.215). Although that incident is, along with the Spanish pastoral romances already described, clearly a source for this episode, its instance of sexual inversion does not diminish the even greater degree of inversion in Góngora's poem.

11. Góngora may have had in mind the commentary to Garcilaso's sonnet 22, and the anecdote about the beloved injuring herself with a pin; fulfilling El Brocense, Góngora really did write a poem about a pricked finger.

12. The classic study of the effect of Góngora's poetry on the evolution of Spanish poetic theory remains Collard's; for more recent and more limited discussions, see Darst, "Las palabras"; Romanos.

13. For other theoretically informed discussions of Góngora as a parodist, see Ball's studies, which emphasize the poet's ballads; and Quintero, esp. 8–18, where she emphasizes the continuing vitality of Petrarchism in general and of Gongorism in particular as a force in seventeenth-century Spanish drama.

14. Fourteen more sonnets also dedicated to Lisi appeared in a second volume, *Las tres Musas últimas castellanas*, published after González de Salas's death by Quevedo's nephew Pedro Aldrete in 1670; the common practice among modern editors of including them together with the Lisi poems in the *Parnasso* volume presupposes their inadvertent exclusion by González de Salas rather than a deliberate decision made in the course of organizing the collection.

15. Quotations are taken from José Blecua's critical edition, *Obra poética*, which modernizes spelling and punctuation; references to notes and introductions are by page number. References to poems include both the sonnet's place in the Lisi cycle, and its number in the Blecua *Obra poética* edition (thus "L1/B442," etc.). Where my readings differ from Blecua's, I so indicate. In preparing my translations I benefited from those in the studies by Walters and Olivares.

16. Commenting on this passage, Mas quotes the nineteenth-century critic Ernest Merimée: "Ce qui inspirerait des doutes sur l'existence de Lisis, c'est précisément cette prétension, aussi peu dissimulée que mal justifiée, d'imiter Pétrarque. Ce qui n'est que trop certain, c'est que Lisis a induit le poète en bien des défauts dont il s'est moqué maintes fois. Outre la clarté, ce qui manque le plus dans ces laborieuses vétilles, c'est la sincérité, l'émotion, la mesure" (That which would inspire doubts about the existence of Lisi is precisely this pretense, as little dissimulated as it is badly justified, of imitating Petrarch. What is all too certain is that Lisi induced the poet to all of the faults that he has mocked so many times. Other than clarity, what is most lacking in these overworked bagatelles is sincerity, emotion, and measure, 289). On González de Salas's introduction see also Consiglio; Walters, *Francisco de Quevedo*, 113–15; and recall Anne Cruz's discussion of the role of an *imitatio vitae* in Bembo and Boscán (*Imitación*, 26–29).

17. In the González de Salas edition, the Lisi cycle consists of fifty-one

sonnets followed by a madrigal and four idylls; while thematic argument could be made for having the madrigal and the final idyll (metrically a *silva*) at the end, the other three idylls (metrically a *canción* and two sets of octave stanzas) would seem to belong in the midst of the sonnets. Blecua preserves González de Salas's generic arrangement but adds sonnets dedicated to Lisi from *Las tres Musas* and other sources, inserting them between the *Parnasso* sonnets and the madrigal. Thus he preserves González de Salas's ordering of the sonnets in *El Parnasso* but cuts them off from the poems in other genres. Recently Walters, in a new edition of the collection (*Poems to Lisi*), has proposed a rearrangement that incorporates all of the Lisi poems; and in *Francisco de Quevedo*, 104–30, he analyzes the collection in terms of his new ordering. As he preserves the order of the beginning and the ending sonnets from the *Parnasso* and the central position of "Cerrar podrá," the trajectory he traces is similar to mine, though his interests are different. His proposed reordering, while intriguing, has yet to win widespread acceptance.

18. Although, as in Petrarch's *Rime sparse*, several poems in the collection refer to the supposed anniversaries of the poet's first encounter with Lisi, these poems are merely one more aspect of Quevedo's elaborate attempt to draw attention to his imitation of Petrarch. Nonetheless, the efforts by some critics to reconstruct on the basis of the collection the story of a love affair lasting twenty-two years with a woman code-named "Lisi" point to the tremendous affective power and poetic force of the poems, what Paul Julian Smith has called their rhetoric of presence (*Writing*, 43–49).

19. For summaries of the debate over the issue of "excess," see Collard; and, more recently, Paul Julian Smith, *Writing*, 19–42.

20. See Walters, *Francisco de Quevedo*, 82–83, 115; and Close, who sees in this poem the *cancionero* theme of enslavement by Lisi, invoked through Petrarchan synecdoches and in an emotional range similar to that of Petrarch, Bembo, and Herrera.

21. For line 6 Blecua prefers the reading from the *Cancionero antequerano* of the 1620s, "porque en tus llamas, Lisi, está encendido," to González de Salas's "porque en tus llamas, Lisis, encendido." The latter, however, by eliminating the synalophas, is harsher and grammatically more condensed, features typical of Quevedo's revisions (see Georgina Rivers, "Quevedo, Floralba").

22. Indeed, the line is a variation on the familiar *cancionero* trope, "muero porque no muero."

23. For additional discussion of this poem see Naderi, who emphasizes Quevedo's borrowing from Petrarch of visual images and symbolic situations transferred to extreme emotional contexts, and in this poem, the function of the eagle, sharp-sighted bird of prey, as a mediator between eyes and mouth, and the reconciliation of opposites in the tercets; also Walters, *Francisco de Quevedo*, 16–17, 22–23, 106, 117; and Olivares, 93–96.

24. For an exhaustive discussion of the poem see Molho, "Sobre un soneto."

25. See the article by Blanco-Morel, who analyzes Quevedo's use of the

hair/gold metaphor and his use of the Midas myth to achieve a mineraliza-
tion of Lisi. See also ter Horst, "Death and Resurrection," who underlines
the erotic dimension of Lisi undoing her hair and sees in the poem a re-
enactment of sexual intercourse; Paul Julian Smith, *Quevedo* (77–84), who
argues that the rhetoric demands an active reader, and notes allusions to
Marino (whose source was in turn Lope de Vega), and to the Latin elegiac/
erotic tradition where unfastened hair is a prelude to intercourse; and on
Quevedo's use of the Midas myth, Walters, *Francisco de Quevedo*, 94–98.

26. Paul Julian Smith, *Quevedo* (84–89), sees in this poem an attempt to
protect the love sonnet from the licentiousness of the *seicento* Italians: "The
tension between variety and dignity, then, is also the tension between plea-
sure and profit, low and high, Italian and Spanish. . . . The 'brief prison' of
the sonnet, Quevedo's most successful verse form, is also that of an anxious
traditionalist, enclosed, and indeed besieged, by the sensuous exempla of
Latin authority and Italian novelty" (89).

27. For discussions of Quevedo's rhetoric in this poem, see in particular
Blanco Aguinaga, who analyzes the patterns of division, opposition, and
contradiction in the poem: *ojos* opposed to *sombra*; *sombra* to *blanco día*; qua-
trains are opposed to the tercets; the first quatrain to the second; lines 5–6
to lines 7–8; line 7 to line 8; *mas no* (line 5) to *no . . . mas . . . mas* (lines 12–14);
and the *bimembres* of the final three lines, each consisting of an assertion
and a negation. See also Fernando Lázaro Carreter, "Quevedo," who argues
that the poem's future/subjunctive structure goes beyond logic; and Paul
Julian Smith, *Quevedo*, 171–75, who emphasizes the presence of synec-
doches, metonymy, and metaphor, along with misleading argumentation:
"Dialectically, the poem is based on a temporal variant of the connexive or
hypothetical proposition, cited by Ramus: 'When/if I die, then my love will
live on.' The unstated syllogism which may be predicated from this contin-
ues: the first term is true; therfore, so must the second. Logically, however,
the relationship between the *antecedens* and the *consequens* is 'unnecessary'.
Other consequents are equally possible" (172–73). See also Mas, who con-
cludes that the living source of this poetry is to be seen less in its originality
of intuition and the exceptional force of sentiment than in its conceptual
logic and verbal invention (293). For other recent discussions see also Oli-
vares, 128–41; Walters, *Francisco de Quevedo*, 122–27.

28. Yet the soul alone cannot be the subject, for the verb is plural. Even
Blecua, ordinarily scrupulous in his editing, recognized the problem and
emended the reading to *dejará*.

29. As Close goes on to say, "By means such as these Quevedo elo-
quently conveys the contradictions of the lover's state, where the power and
glory of the feeling can be measured by its seeming capacity to wrest mo-
mentary triumph over and *through* reason itself," with poignancy height-
ened rather than nullified by our awareness of its impossibility (854).

30. Consiglio connects this theme in Quevedo to Petrarch's sonnet 36:
"'S' io credesse per morte essere scarco / del pensiero amoroso che
m'atterra, / colle mie mani avrei già posto in terra / queste membra noiose

et quello incarco" (If I thought that by death I would be lightened of this amorous care that wears me down, with my own hands by now I would have consigned to earth these burdensome members and that weight, 1–4). See also Olivares, 122–27.

31. The most notable exception is itself instructive. Sonnet 39 begins with lines that, to Blecua, are an echo of Góngora's *Soledades:* "Por yerta frente de alto escollo, osado, / con pie dudoso, ciegos pasos guío" (Along the hard face of a high cliff, boldly but with uncertain steps, I guide my steps, L39/B480.1–2). Yet the first tercet emphasizes, in the most direct way of any poem from the Lisi cycle, Quevedo's belatedness: "En muda senda, obscuro peregrino, / sigo pisadas de otro sin ventura, / que para mi dolor perdió el camino" (On this mute path, an obscure pilgrim, I follow the steps of another unfortunate one, who to my sorrow lost his way, L39/B480.9–11). Thus he presents his poetry as a secondary phenomenon, dependent for its motivation and nature on the work of his predecessors, who themselves had strayed from the path.

32. On Quevedo's self-conscious awareness of being at the end of a literary tradition, and the need for defamiliarization, see Pozuelo Yvancos (12–18).

33. See Mariscal: "Despite the caveats issued by the New Critics and others, theories of expression continue to collapse the speaker of the poem into the biographical poet, so that the preoccupation with a fully embodied presence ... still effaces the fact that the poetic voice is a linguistic construct" (99).

34. See for example Blecua's introduction to Quevedo's *Poesía metafísica y amorosa;* also Close; Olivares; and Walters, *Francisco de Quevedo,* 131–57. Under the category "metaphysical poetry" Blecua includes those poems "en los que se plantea el angustioso problema de la vida como muerte y de la inexorabilidad del tiempo" (those poems in which he plants the anguishing problem of life as death, and of the inexorability of time; *Poesía metafísica,* xxxvi); most of these poems appeared in the original *Parnasso,* classified by González de Salas under the muse Polymnia, "poesías morales que descubren i manifiestan las pasiones i costumbres del hombre" (who sings moral poems that uncover and display human passions and habits; Quevedo, *Obra,* 1.103). In addition to the metaphysical poems, this section of the *Parnasso* also contains moral and satirical works. The dedication of the *Heráclito,* dated 1613, survives in several seventeenth-century manuscripts (see Blecua's notes in Quevedo, *Obra poética,* 1.167–97; Manley); the collection itself consists of twenty-six poems, many of them sonnets, but all characterized as psalms.

35. See Close: "The allegory of their arduous 'road', and the analysis of their alternating states of hope and despair, self-control, and passion, acquire among the first generation of Spanish Petrarchists a characteristic tone of tragic introspection, despair, and fatalism, combined with sober plainness of expression and an occasional dramatic harshness in the imagery. These qualities are anticipated by numerous poems in the *cancioneros* on

the theme of *amar muriendo* and also by . . . poems of Ausías March" (850–51). On the Herrera-Quevedo relationship, see the comments of Mariscal, 122–24.

36. An exception is Elias Rivers, "Language and Reality," to whom the conflict between reality and linguistic aesthetization is at the heart of all Quevedo's poetry. Rivers's examples are taken from the *Heráclito cristiano* ("¡Ah de la vida!"), the Lisi cycle (two poems, the "courtly" "¿Cómo es tan largo . . . ?" and the "erotic" "Si mis párpados"), and the burlesque sonnets ("La voz del ojo que llamamos pedo"). See also Bergmann, 255–57.

37. See Molho, "Una cosmogonía antisemita," who also finds an anti-Semitic reference in line 7, "érase una nariz sayón y escriba" (it was a nose executioner and scribe) and compares it with two lines from an anti-Góngora sonnet, "aunque aquesto de escribas se te pega, / por tener de sayón la rebeldía" (although this being a scribe sticks to you, for you have the executioner's insubordination, B829.13–14). On phallic and homosexual images in the poem see Profeti, 214–25.

38. On Quevedo's Daphne poems see Barnard, *Myth of Apollo*, 131–55; and Alvarez Barrientos.

39. See Profeti on "Este ciclope" (210); and Morel D'Arleux on Quevedo's use of obscenity.

Bibliography

Alatorre, Antonio. "Garcilaso, Herrara, Prete Jacopín y Don Tomás Tamayo de Vargas." *MLN* 78 (1963): 126–51.

Alcina Rovira, Juan F. "Herrera y Pontano: La métrica en las *Anotaciones.*" *Nueva revista de filología hispánica* 32, no. 2 (1983): 340–54.

Almeida, José. *La crítica literaria de Fernando de Herrera.* Madrid: Gredos, 1976.

Alonso, Amado. *Castellano, español, idioma nacional: Historia espiritual de tres nombres.* Buenos Aires: Facultad de Filosofía y Letras de la Universidad de Buenos Aires, Instituto de Filología, 1938.

Alonso, Dámaso. *Poesía española: Ensayo de métodos y límites estilísticos.* Madrid: Gredos, 1950.

Alonso Hernández, José Luis. *Léxico de marginalismo del Siglo de Oro.* Acta Salmanticensia, Filosofía y Letras 99. Salamanca: Universidad de Salamanca, 1976.

Alvarez Barrientos, Joaquín. "Dafne y Apolo en un comentario de Garcilaso y Quevedo." *Revista de literatura* 46, no. 92 (1984): 57–72.

Alzieu, Pierre, Robert Jammes, and Yvan Lissorgues, eds., introduction, and glossary. *Poesía erótica del siglo de oro.* Barcelona: Editorial Crítica, 1984.

Andrews, J. Richard. *Juan del Encina: Prometheus in Search of Prestige.* University of California Publications in Modern Philology 53. Berkeley and Los Angeles: University of California Press, 1959.

Argote de Molina, Gonzalo. *Discurso sobre la poesía castellana.* Edited by Eleuterio F. Tiscornia. Madrid: Suarez, 1926.

Armisén, Antonio. *Estudios sobre la lengua poética de Boscán: La edición de 1543.* Saragossa: Departamento de Literatura de la Universidad de Zaragoza; Libros Pórtico, 1982.

Asensio, Eugenio. "El Brocense contra Fernando de Herrera y sus *Anotaciones* a Garcilaso." *Crotalón* 1, no. 1 (1984): 13–24.

———. "La lengua compañera del imperio: Historia de una idea de Nebrija en España y Portugal." *Revista de filología española* 43 (1960): 399–413.

Azar, Inés. *Discurso retórico y mundo pastoral en la "Égloga segunda" de Garcilaso.* Purdue University Monographs in Romance Languages 5. Amsterdam: John Benjamins, 1981.

Azara, José Nicolás de. *Obras de Garcilaso de la Vega, ilustradas con notas.* 1st ed. Madrid, 1765. In *Garcilaso de la Vega y sus comentaristas,* edited by Antonio Gallego Morell. 2d ed., 667–80. Madrid: Gredos, 1972.

Bakhtin, M. M. *The Dialogic Imagination: Four Essays.* Edited by Michael Holquist, translated by Michael Holquist and Caryl Emerson. University of Texas Press Slavic Series 1. Austin: University of Texas Press, 1981.

———. *Problems of Dostoevsky's Poetics.* Edited and translated by Caryl Emerson, with an introduction by Wayne C. Booth. Theory and History of Literature 8. Minneapolis: University of Minnesota Press, 1984.

Ball, Robert. "Góngora's Parody of Literary Convention." Ph.D. diss., Yale University 1976. Ann Arbor, Mich.: University Microfilms International, 1977. UMI 76-28547.

———. "Imitación y parodia en la poesía de Góngora." In *Actas del Sexto Congreso Internacional de Hispanistas,* edited by Alan M. Gordon and Evelyn Rugg, 90–93. Toronto: Department of Spanish and Portuguese, University of Toronto, 1980.

Barnard, Mary E. "Garcilaso's Poetics of Subversion in the Orpheus Tapestry." *PMLA* 102 (1987): 316–25.

———. *The Myth of Apollo and Daphne from Ovid to Quevedo: Love, Agon, and the Grotesque.* Duke Monographs in Medieval and Renaissance Studies 8. Durham, N. C.: Duke University Press, 1987.

Battaglia, Salvatore. "Per il testo di Fernando de Herrera." *Filologia romanza* 1 (1954): 51–88.

Bayo, Marcial José. *Virgilio y la pastoral española del renacimiento (1480–1550).* 2d ed. Madrid: Gredos, 1970.

Beach, R. M. *Was Fernando de Herrera a Greek Scholar?* Philadelphia: University of Pennsylvania Press, 1908.

Bell, Aubrey. *Francisco Sánchez El Brocense.* Hispanic Society of America, Notes and Monographs 8. [London]: Oxford University Press, Humphrey Milford, 1925.

Bembo, Pietro. *Prose e rime.* Edition and introduction by Carlo Donisotti. 2d ed. Turin: UTET, 1966.

Benedetto, Ubaldo di. "Fernando de Herrera: Fuentes italianas y clásicas de sus principales teorías sobre el lenguaje poético." *Filología moderna* 25 (1966): 21–46.

Bergmann, Emilie L. *Art Inscribed: Essays on Ekphrasis in Spanish Golden Age Poetry.* Harvard Studies in Romance Languages 35. Cambridge, Mass.: Harvard University Press, 1979.

Berman, Antoine. "Critique, commentaire, et traduction: Quelques réflexions à partir de Benjamin et de Blanchot." *Po&sie* 37 (1986): 88–106.

Bianchini, Andreina. "The *Anotaciones* of Fernando de Herrera." Ph.D. diss., Rutgers University, 1973. Ann Arbor: University Microfilms International, 1974. DDJ74-08763.

———. "Fernando de Herrera's *Anotaciones*: A New Look at His Sources." *Romanische Forschungen* 88 (1976): 27–42.

———. "Herrera and Prete Jacopín: The Consequences of a Controversy." *Hispanic Review* 46 (1978): 221–54.

————. "A Note on Boscán's 'Carta-prólogo' to the Duchess of Soma." *Hispanófila* 94 (1988): 1–7.

Blanco Aguinaga, Carlos. "'Cerrar podrá mis ojos': Tradición y originalidad." In *Francisco de Quevedo,* edited by Gonzalo Sobejano, 300–318. Madrid: Taurus, 1978.

Blanco-Morel, Mercedes. "Métaphore et paradoxe dans deux sonnets de Quevedo." *Bulletin hispanique* 85 (1983): 83–103.

Blecua, José Manuel. "Un soneto de Góngora." In *El comentario de textos,* edited by Emilio Alarcos et al., 2d ed., 52–61. Madrid: Castalia, 1973.

Bloom, Harold. *The Anxiety of Influence: A Theory of Poetry.* London: Oxford University Press, 1975.

————. *The Breaking of the Vessels.* Chicago: University of Chicago Press, 1982.

————. *A Map of Misreading.* Oxford: Oxford University Press, 1975.

Borges, J. L. *Otras inquisiciones (1937–1952).* Buenos Aires: Sur, 1960.

Boscán, Juan. *Las obras de Boscán y algvnas de Garcilasso de la Vega repartidas en quatro libros.* Barcelona: Carles Amorós, 1543.

————. *Las obras de Juan Boscán repartidas en tres libros.* Edited by William I. Knapp. Madrid: Murillo, 1875.

————. *Obras poéticas.* Critical edition by Martín de Riquer, Antonio Comas, and Joaquín Molas. Barcelona: Facultad de Filosofía y Letras, Universidad de Barcelona, 1957.

Brancaforte, Benito. "Valor y límites de las *Anotaciones* de Fernando de Herrera." *Revista de archivos, bibliotecas y museos* 79 (1976): 113–29.

Breitenbürger, Gerd. *Metaphora: Die Rezeption des Aristotelischen Begriffs in den Poetiken des Cinquecento.* Kronberg: Scriptor, 1975.

Brockhaus, Ernst. *Góngoras Sonettendichtung.* Druck: Heinrich Pöppinghaus o. H. -G., Bochum-Langendreer, 1935.

Bromwich, David. "Parody, Pastiche, and Allusion." In *Lyric Poetry: Beyond New Criticism,* edited by Chaviva Hošek and Patricia Parker, 328–44. Ithaca, N. Y.: Cornell University Press, 1985.

Buceta, Erasmo. "La tendencia a identificar el español con el latín." In *Homenaje ofrecido a Menéndez Pidal,* 1.85–108. Madrid: Hernando, 1925.

Calcraft, R. P. *The Sonnets of Luis de Góngora.* Durham Modern Language Series HM 1. Durham, England: University of Durham, 1980.

Carron, Jean-Claude. "Imitation and Intertextuality in the Renaissance." *New Literary History* 19 (1988): 565–89.

Castiglione, Baldesar. *El cortesano.* 1st ed. 1534. Translation and preface by Juan Boscán, with a preface by Garcilaso de la Vega and an introduction by M. Menéndez y Pelayo. Madrid: CSIC, 1942.

————. *Il libro del Cortegiano con una scelta delle opere minori.* Edited by Bruno Maier. 3d ed. Turin: UTET, 1981.

Castillejo, Cristóbal de. "Represión contra los poetas españoles que escriben en verso italiano." In *Obras,* 2.188–96. Clásicos castellanos 79. Madrid: Espasa-Calpe, 1957.

Castro, Américo. *The Structure of Spanish History.* Translated by Edmund L. King. Princeton: Princeton University Press, 1954.

Cave, Terence. *The Cornucopian Text: Problems of Writing in the French Renaissance.* Oxford: Oxford University Press, Clarendon Press, 1979.

Celt, Sandra. "Boscán's Poetics: The Trouble with Troubadours." *The Linguist* 25, no. 2 (1986): 83–86.

Clarke, Dorothy Clotelle. *The Morphology of Fifteenth Century Castilian Verse.* Duquesne Studies, Philological Series 4. Pittsburgh: Duquesne University Press, 1964.

———. "On Juan del Encina's 'Un Arte de Poesía Castellana.'" *Romance Philology* 6 (1953): 254–59.

Close, Lorna. "Petrarchism and the 'Cancioneros' in Quevedo's Love-Poetry." *Modern Language Review* 74 (1979): 836–55.

Collard, Andrée. *Nueva poesía: Conceptismo, culteranismo en la crítica española.* La lupa y el escalpelo 7. Madrid: Castalia, 1967.

Colombí-Monguió, Alicia de. *Petrarquismo peruano: Diego Dávalos y Figueroa y la poesía de la "Miscelanea austral."* London: Támesis, 1985.

Consiglio, Carlo. "El poema a Lisi y su Petrarquismo." *Mediterraneo* 4 (1946): 76–94.

Corti, Maria. *Principi della communicazione letteraria.* Milan: Bompiani, 1976.

Coster, Adolphe. *Fernando de Herrera (el Divino) 1534–1597.* Paris: Champion, 1908.

Covarrubias, Sebastián de. *Tesoro de la lengua castellana o española.* Edited by Martín de Riquer. Barcelona: Horta, 1943.

Crawford, J. P. W. "Notes on the Chronology of Boscán's Verses." *Modern Philology* 25 (1927): 29–36.

Croce, Benedetto. *España en la vida italiana del Renacimiento.* Translated by Francisco González Ríos. Buenos Aires: Ediciones Imán, 1945.

Cruz, Anne J. *Imitación y transformación: El petrarquismo en la poesía de Boscán y Garcilaso de la Vega.* Amsterdam and Philadelphia: John Benjamins, 1988.

———. "La mitología como retórica poética: El mito implícito como metáfora en Garcilaso." *Romanic Review* 77 (1986): 404–14.

Cuesta Gutiérrez, Luisa. *La imprenta en Salamanca: Avance al estudio de la tipografía salmantina (1480–1944).* Salamanca: Diputación Provincial de Salamanca, 1960.

Curtius, Ernst Robert. *European Literature and the Latin Middle Ages.* Translated by Willard R. Trask. Bollingen Series 36. Princeton, N. J.: Princeton University Press, 1973.

Darst, David H. "Garcilaso's Love for Isabel Freire: The Creation of a Myth." *Journal of Hispanic Philology* 3 (1979): 261–86.

———. *Imitatio: Polémicas sobre la imitación en el siglo de oro.* Tratados de Crítica Literaria. Madrid: Orígenes, 1985.

———. *Juan Boscán.* Twayne World Author Series 475. Boston: Twayne, 1978.

———. "Las palabras y las cosas en la iniciación del cultismo español." In *Studies in Honor of William C. McCrary,* edited by Robert Fiore, Everett W.

Hesse, John E. Keller, and José A. Madrigal, 91–114. Lincoln, Nebr.: Society of Spanish and Spanish-American Studies, 1986.

Dasenbrock, Reed Way. *Imitating the Italians: Wyatt, Spenser, Synge, Pound, Joyce.* Baltimore, Md.: The Johns Hopkins University Press, 1991.

Díaz de Toledo, Pero. "Diálogo e razonamiento en la muerte del Marqués de Santillana." In *Opúsculos literarios de los siglos xiv a xvi,* edited by Antonio Paz y Melia, 247–360. Madrid: Sociedad de Bibliófilos Españoles, 1892.

Díaz Rengifo, Juan [pseud. for García Rengifo, Diego]. *Arte poética española.* Facsimile of 2d ed., with an afterword by Antonio Martí Alanis. Colección Primeras ediciones 7. Madrid: Ministerio de Educación y Ciencia, Dirección General del Patrimonio Artístico y Cultural, 1977.

Díaz y Díaz, Manuel C. "Imagen de España en E. R. Curtius." In *Ernst Robert Curtius: Werk, Wirkung, Zukunftsperspektiven,* edited by Walter Berschin and Arnold Rothe, 195–205. Heidelberg: Carl Winter Universitätsverlag, 1989.

Di Camillo, Ottavio. *El humanismo castellano del siglo xv.* Valencia: Fernando Torres, 1976.

Du Bellay, Joachim. *La deffence et illustration de la langue francoyse.* Edited by Henri Chamard. 4th ed. Société de textes français modernes. Paris: Didier, 1970.

Dunn, Peter. "La oda de Garcilaso 'A la flor de Gnido.'" In *La poesía de Garcilaso: Estudios críticos,* edited by Elias Rivers, 131–62. Barcelona: Ariel, 1974.

Durling, Robert M. *The Figure of the Poet in the Renaissance Epic.* Cambridge, Mass.: Harvard University Press, 1965.

————. "Introduction." In *Petrarch's Lyric Poems: The "Rime Sparse" and Other Lyrics,* 1–33. Cambridge, Mass.: Harvard University Press, 1976.

Egido, Aurora. "La poética del silencio en el Siglo de Oro." *Bulletin hispanique* 88 (1986): 93–120.

Encina, Juan del. *Cancionero.* Facsimile of 1st ed., Salamanca, 1496. Edited with an introduction by Emilio Cotarelo. Madrid: Real Academia Española, 1928.

————. *Obras completas.* 4 vols. Edited with an introduction by Ana M. Rambaldo. Clásicos Castellanos 218–20, 227. Madrid: Espasa-Calpe, 1978–83.

Even-Zohar, Itamar. *Papers in Historical Poetics.* Tel Aviv: The Porter Institute for Poetics and Semiotics, Tel Aviv University, 1978.

Farinelli, Arturo. "Petrarca en España y Portugal." In *Poesía y crítica (temas hispánicos),* 37–54. Madrid: CSIC, 1954.

Ferguson, Margaret. *Trials of Desire: Renaissance Defenses of Poetry.* New Haven, Conn.: Yale University Press, 1983.

Ferguson, Wallace K. *The Renaissance in Historical Thought.* Boston: Houghton Mifflin, Riverside Press, 1948.

Ferguson, William. "De lo *suave* a lo *aspero:* Notas sobre la estética de Herrera." *Revista de estudios hispánicos (Rio Piedras)* 8 (1981): 89–96.

Fernández Alvarez, Manuel. *Charles V: Elected Emperor and Hereditary Ruler.* Translated by J. A. Lalaguna. London: Thames and Hudson, 1975.

Fernández-Morera, Dario. *The Lyre and the Oaten Flute: Garcilaso and the Pastoral.* Monografias 81. London: Támesis, 1982.

Foley, Augusta. "Petrarchan Patterns in the Sonnets of Garcilaso de la Vega." *Allegorica* 3 (1978): 190–215.

Foster, David William, and Virginia Ramos Foster. *Luis de Góngora.* Twayne World Authors Series 266. New York: Twayne, 1973.

Freccero, John. "The Fig Tree and the Laurel: Petrarch's Poetics." *Diacritics* 5 (1975): 35–40.

Fucilla, Joseph. *Estudios sobre el Petrarquismo en España.* Madrid: CSIC, 1960.

Gadamer, Hans-Georg. *Truth and Method.* Translated by Garret Barden and John Cumming. New York: Seabury Press, Continuum, 1975.

Gallagher, Patrick. "Locus Amoenus: The Aesthetic Centre of Garcilaso's Third Eclogue." In *Hispanic Studies in Honour of Frank Pierce,* edited by John England, 59–75. Sheffield: Department of Hispanic Studies, University of Sheffield, 1980.

Gallego Morell, Antonio. "Estudio crítico." In *Églogas* [by Garcilaso de la Vega], 15–44. Madrid: Narcea, 1972.

———. *Estudios sobre poesía española del primer Siglo de Oro.* Madrid: Insula, 1970.

———. "Garcilaso de la Vega en los 'Cronistas' de Carlos Quinto y en las 'Vidas' de San Francisco de Borja." *Boletín de la Real Academia de Historia* 173 (1976): 65–96.

———. *Garcilaso de la Vega y sus comentaristas.* 2d ed. Biblioteca Románica Hispánica IV Textos 7. Madrid: Gredos, 1972.

García Berrio, Antonio. "Poesía galante, poesía amorosa, y poesía erótica: sistemas literarios de legitimación." In *Amours légitimes, amours illégitimes en Espagne (XVIe et XVIIe siècles),* edited by Augustin Redondo, 241–49. Travaux du Centre de Recherche sur l'Espagne des XVIe et XVIIe Siècles. Paris: Publications de la Sorbonne, 1985.

Garcilaso de la Vega. *Obras completas con comentario.* Critical edition by Elias L. Rivers. Columbus: Ohio State University Press; and Madrid: Castalia, 1974.

Gargano, Antonio. *Fonti, miti, topoi: Cinque saggi su Garcilaso.* Romanica Neapolitana 21. Naples: Liguori, 1988.

Gemmingen, Barbara von. "Du bon ton au bon usage: L'importance des traités de bienséance pour la constitution d'une norme linguistique au XVIe siècle." *Textes et langages* 12 (1986): 41–51.

Genot, Gérard. "Strutture narrative della poesia lirica." *Paragone* 212 (1967): 35–51.

Góngora, Luis de. *Góngora y el "Polifemo."* Edition with introduction and commentary by Dámaso Alonso. 5th ed. 3 vols. Madrid: Gredos, 1967.

———. *Obras en verso del Homero español.* Facsimile ed. Compiled by Juan López de Vicuña, edited by Dámaso Alonso. Madrid: CSIC, 1963.

———. *Sonetos.* Critical edition by Biruté Ciplijauskaité. Madison, Wis.: Hispanic Seminary of Medieval Studies, 1981.

———. *Todas las obras de Don Lvis de Gongora en varios poemas.* Compiled by Gonzalo Hoces y Córdoba. Madrid: Imprenta del Reino, 1633.

Goodwyn, Frank. "New Light on the Historical Setting of Garcilaso's Poetry." *Hispanic Review* 46 (1978): 1–22.

Greene, Thomas M. *The Light in Troy: Imitation and Discovery in Renaissance Poetry.* New Haven, Conn.: Yale University Press, 1982.

Guerrero Ramos, Gloria. "Antigüedad y modernidad en Nebrija." *Español actual* 45 (1986): 27–58.

Guidi, José. "L'Espagne dans la vie et dans l'oeuvre de B. Castiglione: De l'équilibre franco-hispanique au choix impérial." In *Présence et influence de l'Espagne dans la culture italienne de la Renaissance,* 113–202. Centre de Recherche sur la Renaissance Italienne 7. Paris: Université de la Sorbonne Nouvelle, 1978.

———. "Reformulations de l'idéologie aristocratique au XVIe siècle: Les différentes rédactions et la fortune du «Courtisan»." In *Réécritures 1: Commentaires, parodies, variations dans la littérature italienne de la Renaissance,* 1.121–84. Centre Interuniversitaire de Recherche sur la Renaissance Italienne 11. Paris: Université de la Sorbonne Nouvelle, 1983.

Guillén, Claudio. "Quevedo y el concepto retórico de literatura." In *Homenaje a Quevedo: Actas de la II Academia Literaria Renacentista,* edited by Victor García de la Concha, 483–506. Biblioteca academica. Salamanca: Biblioteca de la Caja de Ahorros y Monte de Piedad, 1982.

Haebler, Konrad. *The Early Printers of Spain and Portugal.* London: The Bibliographic Society, 1897.

Hall, R. A. *The Italian "Questione della lingua."* Chapel Hill: University of North Carolina Press, 1942.

Hanning, Robert W., and David Rosand, eds. *Castiglione: The Ideal and the Real in Renaissance Culture.* New Haven, Conn.: Yale University Press, 1983.

Hernández Esteban, María. "Procedimientos compositivos de la sextina: De Arnaut Daniel a Fernando de Herrera." *Revista de literatura* 49, no. 98 (1987): 351–424.

Herrera, Fernando de. *Algunas obras de Fernando de Herrera.* 1st ed. Seville: Andrea Pescioni, 1582.

———. *Obras de Garci Lasso de la Vega con anotaciones de Fernando de Herrera.* 1st ed. Seville, 1580. In *Garcilaso de la Vega y sus commentaristas,* edited by Antonio Gallego Morell, 2d ed., 307–594. Madrid: Gredos, 1972.

———. *Poesía castellana original completa.* Edited by Cristóbal Cuevas. Letras hispánicas 219. Madrid: Cátedra, 1985.

———. "Respuesta a las observaciones de Prete Jacopín." In *La controversia sobre las "Anotaciones" Herrerianas,* edited by Juan Montero, 185–246. Seville: Servicio de Publicaciones del Excmo. Ayuntamiento de Sevilla, 1987.

————. *Rimas inéditas*. Edition of MS 10.159 of the Biblioteca Nacional, Madrid, by José M. Blecua. Madrid: CSIC, 1948.

————. *Versos de Fernando de Herrera emendados i divididos por él en tres libros*. Prepared by Francisco Pacheco, dedication by Francisco de Rioja, with a preface by Enrique Duarte. 1st ed. Seville: Gabriel Ramos Vejarano, 1619.

Hirsch, E. D., Jr. *The Aims of Interpretation*. Chicago, Ill.: University of Chicago Press, 1976.

Horst, Robert ter. "Death and Resurrection in the Quevedo Sonnet 'En crespa tempestad.' " *Journal of Hispanic Philology* 5 (1980): 41–49.

————. "The Duke and Duchess of Alba and Juan del Enzina: Courtly Sponsors of an Uncourtly Genius." In *Studies in Honor of William C. McCrary*, edited by Robert Fiore, Everett W. Hesse, John E. Keller, and José A. Madrigal, 215–20. Lincoln, Nebr.: Society of Spanish and Spanish-American Studies, 1986.

Hutcheon, Linda. *A Theory of Parody: The Teachings of Twentieth-Century Art Forms*. New York: Methuen, 1985.

Ingarden, Roman. *The Cognition of the Literary Work of Art*. Translated by Ruth Ann Crowley and Kenneth R. Olson. Northwestern Studies in Phenomenology and Existential Philosophy. Evanston, Ill.: Northwestern University Press, 1973.

————. *The Literary Work of Art*. Translated by George Grabowicz. Northwestern Studies in Phenomenology and Existential Philosophy. Evanston, Ill.: Northwestern University Press, 1973.

Jammes, Robert. *Études sur l'oeuvre poétique de Don Luis de Góngora y Argote*. Bibliothèque de l'École des Hautes Études Hispaniques fasc. 40. Bordeaux: Féret et Fils, 1967.

Jauss, Hans Robert. *Toward an Aesthetic of Reception*. Translated by Timothy Bahti, with an introduction by Paul de Man. Theory and History of Literature 2. Minneapolis: University of Minnesota Press, 1982.

Javitch, Daniel. "Imitations of Imitations in *Orlando Furioso*." *Renaissance Quarterly* 38 (1985): 215–39.

————. *Poetry and Courtliness in Renaissance England*. Princeton, N. J.: Princeton University Press, 1978.

————. *Proclaiming a Classic: The Canonization of "Orlando Furioso."* Princeton, N. J.: Princeton University Press, 1991.

————. "The Shaping of Poetic Genealogies in the Late Renaissance." In *Comparative Literary History as Discourse: In Honor of Anna Balakian*, edited by Mario J. Valdés, Daniel Javitch, and A. Owen Aldridge, 265–83. Bern and New York: Peter Lang, 1992.

Johnson, Carroll B. "Personal Involvement and Poetic Tradition in the Spanish Renaissance: Some Thoughts on Reading Garcilaso." *Romanic Review* 80 (1989): 288–304.

Jones, R. O. *The Golden Age: Prose and Poetry*. American Edition. Vol. 2 of *A Literary History of Spain*. New York: Barnes and Noble, 1971.

————. "Juan del Encina and Renaissance Lyric Poetry." In *Studia Iberica: Festschrift für Hans Flasche*, edited by K.- H. Kürner. Bern: Francke, 1973.

Kamen, Henry. *Spain 1469–1714: A Society of Conflict.* 2d ed. London: Longman, 1991.

Kennedy, William J. *Rhetorical Norms in Renaissance Literature.* New Haven, Conn.: Yale University Press, 1978.

Kerrigan, William, and Gordon Braden. *The Idea of the Renaissance.* Baltimore, Md.: The Johns Hopkins University Press, 1989.

Kinney, Arthur R. *Continental Humanist Poetics.* Amherst: University of Massachusetts Press, 1989.

Komanecky, Peter M. "Quevedo's Notes on Herrera: The Involvement of Francisco de la Torre in the Controversy over Góngora." *Bulletin of Hispanic Studies* 52 (1975): 123–33.

Kossoff, A. David. *Vocabulario de la obra poética de Herrera.* Madrid: Real Academia Española, 1966.

Lapesa, Rafael. *Historia de la lengua española.* 8th ed. Madrid: Gredos, 1980.

———. "Poesía y realidad: Destinatarias y personajes de los poemas Garcilasianos de amor. Isabel Freyre, la ninfa «degollada»." In *Garcilaso: Estudios completos,* 199–210. Madrid: Istmo, 1985.

———. *La trayectoría poética de Garcilaso.* Reprinting of 2d ed. Madrid: Alianza, 1985.

Lázaro Carreter, Fernando. "La 'Ode ad Florem Gnidi' de Garcilaso de la Vega." In *Garcilaso,* edited by Victor García de la Concha, 109–26. Academia Literaria Renacentista 4. Salamanca: Ediciones Universidad de Salamanca; Biblioteca de la Caja de Ahorros y Monte de Piedad de Salamanca, 1986.

———. "Poética del arte mayor castellano." In *Studia hispanica in honorem R. Lapesa,* 1.343–78. Madrid: Cátedra-Seminario Menéndez Pidal; Gredos, 1972.

———. "Quevedo entre el amor y la muerte: Comentario de un soneto." In *Francisco de Quevedo,* edited by Gonzalo Sobejano, 291–99. Madrid: Taurus, 1978.

Lentricchia, Frank. *After the New Criticism.* Chicago, Ill.: University of Chicago Press, 1980.

Lerner, Lía Schwartz. *Metáfora y sátira en la obra de Quevedo.* Madrid: Taurus, 1983.

———. "Quevedo junto a Góngora: Recepción de un motivo clásico." In *Homenaje a Ana María Barrenechea,* edited by Lía Schwartz Lerner and Isaias Lerner, 313–25. Madrid: Castalia, 1984.

Levisi, Margarita. "La interioridad visualizable en Garcilaso." *Hispanófila* 73 (1981): 11–20.

Lida de Malkiel, María Rosa. "Para las fuentes de Quevedo." *Revista de filología hispánica* 1 (1939): 369–82.

———. "La tradición clásica en españa." *Nueva revista de filología hispánica* 5 (1951): 183–223.

López Barralt, Luce. "San Juan de la Cruz: Una nueva concepción del lenguaje poético." *Bulletin of Hispanic Studies* 55 (1978): 19–32.

López Estrada, Francisco. " 'El Arte de poésia castellana' de Juan del Encina." In *L'Humanisme dans les lettres espagnoles,* edited by Augustin Redondo, 151–68. Paris: Vrin, 1979.

Ly, Nadine. "Garcilaso: Une autre trajectoire poétique." *Bulletin hispanique* 83 (1981): 263–329.

Lynch, John. *Spain Under the Habsburgs.* 2d ed. 2 vols. Oxford: Basil Blackwell, 1981.

McCallum, Thomas, and Anthony N. Zahareas. "Toward a Social History of the Love Sonnet: The Case of Quevedo's Sonnet 331." *Ideologies and Literature* 2, no. 6 (1978): 90–99.

McInnis, Judy B. "The Moral and Formal Dimensions of Herrera's Purist Aesthetics." In *Classical Models in Literature: Proceedings of the IXth Congress of the International Comparative Literature Association,* edited by Zoran Konstantinović, Warren Anderson, and Walter Dietze, 153–88. Innsbruck: Institut für Sprachwissenschaft der Universität Innsbruck, 1981.

Macrí, Oreste. *Fernando de Herrera.* Revised ed. Madrid: Gredos, 1972.

Manero Sorolla, María Pilar. *Introducción al estudio del petrarquismo en España.* Estudios de literatura española y comparada. Barcelona: Promociones y Publicaciones Universitarias, 1987.

Manley, Joseph. "Quevedo's *Heráclito Cristiano* as Poetic Cycle." *Kentucky Romance Quarterly* 24 (1977): 26–34.

Manrique, Gómez. "Carta que enbió Gomez Manrique al obispo de Calahorra sobre la muerte del Marqués." In *Obras de Don Iñigo López de Mendoza, Marqués de Santillana,* edited by José Amador de los Ríos, clii–cliv. Madrid: José Rodríguez, 1852.

Marasso Rocca, Arturo. "Juan Boscán." In *Estudios de literatura castellana* 1–34. Buenos Aires: Ediciones Kapelusz, 1955.

Maravall, José Antonio. *Culture of the Baroque: Analysis of a Historical Structure.* Translated by Terry Cochran, with a foreword by Wlad Godzich and Nicholas Spadaccini. Theory and History of Literature 25. Minneapolis: University of Minnesota Press, 1986.

Mariscal, George. *Contradictory Subjects: Quevedo, Cervantes, and Seventeenth-Century Spanish Culture.* Ithaca, N. Y.: Cornell University Press, 1991.

Martí, Antonio. *La preceptiva retórica española del siglo de oro.* Madrid: Gredos, 1972.

Martínez-López, Enrique. "Sobre 'aquella bestiliadad' de Garcilaso (égl. III.230)." *PMLA* 87 (1972): 12–25.

Mas, Amédée. *La caricature de la femme du mariage et de l'amour dans l'oeuvre de Quevedo.* Paris: Ediciones Hispano-Americanas, 1957.

Mazzacurati, Giancarlo. *La questione della lingua dal Bembo all'Accademia Fiorentina.* Naples: Liguori, 1965.

Mele, Eugenio. "In margine alle poesie di Garcilaso." *Bulletin hispanique* 32 (1930): 218–45.

Menéndez y Pelayo, Marcelino. *Juan Boscán.* Vol. 13 of *Antología de poetas líricos castellanos.* Madrid: Librería de los Sucesores de Hernando, 1908.

Micó, José María. "Norma y creatividad en la rima idéntica (a propósito de Herrera)." *Bulletin hispanique* 86 (1984): 257–308.

Miller, David M. *The Net of Hephaestus: A Study of Modern Criticism and Metaphysical Metaphor.* The Hague: Mouton, 1971.

Il «minore» nella storiografia letteraria. Convegno Internazionale Roma, 10–12 Marzo 1983. Edited by Enzo Esposito. Classici italiani minori 14. Ravenna: Longo, 1984.

Molho, Maurice. "Una cosmogonía antisemita: 'Érase un hombre a una nariz pegado.' " In *Quevedo in Perspective: Four Essays for the Quadricentennial,* edited by James Iffland, 57–79. Newark, Del.: Juan de la Cuesta, 1982.

———. "Sobre un soneto de Quevedo, 'En crespa tempestad . . .': Ensayo de análisis intratextual." In *Francisco de Quevedo,* edited by Gonzalo Sobejano, 343–77. Madrid: Taurus, 1978.

Montero, Juan. *La controversia sobre las "Anotaciones" Herrerianas.* Seville: Servicio de Publicaciones del Excmo. Ayuntamiento de Sevilla, 1987.

Montgomery, Robert L. *The Reader's Eye: Studies in Didactic Literary Theory from Dante to Tasso.* Berkeley, Los Angeles, and London: University of California Press, 1979.

Moore, Roger. "Conceptual Unity and Associative Fields in Two of Quevedo's Sonnets." *Renaissance and Reformation* o.s. 14 (1978): 55–63.

Morales, Ambrosio de. "Discurso sobre la lengua castellana." Critical edition by Valeria Scorpioni. *Studi ispanici* 3 (1977): 177–94.

Morel D'Arleux, Antonia. "Obscenidad y desengaño en la poesía de Quevedo." *Edad de Oro* 9 (1990): 181–94.

Moreno Castillo, Enrique. "Melancolía y utopía en Garcilaso de la Vega: Lectura de las églogas I y III." *Cuadernos Hispanoamericanos* 439 (1987): 29–45.

Morreale de Castro, Margherita. *Castiglione y Boscán: El ideal cortesano en el renacimiento español.* 2 vols. Madrid: Anejos del Boletín de la Real Academia Española, 1959.

Naderi, Georgia. "Petrarchan Motifs and Plurisignative Tension in Quevedo's Love Sonnets: New Dimensions of Meaning." *Hispania* 69 (1986): 483–94.

Naumann, Walter. " 'Polvo enamorado': Muerte y amor en Propercio, Quevedo, y Goethe." In *Francisco de Quevedo,* edited by Gonzalo Sobejano, 326–42. Madrid: Taurus, 1978.

Navarrete, Ignacio. "Boiardo's *Pastorali* as a Macrotext." *Standford Italian Review* 5 (1985): 37–53.

———. "The Renaissance Preface as a Platform for Theories of Translation." *Publishing History* 16 (1984 [1986]): 21–32.

———. "Strategies of Appropriation in Speroni's *Dialogo delle lingue* and Du Bellay's *Deffence et illustration.*" *Comparative Literature* 41 (1989): 141–54.

Navarro Durán, Rosa. "La oda 'Diffugere nives' de Horacio, traducida por Fernando de Herrera." *Boletín de la Real Academia Española* 62 (1982): 499–541.

Nebrija, Antonio de. *Gramática de la lengua castellana.* Edited by Antonio Quilis. Madrid: Editora Nacional, 1981.

Nordstroem, Johan. *Moyen âge et Renaissance.* Translated by T. Hammar. Paris: Stock, 1933.

Norton, Glyn P. *The Ideology and Language of Translation in Renaissance France and Their Humanist Antecedents.* Geneva: Droz, 1984.

Olivares, Julián. *The Love Poetry of Francisco de Quevedo: An Aesthetic and Existential Study.* Cambridge Iberian and Latin American Studies. Cambridge, England: Cambridge University Press, 1983.

Ong, Walter J. "The Writer's Audience Is Always a Fiction." In *Interfaces of the Word: Studies in the Evolution of Consciousness and Culture,* 53–81. Ithaca, N. Y.: Cornell University Press, 1977.

Orozco Díaz, E. "El sentido pictórico del color en la poesía barroca." In *Temas del barroco,* 71–109. Anejos del Boletín de la Universidad de Granada, Estudios y Ensayos 3. Granada: Universidad de Granada, 1947.

Panofsky, Erwin. *Meaning in the Visual Arts.* Paperback Edition. Garden City, N. Y.: Doubleday, Anchor, 1955.

Parducci, Amos. *Saggio sulla poesia lirica di Juan Boscán.* Vol. 3 (1951) of *Memorie.* Classe di Scienze Morali, ser. 5. Bologna: Accademia delle Scienze dell'Instituto di Bologna, 1952.

Parker, Patricia. *Literary Fat Ladies: Rhetoric, Gender, Property.* London: Methuen, 1987.

Partner, Peter. *The Pope's Men.* Oxford: Oxford University Press, Clarendon Press, 1990.

Paterson, Alan K. G. "Ecphrasis in Garcilaso's 'Egloga Tercera.'" *Modern Language Review* 72 (1977): 73–92.

Pepe Sarno, Inoria. "'Bianco il ghiaccio, non il velo': Ritocchi e metamorfosi in un sonetto di Herrera." *Strumenti critici* 15 (1981): 458–71.

———. "La 'luz' de la 'aurora': Variantes en dos sonetos de Fernando de Herrera." In *Actas del VIII Congreso de la Asociación Internacional de Hispanistas,* edited by A. David Kossoff, José Amor y Vázquez, Ruth H. Kossoff, and Geoffrey W. Ribbans, 2.409–18. Madrid: Istmo, 1986.

———. "Se non Herrera, chi? Variante e metamorfosi nei sonetti di Fernando de Herrera." *Studi ispanici* (1982): 33–69.

Petrarch [Francesco Petrarca]. *Letters on Familiar Matters.* 3 vols. Translated by Aldo S. Bernardo. Baltimore, Md.: The Johns Hopkins University Press, 1975–85.

———. *Petrarch's Lyric Poems: The "Rime Sparse" and Other Lyrics.* Translated and edited by Robert M. Durling. Cambridge, Mass.: Harvard University Press, 1976.

Phillips, Katherine K. "Structuralism and Some Sonnets by Góngora." *Romanic Review* 65 (1974): 294–307.

Piedra, José. "Literary Whiteness and the Afro-Hispanic Difference." *New Literary History* 18 (1987): 303–32.

Pigman, G. W., III. "Versions of Imitation in the Renaissance." *Renaissance Quarterly* 33 (1980): 1–32.

Pinto, Mario di. "Mientras por competir con Garcilaso." *Cuadernos hispanoamericanos,* no. 461 (November 1988): 77–87.

Pound, Ezra. *How to Read.* 1st ed. London: Desmond Harmswirth, 1931.

Pozuelo Yvancos, José María. *El lenguaje poético de la lírica amorosa de Quevedo.* Murcia: Universidad de Murcia, Secretariado de Publicaciones, 1979.

"Prete Jacopín" [Juan Fernández de Velasco]. "Observaciones del Licenciado Prete Jacopín, vecino de Burgos, en defensa del Príncipe de los Poetas Castellanos Garci-lasso de la Vega, natural de Toledo, contra las Anotaciones de Fernando de Herrera, Poeta Sevillano." In *La controversia sobre las "Anotaciones" Herrerianas,* edited by Juan Montero, 105–47. Seville: Servicio de Publicaciones del Excmo. Ayuntamiento de Sevilla, 1987.

Pring-Mill, R. D. F. "Escaligero y Herrera: Citas y plagios de los *Poetices libri septem* en las *Anotaciones.*" In *Actas del segundo congreso internacional de hispanistas,* edited by Jaime Sánchez Romeralo and Norbert Poulussen, 489–98. Nijmegen: Asociación Internacional de Hispanistas; Instituto Español de la Universidad de Nimega, 1967.

Profeti, Maria Grazia. *Quevedo: La scrittura e il corpo.* Letterature Iberiche e Latino-Americane. Rome: Bulzoni, 1984.

Quevedo, Francisco de. *Obra poética.* Edited by José M. Blecua. 4 vols. Madrid: Castalia, 1969–81.

———. *El Parnasso español, monte en dos cvmbres dividido, con las nveve Mvsas castellanas. Dondese contienen poesias de Don Francisco de Qvevedo Villegas.* Compiled and edited by Ioseph Antonio González de Salas. 1st ed. Madrid: Diaz de la Carrera, 1648.

———. *Poesía metafísica y amorosa.* Edited with an introduction by José Manuel Blecua. Hispánicos Planeta. Barcelona: Planeta, 1976.

———. *Las tres musas ultimas castellanas.* Compiled and edited by Pedro Aldrete. Madrid: Imprenta Real, 1670.

Quilis, Antonio. "Nebrija y Encina frente a la métrica." *Revista de estudios hispánicos* [San Juan, P. R.] 7 (1980): 155–65.

Quintero, María Cristina. *Poetry as Play: "Gongorismo" and the "comedia."* Purdue University Monographs in Romance Languages 38. Amsterdam: John Benjamins, 1991.

Randel, Mary Gaylord. *The Historical Prose of Fernando de Herrera.* London: Tamesis, 1971.

Read, Malcolm M. "Language and the Body in Francisco de Quevedo." *MLN* 99 (1984): 235–55.

Redel, Enrique. *Ambrosio de Morales.* Córdoba: Imprenta del Diario, 1908.

Regosin, Richard L. "The Name of the Game/the Game of the Name: Sign and Self in Castiglione's *Book of the Courtier.*" *Journal of Medieval and Renaissance Studies* 18 (1988): 21–47.

Reichenberger, Arnold. "Boscán and the Classics." *Comparative Literature* 3 (1951): 97–118.

Rico, Francisco. "De Garcilaso y otros petrarquismos." *Revue de littérature comparée* 52 (1978): 325–38.

Ricoeur, Paul. *La métaphore vive.* Paris: Éditions du Seuil, 1975.

Rigolot, François. *Poétique et onomastique: L'example de la Renaissance.* Histoire des idées et critique littéraire 160. Geneva: Droz, 1977.

Rivers, Elias. "L'humanisme linguistique et poétique dans les lettres espagnoles du seizième siècle." In *L'humanisme dans les lettres espagnoles*, edited by Augustin Redondo, 169–76. Paris: Vrin, 1979.

———. "Language and Reality in Quevedo's Sonnets." In *Quevedo in Perspective: Four Essays for the Quadricentennial*, edited by James Iffland, 17–35. Newark, Del.: Juan de la Cuesta, 1982.

———. "Nota sobre Bernardo Tasso y el manifiesto de Boscán." In *Homenaje al profesor Antonio Vilanova*, coordinated by Adolfo Sotelo Vazquez, edited by Marta Cristina Carbonell, 1.601–5. Barcelona: Departamento de Filología Española, Universidad de Barcelona, 1989.

———. "The Pastoral Paradox of Natural Art." *MLN* 77 (1962): 130–44.

———. "Some Ideas About Language and Poetry in Sixteenth-Century Spain." *Bulletin of Hispanic Studies* 61 (1984): 379–83.

Rivers, Georgina Sabat. "Quevedo, Floralba, y el Padre Tablares." *MLN* 93 (1978): 320–28.

Robles, Juan de. *Primera parte del culto sevillano.* Sevilla: El Mercantil Sevillano, 1883.

Rodríguez-Moñino, Antonio. *Critical Reconstruction Vs. Historical Reality of Spanish Poetry in the Golden Age.* Introduction by Marcel Bataillon, translated by Lesley Byrd Simpson. [San Francisco]: [Lawton and Alfred Kennedy], 1968.

Rodríguez-Salgado, M. J. *The Changing Face of Empire: Charles V, Philip II and Habsburg Authority 1551–1559.* Cambridge Studies in Early Modern History. Cambridge, England: Cambridge University Press, 1988.

Romanos, Melchora. "Sobre aspectos de la elocutio gongorina en el enfoque de uno de sus comentaristas." *Filología* 22, no. 1 (1987): 119–35.

Russell, Peter. "Arms Versus Letters: Towards a Definition of Spanish Fifteenth-Century Humanism." In *Aspects of the Renaissance*, edited by Archibald R. Lewis, 47–58. Austin: University of Texas Press, 1967.

Sacks, Norman P. "Antonio de Nebrija: Founder of Spanish Linguistics." *Hispanic Linguistics* 1 (1984): 1–33, 149–76.

Salcedo Coronel, Garcia, ed. *Obras de don Luis de Gongora, comentadas* (by Luis de Gongora y Argote). Madrid: Imprenta real [vol. 1] and Diaz de la Carrera [vols. 2–3], 1636–48. 3 vols.

Sánchez de las Brozas, Francisco ("El Brocense"). *Obras del Excelente Poeta Garci Lasso de la Vega. Con anotaciones y enmiendas del Licenciado Francisco Sánchez, Cathedrático de Rhétorica en Salamanca.* 1st Ed. Salamanca, 1574. In *Garcilaso de la Vega y sus comentaristas*, edited by Antonio Gallego Morell, 2d ed., 265–303. Madrid: Gredos, 1972.

———. *Opera omnia, una cum ejusdem scriptoris vita auctore Gregorio Maiansio.* 4 vols. Geneva, 1766.

Sánchez de Lima, Miguel. *El arte poética en romance castellano.* 1st Ed. Alcalá, 1580. Edited by Rafael de Balbín Lucas. Biblioteca de antiguos libros hispánicos, ser. A, 3. Madrid: CSIC, 1944.

Sánchez Robayna, Andres. "Petrarquismo y parodia (Góngora y Lope)." *Revista de filología de la Universidad de La Laguna* 1 (1982): 35–45.

Santangelo, Giorgio. *Il Bembo critico e il principio d'imitazione.* Florence: Sansoni, 1950.

Saulnier, Verdun. "Sebillet, Du Bellay, Ronsard: L'entrée de Henri II à Paris et la revolution poétique de 1550." In *Les fêtes de la Renaissance,* edited by Jean Jacquot, 1.31–59. Paris, CNRS, 1956.

Schiff, Mario. *La bibliothèque du Marquis de Santillane.* Bibliothèque de l'École des Hautes Études, IVème section: Sciences historiques et philologiques 153. Paris: Bouillon, 1905.

Schulz-Buschhaus, Ulrich. "Der frühe Góngora und die italienische Lyrik." *Romanistisches Jahrbuch* 20 (1969): 219–38.

Scott, Izora. *Controversies over the Imitation of Cicero.* New York: Teacher's College, Columbia University, 1910.

Segre, Cesare. "Edonismo linguistico nel cinquecento." *Giornale storico della letteratura italiana* 130 (1953): 145–77.

Selig, Karl-Ludwig. "Garcilaso and the Visual Arts." In *Interpretation und Vergleich: Festschrift für Walter Pabst,* edited by Eberhard Leube and Ludwig Schrader, 302–9. Berlin: Erich Schmidt, 1972.

Semiotics and Structuralism: Readings from the Soviet Union. Edited with an introduction by Henryk Baran. White Plains, N. Y.: International Arts and Sciences Press, 1976.

Shepard, Sanford. *El Pinciano y las teorías literarias en el siglo de oro.* Biblioteca Románica Hispánica II: Estudios y ensayos 58. Madrid: Gredos, 1962.

Shklovsky, Victor. "Art as Technique." In *Russian Formalist Criticism,* translated and edited by Lee T. Lemon and Marion J. Reis, 3–24. Regents Critics Series. Lincoln: University of Nebraska Press, 1965.

Smith, C. C. "Fernando de Herrera and Argote de Molina." *Bulletin of Hispanic Studies* 33 (1956): 63–77.

Smith, Paul Julian. *The Body Hispanic: Gender and Sexuality in Spanish and Spanish American Literature.* Oxford: Oxford University Press, Clarendon Press, 1989.

———. *Quevedo on Parnassus: Allusive Context and Literary Theory in the Love-Lyric.* Texts and dissertations 25. London: Modern Humanities Research Association, 1987.

———. *Writing in the Margin: Spanish Literature of the Golden Age.* Oxford: Oxford University Press, Clarendon Press, 1988.

Snell, Ana María. "Tres ejemplos del arte del soneto en Garcilaso." *MLN* 88 (1973): 175–89.

Snell, Bruno. *The Discovery of the Mind: The Greek Origins of European Thought.* Cambridge, Mass.: Harvard University Press, 1953.

Spitzer, Leo. "Garcilaso, Third Eclogue, Lines 265–271." *Hispanic Review* 20 (1952): 243–48.

Strum-Maddox, Sara. *Petrarch's Metamorphoses: Text and Subtext in the "Rime Sparse."* Columbia: University of Missouri Press, 1985.

Tamayo de Vargas, Tomás. *Garcilasso de la Vega, natural de Toledo, Príncipe de los Poetas Castellanos. De don Thomás Tamaio de Vargas.* 1st ed. Madrid, 1622. In *Garcilaso de la Vega y sus comentaristas,* edited by Antonio Gallego Morell, 2d ed., 597–664. Madrid: Gredos, 1972.

Terracini, Lore. *I codici del silenzio.* Turin: Edizione dell'Orso, 1988.

———. *Lingua come problema nella letteratura spagnola del cinquecento.* Turin: Stampatori, 1979.

Thompson, Colin P. *The Strife of Tongues: Fray Luis de León and the Golden Age of Spain.* Cambridge, England: Cambridge University Press, 1988.

Todorov, Tzvetan. *Mikhail Bakhtin: The Dialogic Principle.* Translated by Wlad Godzich. Theory and History of Literature 13. Minneapolis: University of Minnesota Press, 1984.

Ulivi, Ferruccio. *L'imitazione nella poetica del rinascimento.* Milan: Marzorati, 1959.

Valdés, Juan de. *Diálogo de la lengua.* Edited by Juan M. Lope Blanch. Madrid: Castalia, 1969.

Vian Herrero, Ana. "La mimesis conversacional en el *Diálogo de la lengua* de Juan de Valdés." *Criticón* 40 (1987): 45–79.

Vickers, Brian. "Leisure and Idleness in the Renaissance: The Ambivalence of *otium.*" *Renaissance Studies* 4 (1990): 1–37, 107–54.

Vickers, Nancy. "Diana Described: Scattered Woman and Scattered Rhyme." *Critical Inquiry* 8 (1981): 265–79.

Vilanova, Antonio. "Fernando de Herrera." In *Historia general de las literaturas hispánicas,* edited by Guillermo Díaz Plaja, 7 vols., 2.689–751. Barcelona: Barna, 1949–67.

———. *Las fuentes y los temas del Polifemo de Góngora.* 2 vols. Revista de filología española. Madrid: CSIC, 1957.

Waley, Pamela. "Garcilaso, Isabel and Elena: The Growth of a Legend." *Bulletin of Hispanic Studies* 56 (1979): 11–15.

Waller, Marguerite. *Petrarch's Poetics and Literary History.* Amherst: The University of Massachusetts Press, 1980.

Walters, D. Gareth, ed. *Poems to Lisi,* by Francisco de Quevedo. Exeter, England: Exeter University Press, 1988.

———. *Francisco de Quevedo, Love Poet.* Washington, D. C.: The Catholic University of America Press; and Cardiff: University of Wales Press, 1985.

Warnke, Frank J. *Versions of Baroque: European Literature in the Seventeenth Century.* New Haven, Conn.: Yale University Press, 1972.

Weinrich, Harald. "Das spanische Sprachbewußtsein im Siglo de Oro." In *Spanische Literatur im goldenen Zeitalter,* edited by Horst Baader and Erich Loos, 524–47. Frankfurt an Main: Klostermann, 1973.

Weiss, Julian. *The Poet's Art: Literary Theory in Castile c. 1400–60.* Medium Aevum Monographs n.s. 15. Oxford, England: Society for the Study of Medieval Languages and Literatures, 1990.

Welsh, Andrew. *Roots of Lyric.* Princeton, N. J.: Princeton University Press, 1978.

Whigham, Frank. "Interpretation at Court: Courtesy and the Performer." *New Literary History* 14 (1983): 623–39.

Whinnom, Keith. "Hacia una interpretación y apreciación de las canciones del *Cancionero general* de 1511." *Filología* 13 (1968–69 [1970]): 361–81.

Wilhelmsen, Elisabeth. "San Juan de la Cruz: 'Percepción' espiritual e imagen poética." *Bulletin Hispanique* 88 (1986): 293–319.

Williams, Raymond. *Marxism and Literature*. Oxford: Oxford University Press, 1977.

Woods, M. J. "Herrera's Voices." In *Mediaeval and Renaissance Studies on Spain and Portugal in Honour of P. E. Russell*, edited by F. W. Hodcroft, D. G. Pattison, R. D. F. Pring-Mill, and R. W. Truman, 121–32. Oxford: Society for the Study of Mediaeval Languages and Literature, 1981.

Yarbro-Bejarano, Yvonne. "The New Man and the Shepherd: Juan del Encina's First Dramatic Eclogue." *Revista canadiense de estudios hispánicos* 11 (1986): 145–60.

Zamora, Juan C. "Ideología, filología y lingüística en la gramática española del renacimiento." *Hispania* 70 (1987): 718–23.

Zimic, Stanislav. "Las églogas de Garcilaso de la Vega: Ensayos de interpretación." *Boletín de la Biblioteca Menéndez y Pelayo* 64 (1988): 5–107.

Index

Weinrich, Harald, 256n. 19
Western culture, *translatio studii* theory
 of, 16, 242n. 10
Whigham, Frank, 52

Wit: Castiglione on, 50–51; in Garcilaso,
 98–99, 101; in Góngora, 194

Zimic, Stanislav, 251n. 28, 252n. 34

Compositor: Graphic Composition, Inc.
Printer: Braun-Brumfield, Inc.
Binder: Braun-Brumfield, Inc.
Text: 10/13 Palatino
Display: Palatino